The Lancashire Cotton Industry and Its Rivals

LTCB International Library Selection No. 10

The Lancashire Cotton Industry and Its Rivals

International Competition in Cotton Goods
in the Late Nineteenth Century:
Britain versus India, China, and Japan

Heita Kawakatsu

 LTCB International Library Trust/International House of Japan

Transliteration of Foreign Words

The Hepburn system of romanization is used for Japanese terms, including the names of persons and places. Except in familiar place names, long vowels are indicated by macrons.

With regard to Chinese personal names, we have followed the local custom of placing the family name first. Japanese names, however, are presented in Western order, with family name last in the main text but not in the Epilogue.

This book originally appeared in English as 'International Competition in Cotton Goods in the Late Nineteenth Century with Special Reference to Far Eastern Markets.' A Thesis Submitted for the Degree of D.Phil. of the University of Oxford (Oxford, 1984). International House of Japan retains the English-language publication rights under contract with Heita Kawakatsu.

First English edition published March 2018 by International House of Japan
5-11-16 Roppongi Minato-ku, Tokyo 106-0032, Japan
Tel: +81-3-3470-3211   Fax: +81-3-3470-3170

Printed in Japan
ISBN 978-4-924971-44-8

In Memoriam

Professor Yoshitaka Komatsu (1906–2000)

Professor Peter Mathias (1928–2016)

CONTENTS

Foreword
1. Peter Mathias
xiii

2. A.J.H. Latham
xv

Preface and Acknowledgements
xvii

Illustrations
xxv

Prologue
1

Introduction
7

PART ONE

TYPES OF RAW COTTON AND THEIR EVOLUTION

Chapter One
THE EASTWARD AND WESTWARD SPREAD OF COTTON CULTIVATION

Chapter Two

THE SPREAD OF COTTON TEXTILES TO THE WEST:
INDIA'S ROLE IN THE INDUSTRIAL REVOLUTION

PART TWO

SPECIALISATION IN COTTON GOODS IN
FAR EASTERN MARKETS, 1870–1900

Chapter Three
BRITISH EXPANSION INTO ASIAN MARKETS

Chapter Four
COMPARISON OF PRICES BETWEEN BRITISH AND
JAPANESE COTTON CLOTHS

Chapter Five
QUALITY DIFFERENCES BETWEEN COTTON GOODS

Chapter Six
QUALITY DIFFERENCES IN RAW COTTON

CONCLUSION
183

Epilogue
TWO MODES OF 'ESCAPE-FROM-ASIA'

Appendices

FOREWORD

by

Peter Mathias
Downing College, Cambridge

I am delighted to add a foreword to Heita Kawakatsu's book. The study, based on his original research, undertaken in Oxford and subsequently in Japan, covers the important nexus established between Japan and the United Kingdom in the nineteenth century with the export of cotton textiles (of higher quality) from Britain to Asia. This historical link between key industries in our two countries is now happily mirrored in current scholarship, of which this is a prime example. It is no function of a brief preface to replicate the conclusions of detailed research but to emphasise the wider context of the research which lies behind the text of this book, which I am most happy to endorse.

Doctor Kawakatsu's career, uniquely, embraces distinction as a scholar and now as a diplomat, which gives his work both depth and width of perception. It will stand as authoritative evidence of his major status in this field of research, both in Britain and Japan.

by

A.J.H. Latham

Sometime Postmaster of Merton College, Oxford

H eita Kawakatsu's 1984 Oxford Doctoral Thesis marked the start of a new wave of research on the development of East Asia stressing market forces. This book, based on his original dissertation, reminds us of the force of his argument of some thirty years ago, and still valid today. It also shows us the impetus which energised so many subsequent scholars in Japan and elsewhere, and revolutionised our understanding of the industrialisation and economic development of Asia.

The issue which Professor Kawakatsu examines here is the conundrum that although in the late nineteenth century cotton textiles from Lancashire were imported in vast amounts to India, and in lesser amounts to China and Japan, these countries were able to industrialise successfully despite this competition. The fact that they did so flies in the face of those who argue that industrialisation in Britain destroyed local industries abroad and turned these countries into suppliers of raw materials.

By examining the actual cloths produced in Lancashire and comparing them with those produced in India, China, Korea, and Japan, Kawakatsu has been able to show that the market for cloth in these countries differed essentially in character. In essence the argument is that whilst India did consume large quantities of fine cottons, made from thin yarn spun from long staple American cotton, China, Korea, and Japan needed a coarser cloth made from thicker yarn, which was spun from short staple indigenous cotton. Paradoxically, India, whilst consuming fine cottons made from American cotton and imported from Lancashire, actually exported to East Asia its own short staple indigenous cotton, and the yarn made from it. The industrialisation of its own cotton industry was based upon producing these yarns. In China and Japan this yarn, and similar yarns produced from local cotton by their own industries, was woven into coarse cloths for local use. This was needed in these countries particularly for winter wear, as they did not have woollen cloths to keep them warm. So the industrialisation of these East Asian countries was based upon spinning short staple local cotton into thick yarn, and then weaving it into robust coarse cloth for everyday use. It was the differing requirements of consumers, and hence the market for cloth, which determined the development of the cotton industry in Asia, and ultimately its success. China and Japan industrialised making coarse cottons for local consumers, whilst Lancashire continued to make fine fabrics for elegant use by consumers who had other textiles for winter wear, or lived in India where demand for winter clothing was not so great. The markets for Lancashire and East Asian cotton manufacturers were different, because consumers in their respective markets required essentially different products. The market dictated, and the respective cotton industries complied. The market ruled!

PREFACE AND ACKNOWLEDGEMENTS

This book is based on my doctoral thesis, 'International Competition in Cotton Goods in the Late Nineteenth Century with Special Reference to Far Eastern Markets', submitted to Oxford University in 1984. Thus some mention must be made as to how the International House of Japan came to publish this book now and about the epilogue, which is not included in the original thesis.

Upon my return to Waseda University from Oxford, I wrote an essay on Japanese civilisation versus the British-centred and capitalist-oriented world economy. This essay, based on the essence of my doctoral thesis findings, offered a new outlook from a Japanese perspective on world economic history from 1600 to 1800. It won second prize when submitted to the Japan Foundation's tenth anniversary essay competition. As a result of this positive public attention, this essay became the basis of my first book in Japanese, *Nihon Bunmei to Kindai Seiyō: Sakoku Saikō* (Japanese Civilisation and the Modern West: Reassessing Japan's Isolation Policy), Tokyo: NHK Books, 1991. *Nihon Bunmei to Kindai Seiyō* is currently in its nineteenth reprint, and its Korean translation was published in 2005.

The present book project emerged when *Nihon Bunmei to Kindai Seiyō* was selected for translation into English for the LTCB International Library. The library, established by the Long-Term Credit Bank of Japan in 1994 and managed by the International House of Japan since 2000, has been publishing English translations of outstanding Japanese nonfiction titles. Ms. Jean Connell Hoff completed the English translation of the entire text; however, we came across a problem when it came to including references. Academic writing must include citations and a bibliography, but the NHK Books series, intended for a general readership, had space limitations. When *Nihon Bunmei to Kindai Seiyō* was written, there was no choice but to exclude the tables and all of the references found in the thesis. Ms. Hoff went beyond the call of duty and took on the onerous task of adding citations and footnotes where needed by referring back to my thesis and other sources. As we worked, however, we began to realise that it was better to utilise the thesis itself rather than to work with the English translation. This went against the aim of the LTCB International Library, which was to provide works in Japanese to an English readership, but all graciously agreed to use the thesis to enhance the academic value of the book.

I also wish to acknowledge that this book does not cite other relevant academic literature that has been published since the completion of my thesis. To name but a few, these include Beverly Lemire, *Fashion's Favourite: The Cotton Trade and the Consumer in Britain 1660–1800*, Oxford: Oxford University Press, 1991, and her *Dress, Culture and Commerce: The English Clothing Trade before the Factory, 1660–1800*, New York: St. Martin's Press, 1997; Maxine Berg, *Luxury and Pleasure in Eighteenth-Century Britain*, Oxford: Oxford University Press, 2005; and Maxine Berg, et al., eds., *Goods from the East, 1600–1800: Trading Eurasia*, Basingstoke: Palgrave Macmillan, 2015. These are all important academic contributions and are closely related to my second chapter, which is largely based on secondary sources.

Lastly, the epilogue is an excerpt from *Nihon Bunmei to Kindai Seiyō*, which Ms. Hoff translated into English and added the references. Unfortunately, a great portion of her translation has gone unused, and no words can fully express my utmost gratitude to her for permitting this drastic change of course so generously. She remained very dedicated to this project, editing and commenting on the entire manuscript. She suggested important revisions and improved the text.

I also owe a special debt to an important editorial staff member, Mr. Yasuo Saji, for keeping track of this project that has extended over a few decades. Not only did the nature of the project change from publishing a translation to publishing the thesis itself, the Long-Term Credit

Bank went bankrupt, and the library's publishing unit was transferred to the International House. Despite all of these tumultuous changes, Mr. Saji's steadfast support and passion to see this book published remained unchanged from the very beginning. It is because of him that this book has been published, and I wish to sincerely thank him.

In 2009, I was elected as the governor of Shizuoka Prefecture, located at the foot of Mount Fuji. Now into my third term, my work as governor has kept me quite busy over these years. I am grateful to my office staff and wish to recognise among others: Ms. Toshimi Suzuki, Ms. Ryoko Nakagawa, and Ms. Yoshie A. Oya for helping me manage my time and providing logistical assistance.

1 January 2018

ACKNOWLEDGEMENTS

My research in England, based at Wolfson College, Oxford, extended over a little more than four years from August 1977 to October 1981. This was made possible by a two-year scholarship from the Ishizaka Foundation, Tokyo, and by a three-year fellowship from Waseda University, Tokyo. To both of them I am very grateful for their financial help. I am also obliged to the following companies, institutions, libraries, and their staffs in Tokyo: Waseda University Library, the University of Tokyo Library, the National Diet Library, the Tokyo Metropolitan Archives, the Statistics Bureau of the Prime Minister's Office, and the Institute of Developing Economies; and in England: Jardine, Matheson & Co., the Liverpool Chamber of Commerce, the Greater Manchester Chamber of Commerce, the Bodleian and its dependent libraries, Cambridge University Library, SOAS Library, the British Library, Manchester Central Library, the University of Manchester Library, and Oldham City Library. I should like to thank especially three archivists: Mr. Shōjirō Ishiyama of Waseda University for his tremendous help in sorting out contemporary newspapers and other materials of Meiji Japan; Mr. A. Roberts, the keeper of the Oriental Reading Room of the Bodleian for allowing me to read Japanese materials in the library stacks; and Miss M. Pamplin of the archives department of Cambridge University Library for her help in locating the relevant archives in the Jardine Matheson collection.

But the most far-reaching of all sources of inspiration for my research has been my supervisor, Professor Peter Mathias. Not imposing his own view, even when I became less confident of my argument, he was always able to show me the dimensions that the subject might have, and to place it in a more general perspective. He also kindly took the time to improve my written English. Even my best Japanese is not competent enough to convey my deep gratitude to him; still less to his family whenever I remember the happy occasions with them at their home. In the Michaelmas term of 1979 when Professor Mathias was away from Oxford, Dr. Patrick O'Brien kindly supervised me. He very carefully read a section of the thesis, which eventually became Chapter IV, and made most constructive comments on it, for which I owe a profound debt to him.

Research in Liverpool, Manchester, and Cambridge gave me valuable opportunities to listen to Professor S. A. Broadbridge, Professor W. H. Chaloner, Dr. D. A. Farnie, and Dr. W. J. Macpherson. Dr. Farnie was generous enough to reply in detail to all the questions I asked and even let me use his own notebook for some sources which I could not otherwise locate. I have always been stimulated by his talks and letters. I am also grateful to Professor Barry Supple, who presided at the economic history seminar at All Souls College, on 23 November 1980, at which I had the opportunity to read a paper entitled, 'International Competition in Cotton Textiles in the Late Nineteenth Century, with Special Reference to the Far Eastern Markets', which eventually became Chapter V; I am thankful to all who made comments and criticisms at the seminar, especially Dr. J. F. Wright, Mr. Christopher Lloyd, and Miss Anne Wilkinson. Mr. Lloyd also provided fruitful discussions on the theory and practice of social science. Many friends helped to check my English and/or give comments; I am especially indebted to Dr. Allan Barr, Mr. Chen, Miss Jill Haas, Dr. Pamela Asquith, and Mr. Paul Snowdon. I have also benefited from discussions with the late Emeritus Professor of Oxford University, Richard Storry, the late Emeritus Professor of the University of London, G. C. Allen, Dr. Mark Elvin, Dr. Gopal Krishna, Professors Louis Cullen,

John Stoye, W. Woodruff, Sakae Tsunoyama, Eiichi Funayama, Kaoru Sugihara, and Hajime Shimizu.

I also want to set down here my especially deep obligation to senior colleagues at Waseda University, among others, to Professor Ken'ichirō Shōda who supervised me when I was in Tokyo, to Professor Tadao Horie for putting at my disposal his fundamental critical studies of Marx's *Capital*, and to the Emeritus Professor of Waseda University, Yoshitaka Komatsu, for his everlasting encouragement which remains fresh in the nearly 200 letters he wrote to me while I was in Oxford.

Last but not least, to my wife, Kimi, who acted throughout as a typist and superb all-round assistant, I am especially indebted. Because of my father's untimely death on 31 December 1980, my work is dedicated to him, Hiromu Kawakatsu, in memoriam.

31 December 1983

. . .

More than three decades have passed since the completion of my Oxford thesis. Over the years, I have had opportunities to share and publish parts of it. Professor Mathias made it possible for me to present an overview at the Ninth International Economic History Congress in Bern, Switzerland in 1986.[1] I also offered an essay based on the thesis, 'The Lancashire Cotton Industry and Its Rivals,' to the Festschrift honouring Professor Mathias's seventieth birthday.[2] As a tribute to Professor Mathias, I have used the Festschrift essay title for this book.

Sadly, Professor Mathias, my Oxford mentor, and Professor Yoshitaka Komatsu, my Waseda mentor, have both passed away. I am eternally grateful to them both and miss them dearly. Professor Komatsu's recommendation and introduction to Professor Mathias led to my studies at Oxford. Professor Mathias was known for his notable work, *The First Industrial Nation* (London: Methuen, 1969, 2nd edn., 1983), both of which Professor Komatsu translated into Japanese (Tokyo: Nippon Hyōronsha, 1972 and 1988). When I was awarded the Keidanren-established Ishizaka Memorial Foundation scholarship to study abroad, I was enrolled in Wolfson

College, Oxford and was the first Japanese student Professor Mathias supervised. His second Japanese student was H.I.H. Crown Prince Naruhito, who studied for two years (1983–85) at Merton College, Oxford. Under the supervision of Professor Mathias, the Crown Prince completed a very fine work, *The Thames as Highway: A Study of Navigation and Traffic on the Upper Thames in the Eighteenth Century* (Oxford: Oxford University Printing House, 1989). Professor Mathias did most of his graduate student supervising in his capacity as Chichele Professor of Economic History at All Souls College, Oxford for nearly two decades (1968–87). He subsequently became Master of Downing College, Cambridge (1987–95), making Crown Prince Naruhito and myself the only two Japanese who received his direct supervision. However, Professor Mathias was widely respected among economic historians in Japan, and he had a wide academic circle of Japanese friends. A memorial volume to honour Professor Mathias that A. J. H. Latham and I co-edited was recently published with contributions from Crown Prince Naruhito and friends including Professor Masami Kita, Professor Katsuhiko Kitagawa, Professor Toshio Kusamitsu among others.[3] It is absolutely my greatest honour to have this book open with a foreword from Professor Mathias, which he had so generously written some time ago.

I am also very grateful to my long-time friend, Dr. A. J. H. Latham, for writing this book's second foreword. It was almost four decades ago in the spring of 1978 when I first met John at an annual economic history conference in Swansea, Wales. Another memorable conference anecdote was Professor Mathias's impressive high-speed lift to the conference luncheon, which I am glad he made to on time, for it was delicious. I had just arrived in the UK and have loved English cuisine ever since. At the conference, I heard John's presentation, which inspired me very much, and this work was soon after published as *The International Economy and the Undeveloped World 1865–1914* (London: Croom Helm Ltd., 1978). Having concurred with John's conclusions, I translated this book into Japanese (Tokyo: Nippon Hyōronsha, 1987). Our friendship grew, and we have worked together on many book projects over the years.[4]

My friendship with John is similar to the friendship shared by Professor Komatsu and Professor Mathias. Academic collaboration has enhanced Japan-UK relations over generations. With great gratitude, I dedicate this book to my two mentors and hope that this work in a small way contributes to mutual understanding and deepens the friendship between our two countries.

15 December 2017

Notes to Acknowledgements

1. H. Kawakatsu, 'International Competition in Cotton Goods in the Late Nineteenth Century: Britain versus India and East Asia', in *The Emergence of a World Economy 2, 1850–1914*, W. Fischer, R. M. McInnis, and J. Schneider, eds., Wiesbaden: Franz Steiner Verlag, 1986.

2. H. Kawakatsu, 'The Lancashire Cotton Industry and Its Rivals', in *From Family Firms to Corporate Capitalism: Essays in Business and Industrial History in Honour of Peter Mathias*, K. Bruland and P. O'Brien, eds., Oxford: Clarendon Press, 1998.

3. A. J. H. Latham, and H. Kawakatsu, eds., *Asia and the History of the International Economy: Essays in Memory of Peter Mathias*, Abingdon: Routledge, 2018.

4. We have jointly edited the following: *Japanese Industrialization and the Asian Economy*, London: Routledge, 1994, repr. Routledge Paperback 2014; *The Evolving Structure of the East Asian Economic System since 1700: A Comparative Analysis*, Proceedings, Eleventh International Economic History Congress: B6, Milan: Università Bocconi, 1994; *Asia Pacific Dynamism*, 1550–2000, London and New York: Routledge, 2000, repr. Routledge Paperback 2016: *Intra-Asian Trade and the World Market*, Abingdon and New York: Routledge, 2006, repr. Routledge Paperback 2009; *Intra-Asian Trade and Industrialization: Essays in Memory of Yasukichi Yasuba*, Abingdon and New York: Routledge, 2009, repr. Routledge Paperback 2014; *The Evolving Structure of the East Asian Economic System since 1700: A Comparative Analysis*, Abingdon and New York: Routledge, 2011, repr. Routledge Paperback, 2016.

ILLUSTRATIONS

Prologue

MEIJI-ERA JAPAN'S COTTON GOODS FROM A COMPARATIVE ECONOMIC HISTORY PERSPECTIVE

Britain was the 'first industrial nation' in the world, and Japan was the first in Asia. When Japan concluded commerce treaties with Britain and other nations in 1858, it effectively dissolved its long-standing national isolation policy established during the Tokugawa era (1603–1868). From that time on, Japan was virtually open to free trade until 1911 at the end of the Meiji era (1868–1912) when Japan gained autonomy to impose tariffs. Thus Meiji-era Japan, largely accessible through free trade, was able to quickly usher in the first industrial revolution in Asia.

Both Britain and Japan had industrialised under free trade, but the difference was that Japan's free trade had been forced upon it while Britain had embraced laissez-faire as a national policy. When the wave of industrialisation hit the rest of Europe and the United States at around the same time, rather than opening themselves up, they had adopted protectionist measures by imposing tariffs on imports to safeguard their home industries. This was in stark contrast with Japan, which was in no position to take protectionist measures.

Japan achieved industrialisation by the end of the nineteenth century, and economic growth continued well into the twentieth century much to the amazement of Great Britain. This book concerns how Japan was able to accomplish this level of development unlike other countries such as India, which became the biggest market for British products.

Since the opening of its ports, Japan's largest trading partner was Britain. In the second half of the nineteenth century, British cotton goods (textiles and yarns) were Britain's main export commodities and also what Japan imported the most. Japan's handicraft industry had commercially produced cotton wool, yarns, and textiles, which were leading products of Tokugawa Japan. The Japanese population of 30 million in early Meiji utilised vast quantities of cotton textiles. The industry matured and was far from the so-called 'Asiatic mode of production' by the time the population reached 50 million at the end of Meiji. Japanese cotton goods, as with the British ones, were price sensitive, thus the conditions were ideal for perfect competition between British and Japanese cotton markets. Given that protectionist measures were not in place, all would assume that Japanese cotton goods would not stand a chance with those produced in Britain, which boasted the most productive cotton industry in the world.

What happened was quite the contrary: Japanese cotton spinning and textile industries led Japan's industrialisation in the late nineteenth century. In the early Meiji era, Japan began manufacturing its own textile machinery and by the early twentieth century was referred to as the 'Britain of the East'. In 1929, Sakichi Toyoda (1867–1930), the founder of Toyota Industries Corporation and the greatest inventor of textile machinery in Japan, sold the license for producing the Type G automatic loom to Platt Brothers & Co. of Oldham in North West England, one of the world's leading manufacturers of textile machinery at the time. This was a clear indication of the superiority of the Type G automatic loom and a huge technological triumph for Japan. Toyota invested the Platt license fee of £100,000 to develop a new automobile manufacturing business, which paved its way to become the highly successful global automobile manufacturer that it is today. The foundation of this success was laid by the Japanese cotton industry, which advanced to the point of challenging Britain's technological position in the world.

This book also attempts to answer why the Japanese cotton industry was able to compete with British cotton imports. The two most important facets of a product are its price and quality; however, this work mainly concerns quality. Although different types of cotton are often not distinguished, quality differences existed between British and Japanese cotton goods, including cotton wool, yarns, and textiles. It was this difference of quality and in practical use that were important, and thus price was not the determining factor for competition between British and Meiji-era Japanese cottons.

A similar phenomenon occurred in post-war Japan with the United States when Japan, under great U.S. pressure, gave in and liberalised the importation of American citrus and beef products. The main U.S. citrus product was grapefruit. When compared with Satsuma mandarins, the citrus fruit of choice among the Japanese people since the Edo period, the two differed in size, shape, flavour, and thickness of the skin. As a result, there was no competition although they were both citrus products. Grapefruits were eventually added to breakfast and other occasions in Japanese life. The same also applied to beef. Japanese and American beef did not compete as they were two different products in terms of quality and taste although Japanese beef was more expensive. Japanese beef is sliced thin for dishes such as sukiyaki and shabu-shabu, and Kobe beef, a well-known brand, is exceptionally tender because of its marbling and has a melt-in-your mouth texture. American beef, often prepared as steaks, are thicker and require a knife and fork to eat. Inexpensive American beef imports did not replace Japanese beef but rather stimulated the creation of new beef dishes such as beef stews and burgers, contributing to more beef consumption that helped build a stronger physique among the Japanese. Removing tariff barriers on U.S. citrus and beef proved to be mutually beneficial.

The situation had been similar in Meiji-era Japan's clothing market. Kimonos were made using Japanese cotton textiles, and British cotton textiles, thin and smooth to the touch, were not viable substitutes to produce them. Instead, British cotton textiles were used as a cheaper alternative to high-quality Japanese silk fabrics. British cotton textiles could not displace Japanese silk, yet they were consumed as affordable substitutes among the lower class.

This book offers an explanation from a historical perspective on the reason for the difference in quality between British and East Asian cotton textiles. Part I covers the origin of the cotton plant and the spread of cotton cultivation and textiles. The heart of this work is in Part II; therefore, the reader would be able to understand the main argument without reading the background found in Part I.

Cotton textiles, which originated in India, clothed the people of India and the greater Indian Ocean Rim region. Britain, captivated by Indian-made muslins and calicoes worn among the upper class, imported Indian cotton textiles from the seventeenth century on. In time Britain's cotton industry, a leading sector of the country's eventual Industrial Revolution, succeeded in the large-scale mechanisation of its cotton textile production process and ultimately surpassed Indian textiles. As a result, production in India was stifled, and India became Britain's greatest market.

Indian cotton textiles, however, had been widely consumed in the Indian Ocean Rim region. Cotton cultivation first spread to the Far East in China during the Yuan dynasty in the fourteenth century. China successfully expanded its production, and cotton cultivation became a national growth strategy in Ming China. Chinese cotton textiles were thick and strong and were issued as clothing to soldiers stationed along the Great Wall to drive out northern invaders. Because China's cotton cultivation had been for military purposes, the transmission of cotton to other countries was prohibited. However, a Joseon envoy secretly brought back cotton seeds, and cultivation quickly spread throughout the Korean Peninsula in the fifteenth century. Cotton textiles, mass-produced in Korea, were used as currency and means of exchange. During the Warring States period in Japan in the sixteenth century, Japan imported Korean textiles to clothe its samurais and use as sailcloth for its battleships. By the seventeenth century, Japan was cultivating its own cotton. Since woollen textiles were not available in Japan, cotton clothing was introduced to the general populace and worn during the winter months for its thickness and warmth.

North America and Europe were not the only competitors of the British cotton industry in the second half of the nineteenth century. The Lancashire cotton industry was alarmed by the sudden rise of Bombay's spinning industry because India was Britain's biggest market for its cotton goods. The Manchester Chamber of Commerce and the British Parliament conducted research to examine this matter and found that there was no real competition. How did the Bombay cotton industry achieve this unprecedented growth? India specialised in producing cotton textiles different in quality to those of Britain's. Bombay's greatest markets were China and Japan, where British cotton goods had limited appeal.

When Japan opened up to the world, it was not the British cotton industry that the Japanese cotton industry competed with, but Asia's. The import of raw cotton from China and India devastated Japan's cotton cultivation, and Japan's spinning industry was exposed to Bombay's cotton yarn imports. However, the industrialisation during Meiji allowed Japan to overcome its Indian competition.

Although the story of the cotton industry is not representative of the Industrial Revolution in its entirety, one cannot deny that the cotton textile industry was one of the leading sectors that triggered that revolution. When we consider how Britain was the first in the world to successfully industrialise and Japan the first to do so in Asia, and how Britain had surpassed India's cotton industry in the late eighteenth century and followed by Japan in the late nineteenth century, we see that it was in fact India's cotton textile industry that spurred technological innovations in both Britain and Japan. The dual revolutions of Britain and Japan occurred in response to pressure from India.

INTRODUCTION

The period between 1873 and 1896 has often been called the 'Great Depression' in Great Britain, or the downswing of a 'Kondratieff' long cycle in the capitalistic economy as a whole, although this is a highly controversial issue.[1] When we turn our attention to East Asia, this period is crucially important because this was when cotton spinning mills in India increased their production very rapidly, and also their yarn exports to overseas markets. These seriously undermined the growth of Lancashire's yarn exports to Asia, especially China and Japan. In 1888, the Manchester Chamber of Commerce compiled a report entitled *Bombay and Lancashire Cotton Spinning Inquiry*, which stated:

> In view of the recent very rapid increase of cotton spinning in India, and the exports of yarn therefrom, more especially to China and Japan, while at the same time there has been a very serious check to the growth of Lancashire yarn exports to those countries, the Directors be requested to examine and report to a Special Meeting of the Chamber as to the causes and circumstances which have thus enabled Bombay spinners to supersede those of Lancashire.[2]

Japan also launched the industrialisation of its cotton industry in the last quarter of the nineteenth century. In 1891, the output of Japan's cotton yarn production exceeded the amount of its yarn imports, and in 1897, Japan's yarn exports greatly exceeded its yarn imports, making inroads into the Chinese market at the expense of Great Britain and India. The Japanese cotton industry was minute compared to its British rival in the middle of

7

the nineteenth century when Japan was forced to open its doors to international trade. But its development after the Meiji Restoration (1868) was
remarkable. In 1894, Thomas Ellison warned Lancashire that Japan would
be one of 'her competitors' in Far Eastern markets.[3] In the following year
Richard Gundry, another commentator, observed that 'Japan has become
practically self-sufficing in the lower counts [of yarn] and has reached a
surplus which she is beginning to send abroad.'[4] In 1896, the number of
spindles Japan possessed was 760,000, and by 1914, it was 2,700,000.[5] By
the turn of the century, she exported 100,000,000 lbs. of yarn to China,
Korea, and other Far Eastern countries;[6] 'indeed, even before World War
I, Japan was the only serious threat to Britain in third markets.'[7]

The whole pattern of the international economy in the late nineteenth
century, as S. B. Saul and A. J. H. Latham have demonstrated, was sustained by Britain's export surplus in her trade with the undeveloped world
in general and Asia in particular.[8] Thus progress in Asia's cotton industry
contrary to British interests had a negative effect upon the British-centred
international economy. My purpose is to examine in detail this aspect of
the international economy in the late nineteenth century with special
reference to Britain's cotton trade in Asian markets.

I focus my attention on cotton goods for the following three reasons.
First and foremost, machine-made cotton goods were the symbol of
wealth of the world's workshop. Lipson wrote: 'it [cotton manufacturing]
was organized from the outset on capitalist lines',[9] and in the middle of
the nineteenth century, Sydney Smith went so far as to proclaim that 'the
great object for which the Anglo-Saxon race appears to have been created
is the making of calico [cotton cloth].'[10] Cotton manufactures constituted
the single greatest export of Great Britain as Table 0.1 shows.

Secondly, in the East, India, China, Korea, and Japan had developed
their cotton industries before Western capitalism reached there, to the
extent that cotton was the most important and common clothing material used by the people. It was to this region that British-made cottons
were increasingly exported towards the end of the nineteenth century,
as shown in Table 0.2. This indicates that there must have been severe
competition in the Asian cotton market.

Thirdly, from a methodological point of view, if we follow a Marxist
approach, as many economic historians of Asia have done,[11] attention

Table o.1 Exports from the United Kingdom

Year	Textiles (total)		Cotton		Total	
	£m.	%	£m.	%	£m.	%
1870–9	118.6	54	71.5	33	218.1	100
1880–9	113.8	49	73.0	32	230.3	100
1890–9	104.3	44	67.2	28	237.1	100

Note: Annual averages per decade in current prices.
Source: P. Mathias, *The First Industrial Nation*, 1st edn., (London, 1969), p. 468.

Table o.2 Relative Share in World Markets of British Cotton Manufactures, 1850–1896

	Proportion of volume of exports of piece goods		Proportion of value of exports of cotton manufactures	
Year	1850	1896	1850	1896
Europe	19.66	7.19	34.26	18.92
The Americas	34.23	17.28	29.10	18.45
United States	7.67	1.06	8.86	3.56
Latin America	23.94	15.69	17.96	14.90
Levant	11.46	8.07	9.20	7.92
Asia	31.39	57.77	24.37	43.42
India	23.15	39.06	18.48	26.58
China	5.39	10.40	3.61	8.48
Africa	2.18	4.96	1.73	5.31
Total	98.92	95.27	98.66	94.01

Source: D. A. Farnie, *The English Cotton Industry and the World Market, 1815–1896* (Oxford, 1979), p. 91.

must be drawn to the goods produced and brought by British capitalists to undeveloped Asia and their impact on Asian producers. Karl Marx stated at the very beginning of *Capital,* in which 'England is used as the chief illustration in the development of my theoretical ideas',[12] that 'The wealth of societies in which the capitalist method of production prevails, takes the form of "an immense accumulation of commodities", wherein individual commodities are the elementary units. Our investigation must therefore begin with an analysis of the commodity.'[13] For the reasons mentioned above, I am going to investigate cotton goods, which were one of the most important commodities for both Britain and Asia, and the world. Many approaches are possible.

According to Marx, 'Every useful object [such as cotton] must be regarded from a twofold outlook, that of quality and that of quantity.'[14] By quantity he meant exchange-value, and by quality a use-value. 'The utility of a thing makes a use-value', continued Marx, 'this utility is not a thing apart . . . [but is] determined by the properties of the commodity'.[15] Although Marx cautioned that 'when the use-values of commodities are left out of the reckoning . . . all the qualities whereby it affects our senses are annulled.'[16] Marx himself and his followers tended to place much emphasis upon something invisible, i.e., the value of labour, abstracted from the material elements of the commodity, and seemed to ignore its physical existence. My primary concern is to fill this vacuum and explore the reality of the white downy fibrous substance of cotton not only in exchange-value terms as Marx did, but also in use-value terms. This study attempts to fill at least some of the existing gaps. Special reference is made to the markets for these goods in East Asia in general and Japan in particular during the late Victorian period, in which the region was integrated into the network of world trade. The inquiry addresses the following points:

1. THE EAST ASIAN MARKETS AT LARGE

One of the pivots of the world payments mechanism in the late nine-teenth century was Britain's ability to maintain a deficit with the rest of the world, which it balanced by means of a trade surplus with Asia. This Asian surplus in commodity trade came largely from exports of Lancashire's cotton manufactures to East Asian markets. Did this influx of British goods into the region have destructive effects on East Asian textile production, as stated by Marx in the following?

> The cheapness of machine-made products, and the revolution in the methods of transport and communication, become weapons for the conquest of foreign markets. By ruining handicraft production in other countries, machinery forcibly converts them into fields for the supply of its raw material. Thus the East Indies have been compelled to undertake the production of cotton . . . for Great Britain.[17]

2. INDIA AND THE FAR EASTERN MARKETS

When China commenced trade with Britain, a great demand for British cotton manufactures was expected. This was exemplified, for example, by Sir Henry Pottinger's remark that 'all the mills in Lancashire could not make stocking-stuff sufficient for one of its provinces'.[18] The Far Eastern markets for British goods, however, remained relatively small compared with the Indian market. The people of India and the Far East (China, Japan, and Korea) all wore cotton clothes. India, with a population about half that of the Far East, imported approximately 40 per cent of total British overseas exports of cotton textiles, while the Far East never exceeded 15 per cent. What caused the big difference in demand between these two cotton-consuming areas?

3. JAPANESE COMPETITION

The Japanese cotton industry was insignificant compared to Britain's when Japan opened its country to foreign trade. But 'the Workshop of the World' failed to subdue this 'late-comer', and Japan emerged as a formidable competitor to Britain. How was this possible?

To tackle these questions, this book does not consider factors involved in the production of cotton manufactures, such as capital and labour, but concentrates on production processes, examining cotton products as commodities. Some explanation is needed to justify this approach. The limit was set because significant work has already been done on supply-side factors such as capital formation, entrepreneurship, business organization, transportation, technological innovation, the comparative profitability of ring and mule spinning, labour disputes, etc.[19]

The reader will not find much mention of these factors here; on the other hand, the reader will not find much about cotton products themselves in other works. But a more important reason is that when comparing the cotton industries in the West and the East, an analysis of production factors does not make sense unless the prices of British and Eastern cotton goods were competitive in the markets concerned. The conventional view has placed much weight upon relative factor prices assuming, in its simplest form, a state of perfect competition between the two types of textiles. This assumption, however, has yet to be proven. In an earlier piece of research, I collected a series of price data for the major varieties of textiles sold in Tokyo, the biggest market in Meiji Japan. This work makes it possible to re-examine the established view.[20] This analysis in fact contradicts the commonly held assumption that price competition was the key instrument for commercial penetration, as in Marx's famous phrase: 'the cheap prices of its [the bourgeoisie's] commodities are the heavy artillery with which it batters down all Chinese walls'.[21] This has important implications for the position of British textiles in Far Eastern markets at large, which were similar to that in Japan: they did not sell well despite their cheaper prices.

Another explanation must be explored. It is easy to suggest that non-economic factors accounted for particular patterns of consumption among the peoples of the Far East, especially in comparison with the British who lived at the opposite side of the world. I try to avoid the temptation of relying upon explanations which resist quantification, such as cultural, climatic, or geographical differences, as these sometimes indicate a lack of rigorous analysis. Instead, I have focussed almost entirely on the cotton products themselves, particularly on the qualities of British and Asian cotton cloth, cotton yarn, and raw cotton. These are physical items that can be analysed numerically. Evidence available in Japan suggests the existence of distinct markets for British and Far Eastern cotton products at each level: raw cotton, cotton yarn, and cotton cloth. Preliminary research on this subject has been published in Japanese.[22] This study will attempt to link what was found in Japan with what has been discovered in England.

The research presented here sets out to demonstrate the difference in qualities between British and Far Eastern cotton products in general, and cotton yarn in particular. By so doing, it will substantiate the existence of distinct markets for the two types of cotton products. Cotton yarn is high-lighted because it is the feature by which the qualities of cotton textiles are distinguished. In addition, cotton yarn is subject to accurate classification according to its 'counts', which indicate the fineness of the yarn. The estimates of British and Far Eastern 'counts' will be a crucial part of this research; at the same time, the 'counts' of Indian yarn will be compared with those of Britain and the Far East.[23]

As a result, three distinct markets for cotton goods in the late nineteenth century are evident as shown in the following table and figure. There was severe price competition within the same type, and there was virtually no competition between West European and East Asian cottons. Use-value or quality mattered more in the case of contemporary world markets.

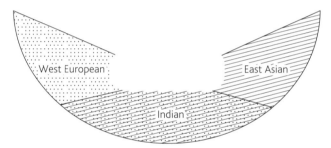

Figure 0.1 The Eurasian Cotton Markets in the Late Nineteenth Century

Table 0.3 Quality Differences of the Eurasian Cotton Markets

Type	Raw Cotton	Cotton Yarn	Cotton Cloth
West European	Long-staple	High-counts*	Thin & light texture
East Asian	Short-staple	Low-counts	Thick & heavy texture
Indian	A mixture of the above two		

Note: * A count represents the number of hanks (of 840 yards) to 1lb. of yarn.

Part I presents a sketch of the origin and evolution of cotton from as early as the Middle Ages. This is included to dispel any impression that the types of cotton introduced in these chapters are static. They are not static at all; they are products of long historical evolution. Part I illustrates how the cotton industry, which originated in India, spread both westward and eastward. This historical background is a prelude to a more detailed discussion in Part II, which deals with cotton specialisation in late nineteenth-century East Asian markets. Raw cotton, cotton yarn, and cotton cloth are examined, and striking contrasts to those found in the Western and Indian markets are revealed.

Concerning the Japanese sources, the price data *par excellence* exist, though scantily, in a contemporary newspaper, *Chūgai Bukka Shinpō*—a predecessor of the present *Nihon Keizai Shimbun* (Japan Financial Times)—and in a journal, *Tokyo Keizai Zasshi* (Tokyo Economist). The latter was long edited by Ukichi Taguchi, a leading economist of the Meiji era who has been called the Japanese Adam Smith. Both of them, issued mostly every other week and overlapping periods of publication, put the relevant data in a similar fashion. The whole series of *Chūgai Bukka Shinpō* is kept by the Tokyo University Library, and *Tokyo Keizai Zasshi* by the Waseda University Library.

So far as the source of data about the quality of yarn is concerned, owing to the urgent need to set up a modern cotton spinning industry in the early Meiji era, both Japanese bureaucrats and entrepreneurs left plentiful records. These contemporary official and non-official mostly Millowners' Association's publications contain invaluable information not only on the exact counts of yarn which each firm was manufacturing at that time, but also occasionally on the quality of yarn imported into Japan. British consular reports from various ports of Japan also sometimes refer to the specific counts of yarn demanded by the country.

My research in England started in autumn 1977. Aside from well-known facts about English yarn such as 'Bolton counts' or 'Oldham counts' and despite my natural optimism, the data on the precise quality of yarn produced in nineteenth-century England were not easy to locate. The voluminous *Proceedings of the Manchester Chamber of Commerce* have few records regarding the qualities of yarn produced in the Lancashire cotton region, and there is much less in the *Minutes of the Liverpool Chamber of Commerce*. Apart from fragmentary information in various writings, the only important source concerning yarn quality was J. Worrall's *Cotton Spinners' and Manufacturers' Directory* (the first publication in 1882, then annually from 1884 up to 1930, and taken over by the *Lancashire Textile Industry* from 1931). This directory contains information on the exact counts which each cotton mill claimed to manufacture, but as it is a directory, such figures cannot be free from bias, for these advertised counts were listed to attract customers; they were not the ones necessarily spun. Despite this apparent defect, it still serves as an indispensable guide, because it was only in 1924 that the overall classification of British-made yarn was first made known by the publication of the *Third Census of Production of the United Kingdom*. As for the quality of British yarn exported to the Far East, China Imperial Maritime Customs Reports contain little information, but a few British consular reports plus thousands of circulars entitled *Prices Current* published by the Chamber of Commerce at various ports of the Far East such as Yokohama, Kobe, Hong Kong, etc., provided detailed infomation. The latter is deposited in the Cambridge University Library as a part of the Jardine, Matheson & Co. Archives. As regards sources of the type of yarn used in late nineteenth-century India, some *Parliamentary Papers* and the annual reports of the Bombay Chamber of Commerce (kept in the India Office Library and Records) were used. Unfortunately, the report of the Bombay Millowners' Association, which contains information on the quality of yarn imported into India in the late nineteenth-century, is not available in England except for copies brought out after the 1920's (these are owned by the Manchester Central Library).

Concerning the classification of cotton plants in terms of botany and genetics, only secondary sources were consulted. Among others, dozens of papers and books by Sir Joseph Hutchinson were the principal and stimulating source of knowledge in a field I was quite ignorant of when I came to England. Concomitantly, and to my good luck, were the talks with members of Wolfson College (roughly 60 per cent of Wolfsonians are natural scientists) on numerous occasions. They have been another source of stimulation, which widened my awareness and range of my thesis. For this I am very grateful to all of them.

PART ONE

TYPES OF RAW COTTON AND
THEIR EVOLUTION

Chapter One

THE EASTWARD AND WESTWARD SPREAD OF
COTTON CULTIVATION

1. INTRODUCTION

Cotton was grown in India for several thousands of years B.C., and for a long time India was the only producer of cotton textiles. By the time Europeans and Japanese ventured into the so-called East Indies, cotton textiles were being used by the people of East Africa, the Middle East, and South and Southeast Asia as clothing materials and a means of exchange. From the Middle Ages to the early modern period, as trade began between the East Indies and the rest of Asia, cotton products found their way from India to the East and the West via various routes.

Two economic revolutions took place in the late eighteenth and early nineteenth centuries, the Industrial Revolution in Britain and the industrious revolution in Japan. These revolutions enabled Britain and Japan to produce their own cotton goods rather than import them. The British textile industry copied Indian goods, and the Japanese copied Chinese goods. What emerged were two separate markets in the West and in the Far East for cotton products with distinct qualities (Table 1.1).

The following account describes how and when particular types of cotton plants spread eastward and westward, creating these two different markets.

Table 1.1 Two Markets for Cotton Products

	Raw Cotton	Cotton Yarn	Cotton Cloth
Western type	Long-stapled cotton	Fine yarn	Thin and light texture
Far Eastern type cotton	Short-stapled	Thick yarn texture	Thick and heavy

2. CLASSIFICATION

The cotton plant belongs to the genus *Gossypium*, of the Hibiscus genus of the Mallow family. From the beginning of the study of *Gossypium*, there was considerable difficulty in drawing up the classification of its species. Notable early botanists who studied cotton included Linnaeus, Parlatore (*Le Specie dei cotoni*; 1866), Bowman, Forbes Royle (*Illustrations of the Botany and Other Branches of the Natural History of the Himalayan Mountains*; 1839), and Todaro (*Relazione sulla cultura dei cotoni in Italia*; 1877–8).[1] These scholars differed greatly in the number of species they recognised. 'The number of species from a botanical point of view', wrote Brooks in 1898, 'is variously stated as from four to eighty-eight.'[2] The disparity arose because, in the period in which cottons had been cultivated, selection had occurred, either consciously or unconsciously. This resulted in the appearance in different places of well-marked forms, probably from the same stock which, in the absence of the history of their origins, had to be regarded as different species.[3]

The most elaborate attempt at classification by the morphological approach was made by Watt in 1907.[4] His main subdivisions of the species were based largely upon the presence or absence of fuzz on the seeds. This character, however, is inherited in simple Mendelian fashion and can be associated with other groups of characteristics. It is not strange, therefore, that of two otherwise similar forms, one may have very fuzzy and the other may have naked seeds. Classification on this basis was necessarily artificial. But the following two decades did not see any significant additional contribution to the taxonomy.[5]

Then in 1928, an article entitled 'A Contribution to the Classification of the Genus *Gossypium*' by Russian botanist G. S. Zaitzev revolutionised the taxonomy of *Gossypium*.[6] Zaitzev used discoveries concerning the minute structure of reproductive cells and adopted a genetic approach for the first time. This was a very different form of analysis from the morphological approach that had been employed previously. What Zaitzev discovered was that the cotton forms of the Old World (Asia and Africa) have a haploid number of chromosomes, 13 in the sexual cells, and the corresponding diploid number in the somatic cells is 26. But the cotton forms of the New World have a haploid chromosome number of 26, and the corresponding diploid number is 52.[7] Crosses between the cotton forms of the Old World and those of the New fail almost completely. When such crosses are made, in a natural or an artificial way, they are very rare and the hybrids obtained from such crosses in the first generation are completely sterile despite their normal appearance. Because of these genetic differences, any interaction between the Old World forms and the New World forms is entirely excluded (regardless of the statements of some botanists, especially Watt), and they are entirely isolated from each other.[8]

Furthermore, experiments indicated that hybrid forms obtained from cotton plants belonging to different sub-groups were of only transitory importance and sooner or later died out or reverted to their ancestral forms. This shows the steadiness and independency of the sub-groups. Zaitzev discovered that the cotton groups of the Old and New Worlds could be divided into two sub-groups, each with its own geographical distribution. Accordingly, he subdivided the Old World cottons into the African and the Indo-China (Asiatic) sub-group, and the New World cottons into the Central American and the Southern American sub-group.[9] The cytological, morphological, and physiological data which he collected, together with the genetic investigations of the genus *Gossypium*, supports the fact that genus *Gossypium* falls phylogenetically into the above four groups.[10]

Successive analyses by botanists have corroborated Zaitzev's findings in respect of the genetic nature of the species and found that only four species embrace the whole vast diversity of cultivated cottons. Zaitzev followed his predecessors' (particularly Watt's) nomenclature. Those who came after him found the original species of each sub-group. S. G. Harland among others, who worked on the New World cotton with 26 chromosomes, established that two species, namely G. *barbadense* and G. *hirsutum*, are good taxonomic species, and long separation had produced profound genetic changes in these two species. In consequence, G. *barbadense* and G. *hirsutum* possess relatively few genetic attributes in common. Geographical isolation over a long period of time had resulted in the production of new alleles at most sites and in a characteristic distribution of the differing alleles between the two species. Although G. *barbadense* and G. *hirsutum* were closely related and their first-generation hybrids were fully fertile, sterile and unviable types appeared in their second generation. The discontinuity between these entities in nature, even in areas where their ranges overlapped, shows they were good taxonomic species.[11]

R. A. Silow made extensive investigations into the genetic aspects of taxonomic divergence in the diploid Asiatic cottons and found that two cultivated Asiatic species, G. *arboreum* and G. *herbaceum*, diverge in their genetic composition. He maintained that taxonomically the relationship existing between G. *arboreum* and G. *herbaceum* was similar to that between the New World cultivated species, with full fertility in the first generation and partial sterility and disintegration in later generations. However, G. *herbaceum* was separated from G. *arboreum* not only by a genetic barrier but also by ecological adaptability.[12]

Three independent lines of evidence confirm Silow's findings. First, the species integrity was maintained when cultivated cottons were grown mixed in commercial crops, for mixtures of G. *arboreum* and G. *herbaceum* were grown commercially in western India and in parts of Madras for many years without breakdown of the species distinction.[13] What is more, before the distinction between G. *arboreum* and G. *herbaceum* was worked out genetically, comprehensive and long-continued efforts were made in South India to breed commercially acceptable cottons from G. *arboreum* × G. *herbaceum* hybrids. These consistently failed to produce material of agricultural value, and it was remarked that 'the better the single plant selection in any generation, the worse the segregates that appeared in its progeny'.[14] Lastly, in crosses made for the genetic analysis of species difference, there arose a wide range of unbalanced and unthrifty types in segregating generations.[15]

3. THE OLD WORLD COTTONS

(i) Origin and spread

According to Watt, 'no species of *Gossypium* is known, in its original habitat, to be an annual.'[16] Historical and botanical evidence is equally emphatic that primitive cottons were perennial.[17] Since cotton plants were originally long-lived perennials, the natural limits of distribution of the genus were fixed by climatic conditions favourable to this habit of growth.[18] The earliest civilisation to spin and weave perennial cotton seems to have been that of the Indus Valley. Fragments of cotton fabrics found at Mohenjo-Daro have been dated at approximately 3000 B.C.[19] As mentioned above, differentiation in the Old World complex of cultivated cottons led to two clearly defined species, *G. arboreum* and *G. herbaceum*. One conjecture about their origins is that the collapse of the Indus civilisation in the middle of the third millennium B.C. effectively divided Sind, the primary centre of origin, into two because there was no well-organised community to maintain irrigation facilities. Sind and Rajputana present an almost complete desert barrier between Persia and peninsular India. This isolation produced an environment under which genetic divergence took place and led to the species distinction between *G. herbaceum* and *G. arboreum*.[20] How they spread to other places is shown in Figure 1.1. This was the first phase of the evolution of cotton.

A radical transformation of cotton cultivation then occurred as a consequence of the intensification of agriculture and the establishment of the supremacy of annual cropping. Selection by man of early-maturing forms suitable for cultivation as an annual crop made possible a great extension of the original geographical limits.[21] However, 'in the thirteenth century all Indian cottons were perennials'.[22] The geographical distribution of these two species in the same period—about the time when Marco Polo was travelling—is shown in Figure 1.2. As the figure indicates, by that time *G. herbaceum* cotton had already spread to Persia and Central Asia, where the spread of the perennial cotton crop must have been very sharply limited by the severity of the winter season.

The development of annual varieties of *G. herbaceum* presented no difficulty once an annual type had been established, able to crop and complete its growth cycle before the onset of cold winters. In Persia, the

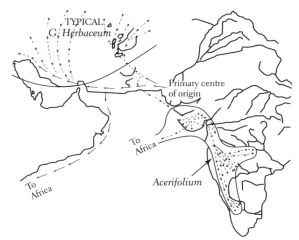

Figure 1.1 (a) The Spread of G. *herbaceum*

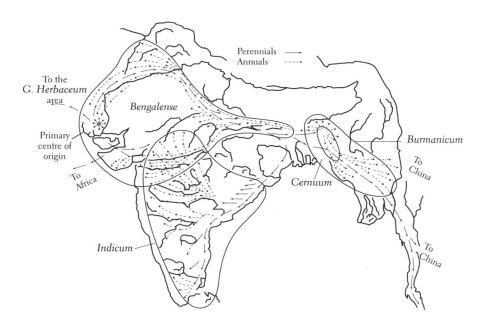

Figure 1.1 (b) The Spread of G. *arboreum*

Source: J. B. Hutchinson, R. A. Silow and S. G. Stephens eds., *The Evolution of Gossypium* (Oxford, 1947), pp. 83, 85.

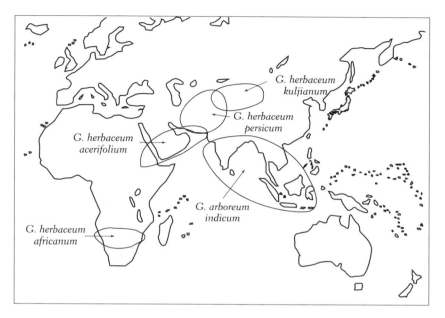

Figure 1.2 Distribution of the Old World Cottons at the Time of Marco Polo (13th century)

Source: Sir Joseph Hutchinson, 'The History and Relationships of the World's Cottons', *Endeavour*, vol. 21 (1962), p. 7.

annual variety *persicum* was developed to meet the limitations imposed by such cold winters. Further north, the very short-season variety *kuljianum* arose by selection in an area of short, hot summers and long, cold winters. Later, when the advantages of the annual varieties became apparent in India, annual *herbaceum* was carried south to replace perennial *arboreum*, giving rise to the variety *wightianum* in western India.[23] The geographical distribution of five varieties of G. *herbaceum* in the modern age is shown in Figure 1.3(a).[24]

It was initially believed that G. *arboreum* arose by differentiation from a cultivated stock of G. *herbaceum*, partly because G. *arboreum* was never truly wild[25] and partly because G. *herbaceum* is cytologically more primitive than G. *arboreum*.[26] This idea has been rejected, and what is now accepted is that the two species were adopted separately from the wild.[27]

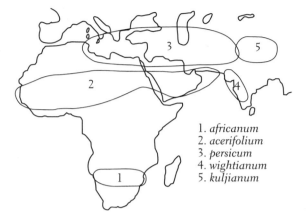

Figure 1.3 (a) Distribution of G. *herbaceum*

1. *africanum*
2. *acerifolium*
3. *persicum*
4. *wightianum*
5. *kuljianum*

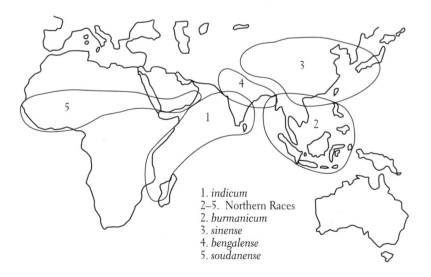

Figure 1.3 (b) Distribution of G. *arboreum*

1. *indicum*
2–5. Northern Races
2. *burmanicum*
3. *sinense*
4. *bengalense*
5. *soudanense*

Source: J. B. Hutchinson, 'New Evidence on the Origin of the Old World Cottons', *Heredity*, vol. 8.2 (1954), pp. 235–6.

According to Hutchinson, G. *arboreum* cottons were first domesticated in Gujarat.[28] G. *arboreum* developed into six geographical varieties: *soudanense* in Africa, *indicum* in western India and the peninsula, *burmanicum* in eastern Bengal, Assam, and Burma, *sinense* in China, and *bengalense* in northern and central India. This distribution is mapped in Figure 1.3(b). The species can be divided into two groups, namely, the *indicum* cottons and the *burmanicum* cottons. From the latter, two annual varieties, *bengalense* and *sinense*, arose.[29] A comparison between Figure 1.1(b) and Figure 1.3(b) shows immediately that *sinense* was the last variety of the three to be developed.

(ii) Levant cottons

The so-called Levant cotton belonged to the form of G. *herbaceum* called *persicum*.[30] The characteristics of the crop are described thus:

> Small, annual sub-shrubs, with stiff stems and few or no vegetative branches. Twigs and leaves sparsely hairy or glabrous. Leaves large, almost fleshy, very broad lobed (not more than half cut), flat. Bolls usually rather large and round, sometimes tapered and prominently shouldered; pale green, generally only cracking and remaining closed when ripe, sometimes opening widely. Seeds large, fuzzy. Lint copious, and of fair quality. Distribution: Iran and Baluchistan, Afghanistan, Russian Turkestan, Iraq, Syria, Turkey, Greece and the Mediterranean islands. It was widely spread round the Mediterranean by the Moslem invasion and was the earliest cotton cultivated in the Nile delta in Egypt.[31]

(iii) Indian cottons

The botanical study of cottons in India provides a clear indication that the ancient Indian cotton plant underwent a change beginning in the eighteenth century. In essence, the old fine cottons (G. *arboreum* var. *neglectum* forma *indica*) were replaced by coarse, high-ginning types of G. *arboreum* var. *neglectum* forma *bengalensis*.[32]

Marco Polo referred to the perennial cotton plant in Gujarat: 'The growth of these trees is such that up to twelve years they produce cotton for spinning, but from twelve to twenty an inferior fibre only.'[33] The incentive to grow annuals was much less in India than in more northern countries, and until the arrival of the British in India, there appears to be no record of the cultivation of annual types.[34] The fine spinning and weaving commonly associated with Dacca muslins was made possible by the selection of fine-quality types among perennials. These cottons were all forms of *G. arboreum*. The cotton from which the famous Dacca muslins were made was fine in staple and seems to have been triennial, as Price reported in Dacca in 1844: 'I found the triennial kind scarcely able to bear the weight of bolls that was on it; it has a fine silky staple, and the *ryots* [peasant farmers] informed me that they get from twelve annas to a rupee per maund more for it than for the annual kind'.[35] Referring to tests carried out on Dacca muslin, Ahmad stated that the mean fibre length of the cotton used in the manufacture of this fine material was found to be just about an inch, the fibre-weight per inch was 0.12 to 0.15 × 10 oz., and the yarn was so fine that there were only ten to fifteen fibres in a cross section of the yarn.[36] Though the Dacca muslins were the best known of India's fine textiles, fine spinning and weaving was carried on in all parts of India, and fine cottons, some of which were exported to Dacca, were grown to meet the demand. These cottons were the cottons of old Hindu India.

But a change occurred in the Indian cotton crop. Stimulated by a developing interest in the potential of growing cotton as an annual variety, *G. herbaceum* cotton was introduced into India, probably from Iraq. This marked 'the beginning of the second phase in the development of the Indian cotton crop.'[37]

In general, the northern cottons were short and coarse, but they possessed a high-ginning out-turn, whereas the *indicum* cottons were comparatively fine in staple, but low in ginning out-turn.[38] The selection of annual types of *G. arboreum* cottons gave rise to the annual *bengalense* of northern India. A variety of the northern cottons, it was 'a rather uniform group of early, high-ginning, relatively coarse cottons'.[39] The penetration of *bengalense* into all parts of India took place as a result of the demand for a high-ginning percentage but produced a deterioration in quality.[40] The reasons for this change are that a large export trade in raw cotton to China created a preference for quantity over quality[41] and that cheap machine-made cotton goods from England began to compete successfully with the fine hand-made local muslins, resulting in a reduction in the cultivation of fine cottons. In 1844, Price, an American planter engaged by the government to investigate the state of cotton cultivation in Bengal, reported:

> Sonergong ... is one of the principal manufacturing places in this district of the fine muslin fabrics, and, I am informed, at one time cultivated a considerable quantity of the Dacca kupas; but whether from the loom becoming more profitable than the plough, or for the want of demand for that article, I cannot say, but the ryots appear to have entirely neglected cultivation, as the lands on which they cultivated cotton at one time are now, and have been for a length of time, a dense jungle.[42]

The mill industry in India, which was concerned with coarse counts, led to the development of a marked premium for ginning percentage as against the comparatively small advantage of high quality. Since there were no safeguards against adulteration, the cultivator grew the high-ginning coarse cottons in place of the low-ginning types.[43]

The coarse-stapled *bengalense* spread in northern India during the nineteenth century and was widely extended at the expense of the finer *indicum* in the Central Provinces and northern Dacca. It displaced *herbaceum* cottons in parts of western India.[44] It also spread south into the peninsula, invading the *indicum* areas of Maharashtra and Andhra Pradesh at the expense of *indicum*.[45] The area covered by *bengalense* greatly increased in the nineteenth century, and the great cotton-growing tract changed over from medium-stapled to coarse-stapled. At the beginning of the twentieth century, the northern *bengalense*, which had displaced the southern *indicum* so successfully in the Central Provinces and Khandesh, was introduced into the *herbaceum* tract of Kathiawar. Under the name of Matthio, it spread until it made up a very large proportion of the Dholleras crop. In the Punjab, the development of a canal irrigation system resulted in a great increase in the area under cotton, and this is where the northern *bengalense* spread. These extensions all involved an increase in the amount of coarse-stapled Indian cottons which seriously weakened India's position in the cotton markets of the West.[46] There were attempts at hybridisation between short-stapled Indian cottons and the American Uplands variety. But because of the sterility barrier mentioned earlier, these were abortive. After the failure of the attempt to introduce American cottons at the time of the cotton famine of 1861–5, 'for the next half-century the Indian crop was grown virtually entirely from G. *arboreum* and G. *herbaceum.*'[47]

(iv) The Far Eastern cottons

Sinense

Of the Far Eastern countries, China was among the first to develop annual forms of *arboreum*, since most of the crop was grown in areas where winter cold would prevent the growing of perennials on a field scale. *Sinense* varieties are the earliest-ripening forms of the species and developed a distinctive character that marked them off from the two main Indian types, *bengalense* and *indicum*.[48]

Silow first noted the botanic classification of the Far Eastern cottons. In their extreme earliness and their glabrous tendency, the Far Eastern cottons were 'establishing a norm distinct from that for the species in general, and they might well be separated under the name *sinense*.'[49] Distribution was restricted to China, Japan, Manchuria, and Formosa. No perennials survived in this area. Although a wide range of variation developed within the limits of the early habit imposed by a short growing season, *sinense* continued to be a new and extremely important variant, which led to the eventual establishment of full varietal distinction within G. *arboreum*.[50] In China, Manchuria, Korea, and Japan, only early annual cottons could survive, and the spread of cotton into that region followed the development of the early annual habit characteristic of *sinense*.[51]

4. THE SPREAD OF COTTON EASTWARDS

At the end of the Middle Ages, Old World cotton, which originated in India, reached its maximum historical extent stretching from Spain to China, and on to Japan. The following pages will briefly describe when and how this expansion took place in the East.

(i) China

China had cold winters where only annual types of cotton could survive. According to Watt, cotton was grown in Chinese gardens as an ornamental shrub towards the end of the seventh century A.D. In fact, *G. herbaceum* var. *kuljianum* had been grown in western China much earlier. The use of this cotton can be dated back as early as the second century A.D. It was adapted to the climate of Central Asia, where the summers are short and the winters cold. *Kuljianum* could 'mature a small crop in three months from sowing',[52] but the cotton fibre was 'scanty and of low quality.'[53] This *G. herbaceum* var. *kuljianum* spread across China along the famous 'Silk Road' but in the reverse direction. In its eastward movement, the further the cotton went, the stronger the competition it would meet. Shenshi (Shaanxi) was the terminal point for cotton coming from Chinese Turkestan, as the city of Sian (Xi'an) in Shensi province was one of the major centres of the silk industry from the Han period (206 B.C.–220 A.D.). However, the quality of this cotton species was not good enough to break the barrier. The G. *herbaceum* would not spread throughout the Far East.[54]

China was the first of the three Far Eastern countries into which cotton was introduced. The others were Korea and Japan. During Marco Polo's stay in China from 1271–92, he observed that the people's clothing was made of silk, not cotton. He mentioned only one place that manufactured cotton goods, the city of Kien-fu in Fukien (Fujian), stating that 'they have no lack of silk', and at the same time, 'so much cotton cloth is woven here of dyed yarn that it supplies the whole province of Manzi [southern China]'.[55] Thus by the end of the thirteenth century, cotton had been established as a commercial crop. Indeed, in the last quarter of the century, cotton inspectors were set up in Fukien and some other provinces, each of which owed an annual tribute of 100,000 pieces of cloth.[56] This cotton is now known as *G. arboreum* var. *sinense*. This was initially thought to have been carried overland from Bengal and Assam or brought by sea from Indo-China.[57] The first route is now accepted as more probable on the authority of Chinese literature, which shows the chronology and diffusion of cotton cultivation in southern China (Table 1.2).[58] It is obvious from the chronology that cotton-growing spread from Yunnan to the adjacent districts of Kwangsi (Guangxi) and Indo-China, then to coastal Kwangtung (Guangdong) and Hainan Island, and finally Fukien. This is mapped in Figure 1.4.

Table 1.2 Chronology and Path of Diffusion of Cotton Cultivation in Southern China

Name of book	Period referred to (AD)	Place
Wu-lu	AD 220–280	Yungch'ang (Yunnan)
		Chiaochou (Indo-China)
Nan-chou i-wu chih	220–280	Nanchou (Kwangsi)
Nan-shih	420–588	Linyi (Indo-China)
Liang shu	502–556	Linyi (Indo-China)
Pai Chu-i's Poems	772–846	Kuei (Kwangsi)
Wen ch'ang tsa-lu	1085	Kwangsi and Kwangtung
Meh-keh hui-si	1023–1064	Kwangsi and Kwangtung
Kuei-hai yu-heng chih	1126–1193	Kueilin (Kwangsi)
Ling-wai tai-ta	1174–1190	Kwangsi and the Hainan Island
Chu-fan chih	1174–1190	Fukien
P'o-tse pien	1180–1200	Fukien and the Hainan Island

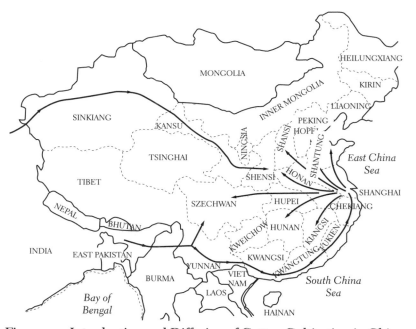

Figure 1.4 Introduction and Diffusion of Cotton Cultivation in China

Source: Kang Chao, *The Development of Cotton Production in China* (Cambridge MA, 1977), p. 17.

A century after Marco Polo, the use of cotton had become universal. When Hongwu established the Ming dynasty in 1368:

> an order was issued that in all private fields from five to ten *mou* [1 *mou* = 0.165 acre] in extent, half a *mou* each was to be planted with mulberry, hemp, and cotton; from ten *mou* and above, the quantity had to be doubled. For hemp, eight ounces were levied per *mou*; for cotton, four ounces per *mou*.[59]

Cotton cloth was also subject to taxation. The government needed the cloth for various purposes. It was exchanged for Mongolian horses and used for military purposes and for the salaries of officials. The use of cotton for military uniforms was most important of all, and it increased year by year as indicated in Table 1.3.[60]

There were two centres of cotton cultivation and manufacturing in Ming China (1368–1644). One in the north centred on the provinces bordering the Yellow River like Hopei (Hebei), Shantung (Shandong), Shansi (Shanxi), and Shensi (Shaanxi). The other in the south was in the Yangtze delta, Chekiang (Zhejiang), Fukien (Fujian), Kwangtung (Guangdong), and Szechwan (Sichuan). These remained major centres into the twentieth century.[61] By the Ming period, local specialisation and commerce had developed, linking the two regions. The north, in which

Table 1.3 Quantity of Cotton Given to Soldiers by the Chinese Government, 1385–96

	Cotton cloth (pieces)	Raw cotton (*kin*)
1385	1,239,900	283,300
1386	1,317,074	424,343
1387	1,159,585	65,600
1388	1,117,800	441,600
1389	1,345,000	560,000
1390	1,489,740	511,100
1396	2,889,900	1,415,200

Source: Nishijima Sadao, *Chūgoku keizai-shi kenkyū* (Studies in Chinese economic history) (Tokyo, 1966), p. 760.

the socio-economic structure was backward and the available technology primitive, exported surplus raw cotton beyond that required for domestic use and tax payments. The south, which had higher levels of textile technology inherited from the traditional silk industry, lacked adequate supplies of raw cotton and so imported it from the north and concentrated on manufacturing cotton goods. Sung-Chiang Prefecture in the Yangtze delta, situated between the northern and southern cotton regions, took advantage of both regions and prospered both by growing raw cotton and manufacturing.[62]

The Chinese cotton industry, which witnessed localisation and the division of labour in the Ming period, did not, however, undergo any further development. According to Elvin:

> Land that was used to grow cotton was land that could be used to grow grain; and by the sixteenth and seventeenth centuries there was very little land available in China for any crop except foodgrains. Any expansion in the supply of raw cotton beyond bare parity with population growth depended on raising higher a per-acre agricultural productivity that was already the highest in the world.[63]

(ii) Korea

There exists a record which shows that by the thirteenth century A.D., cotton cloth was being imported from China into Korea as a luxury used by the upper class. Before the introduction of cotton to Korea, the clothing materials available to Koreans were hemp, ramie (a plant fibre), and silk. It was not until 1364, when Moon Ik-chom was sent as an envoy to China and brought back cotton seed, that it was first introduced to Korea.[64] The strong encouragement of the Korean government then led to the rapid spread of cotton cultivation throughout South Korea within a few decades.[65] Gyeongsang and Jeolla became cotton-growing regions and remained so until the end of the Yi dynasty (1392–1910).[66]

Korea's resources of precious metals were very poor, and so by a decree of King Sejong (1418–50), cotton goods were used as money in home markets. Cotton cloth became one of the most important financial assets of the Korean government,[67] and large amounts were used for the uniforms of soldiers stationed on the northern border.[68]

One of the most important factors which influenced Korean cotton production in the fifteenth and sixteenth centuries A.D. was the demand for these cottons from overseas, particularly Japan, which did not have an indigenous cotton industry. But it did have abundant precious metals. Thus trade between the two countries developed as an exchange of Korean cotton cloth for Japanese precious metals. In 1439, a Japanese trade mission of 1,300 members was sent to persuade the Korean government to export more cotton goods to Japan. Korea declined for financial reasons. Another envoy was sent in 1471. This time Japan was able to secure an increased supply of Korean cotton cloth in exchange for gold. In 1482, 4,532 pieces of cotton cloth were exported to Japan. The volume of cotton cloth exports soon reached 500,000 pieces annually, double the annual tax levy on Korean cotton farmers. The domestic demand for cotton was such that Korea soon had to reduce its export value by half. In 1500, Japan proposed to exchange 110,000 *kan* of copper for Korean cotton cloth (1 *kan* = 3.75 kg.). Korea reversed its policy and accepted the copper in exchange for great quantities of cotton cloth, the bulk of which was provided at the expense of Korean cotton farmers.[69] A rough idea of the quantity of cotton cloth exported from Korea to Japan can be obtained from Table 1.4. The figures in the table cover only exports recorded by the government. The total quantity exported, including consignments not recorded or brought in by illicit traders, would undoubtedly exceed these figures.

Korean exports of cotton goods to Japan declined in the second half of the sixteenth century, as Japan began to increase her imports of cottons from China. They finally ceased in 1592 when the Japanese invaded Korea, and trade between the two countries did not resume until 1609. This cessation of trade damaged Korea more than it did Japan because Japan by that time had succeeded in planting cotton seeds and had begun to manufacture cotton goods. Korea, however, could not obtain precious metals, spices, etc., which had previously been provided by Japan. Also the export-oriented cotton textile industry of Korea suffered a recession because of the abrupt stoppage.[70] After the treaty of 1609, strictly regulated trade was carried on between Korea and a Japanese *daimyō*, the Sō family of Tsushima.[71] Japanese goods up to the equivalent value of 56,000 pieces of Korean cottons could be exchanged at the Korean port of Pusan. This lasted for about forty years. In 1651, the Sō family demanded rice instead

Table 1.4 Korean Exports of Cotton Cloth to Japan

Year		Pieces	Japanese Importer*	Year		Pieces	Japanese Importer*
1418		1,539		1481	Oct.	300	
1419		412		1482	Feb.	3,206	Sō
1420		2,280		1482	May	300	
1421		5,430		1483	Apr.	1,000	Sō
1422		-		1483	Oct.	1,100	
1423		2,640		1486		500,000	
1424		130		1488	Jan.	6,212	Sō
1450	May	998		1488		100,000	
1451	Mar.	2,394		1489	Sept.	1,000	
1453	Jun.	3,860	Doan	1489	Dec.	1,339	Miura
1464	Sept.	1,082		1489	Dec.	480	Taira
1467	Aug.	10,000		1490		10,754	The Government
1468	Mar.	2,000		1490		9,294	Sō
1470	Aug.	500		1491	Feb.	10,906	Sō
1470		1,000	Ise	1492	Mar.	15,245	Sō
1471	Dec.	3,000		1494	Mar.	28,839	The Government
1472	Jan.	100		1500		10,454	Sō
1474	Aug.	200		1525		85,000	The Government
1474	Dec.	500		1528		21,500	Ouchi
1475		27,208		1529		60,000	The Government
1476	Jan.	3,000	Sō	1538		8,000	Ouchi
1476		37,421		1542	Apr.	60,000	The Government
1477	July	400		1544		20,000	Shouni
1479	July	200		1544		45,000	The Government
1480	July	400					

Note: * As far as the name is identified.

Source: Ono Kōji, *Nihon Sangyō hattatsu-shi no kenkyū* (Studies in Japanese industrial development) (Tokyo, 1941), pp. 301–19; Sudō Keikichi, 'Kōrai makki yori Chōsen shoki ni itaru orimonogyō no hatten', (The development of the textile trade from the late Kōryū to the early Joseon) *Shakai keizai-shigaku* (Social-economic history), 12 (1942), pp. 39–45.

of cotton in exchange for Japanese silver, copper, and spices. This was because the rapid development of the cotton industry in Japan had made the country so self-sufficient that imported cotton cloth was no longer profitable. Korea acceded to the request by providing rice to the equivalent to 15,000 pieces of cloth, 26 per cent of the total. A few years later, the share of rice in the total value increased to 36 per cent. The remaining 64 per cent was in cotton cloth, but these cottons were illicitly exchanged by Japanese traders for goods such as *ginseng* and silk fabrics before they left Korea. In 1774, only 5,000 pieces of cotton cloth were brought to Japan. By that time, cotton cloth from Korea had virtually ceased to be used in Japan.[72] The further development of the cotton industry in Korea was impeded by the imposition of increasingly heavy tax burdens.[73]

(iii) Japan

A history compiled in 841 A.D. stated that cotton seed was first brought into Japan by a Malay who came from Pasei (the north-eastern part of Sumatra) to Japan in 799. Another history, compiled in 892, described the method of cotton-growing and the geographical distribution of cotton in the country. But this cotton, believed to be G. *arboreum* var. *indicum*, had become extinct by the Kamakura period (1185–1333).[74]

A new type of cotton seed was brought into Japan during the course of the sixteenth century from China via either Korea or Ryukyu (Okinawa). A number of contemporary records indicate that the introduction had taken place either between the 1490s and the 1510s, or in 1558, or 1592–5. These different dates suggest that the cotton seed was probably brought to Japan on several occasions, and its cultivation attempted in different regions. But by the early sixteenth century, there was cotton cultivation and manufacturing in the Mikawa region (the eastern half of the present Aichi Prefecture) because contemporary records suggest that sales of Mikawa-made cotton were made in Nara from the 1510s onwards, and that Mikawa merchants were trying to expand the markets for their textiles to Kyoto under the protection of their local lord, Tokugawa. Toomi and Suruga (the present Shizuoka Prefecture) are also reported to have developed cotton textile production by the middle of the sixteenth century. In the 1570s, Musashi (the present Tokyo and Saitama Prefecture) had local markets for cotton textiles.

About the same time, tax was collected as cotton textiles at the town of
Kōfu (the capital of the present Yamanashi Prefecture).[75]

These places were all situated in the eastern part of Japan, between
Nagoya and Tokyo. But cotton production throughout the Edo period
(1600–1868) was consolidated in the western half of Japan—Osaka and
the surrounding region and along the coast of the Inland Sea. Production
moved westwards in the late sixteenth century. Cotton is reported in 1591
to have been grown in Yamato (in the present Nara Prefecture). It seems
to have spread from Yamato further westwards to Osaka. Osaka emerges
as a cotton region for the first time according to a 1623 record which states
that a merchant group was organised to obtain *hoshika* (dried sardines or
dried herrings) to use as a fertilizer for growing cotton. In 1644, this trade
organisation developed into a guild that monopolised the trade in *hoshika*,
which was brought from present-day Chiba Prefecture over a distance of
500 kilometers. In 1658, another guild was formed to monopolise sales of
raw cotton for export to northern Japan. *Nōgyō zensho* (General treatise on
agriculture; 1697) and *Hyakushō denki* (Records of the peasantry; 1680–2)
both mentioned Kawachi (eastern part of Osaka), Izumi (southeastern part
of Osaka), Harima (southeastern part of Hyōgo Prefecture), Settsu (Osaka
and the eastern part of Hyōgo), and Bingo (Hiroshima Prefecture) as the
main centres of cotton production in the late seventeenth century. In the
eighteenth century, cotton products brought into Osaka in 1735 consisted
of cotton cloth (74 per cent), cotton yarn (16 per cent), and ginned and raw
cotton (10 per cent). The quantity of ginned cotton amounted to 50,000
kan and that of raw cotton 350,000 *kan*. These figures rose to an annual
average of 2 million *kan* and 1.5 million *kan* respectively between 1804 and
1834. The cotton-growing area in the early nineteenth century was almost
the same as in the early Meiji period (1868–1912).[76]

With reference to the quality of Japanese-made cotton cloth, Ono
states, 'what is certain is that the early home-made cotton fabrics would
have been much thicker than we imagine; because the Japanese had
hemp for summer clothing, cottons were initially employed for winter
clothing; they were very thick.'[77]

The introduction of cotton put Japan on the threshold of a new era in its
industrial history, an era characterised by rising prosperity and productive
energy. The rapid development of the Japanese cotton industry was one of

the most important commercial achievements of the Tokugawa regime.[78] It is now accepted that the transition from an agrarian to a modern industrial society following the Meiji Restoration was based on the industrial and commercial progress already in motion in early modern Japan, in which the cotton industry played a pioneering role. Japan in the sixteenth century was far behind China and Korea in cotton textile production, just as England lagged behind all other European countries in textile production. Both countries, though starting last in the race in quite different historical contexts, subsequently outstripped every other competitor in the West and the Far East respectively in the nineteenth century.

5. THE WESTWARD SPREAD OF COTTON

The westward movement of cotton can be described briefly in comparison to its eastward spread. The spread of Indian cotton to the West was triggered by the so-called Arab Agricultural Revolution, which took place during the period 700–1100.[79] At the heart of the revolution was the introduction of new crops into Arab territory of the Middle East and the Mediterranean. One of these crops was cotton, which spread across Egypt to North Africa, Spain, southern Italy, and Sicily. The commercial contact between the East and the West as a consequence of the Crusades brought large quantities of cotton into Europe.

The dramatic expansion of European cotton imports was closely related to the growth of the handicraft cotton textile industry (mostly fustian, a mixed fabric with cotton weft and linen warp). But there were at least three factors which prevented the medieval cotton (fustian) industry from developing further. Climatic conditions precluded the introduction of cotton cultivation into Europe except in the south, and constant wars, particularly the Thirty Years' War, dealt a heavy blow to the fustian industry. Lastly, the importation of exotic Indian textiles into Europe caused serious damage to the industry.

It was only after inexpensive high-quality Indian cotton textiles were brought to Europe from India that Europeans really became acquainted with pure cotton textiles. Europeans, who used to wear apparel made of woollen fabrics, were charmed by the beautiful thin cotton cloth from India, which people described as 'a web of woven air'. Cotton cloth, unlike

woollen fabrics, could be washed easily and was very cheap. It was treasured by the Europeans, and an enormous demand developed. As a result,
European countries needed to counteract the mounting imports of thin
cotton textiles from India. In Britain, Parliament passed two Calico Acts,
in 1700 and 1720, to ban Indian calicoes. These prohibition laws forced
the East India Company to engage in the re-export business, which led to
the establishment of markets for cotton textiles in the continents bordering the Atlantic Ocean. In order to produce in Europe a 'substitute' for the
thin Indian cotton textiles, fine yarn was necessary. The opportunity for
producing this in Europe came when the New World varieties of cotton
plant with their long, thin staple were discovered. Also, the mule spinning machine, capable of spinning fine yarn, was invented by Samuel
Crompton in 1779. In this way, a link was established between the New
World, which produced the raw material, Britain, which provided the technology, and the Atlantic rim (Europe, the Americas, and Africa), which
constituted the market.

6. THE NEW WORLD COTTONS

(i) Origin and spread

In the New World, cotton fabrics were found in ancient Peruvian tombs[80]
and in the cliff-dwellings of Betatakin, Navaho National Monument in
northern Arizona.[81] The Spanish explorers of the New World found cotton being grown by the natives from the West Indies to Mexico, Brazil,
and Peru. The Coronado expedition of 1540–42 observed cotton-growing
among the Indians of Arizona and New Mexico.[82] Evidence for the existence of a textile industry, perhaps the oldest in the New World, was discovered at the Huaca Prieta in Peru, which radiocarbon dating has proved
to be of the order of 2400 B.C.[83]

It is now accepted that G. barbadense and G. hirsutum existed as
distinct species in the wild. As in the Old World, so in the New, these
ancient cottons were perennial shrubs,[84] and their cultivated derivatives were separately domesticated. Figure 1.5 shows the distribution of
the New World cottons at the time of Columbus. Change in varieties in

Figure 1.5 Distribution of the New World Cottons at the Time of Columbus

Source: Sir Joseph Hutchinson, 'The History and Relationships of the World's Cottons,' *Endeavour* 21, (1962), p. 9.

response to the demands of cultivation was both substantial and rapid, but it went on within the species and did not lead to the emergence of new ones.[85]

Figures 1.6(a) and 1.6(b) show the spread of the two species of G. *hirsutum* and G. *barbadense*. As these figures indicate, perennials of the South American G. *barbadense* spread throughout the continent as far south as northern Argentina. But apart from a Brazilian form, there were no well-defined geographical varieties among the perennials of G. *barbadense*.[86] On the other hand, differentiation among the perennials of G. *hirsutum* is much more pronounced. Two important perennial varieties are recognised. One of these, *Marie-Galante*, includes the largest cottons of all. On the coast of the Spanish Main, from Panama to Trinidad, and thence north to the Greater Antilles and south to northern Brazil, very large shrubs or small trees up to twenty feet in the height were found in house-yards and small cultivations and sometimes growing wild among the dry coastal vegetation. These were the basis for early cotton cultivation in the West Indies. The other important perennial variety is *punctatum*, a very similar, bushy cotton found round the coast of the Gulf of Mexico from Yucatan to Florida and the Bahamas. It was recorded infrequently from Cuba, Haiti, and Puerto Rico, but not from Jamaica or the Lesser Antilles.[87] The introduction of the *hirsutum* cottons into what was later called 'the Cotton Belt' began in the seventeenth century. Cotton was first grown in the colony of Virginia in 1621 soon after Europeans settled there.[88] There are numerous records of subsequent introductions of cottons from Mexico.[89]

(ii) Upland cottons

As indicated in Figure 1.6(a), G. *hirsutum* gave rise to three morphologically distinct varieties: G. *hirsutum* and the two varieties *punctatum* and *Marie-Galante*.[90] The first was the annual type of the *hirsutum* cottons, and this became known as 'Uplands' to distinguish it from the 'Sea Island' cotton of the coastal islands, which belongs to G. *barbadense*.[91] The annual Upland cottons of typical G. *hirsutum* are the cottons of northern continental Mexico and the Cotton Belt of the United States. Their isolation took place in the Aztec state with the development of agriculture in plateau areas where the climate was unsuitable for perennials. After the spread of Upland cottons into the Cotton Belt in the early nineteenth

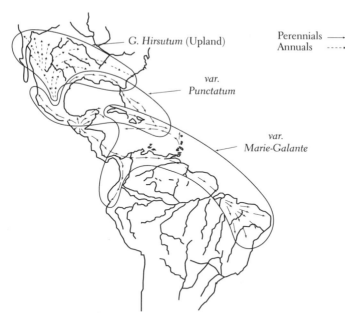

Figure 1.6 (a) Spread of G. *hirsutum*

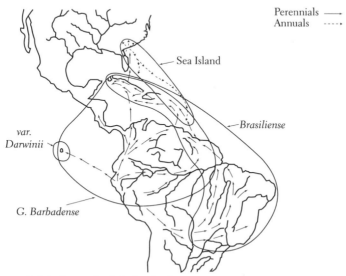

Figure 1.6 (b) Spread of G. *barbadense*

Source: J. B. Hutchinson, et al. eds, *The Evolution of Gossypium*, pp. 100, 105.

century, intensive breeding prevented the separation of distinct types in the United States.[92]

(iii) Sea Island cottons

According to Hutchinson, the Sea Island cottons form a well-defined agricultural type of the species G. *barbadense* and consist exclusively of cultivated annual cottons.[93] There are various accounts of how G. *arboreum* cottons were introduced into the southeastern United States. The most generally accepted is that the best cotton in all the Indies was sent from either the Bahamas or Jamaica to Georgia in 1785–6.[94] Since the original G. *barbadense* cottons were perennials[95] the type introduced must have been one capable of producing a worth-while crop in the first year. Types are known among the *barbadense* cottons of western South America that ripen early and are of good enough quality to have been the source from which the annual cottons of the Sea Islands might have been derived.[96] This finest crop was grown on the Sea Islands off the coast of South Carolina, and the name 'Sea Island' came to be applied to all the G. *barbadense* cottons, both mainland and island.[97] There is no record of the successful introduction of Sea Island cotton into the Old World except Egypt.[98]

(iv) Egyptian cottons

Cotton has been known to Egypt throughout recorded history. The ancient cotton of Egypt, probably of the species G. *arboreum*, was introduced from India, where this species originated.[99] About 2,500 B.C., the seed of true cotton, albeit with a primitive lint, was used as livestock feed in Nubia in the Nile Valley by Neolithic people who did not practice weaving.[100] The cotton grown by the people of this ancient Nubian kingdom was probably what is now known as G. *arboreum* var. *soudanense*,[101] whose distribution was confined to the Sudan and the West African region. Another species, G. *herbaceum*, annual in habit, was introduced into Egypt at a much later date via Arabia.[102]

Until 1820, however, no long-stapled cottons had been grown at all in Egypt.[103] The modern age of the cultivation of fine cottons started in 1820 with the introduction of Jumel cotton although cotton cultivation in Egypt had already received a great stimulus after the French occupation of the country in 1798. It fell to Muhammad Ali, the governor of Egypt and Sudan, to translate the ideas of the French scientists into practice. Among the crops which he vigorously encouraged was Jumel cotton. The exact origin of Jumel is open to debate,[104] but it is believed that the cultivation of Jumel cotton was initiated by a Swiss merchant, M. Jumel, with a perennial type of G. *barbadense* in the years following 1820. Jumel's perennial variety reached the Nile Valley from southern Nigeria by way of the trade and slave routes.[105] Cultivation of Jumel was gradually extended, and production increased from 42 tons in 1820 to 32,000 tons in 1861. It was the American Civil War (1861–5) which gave Egypt its opportunity to expand cotton production to the fullest extent.[106] After the war, Egypt was fully established as an important cotton-growing and exporting country.[107] The success of Jumel cotton led to the introduction of foreign varieties. Sea Island, Peruvian, Brazilian, and Central American varieties were imported and tried, but none was adapted for commercial cultivation except the Sea Island types. Being a form of G. *barbadense* cotton, Sea Island alone of all the types introduced gave vigorous and fertile hybrids with Jumel's perennial. Out of these hybrids, cotton breeders selected types with annual habit and some of the qualities of Sea Island, plus the vigorous cropping characteristics of the old perennial. As a result, new varieties arose such as Ashmouni,[108] a variety of annual G. *barbadense* cotton. They were members of a New World species but bred in and adapted to the Nile Valley.[109] This Egyptian cotton crop is a mixture of Sea Island and perennial G. *barbadense*.[110]

7. SOME REMARKS

As explained above, the cotton plant falls into two main divisions: American cottons and Egyptian cottons with n = 26 chromosomes, and Asiatic cottons with n = 13 chromosomes. They are separated from one another by a virtually complete sterility barrier, which prevents hybridisation. This botanical difference, combined with the fibre properties (= cotton lint) of different cottons, relates to the spinning value of the cotton. The genetic taxonomy, which started in the late 1920s, led in the 1930s to the establishment of the exact measurement and standardisation of a complete fibre test. It was called the 'Combined Stapling Test' and comprised measurements of length, fibre weight, and immaturity.[111] Based on this test, Hutchinson and Govande examined the relationship between the two most important characteristics (fibre length and fibre weight) and the spinning value (the count), then drew the conclusion that the correlation between fibre length and spinning value was greater than that between fibre weight and spinning value.[112] The relationship between fibre length and spinning value was found in the comparison between two types of Indian cotton: G. *arboreum* (northern *bengalense*) and G. *arboreum* (southern *indicum*) as in Table 1.5 below.[113] In the table, three relations are obvious: the longer the length, the lighter the weight; the longer the length, the higher the count; and the lighter the weight, the higher the count.

Table 1.5 Indian Cotton—Fibre Length, Weight, and Spinning Value

	Length of Cotton Fibre (1/100")	Hair Weight (millionths oz./inch)	Highest Standard Warp Count
G. *arboreum* (northern)	77.2	255.0	15.6
G. *arboreum* (southern)	85.0	185.5	28.0

In other words, there is a positive correlation between fibre length and yarn count, and a negative correlation between fibre weight and yarn count. With regard to the relation between fibre weight and spinning value, Hutchinson and Govande found that 'differences between crop varieties in hair-weight affect spinning value only in so far as they are associated with difference in hair-length.'[114] If so, as the fibre length of the New World cottons is far longer than that of Old World (Asiatic) cottons, the fibre weight of the former must be lighter than the latter. This relation was observed very clearly by Hutchinson and Govande as shown in Table 1.6. The table indicates that the fibre weight of G. *barbadense* and G. *hirsutum* cottons (Sea Island, Egyptian, and Uplands) is lighter than that of G. *herbaceum* and G. *arboreum* cottons (Indian and Far Eastern cottons)

Table 1.6 Hair Weight per cm., Standard Hair Weight of Cottons of Different Species

Species	Type	Hair weight per cm.	Standard hair weight	Swollen hair diameter
		(millionths oz./inch)		(1/1000 mm.)
New Word Cottons				
G. barbadense	Nahda	155	152	21.78
(Egyptian & Sea Island)	Sakha 7	125	122	20.31
	Peruvian Pima	160	170	22.56
	Maarad	141	135	21.13
	Sakel Domains	133	132	20.91
	Uppers	188	184	22.62
	Sakel	135	135	21.26
	V 135	171	168	22.28
	Sakha 7	165	161	21.98
	Sakha 7	151	145	21.15
G. barbadense	Ecuador	242	263	27.08
(South American types)	Iquitos	265	267	27.68
G. hirsutum	Texas	226	230	25.11
(Uplands)	Boweds	230	249	25.17
	Sudan American	150	170	22.20
	Nigerian	173	180	22.50
	Texas	207	218	24.46
Asiatic Cottons				
G. arboreum	G. arboreum	356	321	30.94
(Northern Indian)	Oomras improved	274	271	27.58
	Khandoish	319	298	30.26
G. arboreum	Madras Northerns	213	217	24.59
(Southern Indian)	Karunganni	223	222	25.69
	Tinnivelly	232	230	25.25
G. arboreum	Chinese	337	328	32.16
(Burmese & Chinese)	Rangoon	287	324	30.84
	Chinese	412	386	35.39
G. herbaceum var. frulescens	Broach	264	268	28.54
	Surat	303	290	29.75
	Hagari	238	234	25.26

Note: * Measurement of the diameters of hairs swollen in an 18% soda solution, which gives an excellent estimate of the intrinsic fineness of a cotton.

Source: J. B. Hutchinson and G. K. Govande, 'Cotton Botany and the Spinning Value and Hair Properties of Cotton Lint', *The Indian Journal of Agricultural Science*, vol. 8 (1938), pp. 38–39.

and implies that British cotton textiles made of New World cottons are lighter in weight than Far Eastern textiles made from Old World cottons. It also shows that, as the diameters of the fibres of Old World cottons are greater than those of New World cottons, yarns spun from Old World cottons are coarser (thicker) than those from the latter.

Based on these characteristics, the Atlantic market for these cotton products was distinct from the cotton markets of East Asia. In East Asia, short-staple cotton, coarse yarn, and thick textiles were produced and consumed. Thus these two types of cottons did not compete for the same purchasers. It was the East Asian market, demanding qualities for cotton goods distinct from those demanded by the West, that Japan supplied during the late nineteenth and twentieth centuries when she became involved in the intra-Asian trade after the opening of her ports in 1859.

Chapter Two

THE SPREAD OF COTTON TEXTILES TO THE WEST: INDIA'S ROLE IN THE INDUSTRIAL REVOLUTION

G reat Britain was the 'first industrial nation' in the world, and the cotton industry played a vital role in her industrial revolution. What we shall focus on here is the 'challenge and response' relationship between Britain and India, as India had grown cotton for several thousands of years B.C. and had monopolised the industry for millenia. P. J. Thomas once succinctly noted: 'What silk was to China, linen to Egypt, wool to England, that was cotton to India.'[1] This chapter will outline how and when India's cotton industry was overtaken by Britain's and will argue that it was India that initiated the Industrial Revolution and globalisation.

1. THE WEST UNDER THE INFLUENCE OF INDIAN COTTONS: CA. 1680–CA. 1780

Vasco da Gama, on arrival at Calicut in 1498, proclaimed that he had come in search of Christians and spices.[2] Undoubtedly spices and pepper, which were daily necessities as condiments and preservatives in medieval Europe, were of primary importance to the West–East trade.[3]

By the time Europeans arrived in the East Indies, Indian cotton textiles were well established as the principal items in barter for spices in the Malay Archipelago. This Indian Ocean trade was three-way. Ships, mostly manned by Arabs, left the Red Sea and Persian Gulf with bullion, to be exchanged in India for textiles. The textiles were then carried by the same ships to the Malay Archipelago and bartered there for spices. Finally, the ships returned direct to the Middle East laden with spices, which were then converted into bullion for another round of the same journey. The Portuguese, who arrived at the end of the fifteenth century, found this barter trade profitable, and in the following century succeeded in taking it for themselves, diverting the origin of its routes from the Middle East to Western Europe.

In the seventeenth century, the Indian Ocean trade was seized by the English and the Dutch, but its essential three-cornered trade structure remained the same.[4] It was difficult for merchants of any nation to get spices without Indian textiles. The Dutch established factories in India, 'first of all due to the need for Indian textiles', which were 'the only marketable commodities in the exchange with the population of the spice islands.'[5]

At the time the English East India Company was founded, there was no strong incentive to buy Indian textiles. The primary objective of the Company was to sell their woollen textiles in Asia. However, the Company's attempts to exchange their woollens in the spice islands, India, and the Far East proved to be unsuccessful even in China and Japan, where the cold winter climate was thought to favour the sale of English woollen cloth.[6] The Company's second objective was to compete with the Portuguese and the Dutch for spices and pepper from the Malay Archipelago. But few European commodities could be sold in India to obtain the Indian textiles required for barter. As a result, bullion was sent.[7] See Table 2.1.

The normal pattern of trade was that, in order to acquire spices and drugs, it was necessary to take cotton goods to the producing markets, as producers would take little else. But in order to obtain sufficient cotton goods, it was necessary to take gold or silver to India because demand for other imports was small.[8]

After the Portuguese retreat, conflict between the Dutch and the English for control of this trade ended in Dutch victory. The English defeat began after the Amboyna massacre in 1623 and ended when

Table 2.1 English Exports to Asia: 1660–1760

	A	B	B/A
Year	Total	Treasure	(%)
1660	68,388	51,329	75.1
1670	273,177	189,704	69.4
1680	461,206	394,464	85.5
1690	10,239	–	–
1700	579,198	482,219	83.3
1710	508,907	373,351	73.4
1720	697,009	571,195	81.9
1730	756,489	631,066	83.4
1740	575,332	440,319	76.5
1750	1,292,589	1,012,921	78.4
1760	515,144	143,400	27.8

Source: K. N. Chaudhuri, *The Trading World of Asia and The English East India Company 1660–1760* (Cambridge, 1978), Tables C. 1 and C. 4 in Appendix 5, pp. 507 and 512.

they were driven from Bantam in 1682, losing their last foothold in the Malay Archipelago. Compelled to retreat to the Indian subcontinent, the English East India Company was drawn to the possibility of selling Indian textiles at home. In a dispatch of 27 May 1668, the Directors initiated the new policy, saying: 'Encourage the natives and invite them to come thither. . . . We would also have you put the natives upon the making of such Calicoes as they are capable of, . . . and . . . procure the bringing of [cotton] out of the Country, or the conveying of it to them by the sea. . . . The making of Calicoes is that in which people of India are most apt, and a Commodity which is most vendible in Europe.'[9]

Previously, imports to England had largely consisted of indigo, drugs, spices, saltpetre, some calicoes, raw cotton, raw silk, diamonds, and other precious stones.[10] Now, the Company's main interest was transferred to the import of Indian cotton manufactures. See Table 2.2.

The growing volume of Indian cotton imports brought about a revolutionary change in textile fashions in England, which had until then faced no serious challenge to the supremacy of wool. Many factors contributed to the success of Indian textiles. The East India Company devised many

Table 2.2 English Imports from Asia: 1664–1760˙

				(£'000)
Period	A	B	B/A	
Annual average per decade	Total	Textiles	(%)	
1664–1670*	102	64	63	
1671–1680	283	194	69	
1681–1690	380	282	74	
1691–1700	173	119	69	
1701–1710	271	167	62	
1711–1720	478	349	73	
1721–1730	633	415	66	
1731–1740	656	429	65	
1741–1750	778	522	67	
1751–1760	863	419	49	

Note: * Annual average of seven years.

Source: Chaudhuri, *The Trading World of Asia and the English East India Company*, Tables C. 2
and C. 24 in Appendix 5, pp. 510 and 547.

ways to develop a market for cotton textiles at home. The Directors sent
out sample-patterns as models for Indian cotton-printers to copy or adapt
to European needs, or they sent English craftsmen to teach these patterns
directly to local craftsmen.[11] The impact of cottons on English fashion
was due to the fact that the Company manipulated its connections with
the classes that dictated fashion in Restoration society.[12] It was also due
to the contemporary fashion for 'undress', or light-weight clothes.[13] This
fashion was already seen in the first half of the seventeenth century, which
witnessed the expansion of the trade in the so-called new draperies, that
is, 'fabrics made of combed, long-staple wool and characterized by their
light weight and their wide range of patterns.'[14] Cotton was more suited to
this fashion, so it had an obvious place in the trend towards light-weight
fabrics. One writer declared that these light commodities were 'as light as
women and as slight as cobwebs.'[15] In addition, the brilliance and fastness
of Indian dye-colours appealed to the English.[16] Indian cotton textiles were
also cheaper than European textiles[17] and had a wide appeal to consumers
because of their ready washability and easy colour printing.

Thus by the end of the seventeenth century, Indian cotton manufactures had attained a measure of popularity that Khan called 'unrivalled'.[18] Indeed, the last two decades of the century were characterised by 'the Indian Craze'.[19] A pamphlet written in 1699 remarked:

> It was scarce thought about twenty years since that we should ever see Calicoes, the ornaments of our greatest Gallants (for such they are whether we call them Muslins, Shades or anything else) when they were then rarely used . . . but now few think themselves well dressed till they are made up in Calicoes, both men and women, Calico Shirts, Neckcloths, Cuffs, Pocket-handkerchiefs for the former, Head-dresses, Night-royls, Hoods, Sleeves, Aprons, Gowns, Petticoats and what not, for the latter, besides Indian-Stockings for both sexes; and indeed it will be a hard matter to put them out of this Fancy; nothing but an act of Parliament or humour of the Court can do it . . . .[20]

In 1708, Defoe could write, 'Almost everything that used to be wool or silk, relating either to the dress of the women or the furniture of our houses, was supplied by Indian trade.'[21] S. D. Chapman and S. Chassagne's work on the emergence of European cotton textile printing notes that the introduction of light, gaily-patterned Indian cottons created 'a sensation which lasted a century, a consumer craze that overrode the opposition of governments, vested interests (the existing wool and silk industries) and, above all, the centuries-old vernacular traditions in dress.'[22]

England was not the only country in Europe where Indian textiles were used. They were increasingly worn all over the Continent. In France, 'their use spread like wild fire' to the great detriment of the local weavers.[23] The increasing flow of imports of Indian textiles provoked opposition from established textile producers. In almost every country, the ruin of existing manufactures was loudly prophesied.[24] Indian cottons were denounced in England as 'tawdry, pie-spotted, flabby, ragged, low priced, made by a parcel of heathens and pagans that worship the Devil and work for 1/2d. a day'.[25] The sharp conflict of interests between European manufacturers of silk and wool and the East India Company reached a crisis by the end of the seventeenth century.

In England, Parliament introduced the Calico Act of 1700, which prohibited the import of chintzes for domestic use and wear, though it allowed them to be imported for re-export. Muslins and plain calicoes were exempt, and cotton yarn was also free to be imported for use in fustians. The Calico Act of 1720 prohibited domestic consumption of any pure cotton fabric, including calicoes. However, muslin was exempt, and again the Act did not apply to Indian textiles imported for re-export. Although smuggling of Indian cottons continued, the Act had significant effects both internally and externally upon the development of the English cotton industry.

At home, English textile producers were encouraged to manufacture goods similar to Indian calicoes. One of the earliest results of these attempts at imitation was the introduction of colour printing on Indian calicoes.[26] By 1744, colour printing had reached such a state of perfection in England that it could match Indian chintzes although the superiority of English goods was limited to the finest work.[27]

In overseas trade, the prohibition acts forced the Company to engage in the re-export business. There can be little doubt that the English East India Company was Europe's greatest importer and exporter of Oriental textiles. The Dutch East India Company ranked next. See Tables 2.3 & 2.4.

A limited quantity of Indian textiles was also imported by *La Grande Compagnie des Indes Orientales*.[28] English imports of Indian cottons were exported to Germany in exchange for German linens, displacing English woollen goods.[29] Spain was another European country to which the Company exported large quantities of Indian textiles, and many were then re-shipped to the Spanish colonies.[30]

The British colonies in America also provided important markets for such goods, and these markets greatly expanded, along with the growth of the great triangular trade featuring African slave traders, planters in North America and the West Indies, and the merchants of Liverpool, Bristol, and London. This triangular trade was, of course, the core of the 'Commercial Empire of the Atlantic'.[31] Certainly English-made cotton goods were exported to these regions, but 'East India goods only and not those imitated are saleable', reported the Governor of Cape Coast Castle in 1706. 'The box of cloaths in imitation of those . . . are far from being approved on by the natives being so heavy', said his successor in 1724. He thought that if they had been finer, they would have had more chance of success.[32] Exports of English cottons formed less than 10 per cent of total

Table 2.3 Imports of Oriental
Textiles by the English East
India Company (Ten-year
Totals): 1664–1760

Period	Pieces ('000)
1664–1670*	1,988
1671–1680	5,781
1681–1690	7,068
1691–1700	2,958
1701–1710	2,775
1711–1720	5,521
1721–1730	7,827
1731–1740	7,652
1741–1750	7,718
1751–1760	5,275

Note: * seven-year total.

Source: Chaudhuri, *Trading World of Asia
   and the English East India Company
   1660–1760*, pp. 547–8.

Table 2.4 The Dutch Sales of
Asiatic Cotton Textiles at
Kamer Amsterdam (Ten-year
Totals): 1650–1729

Period	Pieces ('000)
1650–1659	449
1660–1669	439
1670–1679	686
1680–1689	1,738
1690–1699	1,388
1700–1709	1,749
1710–1719	2,048
1720–1729	2,449

Source: Glamann, *Dutch-Asiatic Trade
   1620–1740*, p. 143.

British exports of cottons to Africa in 1751, and twenty years later, even though total cotton exports to Africa had increased three-fold, the share of English cottons was still only a little more than 10 per cent. It was Indian goods which took the lion's share of the market.[33] The quantities of Indian textiles imported into the American colonies were also considerable. A great deal was re-shipped from England, but the bulk of Indian textiles used in the colonies were carried there by smugglers. In 1714, for example, New Englanders, who had little respect for the monopoly rights of the East India Company, imported prohibited goods worth £10,523. This was a fraction of the total imports. Smuggling is said to have continued throughout the eighteenth century.[34] According to Ralph Davis, the official value of re-exports of calicoes[35] was £480,000 in 1722/24, £700,000 in 1772/74, and further to £1,440,000 in 1804/06.[36] As indicated in Table 2.5 (a) and (b), showing the overseas markets for English-made cottons and Indian calicoes in the period 1699–1774, Indian textiles had a greater share than English cottons.

Table 2.5

(a) Re-exports of Calicoes from England 1699–1774 (£ '000)

	Northwest Europe	Northern Europe	Southern Europe	British Islands	America	Total
1699–1701	239	2	36	18	45	340
1722–1724	419		14	6	45	484
1752–1754	434	4	24	5	32	499
1772–1774	478	7	116	15	85	701

(b) Exports of English Cottons 1699–1774 (£ '000)

1699–1701	2	1	1		16	20
1722–1724				3	15	18
1752–1754		1		4	78	83
1772–1774	1	1	6	37	176	221

Source: Ralph Davis, 'English Foreign Trade, 1700–1774', *Economic History Review* (2nd series), vol. 15 (1962), pp. 302–3.

Taking into account the imports of Indian textiles by other European nations, plus imports by smugglers, Indian textiles clearly dominated the Atlantic trading world throughout the eighteenth century. Thus the task for entrepreneurs in Britain's nascent cotton industry was to make cotton goods of as good a quality as their Indian competitors and take over the markets previously supplied by Indian products.

2. THE BRITISH RESPONSE TO THE IMPACT OF INDIAN COTTONS: CA. 1780 ONWARD

(i) Change in the supply sources of raw cotton

For about the first three-quarters of the eighteenth century, the expansion of the English cotton industry was restricted by the relatively low productivity of spinners using the hand-wheel. Apart from calico printing, competition was principally focussed on quantity rather than quality.[37] The cotton used in England in the same period came largely from two sources, the West Indies and the Levant. See Table 2.6 (a).

Table 2.6 Sources of Imports of Raw Cotton into England

(Percentage Share)

(a)

Year	Long-stapled West Indies	Short-stapled Misc., Europe & Africa	Levant	Prize	Total
1701–1710	50.5	2.5	46.5	0.5	100
1711–1720	77.8	0.3	21.9	0.0	100
1721–1730	78.8	0.6	20.6	0.0	100
1731–1740	77.7	0.9	21.4	0.0	100
1741–1750	66.3	1.7	26.6	5.4	100
1751–1760	60.0	1.2	33.3	5.5	100
1761–1770	69.3	2.4	27.7	0.6	100
1771–1780	60.8	11.9	23.8	3.5	100

(b)

Year	Long-stapled Latin America	West Indies	U.S.A.	Canada	Europe	Short-stapled Asia	Near East	Total
1784–1786	0	49.0	0.2	0.1	39.7	0.1	10.9	100
1794–1796	0	45.0	4.5	3.7	36.4	1.0	9.4	100
1804–1806	10.4	34.1	37.3	0.1	16.5	1.5	0.1	100

(c)

Year	Long-stapled U.S.A.	Brazil	West Indies & Co.	East Indies & Co.	Short-stapled Mediterranean	Total
1811–1820	38.6	31.6	12.6	16.8	0.4	100
1821–1830	59.1	25.9	3.5	7.3	4.2	100
1831–1840	72.3	11.3	2.0	11.6	2.8	100
1841–1850	75.3	7.1	0.8	13.5	3.3	100
1851–1860	72.6	5.1	0.4	17.6	4.3	100

Source: A. P. Wadsworth & J. de L. Mann, *The Cotton Trade and Industrial Lancashire, 1600–1780* (Manchester, 1931), pp. 520–1 for (a); R. Davis, *The Industrial Revolution and British Overseas Trade* (Leicester, 1979), pp. 110, 113 & 115 for (b); T. Ellison, *The Cotton Trade of Great Britain* (London, 1968), Table No. 1 in Appendix for (c).

Imports varied from year to year, but it is clear from the table that over the course of the eighteenth century, the share of Levant raw cotton was diminishing. The rest came almost entirely from the West Indies. The import of long-stapled cottons from the New World prior to ca. 1780, however, did not result in any improvement in the quality of cotton goods, because 'no attention was paid to the quality of the crop until late in the century'.[38] The advent of mules (1779) made fine spinning possible from good grades of raw cotton.

In 1788 (nine years after the invention of Crompton's mule), Colquhoun wrote:

> the improvements . . . in the culture of this article [raw cotton] in Barbadoes, added to the acquisition of the fine Cotton of the growth of Surinam and the Brazils, has been the means of introducing and extend-ing the Muslin Manufacture, during the last three years, to a height that is almost incredible: And this circumstance has incontestably proved, that nothing is wanted but a fine raw material, to fix in Great Britain, for ever, a decided pre-eminence in the manufacture of Muslins.[39]

In the late eighteenth century, as more and more raw cotton was imported from southern and northwestern Europe, it is difficult to discover where it originated, but by the end of the century, Brazilian cotton seems to have been recognised as supreme above all others. This was shown in the sudden increase in imports from Latin America in Table 2.6 (b).

Imports of cotton from the United States remained insignificant throughout the 1780s and early 1790s. In 1793, Eli Whitney invented the saw-gin, which made it possible to 'cleanse three hundredweight of cotton in a day.'[40] That year, exports of cotton from the United States were 500,000 lbs. But as a result of the coming of the saw-gin, the following year exports rose to 1,600,000 lbs., and five years later (in 1799), they reached 9,500,000 lbs.[41] The Sea Islands, which did not use the saw-gin, increased exports almost simultaneously. Exports of Sea Island cotton from South Carolina were 94,000 lbs. in 1793. This rose to 159,000 lbs. in the following year, then to 2,800,000 lbs., and reached 8,300,000 lbs. in 1801.[42] The bulk of Sea Island cotton was exported to England.[43] The crucial expansion of British imports of cotton from the United States took place during the boom period between 1799–1802, and by 1802, the

United States had become the largest supplier of cotton.[44] As shown in Table 2.6 (c), American cotton formed more than 70 per cent of the total from the 1830s onward. By contrast, Asiatic short-stapled cottons, which had been a quarter to a third of imports for the first three-quarters of the eighteenth century, had effectively disappeared by the end of the century. By 1800, the new British cotton industry had abandoned the cottons of the Old World and had become tied to New World cottons.

(ii) Manufacture of modern types of cotton goods

In 1774, an Act of Parliament made it lawful for British citizens to wear new manufactured stuff made of cotton. This coincided with the advent of spinning machinery including Hargreaves's spinning-jenny (patented in 1770), Arkwright's water-frame (patented in 1769), and above all Crompton's mule (patented in 1779). These technical developments in the cotton industry brought about a spectacular increase in productivity, falling prices, and improvement in the quality of yarn. By the end of the eighteenth century, cotton manufacture was no longer an art and was fast becoming a science.

Cotton yarn is subject to classification by 'counts', which accurately indicate the fineness of the yarn. The counts refer to the number of hanks (a hank = 840 yards) contained in a pound weight of cotton yarn; the higher the count, the finer the yarn. The quality of Indian yarns imported by the East India Company in the middle of the eighteenth century was typified by counts of 60s,[45] while in England, 'the traditional one-thread hand wheel spun "little or no thread finer than 16 to 20" . . . and even-ness depended on the delicacy of the touch of the spinner.'[46] Hargreaves's jenny reached 20s, while Arkwright, at the pinnacle of his achievement, attained 60s.[47] Crompton succeeded in spinning 40s. A short time later, he was able to spin 60s and before long, 80s.[48] Subsequent improvements made it possible to spin yarn of 350s by the 1810s.[49] By 1830, even 350s had become a standard article of commerce sold in substantial quanti-ties.[50] A fine cotton spinning company, McConnel & Co., established in about 1790, was spinning from 60s up to 160s in 1795, and in 1833, they employed 1,545 persons (or about 200 more than any other spinner), with average counts reaching 170s.[51] In the early 1830s, the average counts spun in England and Scotland were estimated at 50s.[52]

Production costs of spinning high counts fell drastically. In the early 1780s, the cost of a pound of 100s was about £2, or 40 shillings, but by 1830, it had fallen to only 3 shillings.[53] This was attributable to the fall in price of raw cotton, the development in the application of steam power to the mule, and the pressure to reduce production costs because of competition among cotton spinners. The number of mule spindles increased rapidly. There were 50,000 in 1788,[54] but in 1811, Crompton provided evidence to Parliament that in England and Scotland, his mule provided 4,500,000 spindles, while Hargreaves's jenny and Arkwright's water-frame accounted for less than 500,000.[55]

Before the mule, fine muslins had been imported from India as were all fine yarns for weaving muslins. But the availability of domestically spun fine yarn of the highest quality at falling prices greatly stimulated demand, and Crompton's mule became known as the 'Muslin Wheel'.[56] Muslin manufacture was permanently established by Thomas Ainsworth at Bolton in 1780.[57] Samuel Oldknow at Stockport and Anderton became a maker of muslins in the spring of 1783, and within three years was recognised as the leading producer in the kingdom.[58] The new availability of long-stapled cottons stimulated further demand. By 1787, Britain was already producing 500,000 pieces.[59]

The result was obvious. The trade between Britain and India was reversed.

As shown in Table 2.7, exports of British-made cottons to Europe, Africa, and America greatly exceeded British re-exports of Indian calicoes to these regions by the 1780s.

To sum up, the British cotton industry made a decisive shift at the end of the eighteenth century from Old World short-staple raw cotton to New World long-staple raw cotton. From 1784–6, cotton goods accounted for only 6 per cent of Britain's exports, but this had increased to 15.6 per cent in 1794–6 and reached 42.3 per cent in 1804–6. Nearly all of these cotton goods found their way to Europe, Africa, and America. Ninety-nine per cent of Britain's cotton exports from 1790 to 1820 were to the Atlantic trading world. English cottons had clearly superseded Indian cottons in this Atlantic market. The Atlantic economy thus became linked to Britain as a market for cotton goods because of the development of improved raw

Table 2.7

(a) Re-exports of Indian Calicoes from England 1784–1816 (£ '000)

Year	Europe	Africa	America	Others	Total
1784–1786	261	86	40	7	395
1794–1796	881	144	113	10	1,148
1804–1806	590	92	89	6	777
1814–1816	293	15	99	9	433

(b) Exports of English Cottons 1784–1816 (£ '000)

Year	Europe	Africa	America	Others	Total
1784–1786	341	164	292		797
1794–1796	823	198	2,432		3,454
1804–1806	5,342	603	7,949	74	13,968
1814–1816	9,207	89	7,005	228	16,529

Source: Ralph Davis, *The Industrial Revolution and British Overseas Trade*, pp. 94–97, 102–5.

materials from the New World and the invention of improved spinning technology.

This commercial relationship came to be characterised by a three-cornered trade network based on exports of British cotton goods to Africa, transportation of African slaves to the Americas, and exports of American raw cotton to Britain. Cotton, once one of the corners of the triangular Indian Ocean trade network, had now become part of the three-cornered Atlantic Ocean trade network. Britain had finally gained ascendancy in the manufacture of one of the products of India and established a production base for global trade.

Meanwhile British imports of Indian textiles declined rapidly, and British-made cloth began to flow into the Indian subcontinent, the quantities growing rapidly. See Table 2.8 below.

Britain's export of cotton cloth to India in 1835 was 65 times greater than it had been in 1814. This increasing dependency of Britain's cotton cloth exports on the Indian markets continued and intensified towards the end of the nineteenth century.

Table 2.8 British Cloth Exports to India and British Imports of Indian Textiles

	British Cloth Exports to India (million yards)	British Imports of Indian Textiles (million pieces)
1814	0.8	1.3
1821	19.1	0.5
1828	42.8	0.4
1835	51.8	0.3

Source: J. G. Borpujari, 'The British Impact on the Indian Cotton Textile Industry, 1757–1865', Cambridge University Ph.D. thesis (1969), pp. 166, 168.

PART TWO

SPECIALISATION IN COTTON GOODS IN FAR EASTERN MARKETS, 1870–1900

Chapter Three

BRITISH EXPANSION INTO ASIAN MARKETS

1. INTRODUCTION

This chapter is concerned with one of the most important manufactures of the nineteenth century for both Britain and East Asia, cotton textiles.

Cotton goods in the markets, as commodities, may be looked at from two viewpoints, their exchange-value and their use-value.[1] The exchange-value of a commodity manifests itself in price, while the utility of a commodity gives it a use-value. In theory, 'the value of commodities is inversely proportional to the productivity of labour'.[2] Thus advanced Britain could have sold her products cheaply to backwards Asia. A comparative analysis of prices of both British and Asian cotton goods, therefore, should be interesting to investigate.

In India, as early as 1834–5, the Governor General is said to have reported, 'the misery hardly finds a parallel in the history of commerce. The bones of the cotton weavers are bleaching the plains of India.'[3] This famous passage, quoted in Marx's *Capital* with the source unrecorded, has not been found by anyone but Marx.[4] However, it is often referred to as an example of cheap machine-made cloth uprooting local handicrafts.[5] If this quotation were true, Far Eastern cotton weavers would have suffered a similar fate. Marx, perhaps with a similar thought in mind, also wrote in the *Communist Manifesto*: 'the cheap prices of its [the bourgeoisie's] commodities are the heavy artillery with which it batters down all Chinese walls'.[6] Since China and Japan were forced to expose themselves to so-called 'Free Trade', having been deprived of tariff protection by the treaties they made with the Western Powers, it has been taken for granted that imports of British manufactures destroyed their handicraft industries too, or pushed them to the brink of collapse. The following sections will examine this generalisation.

2. THE GROWTH OF EAST ASIAN MARKETS

First of all, we shall look at the position of East Asia as a market for British cotton goods.

In the international trading system of the late nineteenth and the early twentieth centuries, in which cottons played such important part, the world's payments mechanism centred on Britain's ability to offset a deficit with the rapidly industrialising countries of Europe and North America by means of a surplus with the primary producers of the underdeveloped world and Asia in particular.[7] According to Saul's rough calculation of Britain's balance of payments in 1910, it had £118 million surplus in its dealings with the rest of the world—to which India, China, and Japan contributed £60 million, £13 million, £13 million respectively (or 70 per cent). On the other hand, Britain had deficits of £145 million, of which £50 million were with the United States, £45 million with Continental Europe, and £25 million with Canada.[8] Thus Britain's surplus with India, and to a lesser extent China and Japan, were vital for it to sustain its deficits with industrial Europe and America. The British cotton trade with Asia was an important part of this international trade, for the British surplus with Asia, as far as visible items are concerned, came largely from its exports of cotton goods to Asia. By 1870, Britain had switched the main outlet of its cotton goods from the Continent and the United States to Asia as the former countries had set up high tariff barriers against British cotton goods and had begun to substitute their own cotton manufactures for British products. In the mid nineteenth century, Asia imported only 25 per cent of British exports of cotton goods including yarns[9] but 50 per cent by the end of the century.[10] These British goods consisted mainly of cotton textiles. Britain exported 43 per cent of its cotton textile exports to Asia in 1870.[11] This proportion gradually increased and fluctuated at around 55 per cent in the 1890s.[12]

Consequently British cotton manufactures became the greatest articles of import to Asian countries in the nineteenth century. The top three importers were India, China, and Japan. The changing share of cotton goods in their total imports are shown in Table 3.1. Did these British goods destroy the Asian cotton industry?

Table 3.1 Imports of Cotton Goods ('000 omitted)

Annual averages for decades

(a) India (a: £; b and c: Tens of Rupees)

Year	Total Imports	Cotton Goods	
		Manufactures	Twist and Yarn
1871–1880 (a)	34,902 (100%)	15,758 (45.1%)	2,810 (8.1%)
1881–1890 (b)	55,915 (100%)	23,299 (41.7%)	3,443 (6.2%)
1891–1899 (c)	69,012 (100%)	25,693 (37.2%)	3,141 (4.6%)

(b) China (Haikwan tael)

Year	Total Imports	Manufactures	Twist and Yarn
1871–1880	73,680 (100%)	21,628 (29.4%)	2,686 (3.6%)
1881–1890	97,473 (100%)	31,644 (32.5%)	9,349 (9.6%)
1891–1900	191,084 (100%)	67,148 (35.1%)	29,290 (15.3%)

(c) Japan (¥)

Year	Total Imports	Manufactures	Twist and Yarn
1871–1880	28,348 (100%)	5,194 (18.3%)	4,921 (17.4%)
1881–1890	43,787 (100%)	3,661 (8.4%)	8,054 (18.4%)
1891–1900	164,539 (100%)	8,739 (5.3%)	7,662 (4.7%)

Sources: Statistical Abstract relating to British India: *Parl. Papers 1881*, XCIII (c. 2976); *Parl. Papers 1890–91*, LXXXIX (c. 6502); *Parl. Papers 1902*, CXII (cd. 802) for India. Hsiao Liang-lin, *China's Foreign Trade Statistics 1864–1949*, pp. 22, 23, 38 for China. *Nippon bōeki seiran* (Foreign trade of Japan: A statistical survey), pp. 2, 230, 241 for Japan.

3. COTTON YARN PRODUCTION IN EAST ASIA

Table 3.2 shows the worldwide distribution of cotton spindles in the last
three decades of the century. It helps us understand the position of the
Asian cotton industry in the world. According to the table, the total number of cotton spindles in the world in 1870 was 59,000,000, distributed in
these proportions: Britain 64 per cent, the Continent of Europe 22 per
cent, America 12 per cent, and Asia 2 per cent. By 1900, total spindlage
had effectively doubled to 107,000,000. But the percentage distribution
had changed significantly. Britain's share had fallen to 43 per cent, while
that of the Continent and America had risen to 30 per cent and 19 per
cent respectively. The Asian share had also increased to 6 per cent. Thus
during the period 1870 to 1900, the relative position of Britain declined as
the industry grew in the rest of the world. Certainly Britain increased its
absolute number of spindles, but the increase was far less than that on the
Continent and in the New World. Particularly of note is the increase of
spindles in Asia, which amounted to two-thirds of the increase in Britain.
The growth of capacity in Asia was the fastest of all. During the thirty
years, 1870 to 1900, the number of spindles on the Continent grew 2.5-
fold, 2.9-fold in the New World, but only 1.2-fold in Britain. Asia, on the
other hand, experienced a six-fold increase. India and Japan (and later

Table 3.2 World Distribution of Cotton Spindles

Year	Great Britain	Continent	Total America	Asia	World
1870	37,700,000	12,838,000	7,132,000	1,130,000	58,800,000
1880	43,000,000	18,885,000	10,653,000	1,492,000	74,000,000
1890	44,500,000	26,353,000	14,188,000	3,659,000	88,700,000
1900	46,500,000	32,225,000	20,610,000	6,802,000	107,395,000
1910	53,397,000	41,167,000	30,804,000	9,126,000	134,434,000
1870	100	100	100	100	100
1880	114	147	149	132	126
1890	118	205	199	324	151
1900	123	251	289	602	183
1910	142	321	432	808	229

Source: W. H. Slater, 'World Cotton Spinning Capacity', in *Textile Recorder* (1930), p. 27.

China) played an important part in the development of the cotton spinning industries of Asia. But it is significant that the industry developed despite growing exports of British cotton goods to Asia at the same time. Some figures will illuminate the remarkable performance of the cotton spinning industry in India and Japan.

In the early 1900s, India's output of cotton yarn was 532 million lbs., of which she exported 234 million lbs. (see Table 3.5). These figures are comparable with those of Britain, whose total output of cotton yarn in 1907 was shown as 1,530 million lbs.,[13] of which she exported 241 million lbs.[14] So as regards output and as regards exports, India's figure matched Britain's. For the thirty years from the early 1870s, Indian yarn output increased ten-fold and her exports a hundred-fold. Japan followed suit. Japanese mill production rapidly developed after the 1880s with output reaching 300 million lbs. By the end of the century, this was 200 times the total of twenty years earlier. No yarn was exported in 1880, but exports reached more than 100 million lbs. in 1899.[15] Asia in the late nineteenth century witnessed conspicuous development in the cotton spinning industry.

Who consumed these vast amounts of yarn? Apart from substantial quantities of yarn for local use, the bulk of Indian yarn was exported to China and Japan, as Table 3.3 indicates. Japan's yarns were also exported mainly to China as Table 3.4 shows. Thus the main customers for Indian and

Table 3.3 **Indian Exports of Twist and Yarn**

	(lbs. '000 omitted)	
	1887–88	1888–89
China	92,571	101,248
Japan	17,391	23,143
Aden	1,354	1,327
Straits Settlements	981	1,844
Asiatic Turkey	365	503
Java	283	327
Arabia	279	261
Persia	79	139
East Coast of Africa	66	64
Ceylon	32	26
Other Countries	50	24

Source: George Watt, A *Dictionary of the Economic Products of India*, vol. 4 (London and Calcutta, 1890), p. 169.

Table 3.4 **Japanese Exports of Twist and Yarn**

	(¥ '000 omitted)
	1893–99
China	52,647
Hong Kong	11,111
Korea	4,930
India	27

Source: *Sen'i*, appendix III-7.

Table 3.5 Yarn Consumption in India, 1873–1914 (million lbs.)

Year	Imports	Indian Mill Production	Exports	Net Consumption of Indian Mill Production	Total Indian Consumption
1873/74	30.5	(48)	2.4	(45.6)	(76)
. . . .	. . . .	. . . .	. . . .	. . . .	. . . .
1876/77	33.2	77	9	68	101
1877/78	36.1	100	17	83	119
1878/79	33.1	92	24	68	101
1879/80	33.2	113	27	86	119
1880/81	45.8	130	29	101	147
1881/82	40.7	135	33	102	143
1882/83	44.8	151	48	103	148
1883/84	45.3	179	53	126	171
1884/85	44.7	205	69	136	181
1885/86	45.9	120	78	42	88
1893/94	42.8	346	135	211	254
1894/95 –1898/99	48.0	(552)	193	(359)	(407)
1900/01 –1904/05	27.6	532	234	298	326
1905/06 –1909/10	34.7	652	251	401	436
1910/11 –1913/14	34.6	651	193	458	493

Note: ( ): My estimates based on S. D. Mehta's proportion of yarn exported to yarn produced.

Sources: *Parl. Papers* 1881, XCIII (c. 2976), *Parl. Papers* 1890–91, LXXXIX (c. 6502), and *Parl. Papers* 1902, CXII (cd. 802): Statistical Abstract relating to British India from 1870/1 to 1879/80, from 1880/1 to 1889/90, and from 1890/91 to 1899/1900 for Imports 1873/74 to 1898/99.
S. D. Mehta, *The Cotton Mills of India 1854–1954* (Bombay, 1954), p. 47 for Exports 1873/74.
T. Ellison, *The Cotton Trade of Great Britain* (London, 1886; New Impression: London, 1968), pp. 317–8 for 1876/77 to 1885/86.
Parl. Papers 1887, LXII (c. 4932): Statement of the Trade of British India with British Possessions and Foreign Countries for the Five Years 1881–82 to 1885–86, p. xlii for 1885/86.
Parl. Papers 1895, LXXII (c. 7602): Papers relating to Indian Tariff Act and the Cotton Duties, 1894, p. 7 for 1893/94.
R. E. Tyson, 'The Cotton Industry' in *The Development of British Industry and Foreign Competition 1875–1914*, ed. D. H. Aldcroft (London, 1968), p. 105 for 1900/1901 to 1913/14.

Japanese yarn were Indian, Chinese, and Japanese cotton weavers. The number of power looms in these countries was small compared to hand-looms. Hence, there must have been a large increase in textile production on handlooms using the newly available machine-made cotton yarn.

4. COTTON TEXTILE PRODUCTION IN EAST ASIA

The following is a brief survey of the development of cotton textile production in India, China, Japan, and Korea from 1870 to 1900.

(i) India

Few statistics exist for textile production in India in the late nineteenth century. But import and export figures of yarn are reliable, and production figures have been estimated by various historians. An estimate is made possible by utilising the formula:

Yarns available for textile production in India = output − exports + imports

Table 3.5 is a summary of statistics concerning internal yarn consumption in India in the late nineteenth and early twentieth centuries. The figures on the following pages are taken from the table unless otherwise stated.

S. D. Mehta wrote that the quantity of yarn exported in 1873/4 was less than 5 per cent of that year's output.[16] As the quantity of yarn exported was 2.4 million lbs.,[17] output can be calculated at 48 million lbs. He also stated that for the 1880s and 1890s, the proportion of yarn exported to yarn produced never fell below 25 per cent between them, and in 1900 accounted for 30 to 35 per cent of total output.[18] Assuming that the maximum 35 per cent of output was being exported in the late 1890s, as export figures are known to be 193 million lbs., we can estimate that approximately 552 million lbs. of yarn were produced (an annual average for 1894/5–1898/9.) Therefore, the internal consumption of yarn in India is:

1873/4   76.1m lbs. (= 48m lbs. − 2.4m lbs. + 30.5m lbs.)

1894/5 to 1898/9   407m lbs. (annual average) (= 552m lbs. − 193m lbs. + 48m lbs.)

Thus the absolute size of the Indian home market for yarn was expanding and remained bigger than the export market.

According to Ellison's figures, which cover the nine years from 1876/7–1884/5, yarn production in India saw an increase from 77 million lbs. to 205 million lbs.[19] Total consumption of yarn in India was:

1876/7 101m lbs. (= 77m lbs. – 9m lbs. + 33m lbs.)

1884/5 181m lbs. (= 205m lbs. – 69m lbs. + 45m lbs.)

Hence, although from 1876/7 to 1884/5, Indian exports of yarn rapidly increased from 9 million lbs. to 69 million lbs., it appears that the absolute size of the internal market continued to be much larger than the export market.

J. O'Conor, Assistant Secretary to the Government of India, had a different opinion from Mehta and Ellison as regards the size of the home market for Indian yarn. His figures are available for only one year, 1885/6. With the proviso that 'this calculation is only an inference', he assumed that 'for every pound of Bombay-made twist used [up] in India two pounds were exported to foreign countries.'[20] The quantity of yarn exported in that year was 78 million lbs., theoretically leaving half that figure for local consumption, i.e., 39 million lbs. O'Conor stated, 'if the other Indian mills are also taken into account, it may be said that about 42 million pounds of Indian yarn are used in the country'.[21] In this case, Indian home consumption of yarn would have been only 88 million lbs. (= 42 million lbs. + 46 million lbs.). This total is still larger than that of exports (78 million lbs.), but by only 10 million lbs.

For the following reasons, however, O'Conor probably overestimated the ratio of yarn exported to yarn internally consumed. In 1894, the Millowners' Association of Bombay for the first time collected statistics for all the production in India; only one mill out of 141 refused to cooperate. The results of the survey were:[22]

	Pounds of Yarn Spun
At Bombay	215,589,414
Elsewhere in India	130,086,279
Total	345,675,693

Out of this total output of 346 million lbs., 135 million lbs. were exported. Therefore, the ratio of exports to the output of yarn was 1:2:6, which was much less than O'Conor's ratio of 2:1. In other words, about 40 per cent of the output of Indian yarn was exported in 1893/4. This proportion of exports to output in the 1900s (when the figures are reliable) was also about 40 per cent (calculated from Table 3.5). Moreover, the ratio in the first half of the 1880s according to Ellison's figure was also 40 per cent. O'Conor's ratio, 200 per cent, is therefore probably much too high, while Mehta's 30 to 35 per cent might be a little low. If we exclude O'Conor's estimates, the conclusion we may draw from these estimated figures is that the size of the Indian home market for yarn was far larger than Indian exports, and home consumption of yarn was expanding from the early 1870s onwards.

Not all Indian yarn retained for local consumption, however, was used by local handloom weavers. Some must have been consumed by mills in their own weaving sheds. In order to calculate the quantity of yarn available for non-mill uses in India, we must subtract the yarn consumed by mills from the total consumption of yarn in India, as calculated above. As regards yarn used by mills, the only information available is the weight in pounds of cloth and other fabrics produced inside mills. The Fact Finding Committee in India (1940–42) and S. D. Mehta attempted to utilise this data for comparable calculations.[23] Although they differed from each other in the ratio by which to convert the weight of the cloth into yarn for the period after World War I, they agreed with each other's figures for the earlier period. These figures are shown in Table 3.6.

Table 3.6 Distribution of Yarn Consumption in India (m. lbs.)

	1896/7 to 1898/9	1906/7 to 1908/9
Free yarn available for consumption initially	258	282
Estimated handloom consumption	249	268
Other consumers	9	14
Exports	173	245
Total free yarn	431	527

Source: Mehta, *The Indian Cotton Textile Industry*, p. 173.

According to these calculations, estimated handloom consumption of yarn was 249 million lbs. between 1896/7 and 1898/9, and rose to 268 million lbs. between 1906/7 and 1908/9. These figures are comparable to the figures for the net consumption of Indian mills in each period, 359 million lbs. and 401 million lbs. respectively (see Table 3.5). This means that approximately 70 per cent of the net consumption of cotton yarn in India was used for handlooms.

As regards the period prior to 1898, Sir James Westland independently collected figures concerning handloom consumption for 1894. He stated that yarn produced in India in that year totalled 373 million lbs., the distribution of which was as follows:[24]

Sold and exported	170m lbs.	(45%)
Sold for handloom weaving	129m lbs.	(35%)
Used for mill-weaving	74m lbs.	(20%)
Total	373m lbs.	(100%)

If the figure of 129 million lbs. is accepted, estimated handloom consumption of yarn in India nearly doubled between 1894 and 1906/7–1908/9.

As to the proportion of yarn used for mill-weaving, Westland's figure of 20 per cent for the year 1894 is comparable to the figure in the early 1870s in *The Report of the Bombay Chamber of Commerce for the Year 1873–74*, which introduced figures for the approximate daily production of yarns of some mills in India as well as the proportion used in weaving cloth in the mills (see Table 3.7).[25] The table does not cover all the mills in India but is useful as a rough guide. As shown in the table, 27 per cent of the output of yarn was used for mill-weaving. The remaining 73 per cent was divided between exports and handloom consumption. As to exports for the year, if we rely on Mehta's 5 per cent of total output being exported, the residual 68 per cent (73 per cent minus 5 per cent) of the output of yarn was available for use by handlooms. This amounted to about 33 million lbs. Thus, over the twenty years between 1874 and 1894, estimated mill-produced yarn available for use by handlooms quadrupled.

Imported yarn was also used by handlooms. A contemporary observed that 'the whole of the imported yarn is used for handloom weaving. The mills take none of it . . . as a matter of fact, no mill does weave, except in minute quantities, from imported yarns.'[26] The quantity of yarn imported

Table 3.7 The Approximate Daily Production of Yarns and the Proportion
Used in Making Cloth in Major Mills in India, 1874

Names of Mills and Localities	Spindles	Looms	Yarn		
			Total Production (A) lbs.	Used in making Cloth (B) lbs.	(B)/(A) %
Ahmedabad					
Ahmedabad Spinning & Weaving Co.	20,000	200	4,500	2,500	56
Becherdas Spinning & Weaving Co.	15,000	100	3,500	800	23
Surat					
Jaffer Ali Spinning & Weaving Co., Ld.	10,000	100	2,700	1,000	37
Broach					
Broach Mills Co., Ld.	17,500	0	3,500	0	0
Alfred Mills Co., Ld.	5,000	0	1,170	0	0
Indore					
Maharajah Holkar's Mill	10,274	225	2,200	1,100	50
Bhownuggur					
Bhownuggur Mills & Press Co.	12,000	0	2,500	0	0
Julgaum					
Khandeish Spinning & Weaving Co.	15,000	200	2,000	500	25
Total	104,774	825	22,070	5,900	27

Source: Report of the Bombay Chamber of Commerce for the Year 1873–74, p. 45.

into India in the 1870s was 34 million lbs. (annual average); this rose to
47 million lbs. in the 1880s and remained at this level in the 1890s. The
highest level of imports of yarn was reached in 1898 when 58 million lbs.
of foreign yarn was brought to India.[27]

From all the figures mentioned above, we may estimate the yarn
available for use by Indian handloom weavers over the thirty years from
the early 1870s to the 1900s as follows:

	Mill Production	Imports	Total
1873/74	33	31	64
1893/94	129	43	172
1896–9 (average)	198	51	249
1906–9 (average)	229	39	268

(in million pounds)

It is evident that the available yarn for handloom consumption increased substantially over the period. Concomitantly, with reference to the estimated handloom cloth production between 1896/7–1898/9 and 1906/7–1908/9, the Fact Finding Committee and Mehta give the same figures based upon their estimates of yarn available for handlooms (see Table 3.8). The output of cotton cloth from handlooms rose from 996 million yards to 1,072 million yards during the period.

This survey of production and export data for the Indian cotton industry yields a most important conclusion. From these figures, it is absolutely impossible to believe the popular view that Manchester's machine-made textiles wiped out the Indian handicraft industry. This point can be emphasised by referring to the debates in the 1968 *Indian Economic and Social*

Table 3.8 Cloth Production and Supply in India 1896–1909 (m. yards)

		1896/7 to 1898/9	1906/7 to 1908/9
Cloth production by mills		393	780
Exports of cloth		98	113
Suppliers	mills	298	667
	handlooms	996	1,072
	imports	1,911	2,154
Total supply		3,202	3,893
Mills share		9%	16%
Handlooms share		31%	27%
Imports share		60%	57%

Source: Mehta, *The Indian Cotton Textile Industry*, pp. 126, 127, 128.

History Review between Morris and other historians in respect to the re-interpretation of nineteenth-century Indian economic history.[28] One of the issues in that debate was the re-assessment of the classical view regarding the fate of the Indian handicraft industry. Morris argued that 'there is evidence of rising demand for cotton cloth during the nineteenth century . . . at worst, the vast expansion of British cloth exports to India skimmed off the expanding demand. The handloom weavers were at least no fewer in number and no worse off economically at the end of the period than at the beginning.'[29] Although criticism of Morris' re-interpretation of the Indian economy by historians such as Matsui Tōru, Bipan Chandra, and Tapan Raychaudhuri covered many issues, as far as Morris' re-assessment of the Indian handicraft industry is concerned, the dissenting historians are not persuasive in their arguments. Chandra's strong words such as 'the destruction', 'the ruin', 'the rapid collapse', 'almost total extinction', of the industry in the nineteenth century are not supported by any statistical evidence. Raychaudhuri, in spite of his critical tone, seems to share Morris' doubts about the claim that the Indian handicraft industry was destroyed by competition from the British machine-made manufactures. He wrote:

> The standard text-book on Indian economics by Jathar and Beri quoted statistics showing the steady growth in the production of hand-woven textiles in the twentieth century. The fact that as late as 1950, the over-whelming bulk of employment in secondary production was in the traditional sector is itself enough to prove that the traditional handicrafts had not withered away.[30]

Further research at the local level still seems to be necessary until enough information on the various regions can be brought together to draw a general picture. In this context, it may be relevant to refer to the conclusions of D. R. Gadgil, who remarked that the sector of Indian industry which was seriously affected by foreign competition was the urban sector like Dacca muslin fine textiles, while the village weaver was more or less untouched by European competition.[31] Some contemporary observations also accord with the thesis that the rural cotton industry underwent a different course from the urban industry. Sir George Watt observed in 1890 that with the 'gradual growth of the Manchester trade the manufacture of the finer textiles by handloom, such as the Dacca muslins, once so famous all over the world, has almost, if not entirely, ceased', and he continued, 'the local manufacture of the coarser kinds, however, for consumption in rural localities, and of ornamental varieties, such as *do-pattas* of Benares, is likely to continue to a much greater extent.'[32] Eighteen years later, he quoted Westland as saying that 'weaving is for the most part the pursuit of the bye-time of the persons who weave', and went on to observe, 'That is doubtless the condition in many parts of the country to-day [in 1908], but here and there centres of professional hand-loom weaving still exist where the village weaver holds an honoured position.'[33]

Given the absence of satisfactory investigations into the process of regional economic growth,[34] it seems too early to generalise from the experience of one particular region like Bengal and to conclude that its fate had been replicated on a national scale. But, from the available statistical and contemporary evidence, it may not be far from the truth to conclude that textile production in India, both mill and handicraft output, was growing, not declining, in the late nineteenth century.

(ii) The Far East

a) China

Imported cotton goods formed 45 per cent by value of China's total imports on average for the thirty years between 1871 and 1900.[35] The products consisted mainly of cotton textiles, which formed three quarters of the total cotton goods imported into China on average for the period. But the three decades witnessed significant changes in the composition of the cotton goods. In the 1870s, the proportion of imported cotton cloth to cotton yarn was 8 to 1, but only 2.3 to 1 in the 1890s. In other words, the proportion of imports of yarn rapidly increased during those thirty years. The main reason for the relatively slow growth of cloth imports in comparison to yarn imports was that the handicraft weaving industry in China increasingly adopted imported yarn.

Koyama Masaki was the first historian who worked on the subject and made clear the positive effect which imported yarn had had upon local textile production.[36] Making extensive use of Japanese and British consular reports, he found that piece goods were primarily introduced to the cities, especially in north and northeast China, where geographical conditions did not permit their manufacturing. He also found that imported piece goods did not penetrate the vast agricultural areas, where local cotton textiles were overwhelmingly used. Lastly, he found that cotton yarn was at first only employed in south China to produce piece goods, but with the inflow of Indian yarn, yarn imports rose rapidly after 1873 and levelled off after 1900 (see Figure 3.1). This resulted in an increased use of foreign yarn

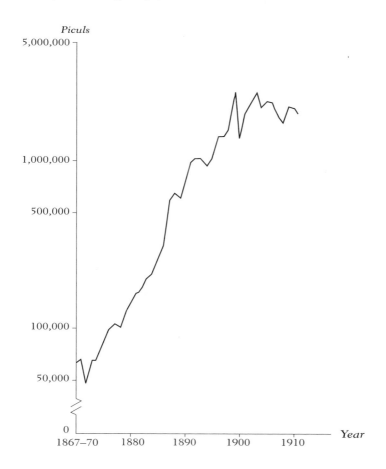

Figure 3.1 Imports of Cotton Yarn into China

Source: Albert Feuerwerker, 'Handicraft and Manufactured Cotton Textiles in China, 1871–1910', *Journal of Economic History*, vol. 30 (1970), data taken from table on p. 344.

in areas such as northeast China, north China, and Szechwan (Sichuan), which had previously relied on the local yarn supplied from the Kiangnan (Jiangnan) delta region and south Hupeh (Hubei). These were the two old centres of the Chinese cotton industry. In due course, these areas also began to use machine-spun yarn.

Imports of yarn rose rapidly in China because hand-spun yarn tended to be expensive. This was due to the rising price of raw cotton as the result of increased demand from foreign countries and Japan in particular. 'The most curious feature in connection with the native cotton industry', reported an English mission to China from Blackburn in 1896/7, 'is the high price of the raw material in comparison with other agricultural produce.'[37] This price rise did not stimulate cotton crop production until new foot-pedal ginning machines imported from Japan later encouraged an increase in supply.[38] The rise in raw cotton prices merely resulted in an increase in the cost of native yarn. For example, in 1877, the Chinese customs bureau in Newchwang (Yinkou) reported that 300 catties of Western yarn sold for 57 taels, while the same quantity of domestic yarn sold for 87 taels.[39] Certainly spinning and weaving with domestic raw cotton for household consumption continued to be important in many areas of rural China, but the significant trend was that the production of handloom piece goods was freed from the limitations of the supply of local yarn and spread throughout China.

Ramon Myers traced the decline of spinning and weaving from 1870 to 1900, and the emergence of new centres specialising mainly in cloth production, some for export. He found that the handicraft industry stretched across China and in many districts became the chief economic activity. During this period, the average annual rate of growth of exports of Chinese cloth was 9.8 per cent.[40] Hou Chi-ming, who examined the available statistics on the production and consumption of raw cotton, arrived at a similar conclusion, i.e., that 'it is by no means clear that there was any severe decline even in hand spinning'.[41] Yet this was the classic evidence for how the handicraft industry was destroyed by machine production.

Although a significant portion of hand-spun yarns were replaced by imported yarn, in fact hand-spun yarns showed strong resilience. Albert Feuerwerker estimated the sources of yarn and cloth consumed in the late nineteenth century,[42] and one of the three results of his calculations was reproduced in an important article of 1980 as shown in Table 3.9.[43] According to the table, although hand-spun yarn was subsequently replaced by imported yarn and by domestic machine-made yarn, in the 1900s it still constituted nearly 42 per cent of total yarn consumed. This persistence of hand-spinning production was observed also in a Japanese report of 1908, which estimated internal production of handicraft yarn at roughly one to two million piculs.[44]

Table 3.9 Sources of Estimated Yarn Consumption in China 1871–80 and 1901–10

	Average year in 1871–80		Average year in 1901–10	
	tan	%	tan	%
Domestic mills	–	–	1,055,040	17.98
Imports	97,451	1.96	2,363,000	40.27
Handicraft	4,882,381	98.04	2,449,715	41.75
Total	4,979,832	100.00	5,867,755	100.00

Source: A. Feuerwerker, 'Economic Trends in the Late Ch'ing Empire', The Cambridge History of China, vol. 11 (1980), p. 25.

The output of textile production in China during the nineteenth century remains undocumented. The absolute amount of cloth woven in China, according to Feuerwerker's estimates, increased from nearly 3,225 million yards on average for the decade of the 1870s to nearly 3,700 million yards for the 1900s, an approximate 15 per cent increase (see Table 3.10).

This would be a good rate of growth and showed the strength of the weaving sector in China. In the first three decades of the twentieth century, there was no decline in hand weaving, suggesting that the industry had not been affected during the latter half of the previous century.[45] The outcome of many recent empirical studies on handicraft textiles in various localities in varying degrees of detail have revealed that the particular areas studied had undergone development.[46]

b) Japan
It is a well-established fact according to Japanese historians that cotton textile production increased rapidly during the Meiji period.[47] A decrease in

Table 3.10 Sources of Estimated Cloth Consumption in China, 1871–80 and 1901–10

	Average year in 1871–80			
	yds.	%	sq. yds.	%
Domestic mills	–	–	–	–
Imports	414,805,000	11.40	376,165,000	18.92
Handloom weaving	3,224,960,440	88.60	1,612,480,220	81.08
Total	3,639,765,440	100.00	1,988,645,220	100.00

	Average year in 1901–10			
	yds.	%	sq. yds.	%
Domestic mills	25,200,000	0.57	24,494,400	0.97
Imports	721,400,000	16.23	654,200,000	25.87
Handloom weaving	3,699,890,434	83.20	1,849,945,217	73.16
Total	4,446,490,434	100.00	2,528,639,617	100.00

Source: A. Feuerwerker, 'Economic Trends in the Late Ch'ing Empire', p. 25.

output, however, was observed during the national depression of 1881–5, though there was an even more rapid fall in cloth imports. A brief reference to some related figures will clarify this point. Satoru Nakamura compiled the available statistics on the output, imports, and exports of cotton products (see Table 3.11).[48] His figures were based upon the official statistics of the cotton crop yield. He attempted to convert the weight of all the cotton yarn and cloth into the weight of the raw cotton from which it was made. The ratio he adopted for the conversion might be questioned, but his figures serve as a rough guide from which to gauge what happened to the market for cotton goods in late-nineteenth-century Japan.

Production of raw cotton increased substantially up to 1887, becoming double the output of 1871. After that, internal production of raw cotton declined, while raw cotton imports rapidly increased. Between 1888 and 1899, raw cotton imported into Japan grew twenty-fold. The trend of yarn imports, on the other hand, showed a contrast to that of raw cotton with a steep rise after 1872, reaching their highest level in 1888. Then, Japanese imports of yarn rapidly diminished. But domestic production of yarn rose.

Table 3.11 Output, Imports, and Exports of Cotton Products in Japan 1870–1899 (in million kin: 1m. kin = 600 tons)

	Raw Cotton			Cotton Yarn			Cotton Cloth		
year	output	imports	exports	output	imports	exports	output	imports	exports
1870	21.0	3.3		12.9	9.7		22.6	8.6	0.0
1871	23.0	0.8		10.6	8.7		19.3	14.2	0.0
1872	25.0	0.5		11.0	14.3		25.3	12.1	0.0
1873	20.0	2.1		13.9	10.4		24.4	15.0	0.0
1874	28.4	8.4		14.1	11.5		25.7	17.2	0.0
1875	29.8	2.8	0.0	16.0	14.8		30.8	14.9	0.0
1876	33.2	3.2		16.6	16.1		32.8	16.3	0.0
1877	36.7	2.7		19.5	16.5		36.0	13.4	0.0
1878	35.6	2.1		17.7	30.1		47.8	15.5	0.0
1879	52.5	0.8		15.5	25.9		41.5	21.3	0.1
1880	35.6	1.4		28.1	31.4		59.6	18.1	0.1
1881	36.2	1.6		16.0	30.5		46.5	17.3	0.1
1882	34.5	3.3		18.6	27.8		46.4	16.2	0.1
1883	41.8	2.1	0.2	17.9	27.1		45.0	10.3	0.2
1884	38.8	4.5	0.0	26.6	23.3		49.9	9.5	0.4
1885	45.0	6.5		25.4	23.5		49.0	11.3	0.7
1886	50.0	4.7		28.7	26.5		55.2	8.9	1.0
1887	55.9	7.6		30.8	36.6		67.5	13.4	0.7
1888	46.0	16.6		37.7	52.1		89.9	15.7	0.5
1889	40.0	39.6		48.7	47.0		95.8	15.7	0.5
1890	35.0	37.5		45.9	35.1	0.0	81.0	14.3	0.5
1891	32.9	72.1	0.2	72.7	19.0	0.0	91.7	11.6	0.8
1892	31.4	92.5	0.2	83.8	26.8	0.0	110.6	14.6	1.1
1893	31.0	102.6	0.3	91.3	21.3	0.3	112.3	16.7	2.0
1894	31.4	113.0	0.5	101.0	17.5	3.8	114.6	15.9	3.2
1895	26.2	155.1	0.7	133.2	16.0	3.8	145.3	16.3	3.9
1896	18.5	171.3	0.8	143.4	22.0	24.1	141.3	24.5	6.2
1897	18.2	224.8	1.0	185.4	17.7	46.2	156.9	20.9	7.0
1898	18.2	251.9	1.3	211.9	17.5	75.7	153.7	24.7	7.7
1899	13.0	339.3	1.1	291.2	9.0	112.6	187.7	19.5	11.7

Source: Satoru Nakamura, *Meiji Ishin no kiso kōzō* (The underpinnings of the Meiji Restoration), Table 3 in Appendix.

Between 1886 and 1899, the increase in output was ten-fold. The effect on weaving was obvious. The output of Japan's woven textile production rose from 22.6 million *kin* in 1870 to 187.7 million *kin* in 1899. On the other hand, the proportion of imported cotton cloth in total consumption of cotton cloth fell from 28 per cent in 1870 to 10 per cent in 1899.

c) Korea

Statistics are not available for Korea's production of cotton textiles in the nineteenth century. But voluminous contemporary Japanese consular reports have been used to construct a picture of foreign trade and the socio-economic conditions of cotton textile production in late-nineteenth-century Korea. Korea was forced by Japan to open her doors in 1876 and soon afterwards, concluded commercial treaties with the Western Powers. Korea's overseas trade was conducted by Japanese and Chinese merchants. The British goods which flowed into Korea were mostly re-exported from China and Japan. The main items of Korea's imports were British cotton textiles, particularly shirting and Victorian lawn (see Tables 3.12 and 3.13).

The pioneering work surveying the effects of the inflow of these goods on the handicraft textile industry was written in 1951 by Sawamura Tōhei, who used consular reports extensively. Sawamura, in a previous article (1944) on the socio-economic pre-conditions in the period before the opening of Korea, assumed that the handicraft industry would have been crushed by the influx of Lancashire textiles.[49] But his figures showed, in fact, that before the Sino–Japanese War, the impact of British textiles upon local textile production was limited.[50] Furthermore, the work by Hideki Kajimura in 1977 concluded that until 1895, the indigenous cotton textile production was growing. Then the Japanese victory in the Sino–Japanese War gave the Japanese cotton industry the impetus to make inroads into Korean markets. Moreover, according to Kajimura's estimates, the British share of cotton goods in the Korean market never exceeded 25 per cent.[51] This view is accepted by practically all Japanese historians working on Korea.[52]

Table 3.12 Imports of Cotton Goods into Korea, 1876–1899 (¥ '000)

	Total Imports (A)	Cotton Goods (B)	(B)/(A) (%)
1876	188	12	6.4
1877	127	54	42.5
1878	245	168	68.6
1879	567	477	84.1
1880	978	768	78.5
1881	1,874	1,495	79.8
1882	1,562	1,283	82.1
1883	2,178	913	41.9
1884	794	498	62.7
1885	1,672	1,122	67.1
1886	2,474	1,306	52.8
1887	2,815	1,894	67.3
1888	3,046	1,962	64.4
1889	3,378	1,709	50.6
1890	4,728	2,675	56.6
1891	5,256	2,875	54.7
1892	4,598	2,185	47.5
1893	3,880	1,733	44.7
1894	5,832	2,495	42.8
1895	8,088	4,714	58.3
1896	6,531	3,479	53.3
1897	10,068	5,273	52.4
1898	11,825	5,185	43.8
1899	10,308	5,384	52.2

Source: Hideki Kajimura, *Chōsen ni okeru shihonshugi no keisei to tenkai* (Formation and development of capitalism in Korea) (Tokyo, 1977), pp. 22–23.

Table 3.13 Composition of Cotton Goods Imported into Korea

	Cotton Manufactures				Cotton (yarn)	Cotton (raw)	Total
	Cambrics & lawns	Shirtings	T-cloths	Various			(yen)
1 July 1877 to 30 June 1878	3,518	92,145	19,902	1,059	1,685	9,164	127,473
1 July to 31 Dec. 1878	8,500	73,584	12,318	1,217	1,151	614	97,384
1879	72,433	354,892	28,573	3,666	14,276	2,250	476,090
1880	105,105	546,788	76,066	12,420	19,243	8,675	768,297
1881	511,952	903,770	14,598	91,492	2,048	–	1,523,860
1 Jan. to 30 June 1882	205,938	334,811	–	35,616	–	–	576,365
Average	907,446	2,305,990	151,457	145,470	38,403	20,703	3,569,469
							(%)
1 July 1877 to 30 June 1878	2.8	72.3	15.6	0.8	1.3	7.2	(100)
1 July to 31 Dec. 1878	8.7	75.6	12.6	1.2	1.2	0.6	(100)
1879	15.2	74.5	6.0	0.8	3.0	0.5	(100)
1880	13.7	71.2	10.0	1.6	2.5	1.1	(100)
1881	33.6	59.3	1.0	6.0	0.1	–	(100)
1 Jan. to 30 June 1882	35.7	58.1	–	6.2	–	–	(100)
Total	25.4	64.6	4.2	4.1	1.1	0.6	(100)

Source: *Parl. Papers* 1883, LXXV (c. 3459): Memorandum respecting the trade between Japan and Korea, p. 10.

5. SUMMARY

In the latter half of the nineteenth century, Britain found its exports to Asia expanding more rapidly than its exports to the United States or industrial Europe, where tariff barriers had been set up against it. Britain earned a considerable surplus on its trade with Asia, which helped settle the deficit in its transactions with the United States and Europe. Cotton textiles were the main item in Britain's earnings from trade with Asia. Much of this increase in earnings came from its textile exports to India, China, and Japan, but the traditional handloom weaving industry in these countries expanded its own textile production with yarns supplied increasingly from India and Japan. The inroad of machine-made yarns had a damaging effect upon handicraft spinners although hand-spun yarn persisted in varying degrees. However, machine-made yarns also had a positive effect, for the handicraft workers could now concentrate on weaving and increase their daily output. Available evidence for each country indicates that the local cotton industry was not destroyed by the influx of British textiles. On the contrary, despite the increase in imports of British cotton textiles into Asia, the traditional weaving sector expanded its own textile production.

Chapter Four

COMPARISON OF PRICES BETWEEN BRITISH AND JAPANESE COTTON CLOTHS

1. INTRODUCTION

As the previous chapter indicates, we face seemingly contradictory phenomena. There was an increasing inflow of British cotton manufactured goods to East Asian markets, on the one hand, and growth and development of indigenous cotton textile production in East Asia, on the other. How can this paradox be explained?

East Asian markets varied according to region. One feature was the difference in size of the Indian and the Far Eastern markets. In marked contrast to the huge markets for British goods in India, the Far Eastern markets never lived up to the great expectations held by the British. Indeed, Japan emerged as the serious threat to Britain in these markets. Our special attention, therefore, will be focussed on the Japanese markets.

The difference in the size of the Indian and Far Eastern markets for British cotton goods can be seen in Table 4.1. Between 1871 and 1900, India's share of British exports of yarn doubled, while the Far Eastern share declined slightly. As regards plain cloth, India took nearly half the total of British exports, while the Far Eastern intake fell from 20 per cent to 12 per cent. As for British exports of printed cloth, the Far Eastern share increased but never exceeded 10 per cent.

Table 4.1 Percentage Composition of Cotton Goods Exported from Britain
to the Far East and India, 1871 and 1900

1. Cotton Yarn

	China and Japan	India
1871	9.5	11.3
1900	8.6	20.3

2. Cotton Piece Goods (printed)

	China and Japan	India
1871	2.1	10.1
1900	9.3	18.3

3. Cotton Piece Goods (plain)

	China and Japan	India
1871	19.9	34.1
1900	12.3	47.8

Source: From *ASTUK* (Annual Statement of the Trade of the United Kingdom with Foreign
Countries and British Possessions) for the relevant years. See also Appendix 1 (iv)–(vi).

The estimated population of India in 1880 was about 217 million, while
that of China and Japan combined was about 514 million in the same year,
more than double.[1] Taking into account the sheer size of the populations
of China and Japan, and the fact that their people traditionally used cottons for clothing, it might well be thought that the quantity imported by
China and Japan was very small. A contemporary British commentator
thought similarly. Mitchell wrote in 1852 at Hong Kong, 'it seems a strange
result, after ten years' open trade with this great country, and after the
abolition of all monopolies on both sides, that China, with her swarming
millions, should not consume one-half so much of our manufactures as
Holland'.[2] Immediately after signing the Treaty of Nanking (1842), the
British representative, Sir Henry Pottinger, had promised his countrymen
that a huge market, consisting of one third of the world's population had
just opened up to cotton goods producers in Britain.[3] He went so far as to
say that even the total output of Lancashire could not turn out stocking-
stuff sufficient for a single province in China.[4]

Yet the great expectation which the British entertained of the Chinese market was never realised. In the case of Japan, the situation was even worse, for British cotton goods were being driven out of this market by the end of the century. Japan became a net exporter of cotton yarn in 1897 and of cotton textiles in 1909. The trend of her imports of cotton goods prior to this needs more careful examination.

2. COTTON GOODS IMPORTED INTO JAPAN

On 1 July 1859, Japan opened three ports (Nagasaki, Kanagawa, and Hakodate) to Britain in accordance with Article III of the treaty concluded between the two countries the previous year.[5] Article XIV of the treaty stipulated a free trade so that 'British subjects shall be at full liberty' to trade directly with the Japanese without the interference of any government officer in all the open ports,[6] and Clause VII of the trade regulations prescribed a low scale of import duty of 5 per cent, *ad valorem*, on English manufactured cotton goods.[7]

At the inauguration of this new Anglo-Japanese trade, the British Consul-General Rutherford Alcock was pessimistic about the prospects for British exports to Japan, a country long self-sufficient and 'even more independent of such supplies than China'. In April 1860, he stated, 'there is no market for imports of European manufactures, nor is it probable that any considerable demand will arise under any circumstances for a long period, if ever'.[8] But such pessimism had gone by the following year when British Acting-Consul Howard Vyse reported, 'there is no denying, that however small the import trade is at present, when compared to that of other countries in the East, it will augment from year to year, and become in due time a profitable branch of commerce with Japan.'[9] As he predicted, Japanese imports increased over the following five years, and in 1866, Sir Harry Parkes confirmed this trend as follows:

> The great expansion of the import trade is attributable to a steadily increasing demand for foreign manufactures in this country, which, having no redundant population, as is the case with China, can obtain clothing more cheaply from foreigners than from its own cottage looms. Under this aspect, therefore, Japan promises to furnish a very satisfactory market for British manufactures.[10]

For the first two decades, Japan, along with other Asian countries, was becoming a leading market for English textiles. These, indeed, formed the greatest share of Japan's imports.

Japanese imports of cotton goods, however, underwent changes in composition. As Table 4.2 shows, three phases are distinguishable. The initial phase, the period between 1860 to 1877, was characterised by cotton cloth as the major import item. Then, during the period from 1878 to 1890, imports of cotton yarn were dominant. Lastly, from 1891 onward, raw cotton became the principal item of import. This sequence of change in imported cottons from finished goods to raw material reflected the industrialisation of the Japanese cotton industry.[11]

In the first phase, the Japanese weaving industry might have been threatened by the inflow of foreign cotton cloth. But the fear of foreign domination had faded by 1878, for from that year on, cotton yarn was the greatest import. Local cotton weavers used it as raw material and supplied the markets with their own product at the expense of British cloth.[12]

This process characterised the next phase. British Acting-Consul Martin Dohmen reported in 1879, 'the enormous consumption of yarn suggests that native wants are rapidly being supplied by native woven cloth, and travellers in the interior of the country report that in various places, attempts are being made to foster cotton weaving.'[13]

In the final phase, the growth of the weaving industry, via the so-called 'backward linkage effect',[14] stimulated the establishment of the modern spinning industry. The first successful cotton mill in Japan started production at Osaka in 1883, followed by other new mills in rapid succession. As shown in Table 4.3, the spinning industry developed by leaps and bounds. Total domestic output exceeded imports in 1891, and exports overtook imports in 1897. Consumption of raw cotton by the mills increased rapidly. As the table shows, exports of yarn were negligible before 1895. Then victory in the Sino–Japanese War gave the industry the impetus to make inroads into other Asian markets. Before the war, Japanese spinning mills were almost entirely dependent on the domestic markets. Thus the development of the modern spinning industry was initially sustained by increasing demand from the traditional weaving sector.[15]

As the British Vice-Consul observed in 1887, 'almost the entire cotton weaving in Japan [is] carried on by means of the old traditional loom.'[16]

Table 4.2 Imports of Cotton Products into Japan, 1860–1893

Year	A	B	C	Percentage Distribution of C			
	Total Imports	Cotton Goods and Raw Cotton	B/A	Cotton Cloth	Cotton Yarn	Raw Cotton	
	¥ '000	¥ '000	%	%	%	%	
1860	946	499	52.8	52.8	–	–	
1861	1,496	795	53.2	46.1	4.9	2.3	
1862	3,074	724	23.6	19.4	4.2	–	
1863	3,701	586	15.8	15.8	–	–	
1864	5,554	2,471	44.5	30.9	13.6	–	
1865	13,153	5,569	42.3	35.8	6.6	–	
1866*	–	–	–	–	–	–	
1867	14,909	5,425	36.4	25.3	9.0	–	
1868	10,693	4,205	39.3	23.8	11.6	4.0	First
1869	20,784	7,132	34.3	12.6	16.5	5.2	Phase
1870	33,742	8,141	24.1	8.8	13.4	1.9	
1871	21,917	9,256	42.2	25.2	16.1	0.9	
1872	26,175	10,313	39.4	18.7	20.4	0.3	
1873	28,107	9,275	33.0	20.2	12.1	0.9	
1874	23,462	10,072	42.9	23.0	15.2	4.7	
1875	29,976	9,483	31.6	16.8	13.5	1.2	
1876	23,965	9,529	39.8	20.5	17.3	1.9	
1877	27,421	8,714	31.8	15.3	14.9	1.5	
1878	32,875	12,627	38.4	15.2	21.9	0.9	
1879	32,953	12,123	36.8	17.7	18.8	0.3	
1880	36,627	13,402	36.6	15.1	21.0	0.5	
1881	31,191	12,513	40.1	16.2	23.3	0.6	
1882	29,447	11,261	38.3	14.3	22.3	1.6	
1883	28,445	9,213	32.4	9.8	21.7	0.9	
1884	29,673	8,215	27.7	8.4	17.4	1.9	Second
1885	29,357	8,893	30.3	9.8	17.7	2.8	Phase
1886	32,168	8,925	27.7	7.2	18.4	2.2	
1887	44,304	12,559	28.4	7.6	18.6	2.0	
1888	65,453	20,577	31.4	7.2	20.8	3.4	
1889	66,104	22,931	34.7	7.1	18.9	8.6	
1890	81,729	19,482	23.8	5.9	12.1	6.6	
1891	62,927	17,211	27.4	5.4	8.9	13.0	
1892	71,326	24,246	34.0	6.5	10.0	17.3	Third
1893	88,257	29,231	33.1	6.4	8.3	18.3	Phase

Note: * No return for the year 1866, owing to destruction of Yokohama records by fire.
Source: Sen'i, p. 59.

Table 4.3 Development of the Japanese Cotton Spinning Industry

	(a)	(b)	(c)	(d)	(e)	(f)
	Number of Spindles	Output lb. ('000)	Imports lb. ('000)	Exports lb. ('000)	(d)/(b) %	Raw Cotton Consumption ('000 picul)
1887	76,600	9,264	44,395			72,680
1888	116,276	12,745	63,253			159,543
1889	215,000	26,818	57,081			369,331
1890	277,895	41,936	42,544	12	0.0	347,701
1891	353,880	57,992	23,117	43	0.1	601,138
1892	385,314	81,980	32,411	44	0.1	902,154
1893	381,781	85,903	25,874	421	0.5	1,011,677
1894	530,074	116,960	21,257	1,118	1.0	1,122,541
1895	580,945	146,676	19,455	4,710	3.2	1,473,630
1896	757,197	160,646	26,685	17,300	10.8	1,707,637
1897	970,567	204,494	21,454	56,046	27.4	2,243,077
1898	1,149,749	257,802	21,240	91,778	35.6	2,516,027
1899	1,189,929	302,926	10,948	136,481	45.1	3,384,699

Source: Sen'i, p. 176, Appendix pp. 44, 50.

The question, therefore, arises as to what would have happened if the handicraft cotton weaving industry had been eradicated by imports of English cotton textiles? Clearly the modern spinning industry could not have come into existence because there would have been no purchasers for its products. Had this happened, not only Japanese industrialisation (in which the cotton industry played a vital part), but also the course of modern Asian economic history generally (in which the expanding economy of Japan played an essential role) would have been totally different.

The following pages aim to shed new light on the peculiar characteristics of the Far Eastern markets, particularly the Japanese market and will attempt to analyse similar types of commodities of different origins. As Marx puts it, the worth of a commodity presents itself as a mixture of two things—exchange-value and use-value—and so our analysis will concentrate on the price and quality of the most important commodities for Britain and the Far East, cotton goods.

3. COMPARISON OF PRICES

The aim of this section is to analyse for the first time a selection of price data for British and Japanese cotton textiles sold in the Tokyo market in the late nineteenth century, and to reassess the view held by historians who have laid special emphasis on the competitive price advantages of Far Eastern cloths in relation to British goods.

(i) Accepted explanation

The accepted explanation for the successful survival of the handicraft textile industry places most weight on relative factor prices. The following reasons are the basis of the argument. As Table 4.4 indicates, foreign yarn was 30 to 40 per cent cheaper than Japanese yarn. By using cheaper foreign yarn, Japanese cotton weavers could cut the price of their products, although in consequence, domestic yarn was driven out of the market.[17] Also, foreign cotton goods were carried by the Japanese throughout the country without any transit duty.[18]

Table 4.4 Prices of Japanese and Foreign Yarn

(per lb.)

Year	Japanese Yarn (¥)	Foreign Yarn (¥)
1874	42.70	29.66
1875	43.54	29.94
1876	40.79	27.42
1877	40.41	26.86
1878	45.00	25.46

Source: Mentō kyōshinkai hōkoku (Report on cotton goods and sugar) No. 2 (Tokyo, 1880), p. 12.

Until the 1870s, the main delivery routes for foreign merchandise were as follows:[19]

In other words, the conditions for open competition in prices between Japanese and foreign goods were satisfied in terms of distribution.[20] It is not surprising, then, that Yamaguchi, Ishii, and the textbooks of other historians based on these authorities argue that while cheaper imported cotton textiles damaged the domestic cotton industry at first, Japanese weavers overcame this by shifting from domestic to imported yarn.[21] Underlying this argument is the assumption that English and Japanese cotton cloths were substitutes for each other. For example, Furushima Toshio states:

> More than half of the imported varieties were white cloth followed by striped cloth, which comprised about 20 per cent of the total. Consequently, weaving areas which specialised in the production of white and striped cloths had to face severe competition in price from the influx of the foreign equivalent.[22]

Takamura Naosuke also notes, 'Japanese white cloth met direct competition from English grey shirting.'[23] All of these authorities assume a state of perfect competition between English and Japanese cotton cloths.[24] However, it has not been shown that they really were perfect substitutes for each other and consequently directly competitive in price.

What has been overlooked is a selection of price data for some of the English and Japanese cotton cloths sold in Japanese markets in the late nineteenth century. Choosing the leading varieties of English and Japanese cotton cloths, we shall compare their prices in a market where both varieties circulated in large quantities between 1878 and 1890 (i.e., the second phase of imports when the imports of cotton cloth decreased but production of Japanese cloth increased). If the prevailing view is correct, the price of Japanese cloth during that period should have been cheaper than English cloth.

(ii) Price comparison between English and Japanese cotton cloths

a) The leading varieties of English cloths

Cotton piece goods imported into Japan consisted of various types of cloth, such as shirting, chintz, drill, handkerchiefs, lawn, satin, taffachelas, turkey red, velvet, T-cloth, singlets, drawers, etc.[25] As shown in Table 4.5, shirtings comprised about 65 per cent of total cloth imports over the initial twenty-five years (see column d). Shirtings were classified into three

Table 4.5 Japanese Imports of Cotton Cloths (¥ '000)

Year	(a) Total Value of Cotton Cloth	(b) Shirtings	(c) Grey Shirting	(d) (Imports of Grey Shirting into Yokohama)	(e) (b)/(a) %	(f) (c)/(b) %	(g) Percentage Share of English Grey Shirting in Total Shirtings
1868	2,543	1,936	1,505	1,557	76	78	
1869	2,623	1,966	1,666	1,531	75	85	
1870	2,982	1,986	1,727	1,458	67	87	
1871	5,525	4,675	4,362	3,072	85	93	
1872	4,888	3,471	3,118	1,765	71	90	
1873	5,609	3,554	3,044	1,922	63	86	
1874	5,405	4,122	3,595	2,463	76	87	
1875	5,046	3,023	2,426	1,853	60	80	
1876	4,908	3,368	2,817	2,268	69	84	
1877	4,195	2,543	1,835	1,776 *	61	72	99.2
1878	5,008	2,891	1,882	1,608	58	65	99.1
1879	5,931	4,299	3,360	2,276	54	78	99.9
1880	5,523	3,120	2,269	2,018	57	71	99.9
1881	5,044	3,034	1,914	1,629	50	63	99.7
1882	4,219	3,343	2,427	2,215	73	73	100.0
1883	2,785	1,785	1,093	1,164	64	61	99.7
1884	2,488	1,578	856	703	63	54	99.9
1885	2,884	2,001	1,234	845	70	62	100.0
1886	2,417	1,519	848	544	66	56	100.0
1887	3,380	1,876	1,170	607	56	62	99.8
1888	4,692	3,152	2,333	1,255 **	67	74	99.1
1889	4,668	3,107	2,011	870	67	65	100.0
1890	4,129	2,494	1,717	903	60	69	100.0

Note: * = $ '000; ** = ¥ '000.

Source: Nihon bōeki seiran (Foreign trade of Japan), pp. 237–241; *Yokohamashi-shi shiryō hen* (History of Yokohama city, Documents), vol. 2, pp. 67, 251.

types: grey (unbleached), white (bleached), and coloured (printed or dyed). Grey shirting comprised three-quarters of these three types, almost all of which was English-made (see column g). From the table, it is fairly clear that the bulk of grey shirting was imported into the port of Yokohama (see columns c, d, and f), but little information exists as regards the destinations to which the goods were sent. Probably the largest market was Tokyo, the nearest city to Yokohama. Data collected by the Tokyo Chamber of Commerce, but only covering the year 1878/9, indicate that 70 per cent of total grey shirting imported into Yokohama was transported to Tokyo. They also show that more than half the grey shirting brought into Tokyo was sold there (see Table 4.6).

Another piece of statistical evidence regarding sales of various shirtings in Tokyo indicates that grey shirting was the commodity most in demand, as shown in Table 4.7, forming 91 per cent of the total in 1884, 85 per cent in 1885, 80 per cent in 1886, 82 per cent in 1887, and 74 per cent in 1888. There were two kinds of grey shirting: one was 44 inches in width, and the other 39 inches, the former being about four times in value the sales of the latter. The bulk of these two types of grey shirtings was sold in Tokyo, as their value brought into Tokyo amounted to 2.23 million yen for the five years 1884–8, while the value exported from the city to other localities was only 0.33 million yen. Thus the principal variety of imported cloths was shirting, especially grey shirting of 44-inch width, and the principal market for this cloth was Tokyo.

b) The leading varieties of Japanese cloths

The earliest information available on the different kinds of cotton cloths woven across Japan is for the year 1894. As shown in Table 4.8, the output of unbleached cotton cloth that year amounted to nearly half the total production of all kinds of cotton textiles throughout Japan. This was followed by striped cotton cloth and bleached cotton cloth. These three varieties formed nearly three-quarters of the total output. Unbleached and bleached cotton cloths were often termed 'white cotton cloth' by the Japanese. White cloth was produced mainly in the following prefectures: Aichi, Ehime, Osaka, Nara, and Saitama, which together produced 86 per cent of this particular type. Aichi produced much more than the other four, weaving 43 per cent of the total amount.

Table 4.6

(1) Deliveries of English Grey Shirting from Yokohama for Local Consumption, 1878–79

	Quantity (*tan*)*	Value (¥)
To Tokyo	501,622	1,112,046
To Osaka	145,812	340,664
To Owari	12,401	26,135
To Kyoto	53,460	112,564
To Uzen	2,300	5,686
To Echigo	13,450	31,564
To Ise	950	3,046
To Mutsu	200	565
Total	730,195	1,642,270

(2) Deliveries of English Grey Shirting from Tokyo for Local Consumption, 1878–79

Consumption from Tokyo	Quantity (*tan*)	Value (¥)
In Tokyo	470,000	1,234,900
To Kyoto	150,000	394,130
To Osaka	50,000	131,370
To Owari	32,000	84,080
To Echigo	48,000	126,120
To Uzen	23,000	60,430
To Shinano	22,000	57,810
To Shimotsuke	20,000	52,550
To Hitachi	15,000	39,410
To Musashi	10,000	26,270
To Kai	10,000	26,270
Total	920,000	2,417,260

Note: * *tan*: a roll of cloth of about 11 1/2 yards in length, and 13 1/2 inches in width.
Source: *Shibusawa Eiichi denki shiryō* (Documents relating to Shibusawa Eiichi) (Tokyo, 1957), 17: 241–284.

Table 4.7

(1) Sales of Shirting in Tokyo from July 1884 to August 1888

(¥)

Year	Grey Shirting		Tenjiku Shirting	Bleached Shirting	Coloured Shirting	Total
	44 inch width	39 inch width				
1884	435,968	69,660	46,610	3,976	4,246	560,460
1885	483,413	102,437	84,932	10,745	4,886	686,413
1886	453,138	109,453	94,530	32,062	4,803	693,986
1887	570,592	134,865	119,877	27,157	8,576	861,067
1888	243,749	81,872	94,195	15,957	6,112	441,885

(2) Exports of Shirting from Tokyo to Other Localities

(¥)

Year	Grey Shirting		Tenjiku Shirting	Bleached Shirting	Coloured Shirting	Total
	44 inch width	39 inch width				
1884	53,401	7,729	-	-	-	61,130
1885	48,984	11,393	16,060	-	-	76,437
1886	38,387	10,724	28,140	1,535	123	78,909
1887	90,979	36,526	44,206	-	-	171,711
1888	57,321	11,087	17,913	-	124	86,445

Note: The figure for 1884 covers six months only, and the figure for 1888 covers eight months.

Source: The Tokyo Chamber of Commerce & Industry, Tōkei hōkoku (Statistical reports), no. 1–5 (Tokyo, 1885–9).

The bulk of Aichi-made cotton cloth was exported from the prefecture to other localities. Yamaguchi estimated that the quantity of cotton textiles shipped out of six ports in Aichi—Handa, Kamesaki, Ohama, Hirasaka, Toyohashi, and Nayagawagishiba—reached 830,000 *tan* in 1883 valued at 700,000 yen, or 28 per cent of the total exports from the prefecture. This formed a larger proportion of total exports than any other single product.[26] Cotton textiles exported from the prefecture consisted of white cotton cloth, striped cotton cloth, etc.; white cotton cloth formed

Table 4.8

(1) Output of Japanese Cotton Cloths by Variety in 1894

Unbleached Cotton Cloth	23,875 *tan*
Bleached	4,927
Striped	8,212
Others	12,581
Total	49,595

(2) Production of White (unbleached and bleached) Cloth by Prefecture in 1894

('ooo *tan*)

Prefecture	Unbleached Cotton Cloth	Bleached Cotton Cloth	Total
Aichi	8,739	4,061	12,800
Ehime	4,242	95	4,337
Osaka	3,083	14	3,097
Nara	2,069	118	2,187
Saitama	1,829	133	1,962
Others	3,913	506	4,419
Total	23,875	4,927	28,802

Source: The 11th *Nōshōmu-tōkeihyō* (Statistics of agriculture and commerce) (Tokyo, 1896).

the bulk of these textiles.[27] The main market for the Aichi-made white cloth was Tokyo. In the early Meiji period:

> Bleached cotton cloth was delivered from Aichi to other districts roughly in the following proportion: 70 per cent to Tokyo, 10 per cent to Osaka, 5 per cent to Shinshu, and 15 per cent to Nagoya plus overseas markets; almost all *mikawa-momen* (cotton cloth produced in the old province of Mikawa in present-day eastern Aichi) were sent to Tokyo, and only a small fraction of it was transported to the Kyoto–Osaka area.[28]

White cotton cloth was produced in such towns as Handa (in the province of Owari), Chiryu, Nishio, and Okazaki (in the province of Mikawa), and the white cloth of Nishio was 'collected by cotton textile dealers and sent to Tokyo'.[29]

This evidence is in accordance with the 1874 *Fuken bussan chōsa* (an official investigation into products delivered into Tokyo from other local areas), which provided a statistical account of the quantity of the main Japanese cotton textiles sent to Tokyo from October 1873 to September 1874.[30] As shown in Table 4.9, the total quantity of Japanese cotton cloths transported to Tokyo during the year reached two million *tan*.[31] The province of Musashi (the present Tokyo Metropolis and Saitama Prefecture) was the greatest exporter to Tokyo, followed by Owari, Mikawa, and Osaka. These four provinces alone provided Tokyo with 88 per cent of its total imports.[32] But as Aichi Prefecture contained the two provinces of Owari and Mikawa, if we add their outputs together, then total delivery from Aichi amounted to 802,000 *tan*, well in excess of that from Musashi (692,000 *tan*). So Aichi was the largest supplier of cotton textiles to Tokyo. The table provides a rough picture of the varieties of cotton textiles sent from Aichi. Those varieties listed were unbleached cotton cloth and white, striped cotton cloth from the provinces of Owari (444,400 *tan*) and Mikawa

Table 4.9 Delivery of Japanese Cotton Cloths into Tokyo, 1874

Province of Origin	Quantity of Imports (*tan*)	Varieties
Echigo	800	
Shinano	16,000	
Mino	7,600	Unbleached, striped.
Kozuke	15,700	Striped.
Musashi	691,500	Unbleached, striped.
Mikawa (Aichi)	357,100	Unbleached.
Owari (Aichi)	444,400	White, striped.
Osaka	313,500	White, coloured, *unzei*.
Yamato	6,100	Striped.
Kii	13,900	*Monpa*.
Saikyo	36,400	Dyed, striped.
Ise	81,000	Bleached, coloured, striped.
Himeji	70,200	*Tamagawa*, bleached.
Total	2,054,200	

Source: Tokyo hyakunen-shi (History of a Century of Tokyo) (Tokyo, 1972), 2: 994–5.

(357,100 *tan*). If we compare the sum of these figures, 801,500 *tan*, with the figure of the total production of the same varieties in Aichi in 1874, 983,622 *tan* (see Table 4.10), we can deduce that 80 per cent of these three varieties produced in Aichi were sent to Tokyo. The total production figure consisted of 939,441 *tan* of white cloth, 5,500 *tan* of bleached cotton cloth, and 38,681 *tan* of striped cotton cloth. Since bleached cotton cloth was listed separately from white cotton cloth, we can assume that the white cotton cloth refers to unbleached cotton cloth and that this formed the major variety of textile exports from Aichi to Tokyo. Thus the leading variety of Japanese cotton textiles was Aichi-made white cotton cloth, more specifically, *Mikawa-kishiro-momen*[33] (unbleached white cotton cloth produced in the province of Mikawa), and its principal market was Tokyo.

c) Comparison
Table 4.11 and Figure 4.1 compare the wholesale prices of comparable

Table 4.10 Production of Cotton Cloth in Aichi Prefecture (1874)

	Quantity
White Cotton Cloth	939,441 *tan*
Bleached	5,500
Striped	38,681
Total	983,622

Source: Meiji-shichinen fuken bussanhyō (Prefectural production in 1874) (Tokyo, 1874), p. 280.

units of English grey shirting and Japanese *Mikawa-kishiro-momen* in the Tokyo market for the period of 1878–90. They clearly show, contrary to the prevailing assumption, that *Mikawa-momen* was far dearer than English grey shirting throughout the period. A brief explanation about the method of comparison is necessary.

One of the greatest difficulties in comparing these two cloths is the difference in their dimensions. The dimensions of *Mikawa-momen* are

Table 4.11   Comparison of Prices between English and Japanese Cotton Cloths

Year	A			B			C		
	English Grey Shirting of 44-inch width			A/11			Aichi-made *Mikawa-kishiro-momen*		
	top quality	medium quality	lowest quality	top	medium	lowest	top	medium	lowest
	yen sen	yen sen	yen sen	sen	sen	sen	sen	sen	sen
1878	2 80	2 64	2 53	25.3	24.0	23.0	44.6	40.7	36.6
1879	3 20	3 08	2 86	29.1	28.0	26.0	46.7	42.5	37.4
1880	3 80	3 72	3 27	34.5	33.8	29.7	56.5	49.1	42.0
1881	4 57	4 44	3 85	41.6	40.3	35.0	77.9	67.1	56.6
1882	4 34	3 85	3 23	37.1	35.0	29.4	68.4	57.2	49.4
1883	3 01	3 02	2 69	27.4	27.4	25.0	60.9	48.4	38.6
1884	2 67	2 54	2 52	24.2	23.1	22.8	45.1	38.0	33.6
1885	2 54	2 44	2 30	23.1	22.2	21.0	46.2	39.6	35.1
1886	2 50	2 44	2 42	22.7	22.1	21.9	42.5	34.4	32.7
1887	2 71	2 63	2 53	24.6	23.8	22.8	44.5	38.3	34.0
1888	2 64	2 60	2 35	24.0	23.7	21.4	46.8	41.3	36.5
1889	2 72	2 70	2 64	24.7	24.4	24.0	39.8	35.4	31.4
1890	2 62	2 55	2 40	23.8	23.1	21.8	32.0	29.5	27.5

Sources: *Chūgai bukka shinpō* (Current domestic and foreign prices, published weekly in Tokyo) for the period between 1878 and 1882; *Tokyo keizai zasshi* (*Tokyo Economic Journal*, published fortnightly in Tokyo) for the period between 1883 and 1890. The figures in the table are annual averages of prices which appeared in these journals near the end of each month.

known, as it was among the samples of Japanese cotton piece goods sent to England in 1887 and described in a consular report as: 'length, 31 feet 11/12 inches; width, 13 1/2 inches'.[34] These measurements conform with those stated in Japanese sources.[35] But the length of 44-inch wide English

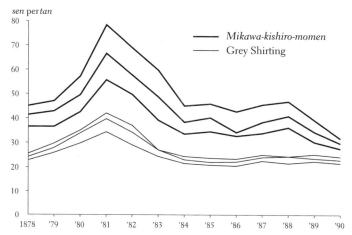

sen per *tan*

Figure 4.1 Comparison of Prices between English and Japanese Cotton Cloths

Source: Same as Table 4.11

grey shirting was 38 to 40 yards.[36] Therefore, the difference in size is as follows:

A roll of grey shirting, therefore, contained roughly twelve times as

Comparison of the Dimensions of the Two Cloths

	Width	Length	Dimensions
Mikawa-momen	0.35 m.	9.48 m. to 9.85 m.	3.31 to 3.44 sq. m.
Grey Shirting	1.12 m.	35.6 m. to 36.6 m.	39.9 to 41.4 sq. m.

The ratios were:

	Width	Length	Dimensions
Mikawa-momen	1	1	1
Grey Shirting	3.21	3.61 to 3.86	11.6 to 12.4

much cloth as a roll of *Mikawa-momen,* and the price per unit can be obtained by dividing the price of grey shirting by twelve. However, if we take into account the way English shirting was cut and made up into

Japanese garments, we should divide by eleven instead of by twelve for the following reason. The standard dimensions of Japanese cloth were traditionally fixed by the *tan*, which provides just enough cloth to make a standard size kimono.[37] The width and length of a *tan* of a cloth is about 13.4 inches and 34.4 feet. This is indicated by the samples of Japanese cotton cloths sent to England in 1887, which show little variation in length or width.[38] The British Vice-Consul who sent the samples noted, 'in many the piece length of the cloth is so rigidly fixed that a very slight departure from it would spoil the prospect of the sale of the piece.'[39] As mentioned earlier, the sales of 44-inch-wide grey shirting in Tokyo were about four times as great as those of 39-inch-wide grey shirting. This was because the former was better suited to traditional Japanese requirements, for the 44-inch-wide cloth was only slightly more than three times the standard Japanese width, so that it was possible to cut out three full pieces with the standard width of the *tan*, leaving only a 2.75 inches remnant. Indeed, the 44-inch-wide grey shirting was called '*mihabamono*', which in Japanese means triple-width cloth. On the other hand, the 39-inch-wide grey shirting was 2.8 times the Japanese width, so that it could provide only two pieces, leaving a full 11 inches of wasted material. This accounted for the small demand for the 39-inch-wide grey shirting.

In contrast to the inflexibility of the width, the length of a *tan* of cloth was more adjustable, for Japanese made up various sorts of kimonos by cutting the length of a *tan* of cloth according to the specific kind of kimono to be made: *haori* (coat), *juban* (underwear), *hitotsumi* (clothes for a baby), *mitsumi* (clothes for a child), *hondachi* (clothes for an adult), and so on. For instance, when making a kimono for a child, they usually used a half length of a *tan* of cloth (and still do). Thus, the length of English grey shirting (40 yards) was adjustable to traditional Japanese needs. Such being the case, a fraction of English grey shirting in excess of three times the standard Japanese length cannot be similarly disregarded. Then the ratio between the two cloths is 1:10.8 to 1:11.6, as $3 \times 3.61 = 10.8$, or $3 \times 3.86 = 11.6$. For the sake of convenience, let us calculate the ratio as 1:11. Even if we employ the ratio of 1:12, on the assumption that there were subsidiary uses for the extra material, the conclusion is not affected, because in this case, the price differences between the two cloths become greater.

The outcome of our comparison of prices between English and Japanese cotton cloths is further supported by a statistical compilation published by the Ministry of Agriculture and Commerce, which investigated prices of a *tan* of Japanese *ki-momen* (unbleached cotton cloth) and

Table 4.12 Prices of Japanese and English Cotton Cloths in the Main Cities of Japan in 1886 and 1887

(sen: ¥1.00 = 100 sen)

	Japanese *ki-momen* (Unbleached cotton cloth) per *tan* of cloth		English Grey Shirting of the Same Dimensions	
	1886	1887	1886	1887
Tokyo	37.0	35.9	23.2	29.4
Kyoto	36.1	42.9	25.4	22.8
Osaka	21.9	22.9	22.3	27.1
Yokohama	41.9	40.2	26.8	28.9
Kobe	41.6	44.5	24.3	24.1
Himeji	17.8	19.6	27.2	30.4
Niigata	31.6	32.3	25.3	27.6
Takada	34.5	33.0	-	-
Nagasaki	25.8	28.1	26.1	22.8
Kawagoe	31.7	27.8	24.1	24.4
Maebashi	42.8	37.7	27.0	36.5
Chiba	29.6	27.8	25.3	26.8
Choshi	34.5	41.0	21.0	27.5
Mito	-	42.2	-	27.5
Utsunomiya	35.8	48.1	26.9	25.2
Nara	-	33.3	-	24.7
Tsu	27.3	41.5	23.1	22.5
Nagoya	27.2	32.9	22.9	23.5
Shizuoka	31.2	38.7	24.0	30.0
Kofu	33.7	38.5	23.9	27.8
Otsu	40.0	49.7	29.0	35.9
Nagahama	39.0	47.4	26.5	32.4
Gifu	32.7	32.3	23.6	29.3
Nagano	48.8	45.0	27.7	29.1
Sendai	39.1	36.2	27.2	27.2
Ishimaki	36.8	35.1	26.7	25.4

Continued on next page

Table 4.12—*Continued*

(sen: ¥1.00 = 100 sen)

| | Japanese *ki-momen* (Unbleached cotton cloth) per *tan* of cloth | | English Grey Shirting of the Same Dimensions | |
	1886	1887	1886	1887
Fukushima	33.5	37.5	30.6	33.2
Morioka	51.5	35.6	32.9	36.7
Miyako	36.7	33.0	21.0	29.4
Aomori	38.8	35.0	23.3	28.0
Yamagata	39.8	35.5	20.0	22.4
Sakata	–	33.7	–	29.5
Akita	34.7	39.0	27.3	35.3
Fukui	28.0	32.4	26.3	27.5
Tsuruga	42.1	44.8	27.6	29.6
Kanazawa	26.3	32.5	27.6	26.1
Toyama	36.5	36.1	30.2	35.9
Matsue	22.8	26.1	24.4	32.0
Tottori	25.7	30.5	27.3	26.8
Okayama	21.3	23.1	27.3	25.9
Hiroshima	29.4	31.8	23.7	32.7
Onomichi	18.9	26.3	33.7	-
Yamaguchi	23.3	24.8	26.0	22.3
Akamagaseki	22.3	20.7	25.5	25.1
Wakayama	24.3	32.3	27.8	31.4
Tokushima	22.5	23.7	25.1	25.6
Kochi	35.0	37.2	28.0	26.1
Matsuyama	-	20.7	-	25.7
Takamatsu	-	35.8	-	28.6
Oita	21.2	22.8	20.9	27.6
Nakatsu	21.3	23.0	25.9	27.1
Saga	22.6	26.4	24.0	26.0
Kumamoto	23.1	23.9	22.4	21.1
Yatsushiro	27.0	25.0	27.6	21.8
Miyazaki	33.0	38.4	27.4	25.6
Nobeoka	33.0	33.3	35.7	35.8
Sapporo	38.9	35.5	17.5	–
Hakodate	47.5	51.5	-	22.6
Otaru	-	42.2	-	31.7
Kagoshima	30.6	30.5	24.8	24.4

Source: Ministry of Agriculture and Commerce, *Nōshōmu tōkeihyō* (Statistics relating to agriculture and commerce), No. 2 and 3 (Tokyo, 1888, 1889).

English grey shirting of the same size in the main cities throughout Japan for the year 1886/7. As is shown in Table 4.12, the Japanese cloth was more expensive than the English equivalent in almost all the cities. These facts contradict the prevailing view, in its simple form, which assumes direct competition between English and Japanese cotton cloths as perfect substitutes for each other in Japanese markets. Moreover, the price data seem to imply that, because cotton yarn was the largest of Japan's imports during that period, Japanese weavers could use less expensive foreign yarn and produce cloth which sold more cheaply than foreign cloth. But this was not, in fact, the case.

4. CONCLUSION

'The Japanese are . . . almost universally clothed in cotton', observed a British consul in the early Meiji period, and he believed, 'when English piece goods were supplied to them at a cost much below that for which they could obtain the produce of their hand-looms, they were not slow to take advantage of them.'[40] We have made it clear, however, that English cotton cloths did not directly compete with their Japanese rivals. The reason the Japanese purchased English textiles in the early Meiji period was something other than their cheapness. But in spite of their relative cheapness, Japanese purchases of English cotton goods gradually declined in the middle of the Meiji era. Japan's imports of cotton textiles decreased in value from 5,404,000 yen in 1874 to 4,129,000 yen in 1890.[41] Yet its production of cotton textiles increased in value from 10,543,000 yen to 31,874,000 yen in the same period.[42] At the same time, the estimated per capita expenditure on clothing by the Japanese more than doubled.[43] We can conclude that in the early Meiji period, on the eve of industrialisation, the Japanese preferred to buy home-made cotton cloth rather than foreign cloth in spite of the higher price of local cloth.It will be interesting at this point to compare the Japanese experience with Chinese cotton textile markets. Mitchell wrote at Hong Kong in 1852.

> It is, perhaps, characteristic of China alone, of all countries in the world, that the loom is to be found in every well-conditioned homestead. . . . The thrifty Chinaman . . . not only cards and spins his cotton, but he weaves it himself with the help of his wives and daughters and farm ser-

vants, and hardly ever confines himself to producing for the mere wants
of his family, but makes it an essential part of his season's operations to
produce a certain quantity of cloth for the supply of neighbouring towns
and rivers. The Fuh-kien [Fujian] farmer is thus not merely a farmer,
but an agriculturist and a manufacturer in one! He produces this cloth
literally for nothing, beyond the cost of the raw material; he produces it,
as shown, under his own roof-tree, by the hands of his women and farm
servants; it costs neither extra labour nor extra time. . . . I have hitherto
spoken of the production of this cloth only in Fuhkien province. The very
same system extends, as far as we know, throughout the whole country.[44]

Based on this sort of contemporary observation, Kang Chao stresses the
significance of family labour, and presents a hypothesis, the so-called
'family (or domestic) production system in China', as distinct from enterprises or firms as production units in the West.[45] By that he means that
'since the family is not based on the wage system and is obliged to accom-
modate all members, it tends to use all available labor until its marginal
productivity drops to zero.'[46]

In practice, however, Chinese cotton cloth was not always cheaper
than English cloth. The English Consul reported in Peking in 1861: 'On
comparing also the prices of native grey cotton cloths with British cotton manufactures, it is reported by the intelligent British merchants who
accompanied the expedition, that the prices of the former cannot be considered low.'[47] Kang Chao himself was unsure about relative prices and
summarises information on prices as follows:

> It would be pointed out that none of the reports cited so far has explic-
> itly and systematically presented price comparisons between imported
> and local cloth. The price information from these reports is rather con-
> fusing. Mitchell implies that native products were lower in price; other
> reports mention that Chinese cloth was more expensive per unit but
> was more durable too; at least one source suggests that the selling price
> was the same for both but the native cloth was narrower (see Chinese
> Maritime Customs, *Trade Reports*, Ningpo, 1871–72, p. 7). The Chinese
> literature, however, always claims that the imported cloth was cheaper.[48]

In the case of Korea, the picture is made much clearer by Kajinishi. He shows from descriptive sources that native cotton textiles were more expensive than British textiles.[49]

Thus the position of British cotton textiles was similar in all the Far Eastern markets. They did not sell well despite their cheap prices. It is clear that an explanation based on price alone fails to explain why Far Eastern weavers held their own against competition from British textiles.

Chapter Five

QUALITY DIFFERENCES BETWEEN COTTON GOODS

1. INTRODUCTION

In the middle of the nineteenth century, the Far East was subject to the influence of the Western Powers, including Great Britain. One of Britain's economic weapons, in the age of 'free trade imperialism', was the low price of cotton textiles. But could that weapon make its influence felt in the Far East? As mentioned in the previous chapter, in Japan, expenditure on native woven cloth increased in preference to British-made cloths. Lancashire cotton piece goods did not sell well in China either. This was one of the reasons why British merchants brought opium into China, resulting in the Opium War of 1839–42. Why, then, were British cotton cloths, which were cheaper in price and finer in quality, not used by local consumers instead of Chinese and Japanese cotton cloths? Several factors determine consumer behaviour—taste and preference, level of household income, and price. As an average Japanese household tended to purchase relatively expensive goods, taste and preference mattered. Why did they prefer Japanese textiles to British goods?

Although British grey shirtings,[1] Japanese *Mikawa-momen*, and Chinese *nankeen* were all categorised as cotton fabric, careful scrutiny will show that the physical properties of British textiles were not the same as those of the other two, and their usage was not exactly alike. Yanagita Kunio, a pioneer of and authority on Japanese folklore, once pointed out that *kana-kin* (imported British shirtings) were popular among the Japanese because they were somewhat similar to silk and because the latter half of the name (*kin*) sounded similar to *kinu* (silk).[2] Indeed some evidence suggests that British cotton textiles were passable substitutes for the local silk fabrics of East Asia. For example, a commercial report from Yokohama in 1887 stated as follows:

> As an illustration of how [British] shirtings were esteemed I [British Vice-Consul Longford] may mention an incident which has been related to me by a Japanese of the class of 'shizoku', or gentry. This person remembers accompanying his lord on a visit to Tokyo in the year 1860. During his stay in the city the lord purchased a quantity of shirtings, had them dyed and emblazoned with his crest and made into coats for the higher ranks of his retainers in preference to the Japanese silk fabric called 'habutai', which was usually employed for that purpose.[3]

Similar accounts also exist in the Japanese records. A report of the Osaka Chamber of Commerce on custom duties in 1879 includes the following statements:

> [British] dyed shirtings are used as substitutes for silk fabrics made in the districts of Chichibu [Saitama] and Kai [Yamanashi] . . . [British] fine shirtings are employed as linings for the kimono and used as substitutes for silk fabrics made in the district of Chichibu . . . . [British] fine unbleached shirtings are used as substitutes for *habutai* [silk] . . . . [British] cotton velveteens are used as substitutes for [Japanese] silk velvets.[4]

The Japanese Foreign Trade Survey of 1890 gives a similar evaluation:

> [British] chintzes are used as substitutes for [Japanese] silk crepes . . . . [British] cotton velveteens are used as substitutes for [Japanese] silk velvets . . . . [British] dyed shirtings, commonly called Tochichibu, are used as substitutes for [Japanese] silk fabrics called Hanachichibu.[5]

When discussing native cotton cloths, however, contemporary records mention such factors as the thickness, durability, and weight to indicate differences in quality with British cotton cloths. These factors would have been closely related to differences in their respective raw materials.

For example, Mitchell's report from Hong Kong in 1852 includes the following paragraph:

> No working Chinaman can afford to put on a new coat which shall not last him at least three years, and stand the wear and tear of the roughest drudgery during that period. Now, a garment of that description must contain at least three times the weight of raw cotton which we put into the heaviest goods we export to China; that is to say, it must be three times as heavy as the heaviest drills and domestics we can afford to send out here.[6]

The commercial report from Hankow (Hankou) in 1861 also stated:

> It is most true, as has been admitted by all best acquainted with this country, that Chinamen of the classes comprising nine-tenths of the immense population of this Empire require cotton cloths containing three times the quantity of cotton that is put into what is imported into this country from Great Britain.[7]

A quarter-century later, another commercial report from Amoy (Xiamen) notes:

> It is well known already that the many millions of lower-class Chinese toiling and moiling throughout the 18 provinces, and in huge territories beyond them, do not wear foreign-made cloths, but homespun. Ask a Chinaman why this is, and he tells you that the poor wear suits of native cotton, because such clothing lasts three, four, or five times as long as foreign cotton cloth, because it wears less easily, and because it is much warmer in winter. Why is it warmer? Because, he says, the yarn of which the native fabric is made is quite different from the foreign, and warmer by nature.[8]

And a report in Yokohama in 1887 states: 'A comparison of the wearing qualities of the two [British grey shirting and Japanese cotton called Moka] shows that the ratio of difference is even greater than the price; i.e., that Moka has more than three times the wearing quality of grey shirting.'[9] Similar accounts are also cited by Kajimura as regards the position in Korea.[10]

Although these alleged differences in foreign and native cloths cannot
be measured, the cotton yarns that constitute their raw materials can be.
Cotton yarn is subject to classification by counts, which accurately indicate the fineness and thickness of the yarn. The counts refer to the number of hanks (a hank = 840 yards) contained in a pound weight of cotton
yarn; the higher the counts, the finer the yarn. Thus, 20 hanks to a pound
is 20s, 40 hanks is 40s, 100 hanks is 100s, etc. Cotton yarn, together with
finish, sizing, length, etc., is a feature by which the quality of cotton textiles is distinguished.[11] If the quality of cotton yarn typically employed for
Far Eastern cotton textiles was different from that of Lancashire yarn, it
will account for much of the difference in quality of British and Japanese
cotton cloths.

2. THE QUALITY OF BRITISH COTTON YARN

Baines estimated that the average count of yarn spun in Britain was
around 40s in the early 1830s.[12] During the following twenty years,
British cotton products underwent a change in quality, and the proportion of coarse to fine yarns actually increased.[13] The spread of Heilmann's
combing machine after 1851, however, marked 'a revolution in the history of fine spinning'.[14] It 'revived the fine-cotton spinning industry'[15]
and 'opened up a new era of fine cotton-spinning'.[16] Also with the rising
pressure of foreign competition in coarse yarns from the 1870s onwards,
British yarns tended to become finer.[17]

Exact figures for counts spun in Britain in the late nineteenth century
are not available, except for some fragmentary information. The reports
of the inspectors of factories for 1863 surveyed the average counts spun in
seventeen districts in Lancashire (see Table 5.1). Of those districts, Bacup,
Bury, Oldham, and Rochdale (and perhaps Haslingden) alone spun low
counts under 20s, although some mills in these districts did produce
higher counts. The simple arithmetical average of the counts enumer-
ated in the table is calculated at around 40s, but is nothing more than a
very rough guide. By 1875, however, the low-count spinning districts such
as Haslingden, Bury, and Oldham had increased their average counts to
above 32s (see Table 5.2). These figures were collected from districts specialising in lower counts and do not include the high-count producing

Table 5.1 The Average Counts of Yarns Spun in Lancashire, 1863

Accrington	30/36s twist,* 32/46s weft
Ashton-under-Lyne	32/46s, a few spun up to 80s
Bacup	16/28s twist, 20/36s weft
Blackburn	30/36s twist, 32/46s weft
Bury	about 26s, varying from 14s to 32s twist, and 16s to 28s weft
Dukinfield	the same as Ashton-under-Lyne
Glossop	30/50s
Haslingden	the lowest counts
Heywood	20/32s twist, 24/36s weft
Manchester	the highest counts
Mossley	50/60s
Mottram	30/90s
Oldham	6/20s using Surat with waste, 20/40s using Surat, 50/70s from Egyptian and mixtures, and up to 80s from better qualities
Preston	50s (30/40s before the Cotton Famine)
Rochdale	18–70
Salford	the same as Manchester
Stalybridge	the same as Ashton-under-Lyne

Notes: * Warp yarn is generally stronger than weft, and hardness is obtained by extra twisting of the thread; owing to this particularity, warp yarn is generally called 'twist'. Brooks, *Cotton Manufacturing*, p. 33.

Source: *Parliamentary Papers 1864*, XXII (c. 8430): Reports of the Inspectors of Factories, 31 October 1863, pp. 16–34.

Table 5.2 The Average Counts of Yarns Spun in Lancashire, 1875

Ashton-under-Lyne	40s
Blackburn	32s twist, 38s weft
Burnley	32s twist, 40/46s weft
Bury	32/40s twist, 40s weft
Darwen	32/60s twist, 36/80s weft
Haslingden	20/32s twist, 40/46s weft
Leigh	50/60s twist, 70/120s weft
Mossley	40s twist
Oldham	32/40s twist, 36/46s weft
Rochdale	mainly weft counts 10/54s and a few twist counts 12/40s
Stalybridge	3/140s (30/45s average)
Stockport	16/32s

Source: Farnie, 'The English Cotton Industry 1850–1896', pp. 170–82. (Original source is Oldham Operative Cotton Spinners' Provincial Association, *A List of Thirty Questions with the Answers Given Thereto, Relating to the System of Payment to Minders etc.*, 1875.)

districts such as Manchester and Bolton. Even so, the simple arithmetical average of the counts listed in the table reaches the fairly high level of 41s. In the 1880s, Oldham's yarn became finer: 32s twist gave way to 34s, and 40s weft to 42s.[18]

In 1888, Brooks noted that Preston and Chorley spun 40–80s twist and 40–90s weft; Manchester 80–200s twist and 80–350s weft; Rochdale 12–24s warp up to 30–40s; Bolton 40–200s; Mossley 20–50s; Stockport 150s.[19] In the early 1890s, many mills in Oldham which used to spin 32s were going in for 50s, 60s, 70s, and 80s, and this movement was spreading.[20] By the end of the century, Stockport had become a centre of fine cotton spinning.[21]

In 1887, evidence was given before the Royal Commission on Gold and Silver that the proportion of the coarse yarn manufactured in Lancashire was only about 10 per cent of the whole. Most of the mills which used to spin coarse yarn had lost business, and some were being filled with new machinery to spin finer counts.[22] Although the report provides no details relating to the proportions of the different counts to the total yarns spun in late-nineteenth-century England, it shows an unmistakable trend toward higher counts. An attempt can be made to calculate the average counts of yarns spun in the whole cotton region of Lancashire and neighbouring areas from J. Worrall's *The Cotton Spinners' and Manufacturers' Directory for the Year of 1887*, which contains a detailed list of the counts spun by each mill.[23] It provides no information on production figures, but only on the number of the spindles at work. For example:

Hargreaves John & Co., Broad Oak Mill; 40,800 spindles, 30s/50s weft, 28s/32s twist; 778 looms, printers and shirtings.

In the 1887 edition of the *Directory*, out of 1,023 mills which operated either spindles only or looms as well, 864, or 84 per cent, presented figures for the counts they spun. Estimating the average counts from these data poses a problem since the mean counts of, for instance, 100s and 50s are not 75s if the output is taken into consideration. But, as no production figures are available, the method used here assumes that the number of spindles is proportionate to the quantity produced. To the extent that this assumption is correct, the proportion of the number of spindles in a mill to that of the total spindles in a district would be similar to the proportion of the quantity produced by a mill to total production for the district. If we multiply that proportion by the average counts spun by each mill, the result will represent the average count in the district. The actual mode of calculation is as follows: on the assumption that a mill with 40,000 spindles would produce twice the output of a mill with 20,000 spindles, the overall average counts of a hypothetical district shown in the table below are calculated at 56s (= 30 × 0.1 + 100 × 0.2 + 60 × 0.25 + 40 × 0.45).

(Example)	X District			
	Counts of yarns	Average counts	Number of spindles (%)	
A mill	20/40s	30s	20,000	(10)
B mill	80/120s	100s	40,000	(20)
C mill	50/70s	60s	50,000	(25)
D mill	30/50s	40s	90,000	(45)
			200,000	(100)

The result of the application of this method to the figures in the *Directory* of 1887 is shown in Table 5.3 (a). These figures, however, do not take into account the extent to which spindles were idle, nor the difference in the operational speed of the spindles. They also assume that the proportion of the spindles producing weft yarns to those producing warp (twist) yarns in a mill is 50 per cent. Unfortunately little information is available on these issues. Still, the figures can serve as a reasonable guide, and they corroborate the other evidence mentioned above. They also demonstrate well-known local differences in the Lancashire cotton region, indicating that Manchester, Bolton, Stockport, and Leigh were centres of the finest cotton spinning whilst Preston, Ashton-under-Lyne, Mossley, and Stalybridge were regions of fairly fine spinning and Rochdale of coarse spinning. They also show that spindles appropriated to the low counts (under 30s) were less than 10 per cent of the total, and the lowest counts (below 25s) were almost negligible. Nearly half of the total spindles were devoted to the counts between 30s and 40s, 27 per cent to the highest counts (above 60s), and 18 per cent to the fairly high counts of 40s to 60s.

Table 5.3 (a) The Average Counts of Yarns Spun in Lancashire in 1887

	Districts	The Average Counts		No.	No.
		weft	warp	of Mills	of Spindles
	Bolton			79 (71)*	4,518,132
	Bolton	81s	80s		
	Others	67	68		
	Manchester			59 (43)	2,994,744
Above 60s	Manchester	110	110		
	Others	37	31		
	Stockport	69	63	58 (48)	1,947,540
	Leigh	71	70	17 (16)	1,164,528
	Chorley	67	61	15 (15)	524,128
					11,149,072 (27.2%)
	Preston	45	40	42 (41)	2,008,356
	Ashton-under-Lyne	47	37	34 (31)	1,756,256
	Mossley	43	42	14 (14)	1,246,384
40–60s	Stalybridge	52	48	18 (17)	1,099,540
	Farnworth	61	42	21 (19)	499,522
	Middleton	44	39	8 (6)	443,696
	Uppermill	49	42	6 (5)	171,000
					7,224,754 (17.6%)
	Oldham			229 (193)	10,258,853
	Oldham	43	34		
	Others	43	36		
	Blackburn	39	32	36 (32)	1,531,449
	Glossop	40	36	17 (14)	1,086,298
	Burnley	45	32	30 (29)	941,373
	Wigan	35	32	14 (13)	759,272
	Heywood	35	31	28 (24)	645,146
30–40s	Hyde	38	34	16 (16)	636,360
	Accrington	47	31	22 (18)	554,916
	Dukinfield	37	39	10 (10)	532,732
	Newchurch	34	34	28 (20)	523,978
	Darwen	37	34	14 (13)	461,710
	Padiham	44	31	9 (8)	223,206
	Denton	32	–	3 (2)	104,088
	Clitheroe & Colne	38	32	6 (6)	189,512
	Great Harwood	45	33	3 (2)	82,626
					18,531,519 (45.3%)

Table 5.3 (a)—*continued*

	Districts	The Average Counts		No.	No.
		weft	warp	of Mills	of Spindles
	Rochdale	39	24	70 (61)	1,725,616
	Bury	33	25	36 (21)	947,410
	Bacup	29	24	19 (12)	432,772
25–30s	Todmorden	31	25	12 (8)	319,510
	Littleborough	30	24	7 (5)	110,292
	Radcliffe	32	24	6 (3)	105,700
	Warrington	31	20	2 (2)	85,000
					3,726,300 (9.1%)
	Ramsbottom	25	23	16 (11)	135,520
	Haslingden	28	14	14 (10)	126,984
Under 25s	Lancaster	23	25	2 (2)	29,496
	Golborne	28	22	3 (3)	21,064
					313,064 (0.8%)
	Average	53s	46s	Total	40,944,709 (100%)

Note: * The number of the mills which presented figures of the counts they spun.
Source: Worrall, *The Cotton Spinners' and Manufacturers' Directory*, 1887.

From these we can compute the overall average of all the counts listed in the table, bearing in mind regional differences in the number of spindles. This calculation reveals that the average counts of weft and warp yarns spun in Lancashire in 1887 were respectively 53s and 46s.

To measure the trend in the qualities of yarns, I have attempted to estimate the average counts of yarn spun in the same region twenty years later. Table 5.3 (b) is the result of the application of the above method to the figures in J. Worrall's Directory of 1908. A comparison of the two tables will immediately show that yarn became finer between 1887 and 1908. Thus, yarn over 30s, which comprised 90 per cent of the total in 1887, rose to 97 per cent in 1908. There were also changes within the over-30s range. The percentage share of spindles spinning the counts above 60s rose to 33.5 per cent from 27.2 per cent in 1887. Spindles operating for counts of 40s–60s increased more rapidly to 44.4 per cent compared with 17.6 per cent in 1887. On the other hand, the percentage of spindles devoted to the 30s–40s range fell to less than 20 per cent from 45.3 per cent. Spindles for 25s–30s also decreased to 1.3 per cent from 9.1 per cent,

Table 5.3 (b) The Average Counts of Yarns Spun in Lancashire in 1908

	Districts	The Average Counts weft	warp	No. of Mills	No. of Spindles
	Bolton	82s	78s	70 (63)*	6,805,165
	Manchester			43 (36)	3,470,668
	Manchester	149s	144		
	Others	40	37		
Above 60s	Stockport	68	60	53 (43)	2,412,462
	Leigh	78	73	16 (14)	1,985,514
	Farnworth	72	59	24 (22)	1,545,072
	Mossley	65	56	15 (15)	1,418,876
	Chorley	66	54	16 (16)	852,512
					18,490,269 (33.5%)
	Oldham	52	39	217 (193)	15,478,045
	Preston	49	45	39 (37)	2,260,182
	Ashton-under-Lyne	54	42	33 (31)	2,135,910
	Stalybridge	54	43	20 (18)	1,242,352
	Middleton	59	49	13 (13)	1,071,880
40–60s	Dukinfield	48	39	10 (10)	813,386
	Accrington	49	33	18 (14)	651,704
	Radcliffe	49	50	8 (5)	288,900
	Darwen	45	40	8 (8)	274,216
	Uppermill & Warrington	47	37	5 (4)	228,746
	Great Harwood	47	38	3 (2)	71,600
	Nelson	45	–	1 (1)	23,200
					24,540,121 (44.4%)
	Rochdale	41	37	80 (70)	3,452,506
	Blackburn	39	32	30 (25)	1,366,168
	Heywood	37	37	29 (26)	1,018,524
	Wigan	40	33	13 (12)	1,017,768
	Bury	35	28	28 (24)	957,294
30–40s	Glossop	39	36	12 (10)	867,834
	Hyde	35	28	12 (12)	735,986
	Burnley	39	35	18 (17)	594,492
	Padiham	42	31	7 (6)	192,650
	Colne	40	34	2 (2)	139,500
	Clitheroe	36	34	4 (4)	120,830
	Denton	36	28	3 (3)	117,750
					10,581,302 (19.2%)

Table 5.3 (b) — *continued*

	Districts	The Average Counts weft	warp	No. of Mills	No. of Spindles
	Bacup	28	23	14 (13)	376,790
25–30s	Rawtenstall	33	25	15 (13)	331,930
					708,720 (1.3%)
	Todmorden	24	24	10 (6)	302,236
	Haslingden	10	22	11 (11)	168,092
	Golborne	24	20	2 (2)	112,296
Under 25s	Waterfoot	29	20	7 (7)	98,070
	Littleborough	21	23	3 (1)	93,084
	Ramsbottom	12	19	9 (8)	74,714
	Lancaster	23	25	2 (2)	31,120
					879,612 (1.6%)
	Average	64	55	Total	55,218,024 (100.0%)

Note: * The number of the mills which presented figures of the counts they spun.
Source: Worrall, *The Cotton Spinners' and Manufacturers' Directory*, 1887.

Table 5.4 British Cloths and Yarns

Varieties	Counts
Shirtings	30–60s
Domestics	18–40s
Printers	32–50s
Tanjibs	32–50s
Jacconetts	32–50s
Mulls	60–100s
Cambrics	80–160s
Sateens	36–80s
Doriah stripes	40–50s

Source: Brooks, *Cotton Manufacturing*, pp. 85–88.

while those devoted to the counts under 25s remained negligible. As a consequence, the spindles for 40s and above comprised 80 per cent of the total in 1908. This was comparable to 45 per cent in 1887. Overall average counts of yarn in 1908 are calculated at 64s weft and 55s twist (compared with 53s weft and 46s twist in 1887). Clearly, the counts of British yarn tended to rise in the period from the late nineteenth to the early twentieth centuries.

The changing quality of British cotton cloths reflected these higher counts yarn. C. P. Brooks detailed the main varieties of British cloths woven in the late 1880s with the counts of yarn used. A summary is shown in Table 5.4. The simple arithmetical average of counts listed on the table is calculated at 55s.

3. THE QUALITY OF YARN USED IN JAPAN

The Japanese in the Meiji period had three sources of supply for cotton yarns, British, Indian, and local. By 1884, the Japanese were using the system of 'counts' for classification of yarn, for an official report called *Kōgyō iken* (Advice on the promotion of industry) published that year stated, 'imported yarns can be classified into three kinds of yarn: No. 1, No. 2, and No. 3. No. 1 yarn consists of 38s, 40s, and 42s; No. 2 yarn consists of 28s, 30s, and 32s; and No. 3 yarn consists of 16s, 18s, 20s, and 24s'.[24] No. 1 yarn referred to fine yarn, No. 2 yarn to medium, and No. 3 yarn to coarse.[25] This distinction of fineness or coarseness, of course, should be understood in a relative sense, as high counts in Japan, such as 40s or 42s, were not particularly high in England, where, to take an extreme example, the average count of yarn produced by McConnel & Co. as early as 1833 was circa 170s.[26]

(i) British yarns

Since, by our estimates, about 90 per cent of the yarn produced in England in 1887 was finer than 30s, one might guess that this type of yarn would have flooded into Japanese markets, as indeed, economic history textbooks have so far assumed. What the available evidence indicates, however, is that the bulk of yarns shipped from England to Japan consisted of yarn of low counts. Table 5.5 (a) and (b) shows the deliveries of British yarns for local consumption in Japan for the twenty years between 1872 and 1891. It shows that fine yarn with counts of 38s–42s constituted only 6 per cent on average of all British yarns delivered in the period. Medium yarn of 28s–32s formed 29 per cent, and the remaining 65 per cent comprised coarse yarn of 24s and under. The relatively high rate of imports of medium yarn in the early 1870s was 'owing to a scarcity of No. 3 [16–24s] throughout the year [1873]', which meant that 'the sales of No. 2 [28–32s], imported in large quantities, improved very considerably'.[27]

This statistical evidence is supported by contemporary observations on Japan's import trade in British yarn: 'There was hardly any demand for No. 1 [38–42s]' at Hyogo and Osaka in 1873.[28] 'There is no market for nos. 38 to 42' at Hyogo and Osaka in 1874.[29] 'The chief demand is for the lower qualities of 16–24' at Kanagawa in 1875.[30] 'The consumption runs chiefly on the 16 and 24 numbers' at Kanagawa in 1878.[31] 'The greater

Table 5.5 (a) Deliveries of British Yarns for Local Consumption at the Port of Yokohama, 1872–91

(piculs)

Year	Coarse Yarn			Medium Yarn	Fine Yarn	Total
	Doubled[#]					
	2/42s	2/32s	16–24s	28–32s	38–42s	
1872 July–Dec.	–	–	24,280	19,001	1,899	45,180
1873	–	–	59,289	33,488	5,120	97,897
1874	–	–	65,620	31,527	5,355	102,502
1875[*]	–	–	67,957	29,515	5,625	103,097
1876	–	–	–	–	–	–
1877	–	–	–	–	–	–
1878 (bales)	–	–	(42,400)	(16,800)	(2,700)	(61,900)
1879	–	–	127,928	48,333	12,613	188,874
1880	–	–	135,741	55,465	14,264	205,470
1881	–	–	137,373	47,332	15,850	200,555
1882 July–Dec.	3,510	2,529	55,149	16,992	3,624	81,804
1883 Jan.–June	3,009	1,581	52,775	14,574	3,093	75,032
1884[**]	5,112	1,865	60,019	29,758	3,767	100,521
1885 July–Dec.	4,257	840	26,367	19,101	3,408	53,973
1886 July–Dec.	5,991	1,311	29,043	23,034	4,308	63,687
1887	10,101	2,514	53,592	39,798	7,437	113,442
1888	16,176	5,493	63,066	39,069	8,694	132,498
1889	19,608	4,080	46,539	36,735	9,096	116,058
1890	18,870	2,460	47,649	29,445	5,883	104,307
1891[***]	21,261	2,334	34,535	19,125	5,534	82,789

Notes: [#] Doubled yarns (two-fold yarns) are numbered according to the single yarn counts. Thus, 2/32s = two ends of 32s twined together, which would warp 16s. In fact, the twist put in the folded yarns contracts it in length and makes it coarser than would appear. Brooks, *Cotton Manufacturing*, p. 145.

   [*] No statistics for the period of November 10–22.

   [**] No statistics for the period of July 16–August 25, October 17–31, and December 16–31.

   [***] No statistics for the period of December 12–31.

Source: *Parliamentary Papers 1878–79,* LXXII (c. 2358): Commercial Report on Kanagawa 1878, p. 35 for 1878; *Parliamentary Papers 1882,* LXXII (c. 3349): CR on Kanagawa 1881, p. 43 for 1879–81; Cambridge University Library, Jardine, Matheson Archives, cl/76, 80, 81, a7/200, *Yokohama Prices Current and Market Report,* Nos. 146–586 for the rest.

part of these yarns in demand are, in the case of English goods, what are termed 16/24s; . . . the finer kinds as 28/32s and 34/42s being in only limited demand' at Hyogo and Osaka in 1882.[32]

(ii) Indian yarns

Few statistics are available in Japan about the quality of Indian yarn imported into the country. But these yarns were undoubtedly coarse counts, judging from the figures in Table 5.6, which shows the output and the counts of yarn produced by 140 mills in India in 1894. Since there were 141 mills throughout the country that year, these figures cover practically all Indian yarn production. According to the table, 80 per cent of all

Table 5.5 (b) Relative Shares of Three Kinds of British Yarns Imported into Yokohama, 1872–91

(%)

Year	Fine Yarn	Medium Yarn	Coarse Yarn
1872	4	42	54
1873	5	34	61
1874	5	31	64
1875	6	29	66
1876	–	–	–
1877	–	–	–
1878	4	27	69
1879	7	25	68
1880	7	27	66
1881	8	24	68
1882	4	21	75
1883	4	19	77
1884	4	29	67
1885	6	35	59
1886	7	36	57
1887	7	35	58
1888	7	29	64
1889	8	32	60
1890	6	28	66
1891	7	23	70
Average	6	29	65

Source: Same as for Table 5.5 (a).

Table 5.6 Production of Yarn in India in 1894

	Pounds of Yarn Spun
At Bombay	215,589,414
Elsewhere	130,086,279
Total	345,675,693

	Percentage of Counts (%)
10s and under	19.7
Above 10s and under 20s	59.6
Above 20s and under 30s	19.1
Above 30s and under 40s	1.5
Above 40s	0.1

Source: Parliamentary Papers 1895, LXXII (c. 7602): Papers relating to the Indian Tariff Act and the Cotton Duties, 1894, p. 7.

Indian yarn was under 20s, 98 per cent was under 30s, and it was estimated that 'at most only 6% of the whole can be put down as over 24s.'[33]
In other words, at least 94 per cent of the amount produced in India was
of 24s and under.

In consequence, Indian yarn exported to foreign countries consisted
almost exclusively of coarser counts. Table 5.7 shows the qualities of
exports of Bombay-made yarn, 99 per cent of which were under 24s. As
more than 90 per cent of Indian yarn exports was carried from the port of
Bombay,[34] the figures in Table 5.7 can be regarded as close to a complete
picture of Indian yarn exports. The main destinations to which Bombay
yarns were exported were China and Japan.[35] As Table 5.8 shows, qualities
of yarn exported to these countries consisted of 24s and under.

These facts are corroborated in commercial reports by the British consul on Japanese trade: 'in Bombay 20s there were large sales' at Yokohama
in 1879,[36] or 'Bombay yarns continued saleable. The bulk of the business was in 20s, but some transactions took place in coarser sizes down
to 10s, and a little was also done in 22s and 24s; finer than that Bombay
yarn finds no favour with Japanese buyers [at Yokohama in 1881]',[37] and
also, 'The greater of these [imported] yarns are . . . in the case of Indian
[goods], 16s and 20s [at Kobe in 1882]'.[38] Thus we can conclude that
Indian yarns imported into Japan were the coarse counts of yarn, the bulk
of which being 20s and under.

(iii) Japanese-made yarn
Figures are available for the counts spun in all the modern spinning mills
in Japan in 1885, 1886, and 1887. These are shown in Table 5.9. As this
table clearly indicates, all the counts are under 20s.

Table 5.10 shows the relative share of the three different types of yarns
used in Japan in the middle of the Meiji era. During the period between
1878 and 1891, i.e., the time when cotton yarn was the major Japanese
import, more than 80 per cent of the total consumption consisted of
coarse counts of 24s and under, whereas the finest range of 38s to 42s
comprised only about 3 per cent.

Production of coarse yarns was the strategy to which the leading mill
owners and the government officials in charge adhered. A conference

Table 5.7 Qualities of Yarns of Bombay Manufacture Exported to Foreign Countries, 1882–1900

(Years ending 31st March)

DESCRIPTIONS	In millions of lbs. (0000s omitted)							
	1899–1900	1898–99	1897–98	1896–97	1895–96	1894–95	1893–94	1892–93
Mule No. 15s and under	125.28	95.82	68.62	50.93	49.37	43.63	35.74	55.99
Mule No. 16s to 24s	92.92	101.21	100.05	124.44	121.65	101.99	88.37	113.70
Mule No. 25s to 32s	.16	.17	.13	.18	.21	.42	.41	.20
Mule No. 33s to 44s	.03	...	...	.15	.02	.10	.05	.02
Total	218.39	197.20	168.80	175.70	171.25	146.14	124.57	169.91
Water No. 20s and under	...	...	.27	.07	.01	.03	.11	.08
Water No. 21s to 30s	...	...	...	...	...	...	.05	...
Water No. 31s to 40s	...	...	...	...	.01	...	.03	.01
Total	...	...	.27	.07	.02	.03	.19	.09
Coloured Yarns Total	1.07	.70	.99	.85	1.10	.86	.70	.78
Total Yarns	219.46	197.90	170.06	176.62	172.37	147.03	125.46	170.78

DESCRIPTIONS	In millions of lbs. (0000s omitted)							
	1889–90	1888–89	1887–88	1886–87	1885–86	1884–85	1883–84	1882–83
Mule No. 15s and under	31.87	23.61	28.82	26.52	22.96	19.33	14.02	11.00
Mule No. 16s to 24s	99.11	98.90	79.37	62.14	52.96	43.52	32.75	30.67
Mule No. 25s to 32s	.39	.09	.01	.02	.08	.05	.02	.03
Mule No. 33s to 44s	.04	.03	...	.02	.01	.01	...	...
Total	131.41	122.63	108.20	88.70	76.01	62.91	46.79	41.69
Water No. 20s and under	.30	.09	.15	.21	.14	.16	.32	.77
Water No. 24s to 30s	.02	...	...	...	...	...	...	...
Total	.32	.09	.15	.21	.14	.16	.32	.77
Coloured Yarns Total	.29	.30	.16	.18	.15	.12	.10	.14
Total Yarns	132.02	123.02	108.51	89.09	76.30	63.19	47.21	42.60

Source: Bombay Chamber of Commerce, *Report of the Bombay Chamber of Commerce for the Year 1900* (1901), p. 463; *Report of the Bombay Chamber of Commerce for the Year 1890* (1891), p. 791.

Table 5.8 Foreign Countries to Which Yarns Spun in Bombay Were Exported

Quality	To	In millions of lbs.							
		1899–1900	1898–99	1897–98	1896–97	1895–96	1894–95	1893–94	1892–93
Mule No. 15s and under	Aden	1.68	.98	1.24	.85	.86	1.50	.99	.71
	Japan	.02	…	…	…	…	…	.03	.20
	China, Hong Kong	57.29	62.75	43.07	32.99	35.78	33.71	24.87	43.95
	China, Treaty Ports*	65.69	31.18	23.63	16.37	12.13	7.74	9.61	10.91
	Other Countries	.60	.91	.68	.72	.60	.68	.24	.22
	Total	125.28	95.82	68.62	50.93	49.37	43.63	35.74	55.99
16s to 24s	Aden	.51	.50	.58	.45	.42	.54	.41	.29
	Japan	.12	.04	.35	.64	1.21	2.58	5.64	6.82
	China, Hong Kong	35.70	49.86	47.74	59.41	53.00	57.12	42.31	53.71
	China, Treaty Ports*	52.98	44.40	46.06	59.44	62.58	35.05	35.54	50.32
	Straits	2.22	3.71	3.16	2.57	2.54	4.25	2.83	1.25
	Other Countries	1.39	2.71	2.16	1.93	1.90	2.45	1.64	1.31
	Total	92.92	101.22	100.05	124.44	121.65	101.99	88.37	113.70
Above No. 24s	Total	.19	.16	.14	.33	.23	.52	.46	.22
	Total Mule	218.39	197.20	168.81	175.70	171.25	146.14	124.57	169.91
Water	Total Water	…	…	.27	.07	.02	.03	.19	.09
Coloured	Total Coloured	1.07	.70	.99	.85	1.10	.86	.70	.78
	Grand Total	219.46	197.90	170.07	176.62	172.37	147.03	125.46	170.78
	Value in Lakhs of Rs.**	625.46	590.69	594.78	648.92	620.60	525.80	465.05	614.08

Notes: *Almost entirely to Shanghai.
         ** 1 lakh = 100,000 Indian rupees.

Continued to next page

Table 5.8 — *continued*

Quality	To	In millions of lbs.							
		1889–98	1888–89	1887–88	1886–87	1885–86	1884–85	1883–84	1882–83
Mule No. 15s and under	Aden	1.14	.85	1.02	.86	1.03	.78	1.28	.97
	Japan	.06	1.29	0.4	.17	.14	.16	.36	.54
	China, Hong Kong	28.24	19.27	26.22	25.30	21.49	18.29	12.26	9.39
	China, Treaty Ports	2.25	2.10	1.44	.19	.30	.10	.12	.10
	Other Countries	.18	.10	.10					
	Total	31.87	23.61	28.82	26.52	22.96	19.33	14.02	11.00
16s to 24s	Aden	.45	.31	.24	.29	.27	.29	.25	.23
	Japan	22.18	21.42	17.20	9.08	6.93	6.34	5.59	4.16
	China, Hong Kong	51.84	57.68	45.09	38.14	37.45	35.52	26.23	25.82
	China, Treaty Ports	22.30	17.23	15.47	13.85	7.82	.92	.39	.46
	Straits	1.31	1.48	1.37	.78	.49	.45	.29	
	Other Countries	1.02	.78						
	Total	99.10	98.90	79.37	62.14	52.96	43.52	32.75	30.67
Above No. 24s	Total	.43	.12	.01	.04	.09	.06	.02	.02
	Total Mule	131.40	122.63	108.20	88.70	76.01	62.91	46.79	41.69
Water	Total Water	.33	.09	.15	.21	.14	.16	.32	.77
Coloured	Total Coloured	.29	.30	.16	.18	.15	.12	.10	.14
	Grand Total	132.02	123.02	108.51	89.09	76.30	63.19	47.21	42.60
	Value in Lakhs of Rs.	587.31	497.12	389.69	324.04	268.35	234.00	182.71	170.60

Source: Bombay Chamber of Commerce, *Report of the Bombay Chamber of Commerce for the Year 1900* (1901), p. 464; *Report of the Bombay Chamber of Commerce for the Year 1890* (1891), p. 792.

Table 5.9 Counts of Yarns Spun by Japanese Mills, 1885–7

Location of Mill	1885	1886	1887
Osaka	11–12	16–18	15–16
Hiroshima	13	12–14	12–14
Nagasaki	14	12–14.5	12–13
Aichi	14	15–19	16–19
Mie	14	12–15	11–14
Sakai	12–17		
Okayama	11–14	12.5–13.5	13
Tamashima	17	13–13.5	13–14
Nagoya		15–16	15–16
Kawasaki		10–16	12–14
Kuwabara		13.4–14.9	14–16
Kagoshima		14–16	12–13
Miyagi		12–14	12–14
Shimada		12.5–14.5	13–14
Nozawa		10–22	13–15
Enshu		13–15	13–16
Dojima		14–18	13–16
Toyoi		12–13	12–13
Shimomura		12–14	12.5–14
Yamato			11–12
Shimotsuke			11–14

Source: S. Minabe, 'Meijishoki ni okeru wagakuni menka seisan no chōraku' (Decline in cotton growing in Japan in the early Meiji period), *Keiō Gijuku Keizaishigakkai Kiyō* (Bulletin of The Keio Economic History Society), 1 (Tokyo, 1937), 33.

on cotton spinning held under the auspices of the government in 1885 discussed various problems that cotton spinners faced at that time, one of which concerned the counts of yarns in demand by local weavers. 'In order to make a profit', said a director of the Osaka spinning company, the first successful mill in Japan, 'we should produce thick yarns of 10s to 20s, which are most in demand.'[39] The counts of yarns spun in 1884 by the Osaka spinning mill were 8s to 24s.[40] Indeed, a government adviser to the mills explicitly warned the mill owners not to spin yarns of 28s and above.[41]

Table 5.10 The Relative Shares of the Three Kinds of Yarns in Japanese Markets, 1878–91

(%)

Year	Coarse Yarn 24s and under	Medium Yarn 28–32s	Fine Yarn 38–42s
1878	74	23	3
1879	74	20	6
1880	71	23	6
1881	76	18	6
1882	83	14	3
1883	86	12	2
1884	81	17	2
1885	81	16	3
1886	80	17	3
1887	83	14	3
1888	85	12	3
1889	88	10	2
1890	90	8	2
1891	94	5	1

Source: Calculated from Table 3.5 in Chapter Three, and M. Kajinishi, ed., Sen'i, Appendix, p. 50.

Table 5.11 Counts of Yarns Demanded by Local Weavers in Japan

Locality	Counts of Yarn
Tokyo	10–16
Iwaki	10–13
Echizen	13–14
Rikuzen	10–24
Osaka	14–16
Izumi	15–16
Suruga	10–16
Kawachi	15–16
Toomi	12–15
Yamato	13–16
Owari	12–20
Mino	16
Ise	10–16
Kai	13–14
Kii	8–10
Shinano	12–16
Tajima	15–16
Echigo	10–13
Iyo	11.5–16
Chikuzen	13–14

Source: Menshi Shūdan-kai kiji (Proceedings of the conference on cotton yarn) (Tokyo, 1885).

There is little doubt that the type of yarns most in demand was precisely the type being provided in vast quantities. Table 5.11 indicates that total demand was concentrated on coarse counts, specifically under 20s, a fact corroborated by contemporary observers. 'There are at present [1887] in various parts of Japan, in all, twenty-one spinning factories worked by foreign machinery. The yarn spun . . . varies from No. 10 to No. 20, but the sizes most in demand are from Nos. 12 to 16'.[42] Japanese concentration on the coarse counts remained unaltered in the 1890s. Yarn with counts under 20s formed 98 per cent of total production in 1892, and was still as high as 92 per cent in 1894.[43] Hand-made yarns produced by the traditional spinning wheel and by an improved version called the *gara-bo* (a clattering spinning machine) were coarser than factory-made.[44] Thus, the quality of yarns typically utilised in Japan in the late nineteenth century was clearly distinguishable from the bulk of cotton yarns manufactured in England. The counts of yarns produced for *Kawachi-momen* (a Japanese cotton cloth produced in the province of Kawachi, the eastern part of modern Osaka Prefecture), for example, were 16s; for *Ashikaga-momen-chijimi* (a Japanese cotton crepe made in the town of Ashikaga, Tochigi Prefecture) they were 20s. Yarns for British cotton cloth were much higher (see Table 5.4).

Naturally the quality of each cotton cloth differed. An episode illustrates the differences. Shimazu Nariakira, perhaps the most enlightened lord in Japan in the last period of the Tokugawa Era,[45] had a foreign yarn presented to him by a merchant around 1853. The lord could not identify the composition of the material and sent it to Japanese weaving experts in Kyoto for examination. But they, too, could not discover what it was made of, and at last suggested that it might be a mixture of raw cotton and silk. The yarn later proved to be a British yarn with a count of 40s spun by throstle spindles.[46] It is no wonder, therefore, that to the Japanese, the texture of British textiles looked different from that of local cotton cloths and rather resembled fine silk goods. This explains why British cotton textiles neither competed with nor were substituted for Japanese cotton cloths. In other words, two separate markets for foreign and native cotton cloths existed in the late nineteenth century in Japan.

(iv) Prices of yarns in Japanese markets

The Japanese market for cotton yarns experienced various changes in composition, and the relative shares of British, Indian, and Japanese yarns varied in different periods. As is shown in Table 5.12, British yarn was dominant until 1886, India then took over between 1887 and 1889, and after 1890, Japanese yarn finally secured its home market. These changes were undoubtedly caused by differences in the prices of each country's yarn, in striking contrast to what happened in the textile markets in which quality mattered more than price. Yarns competed in price, because both foreign and local yarns were of similar quality.

India increased its exports to Japan (and to China even more) in the late 1870s and 1880s.[47] Indian competition was being felt at Manchester already in 1877 as 'an undoubted reality'.[48] But it was ten years later, on 31 October 1887, that the Manchester Chamber of Commerce discussed

Table 5.12 The Percentage Share of
British, Indian, and Japanese
Yarns in Japanese Markets,
1877–92

(in percentage)

Year	British	Indian	Japanese
1877	89	7	4
1878	83	15	2
1879	82	15	3
1880	85	12	3
1881	76	19	5
1882	67	25	8
1883	60	28	12
1884	58	26	16
1885	47	35	18
1886	46	38	16
1887	41	42	17
1888	41	42	17
1889	30	38	32
1890	28	22	50
1891	21	7	72
1892	18	10	72

Source: Calculated from Table 3.5 in Chapter
Three, and M. Kajinishi, ed., *Sen'i*,
Appendix, p. 50.

the matter seriously for the first time at a meeting of the Board of Directors, noting that, 'in view of the recent very rapid increase of Cotton Spinning in India, and the exports of Yarn therefrom, more especially to China and Japan, . . . there has been a very serious check to the growth of Lancashire Yarn exports to those countries.'[49] Thereafter, they held successive meetings about the problem, and set up a special committee to investigate the causes and circumstances which had 'enabled Bombay spinners to supersede those of Lancashire.' The committee's final report made clear that India undersold its main rival, England, in the coarse grade of yarn in Far Eastern markets. India's success was ascribed to her proximity to the cotton fields as well as to consumers' preferences. She may also have been helped by the decline in the value of silver.[50] Table 5.13 shows the prices of British and Indian yarn at Kobe, Japan. Indian yarn was cheaper than British yarn, which doubtless accounts for the rapid increase in the supply of the former at the expense of the latter.

Indian yarn, however, soon disappeared owing to growing competition from Japanese yarn. As Table 5.14 indicates, the years 1889 and 1890 were crucial for the Japanese spinning industry. Until 1889, imported yarns were cheaper than Japanese yarn. But the next year, Japan succeeded in reducing the price to below that of foreign yarn and became dominant in the yarn markets.

Table 5.13 Current Quotations of Yarns at Kobe, 1880–91

(dollars per bale)

Year	British 16–24s		Indian	
	Common to Medium	Good to Best	16s	20s
1880	91–100		89–95	
1881*	89–92	94–98	–	87–92
1882	–	–	–	–
1883**	77–83	84–93	77–83	80–86
1884***	76–84	85–90	73–78	76–84
1885	–	–	–	–
1886	–	–	–	–
1887	83–86	88–96	74–79	75–83
1888	–	–	–	–
1889	91–93	95–98	75–83	78–90
1890	93–96	97–100	66–78	80–90
1891	78–81	83–86	69–73	72–76

Notes: Prices are monthly averages for each year.
    * lacks figures for October and November
    ** lacks figures for November
    *** lacks figures for January, October, and December

Source: Cambridge University Library, Jardine, Matheson Archives, cl/81, cl/82, *Hyogo and Osaka Prices Current and Market Reports*, No.136–308, 31 January 1880 to 31 December 1891.

Table 5.14 Prices of Japanese and Foreign Yarns

(yen per 100 kin)

Year	Japanese	Foreign
1888	32.37	31.52
1889	31.63	30.54
1890	28.17	29.61
1891	26.27	27.48
1892	26.95	28.58

Source: Sen'i, p. 93.

This success was the result of the introduction of double shifts employing young female operatives whose wage level was lower than that in India. Coal was also cheaper in Japan due to the infamous exploitation of prisoners as the labour force in coal mining.[51] These two advantages can be observed in the first and the third columns of Table 5.15.

Table 5.15 Comparison of Costs between Japanese and Indian Yarns in 1891

(sen per 100 kin)

	Manufac-turing	Coal	Deprecia-tion	Packing	Miscella-neous	Interest	Total
Japanese Yarn	135.5	50.7	65.5	17.1	45.2	50.0	306.4
Indian Yarn	151.9	86.7	91.1	40.3	44.3	45.5	458.7

Source: E. Soejima, 'Nihon bōsekigyō to Chūgoku shijō' (The Japanese spinning industry and its Chinese markets), *Jinbun Gakuhō* (Journal of Humanistic Studies), 33 (1972), 92.

4. COTTON YARNS USED IN EAST ASIA

(i) The Far East

The quality of cotton yarn in demand in China in the late nineteenth century was similar to that in Japan. Chinese weavers used three types of yarns, their own handicraft yarn, Indian yarn, and British yarn. As was indicated earlier in Table 3.9, handicraft yarn comprised 98 per cent of total consumption in the 1870s. Whilst its share declined towards the end of the century, it still held the largest share in the 1900s. This homespun yarn was undoubtedly coarse. As regards Indian yarn, we have shown that it consisted exclusively of coarse counts under 24s. As to the quality of British yarn, Table 5.16 compiles the figures for the counts of British imports to China from *Prices Current and Market Report*, a circular published every other week in Hong Kong. Seventy per cent of British yarn was of low counts under 24s, 20 per cent of medium range between 28s and 32s, and only 10 per cent of the finest counts of 38s to 42s. Exact information is not available on the quality of British yarn imported at the other treaty ports. But there is little doubt that it would have been the same as that imported at Hong Kong, because the unit-values of yarns exported from Britain to Hong Kong and to the treaty ports were almost the same

Table 5.16 Sales of Cotton Yarn in Hong Kong

(bales)

Year	Bombay Yarn	British Yarn			Total
		16–24s	28–32s	38–42s	
1871	1,025	13,362	4,641	2,340	21,368
1872	1,473	12,202	4,861	1,873	20,409
1873	2,521	14,605	5,057	2,891	25,074
1874	875	14,855	4,625	1,370	21,725
1875*	2,826	13,280	3,897	1,415	21,418
1879	39,677	15,919	5,556	2,644	63,796
1880	45,963	19,198	4,976	2,519	72,656
1881	47,284	13,119	2,755	3,524	66,682
1882**	51,447	7,611	2,306	2,535	66,899
1883	83,613	13,727	3,405	2,528	103,273
1884	105,008	10,996	3,683	2,933	122,620
1885	168,272	15,496	3,553	4,974	182,295
1888	59,474	14,037	2,740	2,711	78,962
1889	46,790	5,351	1,335	2,505	55,981

Note: * No figures for the periods between July 31 and August 26, and between November 25 and December 21.
** No figures for January, November, and December.

Source: Cambridge University Library, Jardine, Matheson Archives, cl/64, cl/71: *Fortnightly Prices Current and Market Report*, Nos. 1–26 for each year, Hong Kong, 1871–89.

(see Figure 5.1). Britain's yarn exports to China, as shown in Figure 5.2, declined in the 1880s, and became negligible in the mid-1890s, whilst both Indian and Japanese yarn exports to China increased rapidly. The yarn of these countries consisted exclusively of low counts under 24s. So the pattern of Chinese consumption was very similar to that of Japan, centring on 24s and under. This meant that the quality of textiles produced in China was thick and heavy.

The cotton yarn used in Korea was similar to that of Japan and China. Apart from her own coarse yarn, foreign yarns were brought into the country via Japan and China.[52] These goods were 'of the coarser class of English

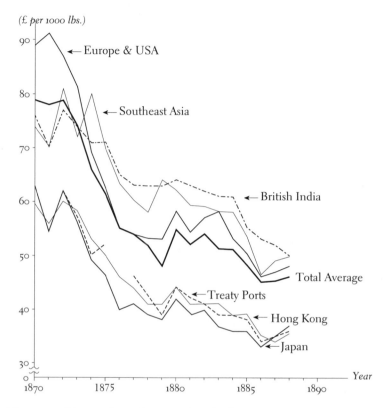

Figure 5.1 Unit-Value of Grey, Bleached and Dyed Yarn Exported from Britain (£ *per 1000 lbs.*)

Note: Europe includes Russia, Denmark, Sweden, Norway, Germany, Holland, Belgium, France, Italy, Spain, Portugal, and Austria; Southeast Asia includes the Philippines, the Straits Settlements, Java, other Dutch possessions in the Indian Sea, as well as Ceylon.
Source: Calculated from ASTUK (Annual Statement of the Trade of the United Kingdom with Foreign Countries and British Possessions).

manufacture . . . purchased in Shanghai and transshipped at Nagasaki to vessels bound for Corea, or else . . . shipped direct from Kobe to Corean Ports',[53] but the amount of yarn imports was very small.[54]

In the Far East as a whole, therefore, the quality of yarns used in the nineteenth century was similar. This particular characteristic of the Far

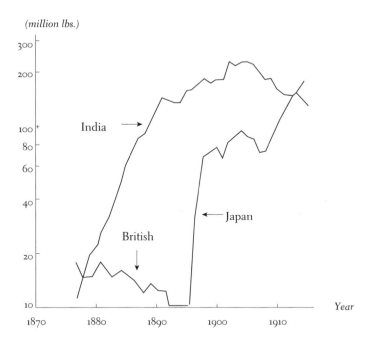

Figure 5.2 Yarn Exports to China from Britain, India, and Japan

Source: K. Koike, 'Indo-mengyō to shijōmondai' (The market structure of Bombay's cotton
mills), *Ajia Keizai* (Asian Economy), 16,9 (1975), 47; Koike, *Keiei dairi seido ron*
(The managing agency system) (Tokyo, 1979), p. 202.

Eastern market, where consumers showed a preference for coarse yarn
below 24s, is emphatically displayed in Figure 5.1, which gives the unit-
values of yarns exported from Britain to its main markets. The figure indicates that Hong Kong, the treaty ports of China, and Japan were similar:
the unit-values of yarn exported to these destinations only were under
the average. In sharp contrast, the unit-values of British yarns exported
to other regions were all higher than the average. The quality of yarn
demanded in the Far East was different not only from that exported to
India and Southeast Asia, but also from that exported to Europe and the
United States. Likewise, the structure of demand for cotton goods in
these regions must have been different from that of the Far East.

Table 5.17

(a) The Counts of Yarn Imported into India

Counts	1875–76	1895–96 Mule & Water	1895–96 Coloured	1896–97 Mule & Water	1896–97 Coloured	1898–99	1899–1900	1899/1900–1901/02 Mule & Water	1899/1900–1901/02 Coloured
20s and under	1,800 ⎱	196	3,303	237	2,987	3,632		886	1,264
21–25s	⎰	18	3,960	7	2,726	2,461	10,283 ⎱	74	1,046
26–30s	21,500 ⎱	4,009	2,003	4,096	1,896	6,838	⎰	9,565	2,580
31–40s		13,302 ⎱	15,109 ⎱	16,126 ⎱	16,686 ⎱	26,580	26,360	27,394	39,377
41–50s	⎰	⎰	⎰	⎰	⎰	1,744	4,241 ⎱	9,158 ⎱	1,870 ⎱
Above 50s		1,569	271	1,998	312	2,170	⎰	⎰	⎰

(b) Relative Proportions of the Different Counts of Yarn Imported into India

Counts	1875–76	1869–73	1874–78	1879–83	1884–88	1889–93	1895–96 Mule & Water	1895–96 Coloured	1896–97 Mule & Water	1896–97 Coloured	1898–99	1899–1900
0–25s	8 ⎱	9	3	2	1	0	1	30	1	23	14	25
26–30s	⎰	54	58	62	54	49	21	8	18	8	16	
Above 30s	92	37	39	37	45	51	78	62	81	69	70	75

*(The bracket marked * spans 1869–73 to 1889–93.)*

Note: * The figures from 1869 to 1893 cover only non-coloured yarn imported into Bombay.

Sources: Report of the Bombay Chamber of Commerce for the Year 1875–76, p. 190 for 1875–76; Parliamentary Papers 1895, LXXII (c. 7602): Papers relating to the Indian Tariff Act and the Cotton Duties, 1894, p. 13 for 1869–93; Parliamentary Papers 1898, LXIV (c. 8692): Review of the Trade of India in 1896–97, p. 22 for 1895–97; Parliamentary Papers 1900, LVIII (cd. 381): Review and Tables relating to the Trade of British India, 1894–95 to 1898–99, p. 21 for 1898–99; Parliamentary Papers 1900, LVIII (cd. 381): Review of the Trade of India in 1899–1900, p. 11 for 1899–1900; and A. K. Bagchi, Private Investment in India, 1900–1939 (Cambridge, 1972), p. 231 for 1899/00–1901/2.

(ii) India

India was one of the largest importers of British yarn, absorbing 15–20 per cent of the total during the last three decades of the nineteenth century. A summary of the figures related to the quality of yarns imported into India is shown in Table 5.17. As the table indicates, yarns (mostly British-made) consisted mainly of types between 26s and 40s, while the lower counts under 25s formed usually less than 10 per cent of the total.[55] A contemporary who reviewed India's import trade of yarn in 1895 concluded his observations as follows:

> There is no doubt that they [the trade figures] indicate with a very near approach to accuracy the relative proportions of the different counts, and they confirm the statements which have frequently been made that, as regard grey yarn, there is hardly any importation below No. 25, and that the bulk of the trade is limited to the numbers from 26 to 50, the real trade being in the numbers from 30 to 40.[56]

Indian yarn imports were in striking contrast to those of the Far Eastern countries, where the bulk consisted of 24s and below.

Unlike the quality of the yarn it imported, the yarn India actually produced centred on 24s and lower counts—below 20s in particular. As Table 5.18 shows, yarn with counts below 20s formed 80 to 90 per cent of production throughout the period. As a result, India had separate markets for foreign and locally made yarns: one was for the finer type exclusively supplied from overseas and the other for the lower grade, which was the monopoly of Indian producers. The counts around 25s to 30s were the dividing points, as the following quotations from contemporary sources corroborate:

> Goods of rather better quality yarns above No. 30s [have] as yet no local competition. . . . No local mills have with success, *at least in a commercial sense,* produced 30s yarn or cloths made from 30s yarn, while on the other hand, the ordinary qualities of grey shirtings, which form the great bulk of the importations, are made of yarns of better quality ranging from No. 32s to No. 38s.[57]

> Speaking generally regarding the numbers of the yarns spun in the Bombay mills, it may be said that they range from 4s as a minimum to 30s as a maximum. For the weaving of T cloths, longcloths, and domestics, the yarns

Table 5.18

(a) Yarn Production in India by Counts

	1894	1895–6	1896–7	1897–8	1898–9	1899–1900	1899/1900–1901/2
20 and under	274	389	365	400	450	451	1,187
21 to 30s	66	42	55	62	62	63	182
Above 30s	5						35

(b) Relative Proportions of the Different Counts of Yarn Produced in India

	1894	1895–6	1896–7	1897–8	1898–9	1899–1900	1899/1900–1901/2
20 and under	79	90	87	87	88	88	84
21 to 30s	19[*]	10	13	13	12	12	13
Above 30s	2						3

Note: * 19% consists of 15% of 21–24s, and 4% of 25–30s.

Sources: Parliamentary Papers 1895, LXXII (c. 7602): Papers relating to the Indian Tariff Act and the Cotton Duties, 1894, p. 7 for 1894; *Report of the Tariff Commission,* vol. 2, part 1, para. 55 (1905), for 1895–1900, Bagchi, *Private Investment in India, 1900–1939,* p. 231 for 1899/1900–1901/2.

employed range from 14s to 18s water and 16s to 22s mule. . . . For hosiery, 26s and 28s are spun.[58]

The facts therefore are that the Manchester trade and the Indian mills trade run on entirely different lines: the trade of the former is confined to goods of higher counts than 24s, and that of the latter to 24s and lower counts.[59]

The conclusion has been amply confirmed by subsequent special inquiries, that the Indian mills rarely, if ever, spin yarn finer than 28s, and that the bulk of their cloths are made of, much lower numbers. With the view of allowing an ample margin for all cases of doubt, 30s was fixed on as the 'quality' or 'fineness' of yarn at which the line of competition should be drawn.[60]

We may conclude, therefore, that there was virtually no competition between Indian and British yarns except for marginal counts between 25s and 30s. This accounts for the paradox that while yarn imports into India rose and reached their highest level in 1898, yarn production developed at the same time without being impeded by the imports. Unlike the Far Eastern countries, yarns of various counts were available in abundance in India, and the types of Indian cotton cloths made from them were also diverse.

A paradoxical feature of the British cotton trade with the Far East was that Britain tended to produce higher and higher grades of yarn in the late nineteenth century, even though demand from Far Eastern cotton weavers continued to be for low counts of yarns. Nor did cheap British textiles sell well in this cotton-using region. This, however, can be explained by the persistent preference of Asian consumers for thick cotton cloths made from low counts of yarn. Far Eastern cloths appear to have been more expensive but were more durable and warmer than the finer, lighter, and thinner British-made cloths. This difference in quality probably derived from their respective requirements for clothing. The British wore woollens in winter, whereas Asians did not, using thick cotton cloth instead. Far Eastern demand for low counts of yarn was based on the need for a raw material suitable for their thick type of cloth.

The Asian market for British products was clearly separate from the market for local cotton products, and there was little direct competition between British and Asian cotton goods. Britain actually faced more severe and direct competition from the textile industries emerging in Europe and the United States.[61]

5. COTTON YARNS PRODUCED IN THE UNITED STATES AND CONTINENTAL EUROPE

Competition from Europe and the United States was most severely felt in medium-range counts between 25s and 40s. According to Sandberg, counts around 40s represented cutoff points at which the relative efficiencies shifted between ring and mule spindles. British mules lost competitive advantage over American rings for counts up to 40s.[62] Furthermore, as Copeland observed around 1910, 'not much yarn finer than 40's, and very little higher than 60's is produced upon the ring-frame in Europe'.[63]

In the United States in the late 1870s, more than half of the warp yarn produced was between 27s and 31s (see Table 5.19).[64] In 1905, over half of the yarn spun in America was still coarser than 20s, but most of the rest was between 21s to 40s.[65] Producers in the Southern States, who specialised

Table 5.19 Average Counts of US Yarn

	Number of Mills	Number of Spindles	Average Counts
1869			
North		6,538,494	28
South		225,063	12.88
Total		6,763,557	27.5
1870			
North		6,851,779	28.88
South		262,221	12.25
Total		7,114,000	28.38
1874			
North		8,927,754	28.56
South		487,629	12.5
Total		9,415,283	27.73
1875			
North	694	9,057,543	28.42
South	181	481,821	12.67
Total	875	9,539,364	27.60

Source: *Encyclopaedia Britannica*, 9th edn., vol. 6 (Edinburgh, 1877), p. 507.

in coarse counts of 12s to 13s in the 1870s, raised their counts gradually, and in 1910, the average counts for the entire southern section reached 20s.[66] The average cloths made from this coarse yarn was considerably heavier in the South than the North, and these qualities dominated US exports. In 1899–1900 when 60 per cent of total exports came from the South, South Carolina alone supplied nearly a half of the entire exports of cotton cloth. One of the main markets for this 'heavy' cloth was China.[67] The United States imported very little yarn, and this chiefly of the finest counts, which were not manufactured in the country.[68] In other words, the United States became self-sufficient in the medium counts and lower.

The situation on the Continent was similar to that in the United States. In the Vosges in France, 28s warp and 37s weft were the common counts.[69] In Germany, too, yarn production centred on medium counts. As Table 5.20 shows, the bulk of yarn produced there was of 45s and under. German imports of yarn counts between 17s and 45s diminished. Imports below 17s became negligible in the 1890s, while imports of 45s and above, and particularly above 60s, increased (see Table 5.21). As other European countries became capable of satisfying their own demand in coarse and

Table 5.20 Yarn Production in Germany by Counts

Year	Output ('ooo ton)	Percentage Distribution (%)				
		0–17	17–45	45–60	60–79	79–
1877	233	42.5	56.1	1.0	0.3	0.1
1900	254	40.9	56.8	1.8	0.4	0.1

Source: S. Tohara, 'Doitsu sangyō-shihon no tokushitsu (2)' (Characteristics of German industrial capital), *Shakai Kagaku Kenkyū* (Journal of Social Science), 15,1 (1963), 76 (original source: W. Lochmüller, *Zur Entwicklung der Baumwollindustrie in Deutschland* (Jena, 1906), pp. 51–2).

Table 5.21 Imports of Cotton Yarn into Germany by Counts

Year	Total	Percentage Distribution of Different Counts				
		0–17s	18–45s	46–60s	61–79s	80s–
	('ooo ton)					
1880/85*	18.1	14.2	57.9	11.6	5.5	10.0
1886/90*	20.3	8.4	60.5	14.0	7.3	9.2
1891/95*	17.2	1.8	57.8	18.3	10.1	10.0
(in million cwt.)			(single yarn)			
1897	191	1.6	60.5	18.2	13.9	5.9
1898	176	1.6	56.8	20.4	13.6	7.5
1899	132	0.5	57.6	18.6	9.3	13.9
1900	118	0.4	50.7	17.6	14.0	17.4
1901	101	0.2	47.4	17.7	17.4	17.2
1902	111	0.1	48.1	17.6	16.0	18.2
1903	123	0.2	47.1	18.0	14.1	20.7
(in million cwt.)			(2-fold yarn)			
1897	207	0.5	56.3	19.0	11.7	12.6
1898	208	0.5	50.1	21.9	12.4	15.2
1899	203	0.6	44.7	24.0	14.1	16.7
1900	199	0.3	41.1	24.7	16.4	17.5
1901	161	0.4	34.9	25.3	18.3	21.1
1902	175	0.6	31.9	26.1	20.8	20.7
1903	191	0.4	35.4	26.7	19.5	18.1

Note: * Annual average of five years.

Sources: Tariff Commission, *Reports of the Tariff Commission*, vol. 2, part 1, para 48 (1905); Tohara, 'Doitsu sangyō-shihon no tokushitsu (2) (Characteristics of German industrial capital)', p. 74 (original source: *Statistik des Deutschen Reichs*).

medium grades, British exports to the Continent shifted to finer yarns, that is 60s and upwards.[70] In 1892, it was 'a matter of common notoriety that the bulk of the export trade [was] done in the medium counts of 30s and upwards'.[71] In 1897, Bolton counts (60s) were said to form nine-tenths of the entire export trade in yarns from Britain.[72] The Tariff Commission of 1905 reported that the exports of cotton yarns from the late nineteenth to the twentieth century increased in fineness of counts.[73] For medium counts (and particularly for counts below 40s), Britain was squeezed out of American and Continental markets, which began to be self-sufficient in this type, protected by tariff barriers.

We can now draw a fairly clear picture of the difference in cotton yarn consumption between the Far East and the industrial West:

	Type of Yarn in Good Demand
Western Pattern	medium and fine
Far Eastern Pattern	24s and below

6. CONCLUSION

As we have seen, there was virtually no competition between Indian and British yarns except at the margin of counts between 25s and 30s. Ninety per cent of yarn produced in England in 1887 was finer than 30s. This

Year	United States	Northern Europe	India	China
1874	159	144	82	88
1883	219	135	87	91
1895	263	159	80	94

Source: L. G. Sandberg, 'Movements in the Quality of British Cotton Textile Exports, 1815–1913', *Journal of Economic History*, 28,1 (1968), 14.

explains why yarn imports to India rose, reaching their highest level in 1898, and why Indian yarn production developed without being impeded by British imports: British and Indian mills produced different yarns.

Consumption patterns for finished goods were closely related to those of raw materials. Sandberg has estimated the average export prices of

British cotton cloth to various areas as a percentage of the average price to all parts to the world.[74]

The industrial West clearly consumed higher grades of cotton cloth compared with East Asia. Much of British yarn exports to India throughout the period were of high counts above 30s, and so India would also have made fine cloth.[75] But China, Japan, and Korea had no source of yarn supply for fine cloth except for a small amount of imports.

British-made goods consumed at home were always much higher quality than those exported. Domestically consumed cloth was 25 per cent more expensive than exported cloth in the period between 1819 and 1821, 14 per cent more expensive in 1829–31, and 38 per cent more expensive in 1844–6.[76] In 1850, British consumers purchased cotton goods with a unit-value one-third greater than that of export goods.[77] In 1872, goods in demand at home were still 33 per cent higher in price than those exported.[78] In 1881, their unit-value was almost double that of export goods.[79] Britain's domestic markets consumed cotton goods of the highest quality in the world. Furthermore, this market was constantly expanding during the last quarter of the century,[80] and from 1882 to 1900, the home market expanded at twice the rate of overseas markets.[81]

But the trend was for the West as a whole, including the United States, to consume higher grades of cotton goods.[82] Britain anticipated this trend conspicuously. Far from being a 'failure of entrepreneurship', Britain's supremacy in Western markets for finer types of cotton goods was the result of British enterprise. Britain's successful response to the changing international economy is striking when compared to Japan's rise to eminence in the Eastern markets for coarser goods. Japan made successful

	Cotton Goods in Good Demand	
Pattern	Cotton Yarn	Cotton Cloth
1. Far Eastern Pattern	24s and below	Heavy and thick texture
2. Industrial Western Pattern	25s and above	Light and thin texture
(British Pattern)	40s and above	the lightest and thinnest texture
3. Indian (Mixed) Pattern	24s and below (native)	Various textures
	25s and above (imports)	

inroads into other Asian markets. But its development was confined to the markets for Far Eastern types of goods consisting of low count yarns and thick and heavy cloth. India, however, had a mixed pattern of consumption including both Western and Far Eastern grades of yarn and cloth. Thus, the main differences in the consumption patterns of cotton goods can be roughly outlined as follows:

India was the largest importer in the world of fine types of British cotton goods. Indian yarn, however, gradually disappeared from the Far Eastern market owing to growing competition from Japan. The emergence of Japan as the first industrial nation in Asia was an outcome of intra-Asian competition. This competition took place outside markets dominated by Britain, although helped by the British policy of free trade in the area. As Peter Mathias perceptively said when he surveyed the British economy during this period of transition:

> [Some] issues lie in the logic of the context facing the British economy in the second half of the nineteenth century. Many problems are just the results of other nations becoming industrialized, over which human agency in Britain can bear no responsibility or incur no blame.[83]

Chapter Six

QUALITY DIFFERENCES IN RAW COTTON

> . . . the quality of the raw cotton has at least as much to do with the quality of the product as with the cost of producing it.
>
> —L. G. Sandberg[1]

1. INTRODUCTION

We have discovered that there were separate markets for cotton goods of British and Far Eastern types. Their use-values differed from each other. A use-value is a product of labour, and the production of use-values is defined by Marx as 'the labour process'. By that he means 'purposive activity carried on for the production of use-values, for the fitting of natural substances to human wants'.[2]

If we look at the labour process from the point of view of its result, the product, the whole process involves the converting of natural substances from raw material to finished goods. Labour is embodied as the raw material is transformed. The change effected on the raw material is not by chance but is the result of a specific series of processes. In these processes, the mechanical, physical, and chemical properties of the raw material are systematically manipulated by human labour with the help of specially prepared equipment and transformed into a product adapted to human needs.[3] We must now trace the relationship between a particular raw material, cotton, and its manufactured form in terms of the technicalities involved.

Technical terms referring to the quality of a product vary according to the manufacturing process, but the basic raw material involved remains the same. In the case of cotton, the quality of cotton cloth is referred to in descriptive terms as 'light', 'heavy', 'thick', 'thin', and so on. Cotton yarn is described in the more accurate terms of 'counts', and raw cotton in terms of 'staple'. These different terms indicate specific characteristics of each product, as variants based on the fibre of cotton wool. This chapter tries to document the connection between the physical properties of cotton as raw material and its final manufactured form. Because the physical properties (or quality) of British yarn and textiles differed from those in Far Eastern goods, the quality of their raw materials would also differ. The following sections show that there was a qualitative relation between raw cotton and cotton yarn, and link it to the different type of cotton goods being used in the Far East and the West.

2. THE COTTON STAPLE

(i) *The length of the staple*

Before ca. 1820, colour distinguished the qualities of cotton in commercial use. Yellow indicated greater fineness, while white was characteristic of secondary quality.[4] By the 1830s, improved processes of manufacturing had reduced the significance of colour. 'As to the distinguishing qualities of cotton-wool in the estimation of the manufacturer', wrote Baines in the early 1830s, 'the quality depends on the length, strength, and fineness of the fibre, or as it is called in the trade, the staple . . . and the broad distinction is therefore into "long-stapled" and "short-stapled."'[5] Almost every private firm or spinning company had one or more brokers on whom they relied for samples and for quotations of prices at which cotton could be bought. The broker became accustomed to the exact length and quality of staple that would best spin the scale of counts their clients or spinners were milling. Certain empirical rules were laid down by the Cotton Brokers' Association, and these had to be adhered to.[6] Even so, selection of the material for a specific use remained an art, which was the domain of a skilled and highly experienced cotton grader or selector. The buying and selling of cotton was mostly based on the grader's or selector's judgement of the grade and staple of a cotton. These depended upon the sight and touch of the grader. His subjective judgement was extremely accurate.[7] Length of cotton fibre played an important part in estimating the quality and price of cotton because longer cottons were generally finer than shorter ones. It was said that 75 per cent of the variation in spinning value could be accounted for by fibre length alone.[8] W. H. Evans wrote in 1896 that the first thing noticed in comparing samples of cotton was the difference in the length and fineness of the fibre, and that the commercial grading of the crop depended almost entirely upon these factors.[9]

(ii) The length of staple and the count of yarn

Some idea of the staple length of various species of cotton cultivated in the late nineteenth century may be obtained from Table 6.1 complied by C. P. Brooks in 1898 after fifteen years' observation and investigation.[10] The table shows where each variety was grown, the length and the diameter of the fibre, and the counts of yarn into which the cotton was usually spun for commercial purposes. Brooks classified and divided 'all the then-known cottons' into four kinds—long-stapled, medium-long-stapled, medium-stapled, and short-stapled.

Several relationships appear from the table. For example, the length of the staples is inversely proportionate to the diameter, and the longer the fibre, the shorter its diameter and hence the thinner the staple.[11] In contrast, the length of the staple is proportionate to the counts of yarn, and the longer the staple (and therefore the thinner the fibre) the higher the counts (i.e., the finer yarn).[12] The length of the long-stapled cottons on average is greater than 1 1/4 inches, whilst that of the shortest-stapled cottons cultivated in the Far East (China, Japan, and Korea) is about half of these and less than 3/4 inches. From the long-stapled cottons, counts as high as 80s to 400s were spun, whereas low counts of 24s and under were spun from the short-stapled cottons. This is significant. Each kind of raw cotton grew in a certain area. Generally, long-stapled cottons were grown in America and Egypt, while short-stapled cottons were cultivated in Asia.[13] The longest-stapled was Sea Island in the United States, and the shortest-stapled cottons grew in Far Eastern countries such as China, Japan, and Korea.

Another important correlation is the relation between the length and the strength of cotton fibres. Although these attributes vary considerably according to the situation and the country in which they were grown, 'as a rule, the thickest fibres, though short in staple, are the strongest.'[14] But

Table 6.1 Table of Cotton

(1) Long Stapled

Trade Name	Where Grown	Length of Staple. Inches	Di. in 10,000fn.	Character of Fibre	Counts or Number of Yarn Usually Used for (Single Yarn)			Remarks
					Twist or Warp.	Weft or Filling.	Doubled or Ply Yarn.	
Sea Island.	Edisto, John, James, Port Royal and St. Helena, S.C.;Cumberland and St. Simon, Ga.	$1\frac{3}{4}$ to $2\frac{1}{4}$	4 to 6	Silky, fine, strong and clean.			150s to 400s	Said to have been spun to 2150s in London in 1851.
Florida Sea Island.	On mainland of Florida, near coast, from Sea Island seed.	$1\frac{1}{4}$ to $1\frac{3}{4}$	5 to 6	Silky and clean.			150s to 200s	Good for lower grade Sea Island yarn.
Peruvian Sea Island.	On Peruvian Mainland, from Sea Island seed	$1\frac{1}{2}$	4 to 7	Silky and strong, but not clean.			100s to 150s	
Fiji and Tahiti Sea Island.	Polynesian Islands, So. Pacific Ocean.	$1\frac{1}{2}$ to 2	4 to 6	Silky, strong and clean.			100s to 200s	Very rarely used and little grown.
Bourbon.	French Island, off coast of Africa.	$\frac{3}{4}$ to $1\frac{1}{2}$		Weak.			80s to 100s	Very rarely used and little grown.

(2) Medium to Long Stapled

Trade Name	Where Grown	Length of Staple. Inches	Di. in 10,000fn.	Character of Fibre	Twist or Warp.	Weft or Filling.	Doubled or Ply Yarn.	Remarks
Brown Egyptian or Mako.	In Lower, Middle, and Upper Egypt.	$1\frac{1}{3}$ to $1\frac{3}{8}$	5 to 7	Golden brown to brown.	50s to 100s	-70s to 150s	70s to 150s	
Mitafifi.	Lower and Middle Egypt.	$1\frac{1}{16}$ to $1\frac{3}{8}$	5 to 7	Rich dark brown: long, strong and fine.				Principal variety.
Ashmouni.	Lower Middle, and Upper Egypt.	$1\frac{3}{16}$ to $1\frac{3}{8}$	5 to 7	Light brown; fine.				
Bamia.	Lower Egypt.	$1\frac{1}{8}$ to $1\frac{1}{4}$	5 to 7	Brown; shorter and weak.				
Abbasi.	Lower Egypt.	$1\frac{1}{8}$ to $1\frac{1}{4}$	5 to 7	Almost white; fine and silky.				Varies from season to season, not reliable.
White Egyptian.		$1\frac{1}{4}$	6 to 7	White.				From American seed. Resembling Gulf or New Orleans cotton. Very rarely seen

Table 6.1—*Continued*

Variety	Country	Length		Character	Yarn counts	Yarn counts	Remarks
Gallini.	Egypt.	1¼ to 1½	5 to 6	White and silky		80s to 150s	From Sea Island seed. Resembling Florida Sea Island. Very rarely grown.
Paraiba.					40s to 60s		The first two are about the best of Brazilian cottons.
Maranham.					40s to 60s		
Ceara.	Brazil.	1 to 1⅜	6 to 8	All Brazilian is harsh, wiry, clean, creamy colored, tree cotton.	32s to 50s		All Brazilian cotton is good for warp yarns, especially yarns for sizing. Gives strength when mixed with American.
Aracaju.					32s to 50s		
Rio Grande.					32s to 50s		
Pernambuco.					32s to 50s		
Bahia.					32s to 50s		
Maceio					32s to 50s		
San Paulo.					32s to 50s		
Santos.	Brazil.	1¼ to 1½	6 to 8	Rougher than Brazil.	40s to 70s		American seed. Some very weak and high colour.
Rough Peruvian.	Peru.						Very little grown or used.
Surinam, Berbice.	British and French Guiana.	1⅛ to 1⅜		Smooth and fine.	Said to spin 160s		
Cayenne, Demerara.							
Guatemala.	Central America.	1 to 1⅓		White and clean.			Resembles the cotton from Guiana.
Honduras.	Central America.						
Colombia.	Central America.						
San Domingo or Hayti.	West Indian Islands.	1 to 1½	6 to 8	Smooth, glossy and clean; variable.	Said to spin 120s		Very little grown or used.
Porto Rico.							
Anguilla.							
Catamarea.	Argentine.	⅞ to 1¼		Reddish.			
Sante Fe.							
Salta.							
San Luis.	Argentine.	1½ to 1⅝		Reddish.			
Rioja.							
Parana.	Argentine.	1 to 1½		White.			
Hawaii.	Hawaii Islands.	1 to 1½					

Table 6.1—*Continued*

(3) Medium Stapled

AMERICAN COTTONS.

	Where Grown						Remarks
Gulf Cotton or New Orleans.	Mississippi, Louisiana and neighboring states.	1 to 1¼	4 to 7		28s to 44s	50s to 70s	
Benders or Bottom Land.	Mississippi River Louisiana and Mississippi.				28s to 44s	50s to 70s	A variety of Gulf or New Orleans cotton.
Mobile.	Varieties originated in Mississippi and grown usually in Mississippi. Louisiana, Arkansas, Alabama.				28s to 44s	50s to 70s	A variety of Orleans or Gulf cotton usually inferior in quality.
Peelers.				Bluish-white usually.	28s to 44s	50s to 70s	Somewhat resembles short Florida Sea Island.
Allan Seed.				Long staple.	28s to 44s	50s to 70s	Ranking among best of New Orleans cotton, usually bad to card.
Uplands.	Georgia, North Carolina, South Carolina, Virginia.	¾ to 1	6 to 7			30s to 40s	A clean, easily manipulated, useful cotton, suitable for weft or filling.
Texas.	Texas.	⅞ to 1	5 to 7		28s to 82s	30s to 40s	Suited for warp.
Georgia.	Georgia. Mississippi or Louisiana.					32s to 40s	A variety of Uplands.
Mississippi or Louisiana					See	above	Varieties of Orleans or Gulf cotton.
Selma.	Alabama.			Generally very clean.	See	above	Variety of Orleans or Gulf cotton.
Arkansas.	Arkansas.				See	above	Variety of Orleans or Gulf cotton.
Boweds.					See	above	Another name for Uplands.
Memphis.	Alabama.			Generally good staple but leafy.	See	above	A variety of Gulf cotton or Orleans.
Norfolk.	North Carolina and Virginia.			Generally very clean.	See	above	Variety of Boweds Uplands.
Savannah.	Georgia.			Generally clean	See	above.	Variety of Boweds Uplands.

Table 6.1—*Continued*

(4) Short Stapled

Trade Name	Where Grown	Length of Staple. Inches	Dia. in 10,000th.	Character of Fibre	Counts or Number of Yarn Usually Used for (Single Yarn)			Remarks
					Twist or Warp.	Weft or Filling.	Doubled or Ply Yarn.	
INDIAN COTTONS.								
Comptah.	Central Provinces.	3/4 to 7/8	7 to 9		14s and below	18s and below		Dirty.
Hinghunghat.	Central Provinces.	1 to 1 1/4	7 to 9		18s and below	24s and below		Very seldom used.
Oonrawattee.	Berars (in Central) India.	7/8 to 1	7 to 9	Good color. Cleaner than Dhollerah.				Glossy.
Dharwar.	Bombay Pres. Extreme South.	3/8 to 1	7 to 9		14s and below	20s and below		
Seinde.	Extreme Western India, Province of Seinde.	5/4 to 7/8	7 to 9	Neppy.	6s to 12s	6s to 12s		
Broach.	Bombay Pres. Western coast.	3/4 to 7/8	7 to 9	Soft fibre and high color.	14 and below	22s and below		
Khandeish.	Bombay Pres.	5/4 to 7/8	7 to 9					
Bilatee.	Bombay Pres.	5/4 to 3/4	7 to 9					
Dhollerah.	Bombay Pres.	1/4 to 1 1/13	7 to 9	White and has considerable dirt.	16s and below	24s and below		
Surat.	Port, Bombay Pres. Dist. of Broach.	3/4 to 1	7 to 9	Creamy.				A name given to all Bombay Presidency cotton.
Tinnivelly.	Presidency of Madras.	5/4 to 7/8		Dirty,	18s and below	24s and below		
Western.	Western Madras.	1/2 to 3/4	7 to 9	Tinged dirty, weak fibre.	Very	low numbers.		
Bengal.	Bengal Pres.				4s to 8s	4s to 10s		Dirtiest cotton grown.
Dacca.	Bengal Pres.	1/2 to 5/4	7 to 9	Short, harsh, rough staple, not very clean, often tinged.	6s to 8s	6s to 12s		Resembles wool.
Coconada.	India.	1/2 to 5/8	7 to 9	Red color, weak, irregular and dirty.	4s to 6s	4s to 10s		
Red Northern.								A high colored variety of Indian cotton.
Assam.	North Eastern India.	1/2 to 3/4		Dull appearance, harsh, stiff fibre, and fairly clean.	6s to 10s	6s to 16s		Resembles wool.

Table 6.1—Continued

OTHER ASIAN COTTONS.						
China and Corea.		**1/2** to 3/4	Rough, but very clean.	6s to 10s	6s to 14s	A variety of China.
Camilla.	China.	1/4 to 3/4	Bright, very clean, harsh and stiff.	6s to 14s	6s to 14s	
Turkestan. Indigenous.	Central Asia. (Russian Provinces)	1	Rough, good color, and clean.			From American seed.
Turkestan. Exotic.	Central Asia. (Russian Provinces)	1	Smooth, good color, and clean.			
Japan.	Japan.	2/4 to 3/4	Very clean.			
Phillipine.	Phillipine Islands.	2/4 to 1	Clean and smooth.			
Java.	Isle of Java.	3/4 to 2/4	Weak and dirty.			
Persian.	Persia.	3/4 to 1 1/13	Bright creamy color, leafy and strong.	4 to 6s	4 to 6s	Resembles Indian but is superior to the best Indian.
Smyrna.	Asia Minor.	3/4 to 1	Creamy, dull and leafy.			
SUNDRY COTTONS.						
Nankin.	United States.	3/4	Clean, high color, weak staple.	4 to 7		Not now grown.
African.	Liberia and West Coast.	About 1	High color and irregular.			Somewhat resembles Brazilian.
Greek.	Greece.	1/2 to 3/4	Short and brittle.			
Caucasian.	Caucasia.	7/4 to 1	Brown and smooth.			Shortest cotton grown.
Queensland.	Australia.	7/4 to 1				
Clarence River.	Australia.	7/4 to 1	Clean.			Gray seed.
Mexican, including Yucatan Laguna. Campeche, and Oajaca.	Mexico.	3/4 to 1	Clean, creamy, not very strong.			
Cyprus.	Isle of Cyprus.					Very little grown.
Malta.	Isle of Malta.					Very little grown.
Turkish.	Roumelia.	3/4 to 1	Dull color.			
Italian.	Neighborhood of Naples.	3/4				Very little grown.
Sicilian.	Isle of Sicily.	3/4				Very little grown.

Source: C. P. Brooks, *Cotton—Its Uses, Varieties, Fibre, Structure, Cultivation* (London and New York, 1898), pp. 79–83.

what is of most significance is the qualitative relation between the staple length and the counts, for to spin a specific count, spinners had to use a cotton staple with a length appropriate to the required count. Figure 6.1 shows the principle that the longer the staple, the higher the count.

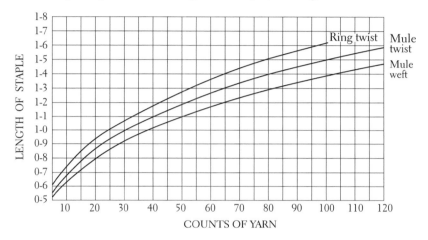

Figure 6.1 The Relation between the Length of Staple and the Counts of Yarn

Source: J. Winterbottom, *Cotton Spinning, Calculations and Yarn Costs* (2nd edn., London, 1921), p. 235.

Corresponding to these figures are the following:[15]
    Length of staple in inches, for ring twist = $0.35 \sqrt[3]{count}$
    Length of staple in inches, for mule twist = $0.325 \sqrt[3]{count}$
    Length of staple in inches, for mule weft = $0.30 \sqrt[3]{count}$
Another formula is given as follows in a Japanese book:[16]
    $C = 37.44 - 4.27S = 0.155s^2$ C: count number
                                         S: staple length in mm.

These figures and formulas clearly indicate that 'staple is the chief determining factor in the matter of the count and the quality of yarn.'[17] Indeed, there are numerous remarks by contemporaries on this relationship between raw cotton and yarn. In Britain, an article written in the middle of the nineteenth century states:[18]

England used three types of cotton. First there was long stapled cotton. This was used for making the *warp*. These threads in the finer sorts—No.

50's and above—*had* to be of long staple. . . . The short stapled cottons were used exclusively for *weft*, for the very lowest counts of *warp*—No. 10's or less—or for candlewicks. . . . The cotton industry could use a limited amount of the long and short varieties. But it could use an unlimited amount of medium stapled cottons . . . *Upland, Mobile* and *New Orleans.* These American cottons were used either for the making of *weft* or *warp*, except in the finer counts.[18]

Evan Leigh wrote in 1871:

It [Egyptian cotton] is used most extensively in the production of No. 60's to 90's yarn, or what are commonly called "Bolton Counts". . . . Whilst the finest Sea Island can be spun practically into No. 200's to 300's yarn, the Egyptian is seldom used so high as No. 150's, and never now without being well combed. . . . The staple, however, of all Brazilian cotton, although long, is much coarser than either Sea Island or Egyptian; hence its unsuitability for very fine numbers of yarn.[19]

And in the early twentieth century, we find an account as follows:

Yarns are spun from Indian, American, Brazilian, Egyptian and Sea Islands cotton. The inferior and coarse classes of yarns are spun from Indian cotton, but there is not much of it used in England at the present time [ca. 1908]. The medium classes of yarns are spun from American cotton, and occasionally Brazilian. The best and finest yarns are spun from Egyptian and Sea Islands cotton.[20]

In India, O'Conor made an investigation in Bombay in 1878 and wrote:

The bulk of the yarns spun consists of Nos. 6, 10, and 20 mule twist. Water twist is spun in smaller quantities, and the highest number spun to any extent seems to be No. 18, but the bulk is 16s. . . . The commoner kinds of short-stapled cottons are not fit for the spinning by machinery of the finer kinds of yarn, and they can be only employed for the lower counts, say up to 22s. Higher than that, from 24s to 26s, 28s, and 30s, the spinner requires a longer stapled cotton, such as Hingunghat and good Coompta, and even such good cotton is not adapted for the proper spinning of yarn above 30s, for which an admixture of Egyptian or American is required. . . . It is quite certain that in the Bombay mills 40s yarn could not be spun from Indian cotton . . . .[21]

Westland wrote in 1894:

The [Indian] mills do not as a matter of fact produce yarns of better class than 30s. . . . The main reason for this is that Indian cotton is not suitable for spinning higher counts; it does not give sufficient length of fibre. The trade, therefore, necessarily follows the limits imposed by the nature of its raw material. . . . Just as the machinery of Indian mills is adapted for the lower counts, so that of Lancashire is adapted for the higher. They use American cotton, which is of such a quality that it would be waste to employ it on goods under about 30s.[22]

Further evidence on the subject is available from Japanese cotton spinners in the nineteenth century. For example:

There are different kinds of cottons in the world which can be used for spinning. It is obviously impossible to spin fine yarn from short-stapled cottons. Japanese cottons like Shimodate and Kawachi are almost the same quality as Indian cottons. By using them we can spin yarn in the range of 10s to 16s. (1885)[23]

Japanese and Chinese cotton is short-stapled and is not suitable for spinning yarn of higher counts than 16s. On the other hand, the staple of Indian and American cotton is long enough to spin fine yarn. (1891)[24]

Chinese cotton is nearly the same as Japanese cotton. Both of them are used for spinning yarn under 16s. In order to spin yarn above 16s, Indian cotton is used, and to spin yarn for higher counts than 24s American cotton is used. (1894)[25]

We faced the problem of raw cotton at that time [ca. 1884]. Although raw cotton was cultivated in some provinces such as Settsu, Kawachi, Hakushū, Hiogo, Owari, Ise, Mikawa, To'omi, Kōshū, Shimotsuke, Sendai, etc., these cottons were too short-stapled to spin by the spinning machinery. Then, a conference on spinning was held in 1885. We put on exhibition the best yarn we could spin from the best Japanese raw cotton, *Sakagamimen*. The count was 17s. Thus it was known that 17s was the highest count at which Japanese cotton could be spun.[26]

The previous chapter noted the trend to spin finer counts of yarn in the West, in marked contrast to the concentration on coarse counts of yarn in East Asian countries. It can, therefore, be maintained that the West tended to use long-stapled cottons, while East Asia used short-stapled. The following pages will look at what kind of cotton was used in each region.

3. RAW COTTON USED IN THE WEST

(i) Britain

Table 6.2 shows the sources of raw cotton imported into Britain in the last three decades of the nineteenth century. The general picture is clear. Imports of long-stapled cottons from the United States, Brazil, and Egypt increased, but short-stapled cottons from India diminished. The share of long-stapled cottons in total cotton imports was 97 per cent in 1900, but short-stapled accounted for only 2 per cent. The increase of long-stapled cottons reflects the fact that British yarn tended to be finer in that period and that long-stapled cottons were necessary to spin high count yarn. It may also reflect the fact that the combing machine 'spread rapidly in the fine-cotton spinning industry of Lancashire' in this period.[27] The function of the combing machine was to 'reject the short and immature fibres and retain only those which are long and perfect.'[28] It was invented in 1845 by Heilmann (1796–1848) of Alsace, and a patent was taken out in England in 1846, but it did not become generally known until exhibited at the Great Exhibition of 1851.[29] That year the patent was bought for £30,000 by the Patent Combing Company, consisting of five Manchester firms. Initially, the Company restricted the making of these machines to supplying its members, but 'after their wants had been provided for, and they had obtained a command of the market, they, on numerous applications from other spinners of fine yarns, consented to supply the trade generally at a price of £500 per machine, £300 of this amount being a charge for royalty.'[30] The machine acted with 'almost the delicacy of touch of the human fingers',[31] and made possible the mechanisation of the main preparation process in the spinning of high counts. In 1866, its use was still in its infancy and for the finer quality of yarn, the 'finisher card' was still used, but by 1880, it had completely supplanted the finisher card for finer yarns. The number of combing machines

Table 6.2 Imports of Raw Cotton into Britain, distinguishing Principal Sources of Supply

Year	Total	Percentage Shares				(%)
	('000 cwt.)	U.S.A.	Brazil	Egypt	India	Others
1871	15,876	58.4	4.8	9.9	24.2	2.7
1872	12,579	44.4	8.0	12.6	31.3	3.7
1873	13,639	54.5	4.8	13.4	24.0	3.3
1874	13,990	55.8	5.1	11.0	26.2	1.9
1875	13,325	56.4	4.8	11.0	25.6	2.2
1876	13,284	62.7	3.6	13.4	18.4	1.9
1877	12,101	67.3	4.0	13.0	14.3	1.4
1878	11,968	76.6	1.6	8.5	12.0	1.3
1879	13,119	73.7	1.2	10.8	12.3	2.0
1880	14,542	75.2	1.5	9.4	12.7	1.2
1881	14,992	72.1	2.4	10.4	11.8	3.3
1882	15,930	64.7	3.0	8.3	22.7	1.3
1883	15,485	71.5	2.8	9.8	15.0	0.9
1884	15,618	69.3	2.3	10.3	17.2	0.9
1885	12,731	73.7	2.5	12.4	10.2	1.2
1886	15,313	75.4	1.8	9.9	11.9	1.0
1887	15,995	70.2	3.9	9.9	15.4	0.6
1888	15,462	77.9	2.8	8.5	9.8	1.0
1889	17,299	73.5	1.5	9.9	14.1	1.0
1890	16,013	73.4	1.6	10.1	13.3	1.6
1891	17,811	81.1	1.5	11.3	5.0	1.1
1892	15,850	79.2	1.0	14.7	3.9	1.2
1893	12,650	74.5	4.0	15.6	4.4	1.5
1894	15,965	77.9	2.2	14.3	4.3	1.3
1895	15,688	79.4	0.8	16.2	2.9	0.7
1896	15,669	79.4	0.6	15.6	3.8	0.6
1897	15,394	80.0	1.0	15.9	2.4	0.7
1898	19,005	84.8	0.3	13.0	1.3	0.6
1899	14,520	75.9	0.3	21.1	1.9	0.8
1900	15,716	77.6	1.7	17.8	2.0	0.9

Source: Calculated from Annual Statement of the Trade of the United Kingdom with Foreign Countries and British Possessions for each year.

in the English cotton industry increased from 1,710 in 1870 (1,467 being in Lancashire) to 2,722 in 1874 (2,283 being in Lancashire). It spread at first mainly in the Manchester and Bolton districts but could also be found in Oldham.[32] In consequence, demand for long-stapled cottons increased.[33]

The import of American cotton increased from 9.3 million cwt. in 1871 to 12.2 million cwt. in 1900 (a 30 per cent increase). Of American cotton, the import of Sea Island (the longest-stapled cotton) was notable, as its export from the United States to Britain saw a 360 per cent increase during the period between 1874/5 and 1896/7 (see Table 6.3). Another characteristic feature of the British cotton trade was the rapid increase in imports of Egyptian cotton. Cotton from Egypt achieved importance as part of the world's cotton supply during the American Civil War, which brought about an almost complete interruption of exports of raw cotton from the United States. As shown in Table 6.4, there was a striking advance in exports of Egyptian cotton to Europe, and to Britain in particular. In the late nineteenth century, Britain took about half. As a rule, English manufacturers took more of the higher grades, while the continental spinners used lower grade Egyptian.[34] The demand for Egyptian was, of course, due to particular characteristics of the cotton, which had long fibre with 'fine, soft quality, silky texture or lustre, and brown colour.'[35] Products for which Egyptian cotton was considered to be particularly suitable included sewing thread, medium-fine yarns, fine underwear and hosiery, and fabrics with a smooth, highly lustred surface and finish. These were competitive with other fabrics such as silk and linens.[36]

Indian cotton exports to Britain also increased dramatically during the American Civil War.[37] In three years, 1862 to 1864, India alone supplied Great Britain with just over 70 per cent of the cotton it imported.[38] But British re-exports of raw cotton also rose every year (1862–66).[39] These probably consisted of Indian cottons, as the stocks of raw cotton in Liverpool in these years were 'increasingly composed of Surat and were not in demand in Lancashire to the extent that they were on the Continent.'[40] With the recovery of the American trade, Indian cotton imports declined, and American cotton re-established its position. As Sir George Watt put it, 'America . . . had gained command of the market, and India was considered only as a supplementary source of supply, resorted to mainly in the event of a short crop from the West.'[41] The price of Indian cotton remained the

Table 6.3 Sea Island Cotton—Crops, Exports and United States
Consumption

Year	Total crop	Exports to Britain	Exports to the Continent	Takings of U.S. Spinners
1874–75	16,687	13,139	1,907	2,192
1875–76	14,515	11,591	1,345	1,915
1876–77	18,352	11,865	1,369	4,068
1877–78	21,510	12,594	3,701	6,451
1878–79	19,601	10,456	2,242	6,688
1879–80	24,862	13,729	3,294	9,389
1880–81	35,021	20,259	4,136	11,270
1881–82	37,862	22,303	2,453	14,762
1882–83	36,709	21,565	1,892	13,573
1883–84	25,490	12,166	1,413	11,674
1884–85	40,452	18,422	3,143	17,358
1885–86	37,778	14,748	1,680	19,973
1886–87	45,137	25,216	1,435	20,515
1887–88	39,479	18,698	1,915	19,560
1888–89	44,089	21,515	1,811	20,132
1889–90	46,803	25,991	2,251	19,124
1890–91	68,133	34,300	4,823	26,602
1891–92	59,134	24,778	2,653	32,279
1892–93	45,418	20,650	1,890	22,927
1893–94	61,052	33,385	4,636	23,516
1894–95	74,628	35,033	5,711	34,765
1895–96	93,045	43,174	7,269	40,092
1896–97	104,557	47,272	11,180	41,676

Source: C.P. Brooks, Cotton Manufacturing, p. 198.

cheapest of all cottons. Yet British manufacturers were always unwilling to use Indian cotton because its staple was short,[42] and there was more breakage in the process of spinning than with long-stapled cottons. It also had to be twisted harder to make a strong thread. 'With Indian it required 12 turns per inch while American needed only 8.'[43] Its spinning value, therefore, was low. It had also other deficiencies such as impurities added by the peasant farmer (ryot) and the village broker in India, and a lower yield of yarn by

Table 6.4 Quantities of Egyptian Cotton Exports 1860/4 to 1910/13

Five Year Average	Total	To Britain	To the Continent* and U.S.A.
1860/64	944	648	
1865/69	1,706	1,270	
1870/74	1,892	1,562	
1875/79	2,230	1,450	
1880/84	2,791		
1885/89	3,031		
1890/94	4,510	2,435 ⌝	1,926 ⌝
1895/1900	5,765	2,929 ⎮	2,757 ⎮
1900/04	5,941	2,934 **	2,668 **
1905/09	6,677	3,385 ⎮	2,978 ⎮
1910/13	6,982	3,261 ⌟	3,358 ⌟

Notes: *The Continent includes Russia, France, Austria-Hungary, Italy, Germany, and Switzerland.
** Calculated from Owen's figures of percentage shares of exports to England and to the Continent and U.S.A.

Source: E.R.J. Owen, *Cotton and the Egyptian Economy 1820–1917* (Oxford, 1969), pp. 161, 198–99.

length as well as weight per pound.[44] In addition, Dr. Vicziany argues that the limited demand for Surat was due also to the very fact that the United States had made such a success of cotton culture, arguing that 'America was a prolific producer and exporter of medium staples, and textile machinery was designed to suit *upland*.'[45] Indeed, from the late eighteenth century on, 'in the vast machine of commerce, the spindles of Manchester are as necessarily tied to the plough and hoe of the Mississippi, as to their own bobbins.'[46] A great quantity of Japanese and Chinese cotton was also imported into Britain during the cotton famine,[47] but because 'it is short staple and can only be used for mixing-up purposes,'[48] exports from Japan ceased in 1865 simply because 'good qualities are scarce'.[49] British spinning machinery was not engineered for short-stapled cottons.[50]

A combination of these factors made Indian (or other short-stapled) cotton a last resort for English manufacturers. About half of the cotton sent to Liverpool was reshipped to the Continent (see Figure 6.2). Indian cotton formed 29 per cent of the import total on average in 1871–4, of which 43 per cent was re-exported. In 1881–4, these import fell to 19 per cent, while re-exports rose to 47 per cent. The delivery of Indian cotton to millers sank to as low a level as 2 per cent in 1901/2–1904/5.[51]

In 1902, E. J. Helm, the secretary of the Manchester Chamber of Commerce, summarised the British cotton trade as follows:

> Much the largest part of the cotton consumed in this country [Britain] is American and Egyptian. Of the former the proportion is about 80.5 per cent, of the latter 15.7 per cent. These two descriptions constitute, therefore, 96.2 per cent of the whole, the small remainder, rather less than 4 per cent, being Brazilian and other growths. Of East Indian cotton the quality used in English mills is now a mere trifle.[52]

(ii) The Continent

The structure of the cotton trade on the Continent was slightly different from that of Britain. For one thing, the proportion of imports of Indian cotton was greater. Deliveries of Indian cotton to consumers on the Continent formed 35 per cent of the total on average in the period between 1871 and 1884 (see Table 6.5), compared to 14 per cent for Britain.[53] But the overall picture of Continental imports of cotton is similar. The delivery of long-stapled cottons (American, Egyptian, and Brazilian) rose from 64 per cent of the whole in 1871 to 91 per cent in 1899/1900. (These figures are comparable to 79 per cent and 98 per cent respectively in Great Britain.[54]) Also, the delivery of Indian short-stapled cottons for local consumption on the Continent declined from 31 per cent in 1871 to 7 per cent in 1899/1900. (These percentages are comparable to 16 per cent and 2 per cent respectively in Britain.[55]) In both Britain and the Continent, the tendency towards the import of long-stapled cottons is unmistakable, though more so in the former. Among long-stapled cottons, Continental imports of Sea Island saw a six-fold increase from 1874/5 to 1896/7,[56] and that of Egyptian cotton also rapidly increased in these years, approaching the level of British imports of this by the end of the century.[57] In France, the import of American, Egyptian, and Brazilian long-stapled cottons was as high as 90 per cent of the total in 1900; by contrast, Indian short-stapled cottons diminished from 23 per cent of the

Figure 6.2. Imports of Indian Cotton into All Europe ('000 bales)

Source: T. Ellison, *The Cotton Trade of Great Britain*, Table Nos. 4 and 5, in Appendix.

total in 1875 to only 2 per cent in 1900.[58] In Germany, too, the import of American and Egyptian cotton formed 91 per cent of the total in 1900, and that of Indian cotton 7 per cent.[59]

Table 6.5 Percentage of Deliveries of Raw Cotton to Consumers for the Continent

| Year | Long Stapled | | | Short Stapled | | |
| | American | Egyptian | Brazilian | East Indian | Others | Total |
	%	%	%	%	%	('000 bales)
1871	47.4	7.9	8.9	30.9	4.9	2,354
1872	34.7	9.4	15.0	36.6	4.3	2,203
1873	41.5	9.2	9.0	36.1	4.2	2,119
1874	42.7	8.2	7.4	37.9	3.8	2,388
1875	42.9	8.2	5.8	40.2	2.9	2,447
1876	47.0	11.0	4.1	35.5	2.4	2,513
1877	47.3	12.1	3.0	35.8	1.8	2,180
1878	61.9	8.3	1.6	26.9	1.3	2,376
1879	61.6	7.0	1.3	29.0	1.1	2,572
1880	56.5	6.3	1.8	33.8	0.6	2,635
1881	58.5	7.9	3.1	29.3	0.2	2,930
1882	51.6	6.3	3.3	37.6	1.2	3,032
1883	53.4	4.3	2.7	38.6	1.0	3,441
1884	51.3	6.8	2.5	38.5	0.9	3,117
1899–900	82.2	8.0	1.2	6.7	1.9	4,473

Source: Calculated, T. Ellison, *The Cotton Trade of Great Britain*, Table No. 5 in Appendix; Ellison's *Annual Review of the Cotton Trade for the Season 1904–5*, p. 3.

A few comments are necessary regarding Continental imports of Indian raw cotton, as they formed a rather high proportion of the total. They consisted of direct imports from India and of re-exports from Britain. The opening of the Suez Canal in 1869 made direct trade possible instead of the old Bombay–Cape of Good Hope–Liverpool–Continent route,[60] raising Indian hopes that it could become 'the cotton field of Europe'. Indeed, in the spring of the next year, shipments of cotton dominated the traffic of the Canal.[61] As shown in Figure 6.2, direct imports gradually rose, while re-exports from Britain declined. Britain lost its position as the main importer of Indian cotton in 1892 when Germany took over.[62] The annual average of Indian exports of raw cotton levelled off at about 5 million cwt. in the last three decades of the nineteenth century.[63] The British share of the trade, which had formed 80 to 95 per cent of the total in the 1860s,[64] then fell to just over 40 per cent in the mid 1880s, to 30 per cent in 1890, and to only 2 per cent in 1900.[65] From the mid 1880s, about half to two-thirds of British imports of Indian raw cotton were re-exported to the Continent.[66]

Meanwhile, the Continental share of Indian raw cotton exports, which was about half of the total in the mid 1880s, rose to 70 per cent in 1890, and reached 82 per cent, its highest level, in 1891/2.[67] On the European Continent, short-stapled cotton was needed for the manufacture of blouses and garments for the peasantry and the working class.[68] But demand from Continental Europe did not last long, as the huge rise of exports to Japan resulted in a notable change in the destination to which Indian raw cotton was exported. Japan's share of Indian cotton exports was nil until the end of the 1880s, then rose to 25 per cent in the mid 1890s and 56 per cent in 1899/1900.[69] This trend continued in the next century.[70] Indian short-stapled cottons were no longer important as a source of supply for Europe by 1900.

(iii) The West as a whole

Table 6.6 shows the consumption of raw cotton in the West as a whole in the late nineteenth and the early twentieth centuries. The United Kingdom, Europe, and the United States all increased their consumption of cotton, though the rate of increase differed for each. The annual consumption of cotton during the period 1901–4 exceeded that for 1876–80 by 3.1 million cwt., or 28 per cent in the United Kingdom, 13.2 million cwt., or 143 per cent on the Continent, and 11.1 million cwt., or 182 per cent in the United States. The consumption of cotton in the United Kingdom was overtaken by the Continent in 1888 and by the United States in 1900.

The source of supply of raw cotton in these regions as a whole is shown in Table 6.7. The figures in the table show that of the total average annual consumption of 26.5 million cwt., American cotton supplied 75 per cent. In the period 1896–1900, total consumption rose to 49.19 million cwt. per annum, of which 83 per cent was supplied from the United States. The consumption of American cotton also increased by 21 million cwt., or 93

Table 6.6 Average Annual Consumption of Raw Cotton in the United Kingdom, Europe, and the United States

(in million cwt.)

Period	United Kingdom	Continent	United States	Total
	(%)	(%)	(%)	(%)
1876–80	11.20 (42)	9.17 (35)	6.13 (23)	26.50 (100)
1881–85	12.88 (40)	11.76 (36)	7.66 (24)	32.30 (100)
1886–90	13.75 (37)	13.98 (38)	9.05 (25)	36.78 (100)
1891–95	14.11 (33)	17.02 (40)	11.26 (27)	42.39 (100)
1896–1900	15.05 (31)	20.11 (41)	14.03 (29)	49.19 (100)
1901	14.32 (28)	21.30 (41)	15.80 (31)	51.42 (100)
1902	15.07 (27)	22.10 (40)	17.83 (32)	55.00 (100)
1903	13.90 (26)	23.69 (44)	16.53 (31)	54.12 (100)
1904	13.99 (25)	22.27 (40)	18.92 (34)	55.18 (100)

Source: *Report of the Tariff Commission*, vol. 2, *The Cotton Industry* (London, 1905), paragraphs 9 and 11.

Table 6.7 Sources of Supply of Raw Cotton Consumed in the United Kingdom, the Continent, and the United States

(in million cwt)

Year	Long-Stapled				Short-Stapled	Total
	America	Brazil	W. India	Egypt	E. India	
	(%)	(%)	(%)	(%)	(%)	(%)
1876–80	19.94 (75.2)	0.39 (1.5)	0.14 (0.5)	2.40 (9.1)	3.63 (13.7)	26.50 (100)
1881–85	24.26 (75.1)	0.48 (1.5)	0.10 (0.3)	2.61 (8.1)	4.85 (15.2)	32.30 (100)
1886–90	28.30 (76.9)	0.47 (1.3)	0.12 (0.3)	2.69 (7.3)	5.20 (14.1)	36.78 (100)
1891–95	33.70 (79.5)	0.45 (1.1)	0.12 (0.3)	4.07 (9.6)	4.05 (9.5)	42.39 (100)
1896–1900	41.01 (83.4)	0.22 (0.5)	0.14 (0.3)	5.14 (10.5)	2.68 (5.4)	49.19(100)

Source: Tariff Commission, *Report of the Tariff Commission*, vol. 2, *The Cotton Industry*, paragraphs 15 and 17.

per cent of the total increase in the requirements of the United Kingdom, the Continent, and the United States. In the same period, consumption of Egyptian cotton more than doubled and increased its share by 1.4 per cent. On the other hand, East Indian cotton supplies, on the whole, tended to diminish, and fell from 14 per cent to 5 per cent of the requirement for Europe and America combined. In both quantity and quality, the West as a whole tended to use longer-stapled cotton in these years.

4. RAW COTTON USED IN EAST ASIA

The principal sources of supply of raw cotton for the cotton industry in East Asia were traditionally indigenous. The relative position of East Asian cotton production to world cotton crops is shown in Table 6.8 compiled by Todd. India and China alone produced a third to two-fifths of the total American crop.

(i) The Far East

Most raw cotton used in China, Japan, and Korea was local, but China and Japan also used cotton imported chiefly from India. Todd's account of Chinese cotton is that 'the staple is generally very coarse and short, averaging about 5/8 inch.'[71] He refers to Korean cotton as being 'apparently similar to the native Chinese cotton, and of about the quality of lower grades of Indian cotton.'[72] As regards Japanese cotton, Consul Vyse reported from Kanagawa in 1862: 'there are several kinds of cotton in Japan, and the better kinds are . . . not inferior to the production of India or China.'[73] Handy observed in 1896: 'the quality of the Japanese cotton is good . . . though the staple is considerably shorter than the ordinary tree or shrub cotton. The staple is seldom more than 1.8 centimeters [i.e., 0.7 inch] in length. The best cotton is also elastic and glossy'.[74]

a) Japan

From the Edo period, cotton was next to rice in importance in Japan's agricultural production.[75] Raw cotton production reached its highest level

Table 6.8 The World Cotton Crops 1902–1912

(Bales of approximately 500 pounds, 'ooo omitted.)

	1902 /3	1903 /4	1904 /5	1905 /6	1906 /7	1907 /8	1908 /9	1909 /10	1910 /11	1911 /12
America	10,758	10,124	13,557	11,320	13,531	11,582	13,829	10,651	12,132	16,043
India	3,367	3,161	3,791	3,416	4,934	3,122	3,692	4,718	3,853	3,288
Egypt	1,168	1,302	1,263	1,192	1,390	1,447	1,150	1,000	1,515	1,485
Russia	342	477	604	759	664	698	686	686	895	875
China	1,200	1,200	756	788	806	875	1,933	2,531	3,467	3,437
Others	801	751	735	781	1,142	916	981	950	965	1,058
Total	17,636	17,015	20,706	18,256	22,467	18,640	22,271	20,536	22,827	26,186

Source: J. A. Todd, *The World's Cotton Crops* (London, 1915), p. 395.

in 1887.[76] This indigenous cotton and Chinese cotton were practically the only sources for the Japanese spinning industry until the end of the 1880s. As shown in Table 6.9, with the development of the cotton spinning industry from the 1890s onwards, imports of raw cotton from India increased rapidly and exceeded Chinese cotton imports in 1896. American cotton was also imported but never exceeded 15 per cent of the total until 1897. Thus Japanese manufactured cotton goods in the key period of the industrialisation of the cotton industry were made from short-stapled cottons.

b) China
China ranked third or fourth among the cotton-growing countries of the world. It exported some but also imported a small quantity of foreign cotton. Table 6.10 shows Chinese imports and exports of cotton. Prior to

Table 6.9 Japan's Imports of Cotton

					(piculs)
	China	India	French Indo-China	U.S.A.	Total
1876	32,308				32,308
1877	27,803				27,803
1878	7,847				7,847
1879	7,434	157			7,640
1880	14,461				14,611
1881	16,584				16,584
1882	32,632				33,097
1883	21,062				21,062
1884	44,061	1,314			45,425
1885	43,984	8			43,994
1886	42,261	172		4	46,438
1887	54,915	709		81	55,706
1888	117,031	442		633	118,932
1889	227,538	3,203		715	231,680
1890	167,862	75,009		17,790	260,843
1891	180,551	265,619		53,044	501,287
1892	327,214	362,131		91,852	786,475
1893	501,838	365,924		61,603	938,357
1894	517,835	423,542		120,568	1,084,156
1895	821,716	466,838	11,192	119,961	1,434,682
1896	436,718	1,034,411	23,013	187,039	1,678,680
1897	491,121	1,350,401	13,434	347,736	2,215,294

Source: *Yokohamashi-shi shiryōhen*, vol. 2, pp. 243–5.

1890, foreign cotton came only from India.[77] But these imports declined because of the availability of yarn from other countries. The annual average total of cotton imports was 170,000 *piculs* in the 1870s, 155,000 *piculs* in the 1880s, and 126,000 *piculs* in the 1890s. These imports were negligible compared with the 5 to 7 million *piculs* which Feuerwerker estimated as the average annual production of ginned cotton in China for the decades 1871–80 to 1901–10.[78] Exports of cotton exceeded imports in 1888. As indicated in the table, most of the cotton exported was shipped to Japan.[79] An attempt to grow American long-stapled cottons in China was first made in 1898, but the experiment ended in failure. Attempts continued in the twentieth century, but it was only from the 1920s and particularly in the 1930s that the cotton improvement programme began to produce significant results.[80] Until then the cotton used in China was exclusively short-stapled.

(ii) *India*

India ranked next to the United States as a cotton-producing country. In 1848, the consumption of cotton per head is said to have been higher than in Europe.[81] But India also imported a small quantity of foreign cotton. Under the provisions of the tariff of 1875, however, the import of raw cotton not from continental Asia or Ceylon (i.e., long-stapled) was made subject to a duty of 5 per cent *ad valorem*, whilst short-stapled cottons from Asia were free of duty.[82] As a result, imports of Asian cotton formed more than 90 per cent of the total up to 1890.[83] The bulk of this was imported from Persia, and almost all of it was landed in Bombay and consumed in the local mills.[84] In the 1890s, long-stapled cottons were imported to foster the spinning of fine yarn, but this was confined to one group of mills. As early as 1886, J. Tata with the help of Sir D. Petit had experimented with Egyptian cotton.[85] In 1892/3, 28,000 cwts. of Egyptian cotton were imported into India, mostly by the manager of the Petit Mills.[86] Other cotton mills confined themselves to short-stapled cottons, and not much success was achieved with imported long-stapled cottons in producing fine yarns.[87] The annual import of long-stapled cotton was 49,384 cwts. in the 1890s,[88] which was negligible when compared with 4.7 million cwt., the annual export from India.[89]

Table 6.10 Chinese Imports and Exports of Cotton — In Volume —

('000 piculs)

Year	A Imports	B Exports	C (to Japan)
1871	348	11	
1872	208	6	
1873	202	25	
1874	12	94	
1875	170	32	
1876	237	43	(32)
1877	155	33	(28)
1878	106	23	(9)
1879	176	12	(7)
1880	87	18	(14)
1871–1880 average	169.5	29.7	
1881	138	23	(17)
1882	178	42	(33)
1883	211	22	(21)
1884	187	54	(44)
1885	131	62	(44)
1886	111	48	(43)
1887	174	69	(55)
1888	157	203	(117)
1889	114	504	(228)
1890	150	299	(167)
1881–1890 average	155.1	132.6	
1891	111	356	(180)
1892	107	509	(327)
1893	53	576	(501)
1894	43	747	(518)
1895	45	896	(822)
1896	99	418	(437)
1897	160	493	(491)
1898	229	274	
1899	278	229	
1900	135	712	
1891–1900 average	126.0	521.0	

Source: Hsiao, *China's Foreign Trade Statistics*, pp. 38, 85; *Yokohamashi-shi shiryōhen*, 2: 243–5 for col. C.

India also ranked second to the United States as a cotton-exporting country. How much raw cotton was left for local consumption can only be guessed.[90] But in the last three decades of the nineteenth century, the quantity appears to have increased. In the 1860s, the outbreak of the American Civil War stimulated Indian cotton exports, which reached the highest level in 1865/6 when India exported 893 million lbs.[91] The rise in the price of cotton also gave an impetus to cotton cultivation, and land under cotton cultivation in India expanded throughout the 1860s. Cotton exports declined in the late 1860s, and levelled off from the 1870s, but cotton crops continued to increase. According to Ellison, cotton consumed in India for spinning was 88.6 million lbs. in 1877. This rose to 234 million lbs. in 1885—a 2.6-fold increase.[92] In 1889, it was reported that Indian cotton was 'now most largely used in India.'[93] Another of Ellison's estimates about production and distribution of cotton in India for the period 1871–94 is shown in Table 6.11. The table shows a gradual decrease in the proportion of the crop exported and an increase in the proportion consumed. Nearly one-third of the crop was consumed in 1871–6 and about a half in 1888–94. Ellison's figures covering India as a whole are supported by the figures in Table 6.12, which show cotton exports from Bombay and mill consumption in the Island of Bombay. The annual total receipts of cotton at Bombay rose from 1.2 million bales in 1871–6 to 1.7 million bales in 1895–1900, while exports fell from 1.1 million bales to 0.9 million bales. Mill consumption rose very rapidly, a nine-fold increase in the period.

Table 6.11 Crops, Exports, and Consumption in India

(Bales of 3 1/2 cwt. or 392 pounds; '000 omitted)

	Crop	Exports	Consumption
1871–76*	2,400 (100%)	1,519 (63%)	881 (37%)
1877–82	2,100 (100%)	1,195 (57%)	905 (43%)
1883–88	2,570 (100%)	1,533 (60%)	1,037 (40%)
1889–94	2,980 (100%)	1,503 (50%)	1,477 (50%)

Note: * Average periods of six seasons each.

Source: T. Ellison, 'The Cotton Trade of India', *Cotton Movement and Fluctuations 1890–1895*, 22nd edn. (New York, 1895), p. 37.

Table 6.12 Indian Cotton Exports from Bombay and Mill Consumption
in Bombay

('ooo bales)

	Exports	Mill Consumption	Total
1871–76	1,109 (93%)	90 (7%)	1,199 (100%)
1877–82	995 (82%)	219 (18%)	1,214 (100%)
1883–88	1,149 (74%)	400 (26%)	1,549 (100%)
1889–94	1,205 (64%)	691 (36%)	1,896 (100%)
1895–1900	886 (52%)	813 (48%)	1,699 (100%)

Source: Bombay Chamber of Commerce, Report of the Bombay Chamber of Commerce
for the Year 1901, p. 465.

Indigenous cottons used by Indian mills and handicraft spinners and
weavers were undoubtedly all short-stapled. G. A. Gammie, who spent
'five years of almost constant observation of a large series of Indian cottons
. . . at Poona' at the beginning of the twentieth century, listed as many as
323 varieties grown there.[94] Of these, the length of staple is known for
302 varieties and varied from 0.38 to 1 inch. Only two varieties, Wardha
(grown in tree cottons) and Assam No. 1, had a staple of 1 inch;[95] the
average length is calculated at 0.68 inch. This can be compared with the
average length of American varieties, for S. M. Tracy, the director of the
Mississippi Agricultural Experiment Station, did research on 129 varieties
of American cottons in the 1890s, and referred to the length of staple of
64 varieties of these.[96] The staple length varied from 18 mm (0.7 inch) to
75 mm (3 inches), and the average length is calculated at 27.98 mm (1.1
inch). On average, then, the staple length of Indian cotton was three-
fifths of that of American cottons. Hence, apart from a small amount of
imported long-stapled cotton, raw cotton used in India consisted exclusively of the short-stapled type.

Attempts were made to grow American long-stapled cottons in India.
These attempts, the so-called 'cotton improvement programme', were
designed to relieve Lancashire's dependence on the United States as the
major source of its raw material. The first extensive experiments were
ordered by the Court of Directors of the East India Company in 1829.[97]

Various kinds of American cotton, Egyptian cotton, and South American cotton were planted in Broach, Khandesh, and Dharwar, but none grew well.[98] In 1838, a new plan was introduced, and, two years later, the cotton improvement programme was launched under the auspices of the East India Company, but this programme also failed.[99]

Despite the failure of the cotton improvement programme in the 1840s, the English continued to be interested in developing a new source of cotton supply in India, and in April 1857, the Cotton Supply Association was formed in Manchester.[100] On 19 June, a public meeting of the Association resolved that:

> The supply of cotton to this country is inadequate to the requirements of manufacturing industry, and being almost entirely derived from one source, is uncertain in quality and unduly fluctuating in price. . . . This meeting believes the colonial and other dependencies of Great Britain afford ample resources for the cultivation and development of the cotton plant.[101]

A plan of action was followed. Prizes and medals were offered to cultivators. Over a thousand tons of seed were distributed in 1857–68, and gins and presses (with instructions on how to use them) were sent to suitable applicants.[102] The outbreak of the American Civil War in 1861 provided the Association with an opportunity to mount a campaign to turn India into a major supplier of good quality cotton. On 1 October 1863, Dr. Forbes was appointed as the first Cotton Commissioner of Bombay. Attempts to introduce new varieties of cotton and to spread the cultivation of selected indigenous varieties continued to the mid 1870s. But this improvement programme also 'failed as its predecessor of the 1840s had failed.'[103]

It is now accepted that the cotton improvement programme in nineteenth-century India was 'a gigantic failure'.[104] The causes of the failure were numerous, ranging from differences in soil and climate to ignorance about Indian economic, cultural, and social factors.[105] As late as 1938/9, only 2 per cent of the Indian cotton acreage was growing long-stapled varieties.[106]

5. CONCLUSION

In the labour process, human activity, with the help of tools and equipment, alters the material worked upon—raw cotton in this case. This change is limited by the physical properties of the cotton plant, which undergo adaptation into a form that meets the wants of humankind. Cotton products take different forms according to the type of raw cotton used. The basic distinction in the forms between cotton products can be represented as below:

	Raw Cotton	Cotton Yarn	Cotton Cloth
I	short-stapled	low counts	thick and heavy
II	long-stapled	high counts	thin and light

This is a rough scheme by which to compare various kinds of cotton products, as 'short-stapled cotton is only adapted for the coarse counts, whilst the longest is applicable for all.'[107] Indeed, in the West where long-stapled cottons were available, various counts of yarn were spun. The Southern states of the United States used long-stapled cottons but spun low counts of yarn. This does not mean that they could not spin higher counts. The cotton industry in New England, which used the same kind of cotton, spun higher counts. It was a matter of specialisation related to the competition within the States. Britain spun the highest counts of yarn in the greatest quantities in the world in the late nineteenth century. This was a result of competition from other European countries, which had begun to spin the middle range of counts, and a consequence of specialisation. Britain used almost exclusively long-stapled cottons, and its industry was equipped with such machinery as combing machines and mules suitable for fine spinning, together with experienced spinners.

In the Far East (China, Japan, and Korea), where only short-stapled cottons were grown, the type of yarn spun in the region was confined to 24s and under. Even though the finer yarn became available through foreign trade in the late nineteenth century, demand was limited to foreign yarn of the same quality as local yarn. The first type of qualitative relation between cotton products (i.e., short-stapled—low counts—thick and heavy) was typical of the Far East. The second type is more typical for the West in general and Britain in particular.

It was difficult to spin fine yarn from short-stapled cottons. But it was not impossible to spin very fine yarn from short-stapled cottons as Winterbottom claims.[108] Short-stapled cottons actually had been spun into one of the finest yarns from ancient times in India (and possibly only in India), not by machinery but by the hands of Hindu girls. Royle relates an episode from as late as the time of the International Exhibition of 1851:

> The local committee of Dacca having given notice that they would award prizes for the best piece of muslin which could be woven in time for the Exhibition, the prize of 25 rupees was awarded to Hubecoolla, weaver of Golokonda [Golconda], near Dacca. The piece is ten yards long and one wide, weighs only 3 oz. 2 dwts. and may be passed through a very small ring.[109]

Such cloth undoubtedly required extremely fine yarns. As this fact relates to our previous argument that the Indian pattern of consumption of cotton goods was a mixed type of the Far Eastern and the Western patterns, we shall discuss it in more detail.

India was once famous for this kind of cotton cloth. The seventeenth-century French traveller, Jean-Baptiste Tavernier, wrote, 'some calicuts are made so fine you can hardly feel them in your hand, and the thread when spun is scarce discernible . . . . The rich have turbans of so fine a cloth that thirty ells of it put into one turban make its weight less than four ounces.'[110] And he says elsewhere, 'when a man puts it on, his skin appears as plainly as if it were quite naked.'[111] In the early nineteen century, William Ward observed, 'when the muslin is laid on the grass to bleach and the dew has fallen upon it, it is no longer discernible'.[112] An English review of the trade in the latter part of the seventeenth century described the same fabrics as 'the shadow of a Commodity'.[113] Baines mentioned that 'some of their muslins might be thought the work of fairies, or of insects, rather than of men'.[114] No wonder it earned the poetic descriptions of 'web of woven air', 'cobweb', and so forth. But 'what is still more astonishing', wrote Ellison, 'is the circumstance that the cotton, with which this wonderful perfection was attained, was [made from] the much despised Surats, and still more despised Bengals, of modern times.'[115]

This fine cotton cloth was indeed made of short-stapled cottons. 'From a careful examination of the cottons grown in different parts of India,' Royle wrote, 'we find that it is not owing to any excellence in the raw material that the superiority in the manufacture is due', for 'the Indian cotton is unfit for their purposes, being not only short but coarse in staple.' The beauty of the fabric is due to 'the first, the best, and most perfect of instruments . . . the human hand.'[116] Writing in 1836, Andrew Ure observed:

> When they [i.e., cotton fibres] are short, and consist of rather broad and flimsy ribands, they will be ill adapted to machine-spinning, though still susceptible of being spun by the tact of delicate fingers. We can thus understand how the Hindoo women manage to spin fine yarn from the Dacca cotton, which is the growth of an unequable wool consisting of flimsy ribands, like most of the India cottons.[117]

In practice, not all Indian-made textiles were 'webs of woven air'. Their quality differed to a considerable extent. Borpujari divides the total output of the traditional Indian textile industry into two broad groups, namely 'the luxury-output' and 'non-luxury-output'. By 'luxury cloth', he means 'cloth using thread of fineness equal to or greater than 250s'.[118] Gadgil also divides the industry into two groups, the urban industry producing fine textiles purchased by the pre-British rulers, and the rural industry producing coarse textiles for local use.[119] Making a piece of superfine cloth took six months.[120] Until the advent of Crompton's mule, no other country could equal or rival Indian fine textiles. Manchester manufacturers in the eighteenth century who deprecated Indian 'webs of woven air' by calling them 'the shadow of a commodity' were at the same time 'doing all they could to imitate the reality'.[121] Chaudhuri argues that 'the development and application of a whole range of machinery from mechanical carding and cleaning of cotton to spinning and weaving was to create an import-substituting industry.'[122] But even as late as the early nineteenth century, Indian textiles enjoyed comparative advantages over English cloth. In 1803, the duties in England on white calicoes reached 60 per cent and in 1813 about 85 per cent *ad valorem*.[123] The price difference mattered between Indian muslins and British machine-made cloths because they were of similar quality. But by the 1830s, the situation was reversed. The muslins and calicoes of India were doomed to be largely replaced by the cheap machine-made fabrics of Lancashire.

At the same time, India also had non-luxury cloths, whose quality was thick and coarse. John Forbes Watson wrote in India in the mid nineteenth century: 'It is an error to suppose that thick and warm fabrics are not required in India. Throughout a great portion of that country the suffering of the poor from cold during certain seasons, particularly at night, is as great as with us in Europe.'[124] These coarse types of cotton 'did not form a considerable object of foreign trades' with the Dutch and the English[125] but were for local use. It was production of this type of cotton that expanded in the late nineteenth century. As we have seen, this coarse type of cloth was made of similar quality yarn to that used in the Far East. British and Far Eastern cotton goods had both similarities and differences when compared with Indian goods. In this sense, the Indian pattern of consumption of cotton goods was a mixture of the two other traditions.

Thus far it has been established that the raw cotton on which the Western cotton industry relied was genetically distinct from that for the Eastern cotton industry and that these different types of cottons correspond with the manufactures made from them. Hence there were three distinctive patterns of specialisation in cotton products in the Western, the Far Eastern, and the South and Southeast Asian markets in the late nineteenth century (see Table 6.13). Britain, Japan, and India represented each of these types.

Table 6.13 Three Types of Markets for Cotton Products

	Raw Cotton	Cotton Yarn	Cotton Cloth
British Markets (Western type)	fine and long- to medium-stapled G. *barbadense* G. *hirsutum*	high-medium counts	thin and light
Japanese Markets (Far Eastern type)	thick and short-stapled G. *arboreum* (*sinense*)	low counts	thick and heavy
Indian Markets (Mixed type)	short-stapled G. *arboreum* (*annual bengalense*) G. *herbaceum*	low counts	thick and heavy

┌─────── British-made ───────┐
high-medium counts   thin and light

Remarks: Cotton with short but fine fibre (G. *arboreum* perennial *indicum*), cotton yarn with high counts, and cloth with thin and light texture existed in the Indian markets prior to ca. 1800–50 when this kind of cotton disappeared and those types of yarn and cloth were superseded by their British rivals.

CONCLUSION

To conclude, let us place the three distinctive cotton markets which we have presented so far into a wider historical perspective.

Cotton has been grown in India from a few thousands of years B.C. (the fragments of cotton fabrics found at Mohenjo-Daro have been dated at approximately 3,000 B.C.), and for a long time India monopolised the product. By the time European explorers and Japanese *wakō* (pirates) launched out into the East Indies, cotton textiles were being used by the peoples of East Africa, the Middle East, and South and Southeast Asia. As trade began between the East Indies, or as Professor Chaudhuri calls it 'the trading world of Asia',[1] and Great Britain and Japan at the two extremities of Eurasia, cotton products found their way from India to the West and the East via various routes.

If Europeans were to develop substitute products for the fine Indian cotton textiles, fine yarns were necessary. This finally became possible when the long-stapled cotton plant was discovered in the New World and also when the mule-spinning machine capable of producing fine yarn was invented in Britain. The result is the well-known 'great triangular trade', in which three regions, i.e., the New World producing the raw materials, Britain creating the technology for textile manufacturing, and the Atlantic perimeter providing the markets for the goods, were linked.

It was around the fourteenth to sixteenth centuries that cotton cultivation spread eastward to China, Korea, and Japan. It took many centuries for cotton growing to reach these countries because of difficulties in developing a species that could withstand the severe cold winters of the region. When the cotton plant, intrinsically a tropical perennial, was successfully transplanted to East Asian soil, a new annual type of the plant, called *Gossypium arboreum* race *sinense,* came into being.[2] This variety, featuring the shortest and thickest cotton fibres in the world, was grown only in China, Korea, Japan, and Taiwan.

The Chinese cotton industry was limited by the need to use the available land for food supplies.[3] In the case of Korea, cotton cloth was used as currency and therefore constituted an important source of revenue for the government. Crushing taxes hindered progress in the industry.[4] In contrast, the development of the cotton industry in Japan was one of the most important industrial and commercial achievements of the Tokugawa era (1603–1868); the centre of cotton production was gradually consolidated in the western part of the country: Osaka and the surrounding region and along the coast of the Inland Sea,[5] with Osaka functioning as the distribution centre.[6] Japan, which had been far behind China and Korea in cotton textile production in the sixteenth century, outstripped the latter during the subsequent two centuries.

As a result, powerful cotton industries emerged at the two extremities of Eurasia, producing goods which had sharply contrasting qualities. These differences were particularly noticeable between the West and the Far East in general, and between Britain and Japan in particular. The British market was for thin cloth, high-count yarns, and long-stapled cotton, and the Japanese market was for thick cloth, low-count yarns, and short-stapled cotton. These differences may have been linked to the different respective uses of cotton clothing: the Europeans had woollens for the winters, whereas the East Asians did not and used thick cottons instead. By the middle of the nineteenth century, each market was built into the conventions of everyday life, and was so distinctive that there was virtually no competition between the respective goods.

The Indian market was a melting pot in which all sorts of cotton products except long-stapled cotton were used. India had dominated the market for 'luxury' types of goods—goods originally made in India alone. But in the nineteenth century, British imitations flowed into India in abundance; 23 per cent of Britain's total export of cotton textiles in 1850, 38 per cent in 1875 and as much as 49 per cent in 1900 was taken by India alone. India also had a market for 'non-luxury' cottons similar to the East Asian types. This particular market in the Far East, which was potentially huge, had been closed to international trade because of the seclusion policy to which East Asian states had adhered for centuries. Only strong external forces like the Western Powers could have broken these barriers down as they did. The latent Far Eastern market, when opened up and finding itself undamaged from competition from the importation of British cotton goods, experienced the momentum to expand. After all, British and East Asian cottons did not compete for one and the same market, but were oriented toward distinctive and noncompetitive ones. The Indian cotton industry took full advantage of the opening of the wider Far Eastern market, which in turn helped the Indians to gain the purchasing power to acquire British goods.[7] India, as the major importer of fine-quality cotton goods from Britain and also as the major exporter of coarse-quality goods to East Asia, was 'the key to the pattern of world multilateral settlement', as Professor Saul put it.[8] By the time of World War I, however, the leading role played by the Indian cotton industry in the Far Eastern market was taken over by a latecomer, her Japanese rival.

Thus, far from the assertion of Marx and others that Asia was exploited by the West, and contrary to the argument advocated by Dr. Andre Gunder Frank that the developed countries created 'the development of underdevelopment',[9] what then-underdeveloped Asia experienced was nothing less than the dynamic development of the cotton industry. This industrial sector undoubtedly played the most strategic role in the process of economic development of Asia in general and of Japan in particular, which, in the light of our findings, can be regarded not so much as a result of the competition between Britain and Asia, but as a consequence of the rivalry among Asian economies.

Supplemental Remarks

THE INTER-WAR YEARS

Finally, in order to dispel any impression the rest of the thesis might convey to the reader that the qualitative correlation in cotton products was polarised at the west and east extremities of Eurasia, tables 7.1 to 7.3 are presented which show the transformation that qualitatively Japanese cottons underwent in the inter-war years from the Far Eastern to the Western type.

Table 7.1 shows that raw cotton imported into Japan gradually changed from short-stapled to long-stapled varieties. Imports of long-stapled cotton superseded those of short-stapled in the 1930s. The increase in imports of long-stapled cotton reflects the tendency for Japanese yarn to become finer in the period. Table 7.2 shows the percentage composition of Japanese yarn; the figures on the table are comparable to those of British cotton yarn on the same table. The comparison immediately shows that in the medium

Table 7.1 Japan's Imports of Raw Cotton: 1907–1935

Year	Short-Stapled		Long-Stapled		Others (%)	Total (in millions of yen)
	China (%)	India (%)	U.S.A. (%)	Egypt (%)		
1907	20.9	51.6	20.6	1.5	5.4	116
1913	8.5	59.5	25.5	1.9	4.6	234
1917	9.0	63.1	23.9	1.7	2.3	335
1925	6.3	56.3	34.7	1.0	1.7	923
1932	4.2	20.6	71.8	3.4	–	447
1935	2.9	36.3	52.1	6.0	2.7	714

Source: K. Ōno, 'Dai Ichiji Taisenzengo no Gaikokubōeki' (Foreign trade around World War I), *Kōza Nihon Shihonshugi Hattatsushiron* (Studies of the development of Japanese capitalism), 2:. 265.

Table 7.2 Percentage Composition of Output of Japanese and British Yarn, by Counts: 1924–1935

Year	Japan				Britain		
	below 20s	20s	medium range*	fine count range*	up to 20s	21s–40s	41s and over
1924	34.2	31.9	30.7	3.2	73.2		26.8
1930	30.9	32.0	33.1	4.0	78.5		21.5
1933	28.3	27.1	38.8	5.9	39.4	41.1	19.6
1934	28.7	32.9	39.0	3.1	40.3	41.5	18.3
1935	28.1	28.8	39.7	3.4	41.8	40.5	17.7

Note: *The exact counts of these ranges are not available, but probably medium range is between 21s–40s.

Source: *Sen'i*, p. 50 for Japan; *Fifth Census of Production*, part 1 (1935), p. 23, for Britain.

range of 21s to 40s, their figures became very similar: 39 per cent for Japan, 41 per cent for Britain in the years 1933 to 1935. In Britain the percentage composition of the finer counts, over 40s, declined, while in Japan that of the medium range increased resulting in the proportionally smaller importance of the coarse counts.

As the Japanese cotton industry tended to produce similar products to those of Britain, Japanese cotton manufactured goods became less in demand and were eventually expelled from the rest of the Far Eastern markets, resulting in a radical change in outlets from the Far East to South and Southeast Asia (see table 7.4).

As table 7.4 (ii) shows, Japan was apparently successful in making an inroad into these markets at the expense of Britain and the Netherlands. Cotton, which originated in this region and spread west- and eastward, now came back, though at the expense of South and Southeast Asia, from the West and the Far East. In other words, the circle was closed.

Table 7.3 Countries to Which Japanese Cotton Textiles Were Exported 1912–1934

(i) *(per cent)*

Year	Far East		South and Southeast Asia			Others
	China	Korea	India	Dutch East Indies	Others	Others
1912	64.3	30.2	1.9	0.5	2.1	1.0
1916	54.9	17.9	14.4	3.0	1.3	9.0
1920	47.1	4.8	19.1	17.1	3.7	8.2

Source: K. Ōno, 'Dai Ichiji Taisenzengo no Gaikokubōeki', p. 247.

(ii)

Year	Far East		South and Southeast Asia		Others
	China	Korea	India	Dutch East Indies	Others
1929	29.6	–	32.5	10.8	27.1
1931	15.4	4.1	28.6	15.0	36.8
1932	9.2	5.1	31.7	17.3	36.5
1933	5.3	8.5	21.6	20.2	44.3
1934	2.3	9.9	17.5	17.1	53.2

Source: *Nihon no Sangyō to Bōeki no Hatten* (Development of Japanese industry and trade), ed. Mitsubishi Institute of Economic Research (Tokyo, 1935), p. 568

Table 7.4 Competition in the South and Southeast Asian Cotton Textile Markets between Japan and Britain: 1927–34

(i) Percentage share between Japan and Britain in India

Year	Japanese textiles	British textiles
1927–28	16.4	78.2
1931–32	43.8	49.4
1932–33	47.3	48.7
1933–34	43.9	53.5
1934–35	39.6	58.5

(ii) Percentage share among Japan, Britain and Netherlands in the Dutch East Indian markets

Year	Japan	Netherlands	Britain	Total
1929	41.0	28.4	19.5	88.9
1932	69.3	15.0	6.5	90.8
1933	83.7	4.7	2.8	91.2
1934	82.2	8.8	1.7	92.7

Source: *Nihon no Sangyō to Bōeki no Hatten*, pp. 620 and 626.

Epilogue

TWO MODES OF 'ESCAPE-FROM-ASIA'

An excerpt from *Nihon Bunmei to Kindai Seiyō* (1991)
(Japanese Civilisation and the Modern West)
translated and edited by
Jean Connell Hoff

1. 'NATIONAL SECLUSION' AND THE 'MODERN WORLD-SYSTEM'

After studying Japanese economic history at Waseda University, I enrolled in the Faculty of History at Oxford University. (I might mention in passing that in Britain economic history tends to be regarded as a field of history; in the United States it is usually considered a branch of economics.) But the history of Japan—to say nothing of East Asia, Southeast Asia, or the Middle East—was not included among the areas of historical research in the Oxford history faculty, and so I ended up reading these subjects in the Faculty of Oriental Studies. And yet, probably one of the most important events prior to the outbreak of the First World War was Japan's emergence in world history as one of the five great powers; for Japan not to be studied in the Oxford Faculty of History seems strange. Even adopting a European perspective, the study of history since the 'Age of Discovery' ought to encompass the entire world. Obsessed with this idea, I fixed my sights on Asia, which stretched out between Britain and Japan. The viewpoint of the present book—to consider the relationship between the decline of the old civilisations of Asia and the rise of modern civilisation in Britain and Japan—took shape at that time.

The traditional attitude of economic historians, however, is also problematic. They have tended to regard the industrial revolution in Britain as a spontaneous development and to assume that other countries are either trying to catch up with Britain, have overtaken it, or are still undeveloped. But even in the case of the industrial revolution in Japan, the situation is not that simple.

Japan's emergence as the first industrial country in Asia took place nearly a century after Britain had emerged as the first industrial country in Europe. The now widely accepted explanation for Japan's success at industrialisation is that Japan, being a late-comer, was able to catch up by adopting technology from the industrially advanced countries of the West. The theory that less advanced countries have an advantage in industrialising because of the very fact of their backwardness is called the Gerschenkron model. This model, however, cannot answer the following two questions.

First, since, like Japan, all the other regions of Asia were late to develop, why didn't they too take advantage of their backwardness? The late nineteenth century, when Japan industrialised, was the period in which the great powers of the West were pursuing their imperialist policies. The course of modern history in Japan was decisively different from that of other Asian countries, which either became colonies of the great powers or were reduced to subordinate positions. Why did Japan alone of all the late-developing regions of Asia escape that unhappy fate?

Secondly, Japan is also different from other late-developing industrial countries in the West. All the Western late-comers who caught up with Britain enacted protective tariffs to counter British imports and protect their domestic industries. In *The National System of Political Economy* (1841), Friedrich List concluded that 'the result of general free trade would . . . be . . . a universal subjection of less advanced nations to the supremacy of the predominant manufacturing, commercial, and naval power', and he used this argument to justify protectionism in 'less advanced' Germany.[1] Japan, however, had been deprived of its rights to impose tariffs by the open port treaties of the Ansei period (1854–60) and did not have protective tariffs. Why did Japan alone among all the late-developing countries in the world succeed in industrialising despite being disarmed, as it were, in this way?

To answer these questions we need to include both Asia and Europe in our perspective and consider the synchronous relationship between

Japan, Europe, and Asia. Up until now, however, most studies have approached Japanese economic history from the perspective of comparisons with the economies of Europe. Under the influence of Marx's materialistic concept of history, Europe, which passed from a feudal system to capitalism, has been taken as the standard, and the question has been when and how did this transition occur in Japan. Or the stages of growth in Western capitalism—from mercantilism to liberalism to imperialism—have been taken as the standard, and the question has been how have these stages manifested themselves in Japan. The reason for this approach is the dominance of a single-track stage-of-growth theory such as the one Marx described in *Das Kapital*: countries that are more industrially developed simply display an image of the future for countries at a lower stage of development. A powerful argument against the Marxist view of history is Walt Rostow's *The Stages of Economic Growth*, which is subtitled 'A non-Communist Manifesto'. (Instead of believing that socialism is the stage that follows capitalism, Rostow argues that socialism and capitalism are merely two different forms of industrialisation [take-off]). But Rostow's work too is a single-track theory, which traces the stages of growth—'the preconditions for take-off, the take-off, the drive to maturity, and the age of high mass-consumption'—at the single-country level.[2] One of the tasks of the present book has been to describe the dynamic interplay between the decline of the old agricultural civilisations of Asia and the rise of the new industrial civilisation in Europe and Japan.

As grist for our argument let us take Morishima Michio's book *Why Has Japan 'Succeeded'?* and Immanuel Wallerstein's *The Modern World-System*. The late Morishima Michio, a professor emeritus at the London School of Economics and a specialist in theoretical economics, was also an expert on Britain, noted for his book (in Japanese) on Britain in the Thatcher Era. In addition, he challenged Japanese perceptions of the 'British disease' in *Igirisu to Nihon* (Britain and Japan), and gave his own views on the Meiji Restoration (1868) in a continuation of the latter work, the English version of which, *Why Has Japan 'Succeeded'?*, has been well received.

Immanuel Wallerstein, a protégé of the late Fernand Braudel, the leader of the French Annales School, has published a four-volume compendium of his research which spans the Middle Ages and the modern period under the title *The Modern World-System*, the capitalist world

economy that first appeared in Europe.[4] With this work, Wallerstein, the
founding editor of the journal *Review*, stirred up a whirlwind of contro-
versy among scholars of social and economic history. Both Wallerstein
and Morishima adopt an international perspective, and there is much in
their arguments that deserves close attention, but instead of introducing
their ideas I will single out those points in need of criticism or supple-
mental explanation in order to make my own sketch of the formation of
Japanese civilisation.

My main topic is the role of Tokugawa Japan (1603–1868) in world
history. The internal conditions that made possible Japan's spectacular
development after it opened itself to the outside world in the latter half
of the nineteenth century were all prepared during the period of national
seclusion that preceded it. And the period that preceded the Tokugawa
era was a time of dazzling internationalism unlike anything Japan had
ever experienced before, a time of openness to the world when foreign
goods from Tang China and the culture of the *Nanban* or 'Southern barbarians' (as the first Europeans were called) entered the country. Thus,
the period of national seclusion (*sakoku*) was sandwiched between two
periods of national openness (*kaikoku*) and corresponds exactly to the
period in which Europe's 'modern world-system', a capitalist European
world economy, took shape. Historians of Japan's early modern period,
regrettably, have been so buried in Japanese documents that their range
of vision has not extended to the rest of the world. In what follows, I will
focus on the, at first glance, seemingly unrelated 'modern world-system'
and Japan's 'national seclusion' and take a hard look at the mutual connections between the two and their place in world history.

2. DID ISOLATIONISM PREVENT THE DESTRUCTION OF JAPAN'S HANDICRAFT INDUSTRY?

Morishima's book *Why Has Japan 'Succeeded'?* is subtitled 'Western
Technology and the Japanese Ethos'. As this title indicates Morishima's
interests are two-fold. First, how did Japan overcome the technology gap
with the more advanced West? Second, what effect did the Japanese
'ethos' have on Japan's modernisation? Ethos refers to the internal
motivation that prompts people to engage in ethical social behaviour;

Morishima describes it as 'an ideological driving force'.[5] In choosing this word, Morishima had in mind Max Weber's *The Protestant Ethic and the Spirit of Capitalism* (1904/5).[6] In that work Weber advanced the idea that capitalism, which arose in the modern West, had its own unique ethos — Weber called it the 'spirit of capitalism' — and that the 'Protestant ethic' played a decisive role in its development.

First, let us review the argument for a Confucian ethic, which is Morishima's main concern. Attempts to explore the relationship between Confucianism and economic growth have been made for quite some time, but interest in the subject increased with the rise in the 1970s and 1980s of the so-called newly industrialising economies of Taiwan, Korea, Hong Kong, and Singapore. This interest centred on the question of whether economic development in Japan and the Asian NIEs was in any way connected to a Confucian ethic. In *The Protestant Ethic and the Spirit of Capitalism*, Weber argued that the 'worldly asceticism' of Puritanism gave rise to the spirit of capitalism; in his *Gesammelte Aufsatze zur Religionssoziologie* (Collected essays on the sociology of religion; 1920/21), he concluded that Confucianism did not have an ethos of this sort from which capitalism might spring.[7] But Japan undoubtedly succeeded in assimilating capitalism. Was it an exception to the Weber thesis? If Japan was not an exception, and given the rise of the NIEs, then it was only natural to examine whether Confucianism, a dominant belief system in these areas which had undergone economic development, was in fact an impediment to capitalism as Weber argued. If the Weber thesis is correct, then Confucianism too must have an ethos of frugality and asceticism that served as a generating force behind the rise of Asian capitalism. It should come as no surprise that efforts have been made to discover just such an ethos.[8]

In fact, however, efforts to put the economic development of the NIEs in the same category as that of Japan pose certain problems. One of these problems has to do with the timing of industrialisation; the other is related to the different historical experiences Japan and the rest of Asia have had. To be more precise, Japan's economic development had already taken place a hundred years before that of the NIEs, a time difference that cannot be ignored. That is not all. The experiences of Japan and the other Confucian countries at the end of the nineteenth century were decisively different. China became a semicolony, Korea was colonised by Japan, Vietnam fell to the French, and Singapore and Hong Kong came under British rule. Though all were part of the Confucian cultural sphere, why did the Confucian ethos work to the advantage of one country and to the disadvantage of all the others? The fact remains that only Japan succeeded in maintaining its political independence and evolving into an industrialised state.

Before applying the Weber thesis, we must first examine the thesis itself. Here, too, there are problems. First, the Weber thesis is based on statistics on Protestants in the state of Baden collected by Weber's student Martin Offenbacher and lacks broad corroborative evidence. Second, whereas Weber identified 'Puritanism' as the motivating factor behind capitalism, Werner Sombart in *Luxury and Capitalism* (1922) advanced the exact opposite view—that luxury and extravagance were the driving forces behind economic growth.[9] The argument has not been settled, but—and this is my third point—assuming that people were only frugal and self-denying, how would an effective demand develop? There are other problems as well, but I will limit myself to pointing out these three reservations.

A pioneering attempt to find the basis of Japanese modernisation in Confucian ethics is Robert N. Bellah's *Tokugawa Religion*.[10] Bellah's effort was not successful. The practical ethics of Ishida Baigan (1685–1744), the founder of Sekimon Shingaku, which Bellah identified as Japan's Calvinism, did provide an ethical basis for commercial activities, but the period in which Baigan was active preceded the Meiji period by more than a hundred years and Sekimon Shingaku itself had declined by the end of the Tokugawa period. Thus, there does not appear to be any temporal cause and effect relationship between Sekimon Shingaku and Japanese capitalism. Bellah's views were roundly criticised by Maruyama Masao, and he later retracted them.[11]

Any attempt to apply the Weber thesis should also take notice of Weber's observation that within the same Christian world Protestant countries made a greater contribution to economic development than Catholic countries did. A comparison between developed and less developed countries in the same Confucian cultural sphere, it is thought, would truly exemplify the Weber thesis. According to Morishima, the Confucian ethos of China is based on 'benevolence' and 'filial piety' whereas the Japanese Confucian ethos is characterised by 'loyalty'.[12] This distinction corresponds to the difference between the Catholic and Protestant ethos in Weber's thesis and should probably be given high marks for isolating a 'Protestant' reformist element in the Confucian cultural sphere.

But there are some problems with this approach. First of all, Morishima nowhere takes into consideration the role of Buddhism in Japan's ancient period and Middle Ages. Sir George Sansom once argued that Nichiren Buddhism corresponded to European Protestantism.[13] Buddhist monks were the most intransigent opponents of the Jesuit missionaries during their proselytising activities at the end of the sixteenth century. And if the Ikkō Sect, which caused difficulties for local warlords in the late fifteenth and sixteenth centuries, had been victorious, Japan might well have become a Buddhist monarchy. How can an ethos as powerful as this be ignored? Secondly, Morishima considers that loyalty first emerged as Japan's quintessential Confucian virtue at the time of Shōtoku Taishi (573–621) and gradually spread to the upper classes, the warrior class, and finally to the Japanese salarymen of today, but a cause and effect relationship between this ethic and the rise of Japanese capitalism is unclear.[14] According to Weber, the Protestant ethic assumed decisive importance at a historical turning point, the transition between feudalism and capitalism. According to Morishima, the Japanese Confucian ethic spread at a sluggish rate, taking more than a thousand years to pass from the upper classes to the general public. As in the case of Bellah, it must be said that Morishima too fails to explain the temporal relationship between the Confucian ethic and Japanese capitalism.

Next, let us test Morishima's argument about the technology gap. Morishima has this to say about the isolationism of Tokugawa Japan: 'By following a policy of national seclusion the Tokugawa Bakufu had, quite unconsciously, implemented a perfect protective trade policy. . . . The isolationist policy . . . was an effective means of controlling imports over a period of 200 years.'[15] Why was an isolationist policy needed to protect trade or control imports?

A comparison of Japanese agriculture and industry with those of the Western countries clearly shows that Japan then had a comparative advantage in mining and agriculture. It would have been more beneficial for her

to specialise in them and exchange their products for foreign manufactured goods than to produce those goods within the country. Therefore,
if free trade had been permitted between Japan and the West, Japanese
handicraft manufacturing industries might have been wiped out. Thus
this isolationist policy prevented the Tokugawa economy from specialising
in primary industries and allowed it to maintain manufacturing industries, though at a primitive level.[16]

Morishima concludes: 'If one looks at it in this way, the isolation does
not express a disregard for Western culture and technology, but rather fear
and admiration of it.'[17]

Various arguments have been made for and against the national seclusion policy of Tokugawa Japan. *Sakoku*, written shortly after the Second
World War by Watsuji Tetsurō, is representative of arguments that view
isolationism negatively because it cut Japan off from scientific developments in the rest of the world. The book begins, 'With their defeat in
World War II, the Japanese people presented a truly sorrowful sight.'
Japan's national flaw, Watsuji believed, could be 'summed up as a lack of
the scientific spirit.'[18] He traced the reason for Japan's failure to develop
a scientific spirit back to the period of isolationism and made a long and
detailed examination of Japanese and Western history to back up his contention. *Sakoku*, which was subtitled 'Japan's Tragedy', concludes with the
sentence: 'It has been left to us today to pay the bill.'[19]

On the other hand, Engelbert Kaempfer, a German physician who
was in Japan between 1690–92, wrote a history of Japan that is said to
have been the basis for Fichte's theory of peace in a closed commercial
state. Kaempfer described Japan as follows:

> . . . civil, obliging, virtuous, in art and industry exceeding all other
> nations, possess'd of an excellent Country, enrich'd by mutual Trade
> and Commerce among themselves, couragious, abundantly provided
> with all the necessaries of life, and withal enjoying the fruits of peace
> and tranquillity. Such a train of prosperities must needs convince them,
> . . . That their Country was never in a happier condition than it now is
> . . . shut up, and kept from all Commerce and Communication with
> foreign nations.[20]

The uniqueness of Morishima's discussion of Japan's seclusion policy lies in its positive assessment of isolationism in terms of economics. It is a new way of presenting the case from an economist's perspective. Morishima uses the idea of a technology gap between Japan and the West as a way of explaining the contribution of the seclusion policy to the Japanese economy. This argument rests on a single theory in economics, the theory of comparative cost of production.[21]

3. WESTERN GOODS WERE UNSALEABLE

Morishima argues that the Tokugawa seclusion policy protected Japan's handicraft industry from being overrun by Western exports and prevented Japan from becoming a purely agricultural country, and that without such a policy 'Japanese handicraft manufacturing industries might have been wiped out' by the more advanced industries of the West. When we look at the economic facts, however, this contention does not seem valid.

What precisely were the manufactured goods that Europe could boast of at the time Japan was implementing its isolationist policy? Woollens, guns, and clocks. Cotton cloth, which would later become the West's most important manufactured product, was not yet being made in Europe at this time. The core of European exports was woollen cloth. But woollens, naturally, did not sell in tropical regions such as India or Southeast Asia and hardly at all in Japan and China, which had been expected to be promising markets. Contemporary reports from the East India Company are filled with the same message: woollens are unsaleable.

But that is not all. Quite the opposite of Morishima's assumptions, it was not the handicraft industries of Asia that were on the verge of destruction, but those of Europe, to which Asian silks and cottons were brought. In a frantic effort to protect their own textile industries, England and the other countries of Western Europe around 1700 began enacting not just protective tariffs but laws prohibiting the import, and even the use of, Asian textiles—how effective these laws were is another story. To imagine that Europe was more industrially advanced than Asia at the time Japan adopted its seclusionist policy is to project onto the past the relationship between the industrialised West and the less advanced countries of Asia in the modern period. This is far from the truth and does not reflect the realities at that time.

As far as Europe's other exports were concerned, Japanese had a different sense of time from what had been developed in Europe. The first mechanical clock to arrive in Japan is said to be the one that Francis Xavier presented to Ōuchi Yoshitaka in 1551. By as early as the beginning of the seventeenth century indigenous clock makers had made the *wadokei*, a distinctively Japanese clock based on Japan's 'indefinite' or 'varying-length' sense of time in which the length of an hour varies with the season. Japan was the only country in Asia to use imported clocks as models from which to make its own mechanical clocks—turret (*yagura*) clocks, pillow (*daimyō*) clocks, pillar (*shaku*) clocks, wall (*kake*) clocks, *inrō* clocks that resembled a pocket watch, even a myriad year clock (*mannen jimeishō*, lit., ten-thousand year self-ringing bell), a kind of astronomical clock perfected by Tanaka Hisashige in 1851 that combined the latest European clock mechanisms and the finest Japanese clock-making craftsmanship. Japan's mechanical clocks based on 'irregular' time were unlike any known elsewhere in the world.[22]

As for guns, the first matchlock is said to have been brought to Tanegashima by the Portuguese in 1543, and Japanese soon mastered the art of making them. Less than ten years later, guns had spread to Bōnotsu (in present Kagoshima Prefecture), Hirado (Nagasaki Prefecture), Bungo (Oita Prefecture), and Sakai (Osaka Prefecture). Around this time Arabs, Indians, and Chinese were all using firearms, but except for Europeans only the Japanese succeeded in mass-producing guns. In less than a half century, Japan had become the largest user of guns in the world. At the battle of Nagashino in 1575, the combined armies of Oda Nobunaga and Tokugawa Ieyasu included 3,000 men armed with matchlocks drawn up in three ranks and firing in volleys against the mounted troops of Takeda Katsuyori. This strategy was the most advanced in the world at that time. Guns were one of the main reasons the Japanese army easily defeated the Korean army during Toyotomi Hideyoshi's invasions of Korea in 1592 and 1597. Indeed, the flintlock, which was a refinement on the matchlock, may well have been introduced into Europe from Japan via the Portuguese.

4. CRITICISM OF MORISHIMA'S 'SECLUSION POLICY' ARGUMENT

At the time Japan implemented its seclusion policy, it was one of the world's 'have' countries.[23] It engaged in technology exchanges and adopted European shipbuilding techniques for its shogun-licenced trading ships. Even more importantly, the country was blessed with natural resources—timber, iron sand, gold, silver, and copper. It would be rash to assume that Japanese industrial resources and technology were inferior to those of Europe in the seventeenth century. Thus Morishima's contention that isolationism was adopted 'to protect Japan's craft industries from the West's export offensive and to prevent Japan's becoming a purely agricultural country' does not hold true.[24]

For the sake of the argument, let us concede this point and suppose, as Morishima suggests, that the significance of Tokugawa isolationism lay in the fact that Japan was able to protect its handicraft industries by closing the country to trade. Even in that case, however, Morishima's assumptions still do not seem valid. Why not? During the more than 200 years that Japan was cut off from the rest of the world, Western Europe experienced the industrial revolution; thus the technology gap was far greater at the end of the Tokugawa period than it had been at the beginning. As a result, when Japan was forcibly integrated into the free trade system by the open port treaties of 1858, Japan was in far greater danger of declining into an exporter of agricultural goods and an importer of manufacturing goods than it had been when isolationism was first imposed. If we follow Morishima's line of argument, the possibility of Japan's being reduced to an agricultural country was much higher at the time the country was opened to the world than it had been at the time of its closure.

Contrary to his intention, Morishima is relying on an argument that explains why Japan should have 'failed' instead of why it has 'succeeded'. Morishima's view that isolation was comparable to import controls or trade protection does not reflect the facts. But that is not all; it is even inconsistent with his stated objective of explaining Japan's 'success'. In short, Morishima's argument is a failure both as a theory and as a proof thereof. This failure is related to the theory of comparative cost of production that Morishima uses. Morishima has tried to apply this theory in a somewhat facile way without considering its limitations. These limitations involve the cultural nature of a commodity. No commodity exists independently of its own inherent value or the capabilities of the people in the society that possesses it.

When Ricardo proposed his theory of comparative cost of production in international trade, he compared the costs of woollens and wine in England and Portugal. This approach was appropriate because wines and woollens were both part of the food and clothing cultures in the two countries. To put it another way, the products that constituted the foods consumed in both countries and the clothes worn there were similar. Both England and Portugal had a clothing culture in which people wore wool, and both had a food culture in which people drank wine. Ricardo's explanation is based on a comparison of quantitative values, and comparing differences in the costs required to produce commodities used in two societies, that is, quantitative differences of price and value, is meaningful when those societies have similar life styles. In places that have similar demand structures, people will probably choose low-cost goods. But when cultures differ in the foods that are eaten, the clothes that are worn, the homes that are lived in, as they do in Japan and in Britain or Western Europe, then the difference between commodities used by each society is too great for a comparison of this sort to have any meaning. Let us take an example.

Vasilii Golovnin, a Russian naval officer who was interned in Japan for more than two years between 1811–13, had this to say about the differences in food and clothing in Japan and the West:

> The chief and most useful productions of Japan are the following: Rice, fish, radishes, salt, cotton, silk . . . . Rice is the chief production, and nearly the only thing the Japanese use for bread; it is to them what rye is to us; nay, it is even more important . . . . Fish are in Japan what meat is in Europe . . . . The radish supplies the place of our cabbage . . . . Silk and cotton, besides the uses to which they are generally applied, supply also the place of our wool, hemp, flax, down, feathers, and furs; for whatever is worn in Japan is made of these two articles. They, likewise, make of cotton stuff travelling cloaks, cases for arms, and other things, and tobacco-pouches, which are varnished in such a manner that they may be taken for leather.[25]

Golovnin compares the significance and use of Japanese goods with the products found in Russia and elsewhere within his own cultural sphere. When peoples with totally different systems of food and clothing trade with one another, it should come as no surprise, for example, that nineteenth-century Britons used imports of Japan's chief food staple, rice, as industrial paste.

For the moment, let us call the assemblage of goods that are the mainstays of the food, clothing, and shelter in a particular society that society's 'product complex'. An object used by a society has a name and a function, or, to put it another way, it has a cultural significance. By giving two sticks of wood the name *hashi*, for example, we imbue them with a cultural significance that expresses the eating habits of the Japanese people. It is possible to go through the respective areas of food, clothing, and shelter and point out the individual items that support each area and the cultural phenomena related to them. If we call the assemblage of items that form the substrate of these cultural phenomena a 'product complex', we can probably call all the cultural phenomena inherent in each item a society's 'culture complex'.

In Japan and the West in those days, both the culture complex of each society and the underlying product complex were different. Ricardo, of course, took no notice of these differences at all. Because they were beyond the scope of his concern, cultural similarities were the unspoken premise of Ricardo's thesis. Morishima's line of argument fails because he never noticed that this premise had broken down.

5. CRITICISM OF THE STAGES-OF-GROWTH THEORY

Under pressure from the Western powers, India and China were forced down the path to dependency; why was Japan able to develop into a capitalist economy and avoid following this same route? The answer according to the linear stage-of-growth argument is that advanced countries (e.g., Europe) provide an image of the future for less advanced countries (e.g., Japan), but this answer contains a number of logical inconsistencies.

First, the differences in the stages of development in Japan, India, and China were insignificant in comparison to their productivity gap with Britain. Compared to the 'workshop of the world', all the Asian countries were still in the handicraft stage. Even though the stage of economic growth in Japan was higher than that in India or China, there was little difference between them when measured against the overwhelmingly high productivity of Western mechanised manufacturing organised along a factory system.

Suppose for the sake of argument that the stages of growth in China and Japan had been significantly different. Even so, there are problems. If we accept the concept that is central to the stage-of-growth theory, then we must assume that Japan escaped colonisation because it was at a relatively high stage of growth. In the back of their minds Japanese economic historians have assumed they could explain the development of capitalism in Japan by proving that Japan was at a high stage of growth in the late Tokugawa period. But this is a subjective assumption on their part. Once again the question needs to be asked: if the high stage of economic development in Japan in the late Tokugawa period was close to that of the West on the eve of capitalism, would this have been a condition for Japan's success in becoming a capitalist economy? Wouldn't this same logic better explain the likelihood that the Japanese economy would fall subject to the Western great powers?

As a matter of fact, the Japanese economy in the late Tokugawa period undoubtedly was at a higher level than other Asian economies; a regional and societal division of labour had developed, and domestic markets had been created. After Japan was opened to trade, the bulk of its imports were from Britain; moreover, Japan had been deprived of its right to enact protective tariffs and thus competed with Britain under a system of free trade. What was the significance of this? During the Tokugawa period Japan had developed a money economy based upon social and regional divisions of labour; thus, in Japan more than in any other country of Asia market conditions and competition conditions were such that any price differences between Western goods and Japanese goods would be meaningful. The fact that Japan had a mature economy in the late Tokugawa period means that the conditions existed which would expose it to direct competition with the West. If that is the case, then the fact that Japan was more economically advanced than the other countries of Asia is a sign that, precisely the opposite of what has hitherto been believed, it faced a higher risk of succumbing to the commodities market of the Western economies.

The opposite argument to this can be made using China as a comparison. China had a higher degree of danger of becoming a colony, it has been argued, because it was at a relatively low stage of growth compared to Japan. In view of the fact that China did not become a colony like India but was only semicolonised and also that it succeeded in opening the way to socialism, some historians have attempted to find the seeds of spontaneous development within China.[26] Still, what needs to be questioned is the premise itself, that the lower the stage of growth the higher the degree of danger. In the beginning Marx clearly made this assumption. Once the Chinese market came in contact with capitalism, he wrote, 'the cheap prices of its [the West's] commodities are the heavy artillery with which it batters down all Chinese walls . . . .'[27] 'The spinners and weavers have suffered greatly under this foreign competition . . . dissolution must follow as surely as that of any mummy carefully preserved in a hermetically sealed coffin, whenever it is brought into contact with the open air . . . . The Chinese revolution will throw the spark into the overloaded mine of the present industrial system and cause the explosion of the long-prepared general crisis.'[28] In short, Marx predicted that Britain, where productivity was high, would cause a revolution in China, where it was low, and lead to proletarianisation.

But contrary to this expectation, British-made commodities did not permeate China. Thus a few years later Marx went so far as to seek the cause in China's hopelessly backward society and economy. 'With the present economical framework of Chinese society, which turns upon diminutive agriculture and domestic manufactures as its pivots, any large import of foreign produce is out of the question.'[29] In other words, he sought the cause in Asian stagnation, that is, the amalgam of farming and industry. Marx's reasoning had undergone a complete change. He now argued that China had escaped the danger of becoming a market for manufactured goods because it was at a low stage of economic growth. This was a 180-degree reversal in the argument. Instead of arguing that a low stage of growth increased China's risk of colonialisation, he shifted to the opposite conclusion: because it was low, there was less likelihood that Western capitalism would penetrate.

Let us take the example of the textile industry. The clothing worn by the general public in Japan's early modern period was made of cotton. The

bulk of the imported goods after the country was opened to foreign trade
was British-made cotton cloth. From the standpoint of both Morishima's
comparative-cost-of-production argument and the stage-of-growth argument, if the cost of a product is in inverse proportion to productivity, then
the cotton cloth made in Japan at a low stage of productivity would be no
match for the cotton cloth made in Britain at a high stage of productivity and would inevitably be driven out of the market. According to the
comparative-cost-of-production argument, it would be more advantageous
for Britain, which had superiority in manufacturing, to specialise in making cloth and for Japan, which had superiority in agriculture, to specialise
in growing cotton. But the historical experience of Japan's textile industry
undermines these logical expectations. Cotton-growing in Japan declined,
and textile manufacturing developed so dramatically that as early as before
World War I, Japan had become the most serious threat to Britain in Asia.

As is clear even from this single example, neither the comparative-
cost-of-production argument nor the stage-of-growth argument is able
to give a satisfactory explanation of the economic relationship between
Japan and the West. At the very least, the idea that the development of
capitalism in Japan can be considered in terms of stages of growth using
the West as a yardstick is superficial and inaccurate.

6. JAPAN AND THE WEST — SIMILARITIES IN PRODUCT COMPLEXES

According to Wallerstein, the 'modern world-system' originated around
the year 1450 and took final shape around 1640 along the perimeter of the
Atlantic Ocean with the establishment of a 'new European division of
labour', a three-tiered structure consisting of 'core states', the 'semiperiphery', and the 'periphery.' That period corresponds to the period in Japanese
history in which the national seclusion system evolved. It began with the
Onin War (1467–77), which marked the start of more than a century of civil
wars, extended through the consolidation of power under Oda Nobunaga,
Toyotomi Hideyoshi, and Tokugawa Ieyasu, and culminated in the expulsion of the Portuguese in 1639. The formative periods for the modern world-
system and the national seclusion system are identical. Nevertheless, they
seem to be unrelated events that occurred separately on the two extremities

of the Eurasian continent. In fact, Japanese isolationism is not included
in Wallerstein's description of the formation of the modern world-system.
In his terminology, Asia as a whole belongs to the 'external arena' and has
nothing to do with the modern world-system. But, as I shall explain below,
one should not go so far as to say that the two are completely unconnected.

According to the often cited quote from Marx, 'The specific task
of bourgeois society is the establishment of a world market . . . . As the
world is round, this seems to have been completed by the colonization
of California and Australia and the opening up of China and Japan.'[30] As
this quote implies, the usual explanation is that Japan's connection to the
modern world-system was the result of the opening of the country in 1858.
For the moment let us accept this commonly accepted view. What, then,
did members of the modern world-system want from Japan that could be
gained by opening the country? The Western great powers forced Japan
to conclude commercial treaties and integrated the Japanese economy
into the free-trade system with Britain at its centre. In other words, they
wanted free trade. What, then, did the great powers want from Japan that
could be gained by free trade? In order to know the answer to that question, we need to examine what the components of free trade were.

The core items sold by the great powers were cotton cloth and sugar,
and the core items they bought—Japan's export goods—were raw silk and
tea. Let us concentrate our attention on these four items, cotton cloth,
sugar, raw silk, and tea and nothing else. At that time, raw cotton was
grown on American plantations, then carried to Britain, where it was
made into cloth that was sold in world markets. Sugar was grown on plantations in Java and the West Indies; tea was cultivated in China until the
mid-nineteenth century, on plantations in India and Ceylon thereafter.
Raw silk was exported in large quantities from China as a raw material
for silk cloth manufacturers in France and Italy and later in the United
States. In short, all these products had been international trade goods
before Japan came in contact with the modern world-system and were in
wide demand within that system.

I would also like to draw attention to the fact that Japan became self-
sufficient in all these items during the period of national seclusion. They
were essential items of food and clothing for Japanese in the Tokugawa

period. This fact does not seem to have attracted much attention. One reason for this is the inadequacy of the dialogue between historians of Japan's modern and premodern periods. As two Japanese economic historians have written, Japan in the early Meiji period had the very good luck to have two major export items, tea and raw silk, and the natural corollary to this good fortune was the appearance of a huge foreign demand for raw silk and tea.[31] The converse to this is that Japan must be regarded as having the very bad luck to have two major import items, cotton cloth and sugar, the influx of which caused a crisis in the indigenous industries that produced them. The problem is that the authors are content to note Japan's good luck or bad luck without ever asking why these items were in demand in the first place.

First of all, isn't it strange that before Japan opened its doors to foreign trade, the products that would be important as items of international commerce would be the very ones that Japan not only already possessed, but that were indispensable to the lives of the Japanese people? That is not all. Cotton thread and cotton cloth became the pivotal commodities in Japan's industrial revolution, and raw silk was important for acquiring foreign currency. Is it proper to relegate the very products that would play the leading role in prewar Japan's economic development to the realm of 'chance'? The problem is this: why were the products that were important to the modern world-system not only available domestically in Japan but indispensable to Japanese life? To put it another way, why did Japan's product complex under the national seclusion system resemble that of the West under the modern world-system?

As a way of exploring the 'accidental' historical 'inevitability' that cotton cloth, raw silk, and the other products in the modern world-system would also exist simultaneously as items indispensable to the lives of the Japanese people in the Tokugawa period, let us try to pose the question in this way: when did these four items begin to be used in Japan, and when did they begin to be traded as international commercial goods within the modern world-system?

It then becomes clear that Japan was completely self sufficient in these products by the Tokugawa period. In the Muromachi period (1336–1573), for example, ordinary Japanese wore clothing made of hemp, silk was a luxury item, and cotton cloth was an import. Cotton textiles began to be made in Japan in the latter half of the sixteenth century, and by the end of the seventeenth century Japan had succeeded in becoming completely self-sufficient in cotton cloth.

Sugar was an imported luxury item in the Muromachi period and was regarded as a medicine; bean paste, honey, and amazura (a syrup made from sweet arrowroot) were used as sweeteners in the period when there was no sugar. Sugar was first made in Japan in 1610 in Amami Ōshima, to which Sunao Kawachi brought sugar cane seedlings from Fuzhou, China. Sugar-making methods were transmitted to the Ryukyus (Okinawa) in the 1620s. Japan succeeded in producing sugar from sugar cane in Kii (Wakayama Prefecture) in the late eighteenth century. By the end of the Edo period, it was also being made in Satsuma (Kagoshima), Sanuki (Kagawa), Awa (Tokushima), Izumi (Osaka), Suruga (Shizuoka), Tōtōmi (west of the Ōigawa-river, Shizuoka) and elsewhere.

The manufacture of silk textiles was introduced into Japan from Korea around the year 1100, but the high-quality, Chinese-made raw silk known as 'white thread' and the fine silk cloth made from it were still being imported in the early modern period. It not until after the eighteenth century that Japan could meet its own demand domestically.

The fashion for tea drinking, which became popular with the warrior class along with Zen Buddhism in the Kamakura period (1185–1333), had spread to the merchant class by the end of the Muromachi period and become an everyday event (in fact, *nichijō sahanji*, the expression which means 'everyday event' in Japanese, contains the character for 'tea'). The standard porcelain for tea use is said to have been Seto ware first made by Katô Shirôzaemon; before then tea masters normally used import ware. Porcelain came to be produced domestically after Korean potters were forcibly taken back to Japan at the time of Hideyoshi's invasions of Korea. Some people even call the Korean campaigns 'the Pottery Wars'. Thereafter, Japanese pottery-making techniques improved dramatically, leading to the indigenous production of porcelain and the creation of special production sites. Eventually, it became possible to supply a complete set of Japanese-made tea utensils for the tea ceremony.

In Europe the beginning of a popular demand for the preceding items took place at roughly the same time as in Japan, that is, the end of the Middle Ages and the beginning of the early modern period. In medieval

Europe, the upper classes had worn silks, linen was also a luxury item, and ordinary people wore woollens or fur. Fustian, a mixture of cotton and hemp, became popular at the end of the Middle Ages, but pure cotton was unknown. When Europeans first saw cotton growing in India, they drew pictures of sheep hanging in a tree—that was how strange cotton seemed to them. Indian cotton cloth was brought into England on a regular basis after the 1660s. Tea and sugar were popularised there at about the same time.[32]

Chinese and Japanese porcelain started to be imported at the beginning of the seventeenth century, but early in the eighteenth century Europeans had succeeded in imitating them. Meissen in Germany, Delft in Holland, Sèvres in France, Chelsea, Worcester, Derby, Wedgwood in England are all famous production sites, but the wares they produced were exceedingly expensive. Mass production became possible in Britain when tariffs on tea dropped from 119 percent to 12.5 percent in 1784, and the increase in tea consumption stimulated the demand for porcelain.

7. 'THE TRADING WORLD OF ASIA'

Where did Japanese and Europeans get these products? Consider the case of Japanese before the period of national seclusion. Japanese activities overseas lasted for nearly three centuries, from around 1350 when *wakō*, Japanese pirates, began full-scale operations to the 1630s when the isolation policy was adopted. Japan's trading partners were not only its neighbours, China and Korea; as time passed, Japanese reached the regions they called 'Tenjiku' and 'Nanban'. Japanese trips to Tenjiku and Nanban took place around the same time that the Europeans also arrived in these places, places the Europeans called the 'East Indies'. The words Tenjiku, Nanban, and the East Indies all refer to the same places, what today is known as South and Southeast Asia. In those days, it was an enormous centre of international commerce. Indians, Southeast Asians, Arabs, Chinese, and many other nationalities gathered there to trade. Tomé Pires in the *Suma Oriental que trata do Maar Roxo ete os Chins* (ca. 1514) described the people trading in the Moluccas at the beginning of the sixteenth century and the places they came from as follows:

Moors from Cairo, Mecca, Aden, Abyssinians, men of Kilwa, Malindi, Ormuz, Parsees, *Rumes*, Turks, Turkomans, Christian Armenians, Gujaratees, men of Chaul, Dabhol, Goa, of the Kingdom of Deccan, Malabars and Klings, merchants from Orissa, Ceylon, Bengal, Arakan, Pegu, Siamese, men of Kedah, Malays, men of Pahang, Patani, Cambodia, *Champa*, Cochin China, Chinese, *Lequeos*, men of Brunei, *Luçoes*, men of *Tamjompura*, Laue, Banka, Linga (they have a thousand other islands), Moluccas, Banda, Bima, Timor, Madura, Java, Sunda, Palembang, Jambi, Tongkal, Indragiri, Kappatta, Menangkabau, Siak, *Arqua* (*Arcat?*), Aru, *Bata*, country of the *Tomjano*, Pase, Pedir, Maldives.[33]

Japanese and Europeans first obtained the products just discussed around the end of the Middle Ages and the beginning of the early modern period through contact with this Asian trading world. What needs emphasising here is that these four international trade goods made up an important part of the large variety of Asian goods imported by both the Japanese and Europeans. Traced back to their origins, the items of international trade in the nineteenth-century modern world-system were all part of 'the trading world of Asia', a vast area that extended from Arabia to India, southeast Asia, and China.[34]

Apart from weapons, the only thing that Europeans were able to offer to the trading world of Asia in large quantities were the gold and silver they had plundered from Latin America. Europeans had large quantities of gold and silver, their spoils from the New World. Conversely speaking, the New World had nothing else except gold and silver that Europeans had any need for. 'Apart from gold and silver, little that could be produced in the Americas during the first century of colonization was marketable in Europe. Unlike the East Indies, which produced articles of great value . . . spices, silks and muslins, the Americas produced nothing that could become the basis of lucrative trade'.[35]

The Japanese too had made advances in mining in the late fifteenth and early sixteenth centuries and had vast quantities of gold, silver, and copper. Output figures for Japanese silver 'at the beginning of the seventeenth century reached forty, sometimes even fifty, thousand *kan* [= 200,000 kilograms or 50 million tael] of silver a year'.[36] 'Moreover, in

those days the entire silver output for the rest of the world is estimated at
between 390,000 and 490,000 kilograms; thus, for a time Japan's annual
silver exports alone easily accounted for 30 to 40 percent of total world
production. Japan's position in the history of world trade at that time
was extremely important'.[37] What then is the relationship between these
facts and the formation of a national seclusion policy and the 'modern
world-system'? In brief outline, neither Japan nor Europe lacked materials
for coinage; they exported these and imported the products of Asia. For
that reason, the components of European and Japanese trade with Asia
were similar: both exported precious metals and imported Asian goods.
As a result of this trading structure, a popular demand for Asia products
was created in Europe and Japan at the two extremities of Eurasia. This
meant that precious metals flowed into the centre of Asia from both ends
of the Eurasian continent, but no matter how large the quantities of coinage materials each had, they would eventually dry up if the outflow continued. To control the outflow of precious metals, the task was to create a production and distribution structure that would meet the demand
structure. In other words, the task facing Europe and Japan was the same:
to produce by their own labour and with their own hands the Asian products imported by their respective societies. To do so, they were forced to
restructure their economies and societies in a rational and efficient man-
ner in order to produce indigenous substitutes for imported goods.

8. SELF-SUFFICIENCY IN ASIAN PRODUCTS

(i) Sugar

The main text has concentrated on cotton and the spread eastward and
westward of a product which originated in the old civilisations of Asia
but whose development in Europe and Japan outstripped anything that
occurred in its place of origin. The introduction of cotton caused a revolution in clothing at both ends of the Eurasian continent, areas that until
the end of the Middle Ages had only been on the fringe of the civilised
world. As the key commodity in bringing about this change in life styles,
cotton has been treated first; here, we will turn to some of the other

import substitutes that Japanese and Europeans learned to produce for themselves, beginning with sugar.

Sugar cane is said to be native to New Guinea and its environs. It was first cultivated some time between 15,000 and 8,000 B.C., and by around 6,000 B.C. the ancestor of the present species began to be grown in Malaysia. Sugar cane was introduced into the Ganges valley in India about 2,000 B.C. and spread throughout the world from there.[38] It spread eastward from India to China, Taiwan, the Ryukyus, and Japan. Taiwan had supplied sugar to Japan even before the Tokugawa period, but after the Dutch East India Company occupied the island in 1624, it encouraged cultivation of sugar cane, most of which was exported to Japan. Production was also encouraged after Zheng Chenggong (Koxinga) occupied Taiwan, and output increased. In 1656, Japan imported 1,320 tons of sugar, much more than the 88 tons imported by Britain in 1665. As Tsunoyama Sakae says:

> Sugar first began to attract attention in Japan about the same time as it did in Europe, namely, from the end of the Muromachi period to the beginning of the early modern period. In other words, by the beginning of the seventeenth century sugar was being brought in on foreign ships, and these imports increased until the end of the eighteenth century. This period was precisely the time of the sugar revolution in Europe and the emergence of sugar as a strategic commodity in international trade.[39]

Sugar imports are discussed in the *Honchō shoku kagami* (The encyclopaedia of food in our country) published in 1697, which notes that 'sugar cane seeds have recently come in from China, Korea, and the Ryukyus, but sugar cannot be grown in Japanese soil. For the most part, it is brought in from foreign countries'. The *Nōgyō zensho* (Encyclopaedia of agriculture) published the same year also reports that 'recently seeds brought in from the Ryukyus are being planted in Satsuma [Kagoshima]', and goes on to say, 'Because [sugar] is used very widely, large amounts of our country's valuable currency is spent on it. . . . If efforts were made to grow it in it large quantities, it would save our country's resources from being paid out unnecessarily to foreign countries.' Arai Hakuseki (1657–1725) conveys the sense of urgency felt at the beginning of the eighteenth century when he writes, 'Every year vast amounts of sugar come in from foreign lands to the south. Even though it is cheaper than it once was, handing over our country's coinage to pay for it mounts up over time and will ultimately destroy Japan's money supply'.

Large quantities of *tōkōmō* (foreign) sugar were imported into Nagasaki by trade with Holland and Qing China. The eighth Tokugawa shōgun, Yoshimune (r. 1716–51), encouraged domestic production: 'In as much as sugar is now indispensable for everyday life, we ought to use our own product rather than wait for it to come from China'. As a result of his incentive policy, by the beginning of the Kansei period [1789–1801] sugar was being grown in several provinces, and more was produced [in Japan] than in China.[40] Satsuma, Sanuki (Kagawa), Suruga (central Shizuoka), Tōtōmi (western Shizuoka), Kii (Wakayama), Izumi (southwestern Osaka), Awa (Tokushima), Tosa (Kōchi), and Hyūga (Miyazaki) were among the sugar-growing areas during the early modern period. Satsuma produced brown sugar, Sanuki and Awa produced white sugar, and by the end of the Tokugawa period Japanese sugar was not inferior to *tōkōmō* sugar in quality. Domestic production surpassed even that of Amami Ōshima and the Ryukyus in terms of quantity. Beginning in the mid Tokugawa period sugar production in Sanuki, Awa, Satsuma, and elsewhere developed to such an extent that domestic sugar overtook *tōkōmō* sugar. At the end of the eighteenth and the beginning of the nineteenth century, production expanded so rapidly that Japan was nearly self-sufficient in sugar by the 1830s.

But when Japan was integrated into the free trade system in 1859, domestic production was hard hit as cheap, foreign sugar flowed into the country through the open ports. Sugar imports rapidly entered Edo (soon to be renamed Tokyo) from the open port of Yokohama and came into the Kansai area from the open ports of Kobe and Osaka. The sugar brought in by the Western great powers was mainly shipped via China and Taiwan from farming areas in Indonesia and can be roughly divided into brown sugar and white sugar. Brown sugar outsold the brown sugar from Kagoshima, and white sugar was refined in Qing China using approximately the same methods as locally produced sugar. After the establishment of modern refineries in Hong Kong, the China Sugar Refinery (1878) and the Taikoo Sugar Refining Company (1881), imports of white sugar jumped from around 100,000 *piculs* (one *picul* = 133.33 pounds) to a million *piculs* by the time of the Sino-Japanese war. In 1894, Japanese consumed four million *piculs* of sugar, only 800,000 of which were produced in Japan.

The turning point was Japan's victory in the Sino-Japanese War and the Japanese occupation of Taiwan. Sugar cane cultivation in Taiwan has been analysed by Yanaihara Tadao in *Teikokushugika no Taiwan* (Taiwan under imperialism).[41] According to Yanaihara, Japan set about improving varieties of sugar cane and promoting the sugar industry as soon as it occupied the country, but the output of Taiwanese sugar actually declined after the occupation. In 1901, Nitobe Inazō presented a paper on reforming the sugar industry, and as a result, the government of Taiwan provided subsidies to improve seedlings. Sugar production increased so much that in 1910 a cartel was formed to deal with the surplus. The total harvest of Taiwanese sugar cane was 700 million *kin* (one *kin* = 1.5 pounds) in fiscal year 1902, 4.4 billion *kin* in FY 1910, 8.6 billion *kin* in FY 1925, and 11 billion *kin* in FY 1930. Harvests per hectare in each of those years soared from 40,000 *kin*, to 50,000 *kin*, 80,000 *kin*, and 110,000 *kin*. In less than thirty years, the total yield had risen sixteen-fold, and land productivity had increased 2.7 times. In 1913/4, exports were negligible, but in 1916, Taiwan began exporting to China, Hong Kong, India, Canada, and Australia. In 1918, it had expanded its trade to Switzerland, and in the following year to Finland, Spain, and Turkey. In FY Shōwa 3–4 [1928/9], sugar production on the island rose to more than 12.96 million *piculs*, enough to supply the entire Japanese empire with sugar. (Total sugar consumption in the Japanese empire had been 12.62 million *piculs* in FY Taishō 14 [1925]). These developments had nothing to do with catching up with Europe but were a classic case of an intra-Asia competition dating back to the Tokugawa period, a competition that Japan won, as it had with cotton.

The westward spread of sugar cane cultivation began when sugar was introduced into Greece after Alexander the Great's invasion of India. By the seventh century A.D., it was being grown in Persia. The 'Arab Agricultural Revolution' subsequently brought it to Syria, Cyprus, Egypt, and Sicily, and by the fourteenth century it had spread throughout the Mediterranean basin. In the fifteenth century the Portuguese introduced sugar into Madeira, the Canary Islands, Cape Verdes Islands, and the Azores. In the New World, Spain established a sugar plantation in Santo Domingo in 1520, and Portugal set one up at Olinda on the northeast coast of Brazil in 1535. By the eighteenth century, England, France, and Holland had sugar plantations in the Caribbean and along the coast of Guyana.

To quote Lucile Brockway:

> Sugar is also an example of the interdependence of the highly centralized and industrializing core area of Western Europe and the tropical periphery. Production and milling, with a labour force imported from Africa and machinery imported from Europe, took place in the New World tropics, but refining and marketing as well as financial control of the trade remained in European hands. In 1556 Antwerp had 19 refineries; in 1600 Amsterdam had 60. In 1750 Hamburg had 350 refineries, and England over 100.[42]

In the West the supply and demand for sugar spanned both sides of the Atlantic.

Blockades of continental Europe during the Napoleonic wars cut off the supply of sugar cane from the colonies, causing prices to soar. At this juncture, sugar beet emerged to compete with sugar cane. Sugar cane is grown in the tropics and semitropical zones, but sugar beets can be grown in temperate and subarctic areas. The use of this plant as a sugar source can be traced back to 1604, but its sugar content in that period was only five per cent. Franz Karl Achard of Germany succeeded in refining sugar beet in 1799. Then its cultivation developed rapidly in continental Europe, especially in countries like Germany, Austria, and Russia that did not have sugar-growing colonies. Of the world's total sugar output in FY 1852 (with the exception of British-occupied India), sugar cane accounted for 86 per cent and sugar beets for 14 per cent. By FY 1899, the situation was reversed, with sugar cane making up 35 per cent of the total and sugar beets 65 per cent. During the latter half of the nineteenth century, Germany and Austria, which both grew sugar beets, were changed from sugar-importing countries to sugar exporters.

Hardest hit by the expansion of sugar-beet sugar were the sugar-cane producing islands of the West Indies. In 1897, Joseph Chamberlain, the British colonial secretary, agreed to provide £60,000 worth of aid to the West Indian colonies. In 1901, an international conference was held in Brussels with the aim of putting an end to sugar competition. Ten European countries participated including Britain, France, Germany, Austria, and Holland.

These developments took place independently of Asia. Europe, which once imported sugar from the Islamic world, succeeded in achieving complete self-sufficiency. They became so productive that they were able to steal each other's markets and had to reach an agreement over the sugar trade.

(ii) Tea and Silk
According to Sombart's *Luxury* and *Capitalism*,

> [the] connection between feminism (old style) and sugar has been of the greatest importance for the history of economic development. Because of the predominant role of women during early capitalism, sugar rapidly became a favorite food; and only because of the widespread use of sugar were such stimulants as cocoa, coffee and tea adopted so readily all over Europe.[43]

Sugar and tea have a close relationship. In Europe sugar is added to tea, in Japan it is eaten with tea in the form of sweets. Japan created a green tea culture and England a black tea culture.[44]

Tea originated in the glossy-leaf forest belts of Assam and Yunnan. These belts, according to Ueyama Shunpei's *Zoku shōyō jurin bunka* (Sequel to The culture of glossy-leaf forests), are places 'in which the original habitats of rice, soy beans, adzuki beans, millet, and buckwheat are clustered'. They were also the source of 'dissemination for various elements of culture such as tea, silk, fermented soybeans, *konnyaku* [yam cake], lacquer, the *shiso* plant, sushi, miso, *kōji* [a fungus used as a fermenting agent], and cormorant fishing.'[45] Tea consumption is said to have developed from the practice of eating the tough leaves of trees grown in glossy-leaf forests. Since tea can be cultivated on the sunny slopes created as a result of the slash-and-burn method of agriculture and is known to grow vigorously there, it is regarded as an undergrowth in glossy-leaf forests.

The original habitat of tea has not yet been established, but since it grows as underbrush in glossy-leaf forests or in stands of cedar and *hinoki* cypress and flourishes in deforested areas because of this trait, Matsushita Satoru, who has studied tea as a cultivated plant, locates the centre for tea in a belt north of the Tropic of Cancer in and around Yunnan province.[46] There is a strong possibility that even the so-called 'mountain tea' (*sancha*), which is native to Japan, was once a cultivated species that later grew wild. The history of tea cultivation in Japan dates to 805, when the Buddhist monk Saichō brought seeds back from China, planted them in Sakamoto in Ōmi (Shiga Prefecture) and opened the Hiyoshi plantation. In Eisai's *Kissa yōjō-ki* (Notes on the curative effects of tea) of 1214, tea is described as 'an elixir; the secret of long life.' As this description indicates, tea was prized for its medicinal purposes. Gen'e's *Kissa ōrai* (Conventions of tea-drinking), which was published about a century later, describes tea-tasting competitions in which participants tried to identify which was the 'true tea', *honcha*, from Toganoo (modern Uji). From this reference, tea drinking is known to have spread to the upper classes.

By the mid fifteenth century, it had become an everyday event, according to the diary of teamaster Yamanoue Sōji of 1592: 'In this period [the reign of the eighth Ashikaga shogun, Yoshimasa, r. 1449–73], anyone who did not practice the tea ceremony was considered a brute in human form. Many daimyō, it goes without saying, all the way down to the merchants especially in Nara, Kyoto, and Sakai, religiously performed the tea ceremony'. The etiquette of the tea ceremony was formalised in that period and established as an art form. The techniques of tea making are generally acknowledged to have been introduced in three stages: the *dancha* (brick tea) method in the Tang dynasty (618–907), the *matcha* (powdered tea) method in the Song dynasty (960–1279), and the *sencha* (green tea) method, which Ingen, founder of the Ōbaku school of Zen Buddhism, is said to have introduced at the end of the Ming dynasty (1368–1644).

Immediately after Japan was opened to trade, Japanese tea was exported to England, but green tea did not appeal to the British, and it ended up in the American market. In 1860, 25,000 pounds of tea were exported to America, ten times that amount three years later, and by 1878 exports had risen ten times more to 2.5 million pounds, but coffee was preferred to green tea in America, and it eventually lost ground to black tea as well. In the 1860s, tea ranked with raw silk as the quintessential Japanese export commodity, but by the 1913, it had plummetted to a mere 2.6 per cent of Japan's total exports. A green tea culture seems to have a weak ability to popularise itself and perhaps can be regarded as profoundly Japanese.

Tsunoyama Sakae's *Cha no sekaishi* (World history of tea) gives a detailed account of the spread of tea to the West. Information about tea reached Arabia by 850, Venice by 1559, Britain by 1598, and Portugal by 1600, but the first tea did not actually arrive in Europe until 1610, when the Dutch East India Company brought in green tea purchased in Macau and Hirado. Tea was first sold in England in 1657 at a London coffee house. This too was green tea. By the eighteenth century, however, the British had acquired a taste for black tea, primarily Bohea, a kind of oolong. At the culmination of a process that had started with coffee and passed from green tea to black tea, a black tea culture, with milk and sugar, became firmly entrenched in British society. In contrast to the coffee houses, which were gathering places for men, tea gardens were built on the outskirts of cities and towns in the eighteenth century for the pleasure of women. Many of these tea gardens were famous for their promenades, music, and fireworks. When the custom of drinking tea in the garden was adopted in the homes of the nobility, tea became an British tradition. The rising demand for tea in the seventeenth and eighteenth centuries and the enormous profits accruing from it led to an increase in the tea trade with China. This in turn stimulated the development of British sailing ships, the training for which was an important factor in creating the traditions of British seamanship. The sailing vessels that carried tea were called 'tea clippers' or 'China clippers', and competitions arose among these majestic ships to be the first to bring the freshly picked tea from China to Britain. This was the golden age of sailing.

The increase in the demand for tea in Britain posed a problem, however, the outflow of silver. How did the British deal with this problem? They brought opium to China with the aim of eliminating their trade deficit. Opium had originally been used as a medicine in China, but because of the large amount being brought in, the number of users increased, and opium addiction became widespread throughout the country. The result was the Opium War. This is a well-known fact. But while the direct cause of the war was undoubtedly Chinese addiction to opium, if we take the process back a step, the problem was the outflow of silver from Britain, and the reason for that was the refusal of the British to give up tea. Thus, it is fair to say that the underlying cause of the Opium War was British addiction to tea.

How did the British succeed in becoming self-sufficient in tea? By operating tea plantations in India and Ceylon. A new variety of tea (Assam tea) was discovered growing wild in Assam in 1823. Plans to cultivate it were drawn up in 1834, and in 1838 samples of the new tea were delivered to London. A business firm was formed the following year. Operations broke even after 1848. The centre of cultivation was Assam, but it later spread to Bengal, and in the second half of the 1870s after the coffee crop in Ceylon was wiped out by rust fungus, tea plantations were opened there as well. As a result, China's share of Britain's total tea imports plummetted, dropping below 30 per cent by the end of the 1880s. After the tax on tea was cut from two shillings and three pence a pound to six pence a pound in 1865, tea could be bought as an everyday commodity. Soon afternoon tea was a national pastime. Thomas Lipton, who succeeded in building a tea store chain, created a sensation in the British tea market and won great public favour by selling tea by the pound in cans at low prices. In 1890, Lipton began cultivating Assam tea in Ceylon on a grand scale, using machinery for everything but the tea picking, and advertising it as good quality tea. Chinese tea was directly affected and disappeared from world markets.

It might be noted in passing that coffee, which had its origins in Ethiopia, was first cultivated by Arabs in Yemen (mocha). In the fifteenth century, many coffee houses sprang up in Mecca, and by the mid sixteenth century there were coffee houses in Cairo, Damascus, and Constantinople. The first coffee house in Europe opened in Venice in 1645. The first in England were in Oxford (1650) and London (1652). Thereafter, coffee houses appeared in Paris in 1669, in Hamburg in 1679, and in New York in 1696. London alone is said to have had 3,000 coffee houses by 1683.

The Dutch were the first to bring the coffee plant to Europe. They had begun cultivating coffee in Ceylon in 1658 and later introduced it into Dutch-occupied India. In 1706, Java coffee seedlings were delivered to the botanical gardens in Amsterdam. Some were transplanted in the Jardin des Plantes at the Paris Museum of Natural History in 1714. The following year, coffee crossed the Atlantic Ocean and was cultivated in Haiti and Santo Domingo. From there it entered Brazil in 1727, Jamaica in 1730, Cuba in 1740, Puerto Rico in 1755, Costa Rica in 1779, Venezuela in 1784, and Mexico in 1790. By the mid eighteenth century the cultivation of coffee had spread to all the prime growing areas known today.[47]

In this way, the West succeeded in meeting its own demand for coffee, which became the typical drink of Europeans.

Coffee was introduced into Japan at the end of the seventeenth century and was drunk by some of the Japanese at Dejima in Nagasaki, but like the British, the Japanese in the Tokugawa period preferred tea. The crucial difference was that the British liked black tea, and the Japanese liked green tea. For that reason, even after Japan was opened up, the two types of tea did not compete in either the British or the Japanese market.

The evolution of the tea business is inextricably linked to the development of the ceramics industry. The Dutch and British at first imported only blue and white ware, cobalt blue designs painted on a white ground. The Chinese succeeded in making blue and white ware at the end of the Yuan period (1271–1368), developed it during the Ming period, and perfected it in the Qing (1644–1912).[48] In Japan, which had hitherto been dependent on imports, production of blue and white ware became possible when the technique was introduced into Hizen (modern Saga and Nagasaki) by the Korean potters who were brought to Japan at the time of Hideyoshi's invasions of Korea in the 1590s. Red-painted Arita ware (Imari), best known from the works of Kakiemon, developed into an export industry in the late seventeenth century. Until Europe succeeded in mass-producing porcelain in the nineteenth century, blue and white ware and red-painted porcelain from China and Japan competed for European markets.[49] The porcelain trade is another example of intra-Asian competition.

The story of silk is similar. The origin of silk can be traced back to China around 3,000 B.C. Silk was carried westward over land (the 'silk road') and sea routes. Sericulture was brought to India around 400 B.C., and spread to western Asia at the time of Alexander the Great's invasion of India. In 552 A.D., during the reign of the emperor Justinian, silkworm eggs were secretly smuggled out of China and brought into the Byzantine empire by Nestorian Christians. At about the same time, Chinese silk looms and the *sorahiki* loom for weaving twill damask and brocade also arrived in the West. Mulberry bushes, silk worms, and silk looms were first introduced into Italy at Palermo and Sicily in the twelfth century. Later the silk industry sprung up in the cities of Florence, Milan, Genoa, and Venice on the Italian peninsula. By 1408, silk weaving had also begun in Tours, France. The status of the French silk industry was assured in the seventeenth century by the protectionist policies of Jean-Baptiste Colbert, the first controller general of France, and Lyon silk soon surpassed that of Italy. Silk weaving was brought to Britain by Belgium and French artisans at the end of the sixteenth century. Although Hernando Cortez's attempt to introduce silkworms to the Americas ended in failure, British efforts during the reign of James I finally met with success in 1619. Silk growing expanded in Virginia, and the first silk weaving factory was built in America in the eighteenth century. In this way, silk spread from the old Asian civilisations to the West during the Middle Ages and the early modern period.

In Japan, the treadle-operated tall loom for weaving brocades was introduced into Nishijin, the textile-weaving district of Kyoto, from China in the 1550s. Thereafter, the high-quality raw silk known as 'white thread', which was used in figured textile weaving, was Japan's largest import throughout the seventeenth century, but by the eighteenth century, Japan was able to meet its own demand domestically. Raw silk thread was Japan's largest export after 1859. It was exported to Europe, where blight had caused a marked decline in the supply of silk, and eventually came to be used in the United States. In the nineteenth century, France was the world's largest importer of raw silk thread. In the twentieth century, the United States occupied this position. The major sources of supply for these two big markets were Italy and China, but after fierce competition Japan worked its way into the ranks of the world's three main producers and exporters of raw silk, Italy, France, and Qing China. By the beginning of the twentieth century, Japan's exports exceeded those of China. Japan had been dependent on imports of 'white thread' until the end of the seventeenth century and was not able to produce a domestic substitute for it until the beginning of the eighteenth century. The reason its silk was regarded as superior to Chinese raw silk after 1859 is that its silk industry had developed during the two and a half centuries of the early modern period to such an extent that Japanese raw silk caught up with 'white thread' in quality and price. This means that in the period of national seclusion, Japan took the lead in the intra-Asian competition for raw silk production.

After Japan awoke from its isolationist slumbers and opened its ports, its imports were mainly cotton and sugar, its exports mainly tea and raw silk. The reason both Japan and the West possessed these important products can be readily understood if we consider their origins in the old civilisations of Asia. These products, which determined modern Japan's economic development, had become indispensable in the period of transition from the Middle Ages to the early modern period. By emerging victorious in the intra-Asian competition, Japan proved that its quest for self-sufficiency in these products was now complete.

9. FROM IMPORTER OF CURRENCY TO SUPPLIER OF CURRENCY MATERIALS

The way in which Japan and Europe began their own production of Asian commodities was also the way in which they dealt with a problem confronting them both: the outflow of currency metals. The reason this outflow became a problem in the first place is that Japan and Europe had a domestic supply of metals useable as money. However, it should be emphasised that the only country in the world that ever had a self-sufficient supply of gold, silver, and copper within its own borders, and had control over its supply, was Japan during the Tokugawa period. This is an extremely unusual situation. What impact did the existence of gold, silver, and copper for making currency in Japan have on economic trends in Asia?

In the beginning Japan did not have a self-sufficient money supply. Quite the contrary, Japan imported copper coins from China until the late sixteenth century. In the ancient period Japan had twelve types of minted coins known as the *kōchō jūnisen* (twelve coinages of the imperial courts of Nara and Kyoto), but these did not circulate, and systems based on rice or on silk were ordinarily used as means of payment. In the mid twelfth century, large quantities of copper coins began to be brought in from China. As many as seventy types of copper coins were imported in the twelfth century, and in 1242, Japan imported ten *kanmon* worth of coins in a single shipment, the equivalent, it is said, of the Southern Song's entire annual output of minted copper coins.[50] The first recorded mention of the use of copper coins in Japan is an entry in the *Tōdaiji monjo* (The documents of Tōdaiji Temple) reporting a purchase of land in 1150 at Tōdaiji village in Yamato (Nara) for twenty-seven *kanmon*. The next is a document contained in the *Tōji hyakugō monjo* showing the sale of rice fields in Kyoto in 1162 and 1176. The circulation of Song coins was prohibited in the late twelfth century, but the order could not be enforced.

In 1226, the use of a cloth-based exchange system was suspended, and payment of the annual land tax was made in copper coins.[51] The use of coins continued to spread, and by the Muromachi period, Ming coins were imported in large quantities. In this period, copper coinage was the international currency of Asia. Chinese copper coins spread through all parts of Asia in trade and were used as money everywhere. Korea, Japan, and the Ryukyus in the East, Java and Vietnam in the South, Islamic countries in the West, even the Tangut empire and the Jin dynasty used Chinese copper coins.

Japan depended on imported coins for its money until the Tokugawa period. Then imported coins disappeared from Japan for the first time in Japanese history. The Japanese currency system in the early modern period had three distinct types of money made of gold, silver, and copper. In 1601, gold and silver coins (*ōban, koban, ichibukin, chōgin, and mameitagin*) were minted for national circulation, and in 1609, one *ryō* of gold = fifty *momme* of silver was established as the official exchange rate. The official copper coinage minted by the Tokugawa government deserves particular mention. Ever since Taira Kiyomori (1118–81) began importing Song coins, Chinese copper coins had been used as money in Japan and as international currency in Japan's trade with Asia. Most of the imported copper coins from the time of the Muromachi period on were the so-called *Eiraku* coins issued during the reign of the Chinese emperor Yongle (r. 1402–24 = Eiraku in Japanese). The Tokugawa government imitated these coins when it minted the Keichō coin in 1606 and the Genna coin in 1617, but neither of these copper coins was accepted for ordinary use in place of the imported coinage.

The acceptance of Japan's copper *sen* as the official coinage was only brought about with the minting of Kan'ei coins over a five-year period between 1636 and 1640. To implement this program, the export of copper was prohibited until 1645. More coins were subsequently minted, 500,000 *kan* (one *kan* = 8.27 lbs.) between 1656 and 1659, and 1.97 million kan between 1668 and 1683.[52] By the end of the seventeenth century, imported coins had finally been driven out of Japan.[53] Thus the Kan'ei coins are worth special mention for the role they played in the history of Japanese currency and indeed of Asian currency. Japan in the Tokugawa period had its own internal sources of all the materials needed to make

its own coinage, gold, silver, and copper. But Japan also became a supplier of currency metals to Asia. According to Arai Hakuseki's *Honchō
hōka tsūyō jiryaku* (Short account of the circulation of currency; 1711) the
amount of silver and gold that flowed out of Nagasaki in the sixty-one
years between 1648 and 1708 was more than 2,397,600 *ryō* of gold and
more than 374,209 *kanme* of silver. Exports of copper are said to have
reached more 114,498,700 *kin* (one *kin* = 1.323 lbs.) in the period between
1636 and 1708. Hence in the Tokugawa period, Japan changed from being
an importer of currency to being an exporter.

Because copper coinage was the international currency of Asia, Japan's
development of the ability to supply its own currency needs did not stop
there. The appearance of Japanese copper in Asian markets was a momen-
tous event both in Japanese economic history and in the economic history
of Asia. The prevailing world order centred on China and was based on the
idea that China was the centre of the civilised world, surrounded by barbarians. Trade within this *Pax sinica* took the form of a Chinese tribute system
in which the tributaries received their supply of coinage exported from
China. But China had become an importer of silver and gold currency.
Thus, the tribute relationship between China and Japan had reversed and,
at least from the Chinese perspective, had become fatally unbalanced.

Copper was the means of exchange in trade with China and the
whole of Asia. It is impossible to understand the economic history of
Asia after the mid seventeenth century without understanding the role
of Japanese copper. Japan was the largest source of copper supply in Asia.
China, Persia, and India also produced copper, but none had enough
to meet their own internal needs. Japanese copper was even shipped to
Amsterdam and had a huge impact on the European copper exchanges,
but the quantities there were small compared with Asian demand.[54]

While Japan was completing the process of producing goods previously
imported from Asia at home, from the middle of the Tokugawa period, it
began to favour internal demand for silver and copper currency and to limit
exports. This led to a shortage of copper in Qing China, which was forced
to increase the zinc content of its copper coins by nearly 40 per cent. In
late Qing China, the copper currency system collapsed completely and was
replaced by *yōgin*, 'silver' coins made of copper, nickel, and zinc. Thus early
modern Japan, with complete control over the currency metals within its

borders and exporting the surplus, occupied a position of economic influence in Asia. By replacing China as the largest supplier of currency metals to Asia, Japan had taken over the role once held by China.

On the other side of the world, none of the countries in Europe, including Britain, could supply its own currency needs domestically. To buy anything produced in the East, they all needed first to import precious metals from Latin America or copper from Sweden. In the early eighteenth century, Britain began shipping Swedish copper to Asia and gradually extended its influence eastwards within the Asian trading network. Eventually Britain seized control of the flow of currency metals from West to East and became the uncontested leader of the modern world-system. Thus in the seventeenth century, Japan and Europe and in particular Britain supplied metals in exchange for Asian products they could not produce themselves. But by the eighteenth century, the changes discussed above were well under way, and as the suppliers of currency metals to Asia, they had acquired control over the economies of Asia.

When Japan opened its ports in 1859, it was self-sufficient in currency metals. The exchange rate of gold to silver on the Japanese currency market at that time was one to five, but the international market rate was one to fifteen. Thus it was possible to acquire gold currency in Japan's open ports for less silver than was required in the international market. As a result of foreign demand, enormous quantities of Japanese gold coins flowed out of the country. The Japanese economy experienced what Shinpo Hiroshi has called a 'price revolution' as the domestic price system was brought into alignment with the international price system. But foreign money did not circulate in Japan. A foreign currency known as *yōgin* did circulate in the open ports and in Asian markets, but it was gradually driven out of both by the yen coinage minted by the Meiji government. By the time the gold standard was adopted in 1897, the dominance of the yen in East Asian markets had been established.[55]

In chapter three of *Capital*, Marx says that money 'on the one hand, . . . represents a sold commodity, on the other, it represents purchasable commodities.'[56] From the early modern period to the Meiji era, Japan had always possessed the metals that were the means of exchange in Asia. Thus, throughout these years, the Japanese economy was in a position where it could obtain all the products of Asia as 'purchasable commodities'. Japan was in a position to make what Marx called the *salto mortale*, the leap from commodity to money. This aided a process that had been going on in the Japanese economy since the early modern period, the 'transformation of money into capital'—industrialisation.

10. TWO FORMS OF PRODUCTION REVOLUTION

Between the Middle Ages and the early modern period, Europe and Japan went from having completely different systems of production to ones that were quite similar. By the eighteenth century, the same Asian products were being used in both. If the product complex of strategic commodities that developed in the Atlantic rim led to the creation of the 'modern world-system' centred around Britain, then *sakoku* Japan (Japan under the system of national isolation imposed by the Tokugawa regime) could be considered the modern world-system in miniature. Yet there were clear differences in the ways these new products from the old civilisations were used. The British used cotton cloth for summer clothes, the Japanese used it for winter wear. Tea in Britain was a luxury enjoyed with milk and sugar, but tea in Japan was associated with tea utensils, tea-ceremony rooms, and the aesthetic of *wabi* and *sabi* with its emphasis on impermanence and imperfection. These differences emerged because of inherent differences in the existing systems of use-value (i.e., the culture/ product complex) in each of these societies.

Even the system of supply and demand for the new products was different in Japan and Europe. The three required factors of production, land, capital, and labour, can be combined in a number of different ways. In the virtually closed economy of Tokugawa Japan, land was clearly limited, but whether one accepts Yoshida Tōgo's or Hayami Akira's population estimates for the Tokugawa era, it is clear that the seventeenth century was a period of population explosion.[57] Put briefly, because Japan was favourably endowed with a large work force, it invested large quantities of labour and fertiliser into its limited territory to increase land productivity. But because the West had a small work force in relation to its vast territory along the perimeter of the Atlantic Ocean, it developed a system that invested large quantities of capital to increase the productivity of labour. *Sakoku* Japan created a labour-intensive system that deepened the regional and societal divisions of labour within a closed economic structure. The West developed a capital-intensive system of supply and demand for products that were supplied to both sides of the Atlantic.

These differences in factor endowments produced differences in the patterns of industrialisation in Japan and the West. Population pressures in Japan reduced the size of agricultural enterprises, resulting in independent small farmers. Industry took the form of rural industries (i.e., proto-industry), and the division of labour between agriculture and manufacturing was characterised by a division within the household (between the sexes) in which the head of the household (the man) was engaged in farming while the woman and children attended to household tasks.[58] Hayami Akira noted this and made a brilliant contrast between the 'industrial revolution' experienced in the West and the 'industrious revolution' experienced in Japan. Please refer to the diagram. To quote Hayami:

> The special feature of agriculture in the Edo period was the investment of large amounts and long periods of gruelling, hard work. Let us consider what this means. Had farmers always been required to work this hard?
>
> First of all, a comparison needs to be made with the state of the work force in agriculture prior to the Edo period. As a rule, this work force was composed of either hereditary vassals with a highly dependent status or long-term apprentices. Although the nature of their work is not adequately known, their standard of living can be readily imagined. No doubt, it was just barely at the subsistence level, and as far as can be made out from historical documents in the early Edo period, most had no families and remained unmarried throughout their lifetime. In the Edo period this sort of labour force gradually disappeared. Operations for which the basic unit was a small family became the general rule, and the labour force is known to have changed to a family work force. In short, the old system of dependent status disappeared, and the farm family now functioned as the unit of operation. Of course, this did not mean that farmers enjoyed freedom in the modern sense of the word. Being an 'independent small farmer' did not mean that at all; there was no possibility of escape from political or social obligations such as the land tax or the family system. Moreover, by functioning as an economic

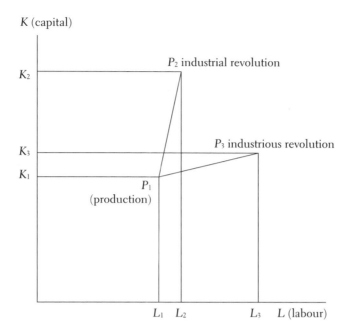

Diagram: The Industrial Revolution and the Industrious Revolution

Production P is indicated by the combination of two factors, capital K and labour L. The industrial   revolution is defined as an increase in production through the investment of large quantities of capital ($P_1 \rightarrow P_2$); an industrious revolution is defined as an increase in production through the investment of large quantities of labour ($P_1 \rightarrow P_3$). Based on Hayami Akira's diagram in *Atarashii Edo jidaishi zō o motomete* (In search of a new image of the history of the Edo period).

unit, they were exposed to the dangers that inevitably accompanied it. All things considered, 'independence' was no bed of roses, but it is possible to make a clear distinction between this way of life and the situation that existed before the Edo period. That granted, might it not be said that 'independence' was compensation for the long periods of gruelling, hard work imposed upon Edo farmers?

Second, this gruelling work was not pure drudgery for the farmers. If the opportunity arose, they could acquire wealth as a reward for their labours, or at least raise their standard of living. During the Edo period, by my estimates, the average life expectancy of the agricultural population increased by between five and ten years, most conspicuously among women and children. Although much of this gain can be accounted for by a decline in the infant mortality rate, some of it, which is not explicable by modern factors such as advances in medicine and public sanitation, may be due to improvements in the living environment, that is, in clothing, food, and shelter. Important tasks remain in finding ways to relate observations in this area with research in social and economic history. Be that as it may, however, it is conceivable that when farmers were able to look forward to an increase, albeit gradual, in their living standards, work ceased to be pure drudgery.

Thus, in the Edo period, these long periods of gruelling, hard work acquired an ethical meaning, 'industriousness'. The industriousness of the Japanese, which has often been noted, impressed the foreigners who visited the country during the Edo period. Might it not be that this is one of the patterns of Japanese behaviour formed within the farming class of that period?[59]

The Hayami thesis provides important insights into the economic history of the Tokugawa period. But because Hayami's 'Japanese industrious revolution' is exclusively a comparison with the European industrial revolution, Japan's relationship with Asia is not discussed. No mention is made of Asia. Why, then, did a labour-intensive industrial revolution occur in Japan in the Tokugawa period? And why did a capital-intensive industrial revolution occur in Britain?

One reason for Japan's labour-intensive industrial revolution was the need to produce items to replace foreign products that entered Japan through trade in the Asian seas. In volume one of *Nihon nōgakushi* (History of Japanese agriculture), Furushima Toshio examines the sixty-volume Chinese encyclopaedia of agriculture compiled by Xu Guangqi (1562–1633), who spent ten years making a thorough study of old and new agricultural treatises after his retirement from government office in 1612, and compares it with the encyclopaedia based on it on agriculture in Japan, the *Nōgyō zensho* (General treatise on agriculture) by Miyazaki Yasusada (1623–97). Furushima's findings suggest that during the period of national seclusion, Japan acquired the competitive edge over China in the latent intra-Asian competition between them.

Xu Guangqi's encyclopaedia is both a compendium of ancient Chinese agriculture and a detailed study of new crops like cotton and sweet potato. The same could be said of the *Nōgyō zensho*, but, as Furushima points out, the influence of the Chinese encyclopaedia appears most pronouncedly in the first volume of the Japanese encyclopaedia, which functions as an introduction but then stops. 'There is no real influence on the discussions of the cultivation of individual crops' except in the entries for sweet potato and mulberry.[60] The uniqueness of Yasusada's discussion of individual crops lies in its emphasis on a fertiliser-intensive method of farming. 'On the whole, the potential for large profits is not limited only to potatoes. It is hard to get much profit from most crops unless they are planted far apart, fertilised thoroughly, and given plenty of attention. You must realise that, as a rule, no profits are possible without expending effort on the land and investing human effort.'[61]

A special feature of the *Nōgyō zensho* is its discussions on the cultivation of commercial crops, first cotton, then white radishes, aubergines, carrots, cucumbers, onions, potatoes, etc. As Furushima says:

> On the subject of vegetables, silk, tobacco, indigo, and other crops for which the main growing areas had been established at that time and for which cultivation techniques were far advanced, the work gives a detailed account of the agricultural methods used in the major growing areas of the Kinai region [Osaka-Kyoto-Kobe], including the use of additional fertiliser and management methods . . . . Even today Japan has its own distinctive methods of cultivation for the most common crops; these methods are characterised by being fertiliser-intensive, which is regarded as the distinguishing characteristic of contemporary Japanese agriculture. The origin of these methods can be traced to the fact that these crops were grown as commercial products.

As early as the end of the seventeenth century when the *Nōgyō zensho* was written, the agricultural methods practiced in the more advanced areas of Japan were already ahead of the technical level being introduced in Chinese agricultural treatises.

Approximately when did the process of import substitution take place? According to Saitō Osamu, the sixteenth and seventeenth centuries in Japan were a period of major land clearing and permanent settlement.[62] The first half of the Tokugawa period was a time of extensive expansion characterised by population growth, the reclamation of alluvial plains suitable for the introduction of imported red rice, and the outflow of gold, silver, and copper. But from the end of the seventeenth century to the beginning of the eighteenth century, and especially during the time of Arai Hakuseki and Tokugawa Yoshimune, the foreign trade regulations of the Shōtoku period (1711–16) and other policies designed to stanch the flow of gold, silver, and copper were adopted. Also, active steps were taken to encourage domestic production of goods previously imported. However, it seems to have taken about a century before these policies were effective and Japan achieved self-sufficiency in sugar, ginseng, and sweet potato, and also cotton and raw silk. In 1811, Hirata Atsutane wrote in *Kodō taii* (True meaning of the ancient way): 'What is gratifying and enviable for the country of Japan, first of all, is that it lacks for absolutely nothing even though it does not trade with foreigners. This is possible because the land is so fertile to begin with that we do not need to procure goods from abroad.'

These words indicate that by the beginning of the nineteenth century, Japanese were aware of the nature of their closed economy. If we consider that the term *sakoku* was first used in Japan in 1801, it can be assumed that Japan's process of import substitution was nearly complete by this period. The word *sakoku* was first used by Shizuki Tadao, the translator and scholar of Dutch. He used it as the title for the Appendix to his translation of Engelbert Kaempfer's *History of Japan*. Although an equivalent expression was not used in the original German, when Kaempfer's book was translated into English, the translator used the words 'to keep it shut up'. These were translated into Dutch, and from Dutch into Japanese.

The period in which Europe succeeded in making import substitutes for the products of the old civilisations, especially Asia, can probably be dated to the English industrial revolution. According to Ralph Davis, this occurred between 1780 and 1850, and he dates it in relationship with overseas trade.[63] Rostow placed the English 'take-off' between 1783 and 1802. A conceptual definition of the industrial revolution is difficult, but there can be no doubt that England had become an industrial society by 1800. This roughly coincides with the completion of the similar import substitution process in Japan.

11. THE CRISIS OF THE FOURTEENTH CENTURY

The main point of the discussion so far is that products which had their origins in the old civilisations spread eastward and westward to Japan and Europe, where rational systems of production were developed that had not existed in the places where they originated. In *Business Cycles*, Schumpeter says that 'new . . . commodities create New Economic Space'.[64] These products did indeed create new economic spaces, the modern world-system in the West and *sakoku* Japan.

But what triggered the appearance of these new civilisations? Immanuel Wallerstein has argued that a 'crisis' led to the formation of the modern world-system. This arose from exhaustion of the soil due to lack of technical progress under the feudal system, frequent wars, and plagues that began sweeping through Europe in the mid fourteenth century. He maintains that Europe's search for a way to overcome this crisis resulted in the modern world-system.

Although Europe was the focus of Wallerstein's interest, the crisis of the fourteenth century was not confined to Europe. Signs of crisis were found elsewhere on the Eurasian continent in the form of a massive loss of human life due to the social and economic factors cited by Wallerstein and the cold climactic conditions noted by other scholars. But the greatest incident was the plague known as the Black Death, said to have killed one-third of the population of Europe. By comparison, in the Second World War, 1.17 million Japanese soldiers and 2.1 million German soldiers died out of a total regular army of 6.09 million soldiers and 10.2 million soldiers respectively. Even this war, which ended in defeat and unconditional surrender, only around 20 per cent of each army died. One can imagine just how disastrous the death of one-third of the entire population would be. In the *Decameron* written in 1353, Boccaccio describes the situation this way:

> In the year of Our Lord 1348 the deadly plague broke out in the noble city of Florence . . . . Neither knowledge nor human foresight availed against it . . . . Nor did humble supplications serve . . . . Toward the

spring of the year the plague began to show its ravages in a way short
of miraculous . . . . At the onset of the disease both men and women
were afflicted by a sort of swelling in the groin or under the armpits. . . .
Almost everyone died within three days of the appearance of the signs
. . . . Even the reverend authority of divine and human law had almost
crumbled and fallen into decay . . . .

A large number perished in their homes, and it was only by the stench
of their decaying bodies that they proclaimed their death to their neigh-
bors . . . . So many bodies were brought to the churches every day that the
consecrated ground did not suffice to hold them . . . . Between March and
the following July it is estimated more than a hundred thousand human
beings lost their lives within the walls of Florence.[65]

Other areas also experienced a precipitous decline in population during the fourteenth century. One-third of the population of the Middle
East died of the plague.[66] In China, the Yuan dynasty collapsed in the
mid fourteenth century. According to McNeill's *Plagues and Peoples*,
between 1353 and 1354:

Epidemic disease raged in eight different and widely scattered parts of
China, and chroniclers reported that up to 'two thirds of the population'
died . . . . The best estimates [of China's population] show a decrease from
123 million about 1200 (before the Mongol invasions began) to 65 million
in 1393, a generation after the final expulsion of the Mongols from China.
Even Mongol ferocity cannot account for such a drastic decrease. Disease
assuredly played a big part in cutting Chinese numbers in half; and bubonic
plague, recurring after its initial ravages at relatively frequent intervals, just
as in Europe, is by all odds the most likely candidate for such a role.[67]

Although it is not known whether the plague occurred in Japan in
the mid fourteenth century, that was the period when the activities of
the *wakō* (Japanese pirates) became prominent. According to the Korean
History of the Koryo Dynasty, *wakō* raids began in 1351 and occurred
nearly every year thereafter, and their frequency increased with every
passing year. The *wakō* are said to have made off with people and food,
which might reflect shortages of food and labour power. The period
of civil wars resulting from the establishment of rival imperial courts

(1336–92) marks a dividing point in Japanese history. The deep cleavages that Japanese society experienced in the fourteenth century are even thought to divide Japanese history as a whole into two distinct parts. According to Amino Yoshihiko, 'this was a major structural turning point that affected the national character and the essential nature of the Japanese people.'[68] With *wakō* raids overseas and civil war at home, the symptoms of crisis were evident in Japanese society.

Wallerstein argues that in the process of overcoming the 'crisis' of the fourteenth century, by around the year 1640, Europe had created a capitalist world-system composed of three tiers, core states, semiperiphery, and periphery along the perimeter of the Atlantic Ocean. He implies that this established the superiority of Europe. But it is worth remembering Woodruff's comment: 'In 1500, Asia, not Europe, was pre-eminent. In the sixteenth century all the major empires in Eurasia were Asian. Whatever aspect of power we consider, whether it is military, economic, or spiritual, it is to Asia, not the West, that we must first turn.'[69] Braudel also argues: 'There was no real luxury or sophistication of eating habits in Europe before the fifteenth or sixteenth centuries. In this respect, the West lagged behind the Old World civilizations.'[70] To Bairoch, in the seventeenth century, indeed even at the beginning of the eighteenth century, 'the most advanced civilization in Asia was ahead of the most advanced civilization in Europe.'[71] And Parker notes: 'Until 1750 . . . (and arguably for some further decades afterwards) the achievements of the great civilisations of Asia were far superior to those of Europe; while those of Africa and the Americas were often comparable.'[72] Between the end of the eighteenth century and the beginning of the nineteenth, however, Britain took control of the Atlantic economic bloc, brought about an industrial revolution, and thereby established the dominance of modern European civilisation.

Out of their efforts to overcome the crisis of the fourteenth century, the first stirrings of rational economic societies began to develop in Europe and Japan, which until then had been on the periphery of the world's civilisations and locked in the superstitious world of the Middle Ages. The beginnings of the historical process that would reverse the power relationship between the old and new civilisations can be found in the unprecedented crisis that struck the inhabitants of the Eurasian continent in the mid fourteenth century. In terms of historical sequence, modern civilisation arose after the crisis. So how was the crisis of the fourteenth century related to the rise of modern civilisation? And what was its significance?

12. TRADE WITH ASIA AND CHANGES IN THE PRODUCT COMPLEX

Although it is true to some extent that the Black Death sent Europeans back to a world of primitive superstition,[73] others undoubtedly rejected superstition and assisted in the birth of modern medicine and other sciences. As Amino Yoshihiko has said, in Japan the period of civil war arising from the conflict between the Northern and Southern Courts 'was a major structural turning point that affected the national character and the essential nature of the Japanese people. . . . Superstition gradually disappeared from society, . . . (and) rationalism gradually gained ascendancy.'[74] Linked to these trends and very conspicuous among them was a rising surge of foreign exploration played out in the Asian seas.

What was the connection between foreign exploration and the crisis of the mid fourteenth century? The crisis was literally a matter of life and death. Deliverance from death and disease was the domain of medicine. To deal with fear of impending death, Europeans sought help from existing medical treatments. In the Middle Ages, medicine was based on black or white magic (the work of God or the Devil) or the esoteric principles of astrology, which associated illnesses of the human body with the movements of the stars. Or it was the medicine practiced in the monasteries by Christian monks, who sold medicinal herbs. The most highly prized of these medicines were pepper and spices. The birth of modern Western medical science based on anatomy would have to wait for the publication of pioneering works by Vesalius, whose book on the structure of the human body was published in 1543, and by William Harvey, the father of modern physiology, whose treatise on the circulation of blood came out in 1628. In the European Middle Ages, however, the Christian church prohibited the dissection of human bodies, and the medical theories of Galen (129–ca. 200/216), dependent on animal dissections to approximate the human body, went unchallenged. Europeans were forced to rely on medicines brought from the East.

Pepper and spices, the traditional textbook explanation tells us, were luxuries that were used as flavourings or as preservatives for meat. Domestic animals in medieval Europe were slaughtered in autumn for food in winter and/or because there was not enough fodder to keep them alive over the winter months. There is no doubt that pepper and spices were used as preservatives or as flavourings to mask the taste of meat that had gone bad after being preserved for long periods of time. But because of the expense, salt was usually used for that purpose. The main use for pepper and spices in the Middle Ages was as medicines. In 1621, at the beginning of the modern period, Thomas Mun was still writing that spices 'haue beene so much desired in all times, and by so many Nations . . . as things most necessary to preserue their health, and to cure their diseases'.[75] Pepper and spices in medieval Europe were sold by an apothecary under the control of a hospital, which was inextricably associated with the Church.

When it is realised that spices were used as medicines in a period of rampant plague that brought death to rich and poor alike, then the Europeans' obsessive search for spices regardless of the risks entailed becomes understandable. The Age of Discovery was motivated by plans to import medicines directly. Spices sold no matter how expensive they might be and were even used instead of money. They brought huge profits because when it is a matter of life and death, people had to buy them despite their high costs. Pepper, spices, and even sugar, tea, and coffee were all used as medicines when they first came to Europe.

Where could these items be obtained? Only from Asia, where they were produced. The largest source for pepper and spices, which were believed to have curative or prophylactic powers, was in Southeast Asia. It was here that the trade routes of the civilised world met, that the civilisations of the Indian Ocean encountered the civilisations of the China seas. The products of these countries, Arabia, Persia, India, and China, were brought to Southeast Asia and exchanged there for pepper and spices.

In those days, Southeast Asia was the centre for the trade of many civilisations. The Mongol invasion of the thirteenth century was a major turning point. Riding southward on the wave of the Khan armies, the Thai people made their appearance in Southeast Asia, creating the Sukhothai empire in the north in 1238 and the Ayutthaya empire in the south in 1350. The Ayutthaya empire was a commercial state and so were Champa and Srivijaya. At about the time the Khan armies were moving southward, the Majapahit kingdom was established in Indonesia (1292). That year, Marco Polo, on his way home to Venice from China, spent five months at Peureulak in northern Sumatra and reported that the Sumatrans were converting to Islam, said to be the oldest record of the Islamisation of Southeast Asia. The acceptance of Islam promoted commercial activity. With the decline of the Majapahit kingdom, the kingdom of the Moluccas founded around 1400 took advantage of its strategic location and flourished as a trading centre in the fifteenth century.

The relationship between Southeast Asia and Japan was mediated by the Ryukyus (present-day Okinawa). After a period of internal strife in the early fourteenth century, the Ryukyus underwent a major transformation. Its three kingdoms were unified in 1429, and an inscription on the 'Bridge of Nations' bell cast in 1458 boasts of the country's prosperity:

> The Ryukyu kingdom adorns the southern seas and gathers in the best from three empires, serving as the wheel for Ming China and the hub for Japan. It has become the new Horai, the fabled Island of Eternal Youth, because of its location between these two. Thanks to its ships it is a gathering place of many countries, and treasures of many kinds fill its hundred thousand temples.

As this inscription shows, the Ryukyus flourished as an entrepôt for Japan, China, and Southeast Asia. In the fifteenth century, the kingdom thrived by shipping pepper, Sappan wood, spices, and ivory from Southeast Asia to Japan, China, and Korea, Chinese silk and porcelain to Japan and Southeast Asia, and Japanese copper, silver, swords, fans, and saltpetre to China and Korea.

The enormous profits that the Ryukyus and the Moluccas enjoyed from the transit trade were snatched away by Portugal and Spain, then by Japanese *wakō*, by merchants from Sakai and Hakata, by the Ōuchis, Hosokawas, and other warlords, and by shogun-licenced trading ships. As a result of their ventures overseas, the Japanese and Europeans came to occupy the same area at the same time. This period was the late sixteenth century, and the area was the South China and East China seas. Contact between these two different cultures was accompanied by outbreaks of violence but also by a spectacular exchange of ideas. The impact of European culture is probably epitomised by Christianity.[76] One of the glories of Japanese culture was the tea ceremony. Tsunoyama Sakae's book *Cha no sekaishi* (World history of tea) contains a description with many interesting episodes, of the spiritual impact that the tea ceremony had on Westerners and how it entered their lives.

What were the results of trade with Asia? It produced enormous changes in the goods used by Japanese and Europeans alike and transformed consumption pattern of their societies. In the words of Tsunoyama:

> Between the seventeenth and eighteenth centuries . . . exotic products of all kinds were imported in great quantities from overseas and brought about major changes in European habits and life styles unlike anything that had ever happened before. Britain was at the centre of this European revolution in life styles, a revolution that took place not only in the area of clothing as a result of the textiles imported from India, but that also covered a wide range of eating habits. The foods appearing on British dining tables in the eighteenth century included potatoes, rice, tomatoes, asparagus, and spinach; fruits began to be served for desserts early in the century. Dates, figs, lemons, limes, watermelons, bananas, plums, strawberries, and pineapples appeared in abundance. Sugar was expensive and hard to come by in the seventeenth century; by the eighteenth century, however, it was no longer a luxury but had become a necessity for rich and poor alike. The drinking of chocolate, coffee, and tea became widespread, and eventually tea overtook cocoa and coffee and became firmly established as the national beverage.[77]

Many of the items that became part of the ordinary diet of modern European society also became food staples in Japan. According to the *Kindai sejidan* (Account of the ways of modern life; ca. 1716–35), watermelon 'came into Satsuma from the Ryukyus in the Kan'ei period [1624–49]'. Pumpkins 'came in in the Tenna period [1681–83]; and seeds were planted in Kyoto in the Enpō-Tenna period [1673–84]'. Maize 'was brought in by barbarian ships at the beginning of Tenshō [1573–91] and is called "Cathay" corn in the area around Edo.' Red peppers 'were first brought in at the time of Hideyoshi's invasions of Korea' although according to the *Bukō nenpyō* (Chronology of Edo), 'they came in at the same time as tobacco from the South in Keichō 10 [1605] and are called Nanban pepper'. Sweet potatoes 'came in to Satsuma from the Ryukyus at the end of the Genroku period [1688–98]'.[78] Other fruits and vegetables which came via Jakarta included potatoes, spinach, Chinese broccoli, a citrus fruit known as Buddha's hand, grapes, peanuts, dates, bananas and even tomatoes, which were highly prized. (See the following chart.)

Crops by Period of Transmission or Period in which Cultivation Began

(Not in chronological order within each period)

Period	Crops
Yayoi period 200 B.C.–A.D. 250	rice plants, foxtail millet, Deccan grass, soy beans, taro, gourds, hemp, rape seed?, peaches, Japanese apricots
Yamato/Nara/Heian periods to 12th century	wheat, barley, Indian and Chinese millet, buckwheat, peas, fava beans, adzuki beans, black-eyed peas, cucumbers, melon cucumber, aubergines, mustard, lettuce, white radish, turnip, leeks, shallots, beefsteak plant, lotus, fennel, garlic, poppy, tea, sesame, safflower, castor oil plant, konnyaku, pears, loquat, apricots, damson plums, citron, persimmon, chestnuts, jujube, Chinese milk vetch, coriander
Kamakura/Muromachi periods to 16th century	Chinese yam, cotton, loofah, kumquats, pomegranate, grapes, kale, maize, watermelon, pumpkin, potatoes, red pepper
Edo period to 19th century	pearl barley, green beans, peanuts, lima beans, cabbage, tomatoes, spinach, parsley, celery, Chinese cabbage, carrots, onions, sweet potatoes, asparagus, moso bamboo, dill, tobacco, sugar cane, sunflower, apples, Western pears, tangerines, natsu mikan, shaddock, figs, walnuts, strawberries, lichee, passion fruit, orchard grass, clover, alfalfa
Meiji period	rye, oats, kidney beans, melon, okra, cauliflower, artichoke, mushrooms, hops, sugar beet, flax, cherries, lemons, oranges, olives, pineapple, rye grass

Sources: N. W. Simmonds, ed., *Evolution of Crop Plants* (London; Longman, 1976); Hoshikawa Kiyochika, *Saibai shokubutsu no kigen to denpa* [The origins and diffusion of cultivated plants] (Tokyo, Ninomiya Shoten, 1978).

These changes in European and Japanese society between the Middle Ages and the early modern period produced a revolution in life styles. Similar items were used in both societies. Each item a society uses has its own unique shape, colour, quality, and function, a name suited to that function, and a cultural meaning attached to it. Any change in the product also produces a change in the culture. The transformation of the product complex causes a transformation of society as a whole. This major transformation took place in Japan and Europe at roughly the same time. The background to these cultural and economic changes were plagues and other shared crises beyond human comprehension and the control of medieval society.

In overcoming these crises, Europe developed the 'modern world-system', and Japan developed the *sakoku* system of national seclusion. The different methods they adopted were the result of different responses to the products they accepted. Though both were alike in being on the periphery of the old civilisations, Japan and Europe clearly differed from one another not only in features such as latitude, climate, and soil conditions but also in their existing cultures. As a result, two different systems were established, one based on a labour-intensive industrial revolution, the other, on a capital-intensive industrial revolution. But both were alike in being production-oriented. The priority given to production was forced on them by necessity. If Europe and Japan had not focussed on increasing and diversifying production, either capital-intensive or labour-intensive, they would not have had anything to exchange with the old civilisations except precious metals. The move toward production was a means to acquire the products of the old civilisations. If the Europeans and the Japanese had had an adequately developed commercial network like the overseas Chinese and had been able to acquire the products they wanted in this way without changing their productivity and product range, then the mentality that focussed on increasing their products and market range might never have happened.

The encounter between these two different production cultures occurred with the opening up of Japan at the end of the Tokugawa period and the destruction of the *sakoku* system. Japan once again faced a crisis. It had been able to escape the crisis confronting it at the end of the Middle Ages by creating what might be called a miniature Chinese system.

This time it escaped the crisis by joining the 'modern world-system'. It brought in the West's labour-saving technology and endowed it with the spirit of hard work cultivated by its own labour-intensive industrial revolution. Japan's rapid economic growth can be understood in these terms. It could not, however, introduce only Western technology. The technology imported from the West also had a cultural significance. Japan's acceptance of Western technology meant its acceptance of the culture inextricably bound with it.

The Japanese of the Meiji period raised the banner of 'civilisation and enlightenment' and set about learning from Western civilisation, making it national policy to 'build a rich country and a strong army'. But Japan grew too strong militarily and ended up being crushed by the West. After the Second World War, it dropped the idea of a 'strong army' and devoted itself singlemindedly to 'building a rich country' through high economic growth and is now universally acknowledged as an economic superpower. Japan's GNP has overtaken each of the European countries that it had once aspired to catch up with and currently threatens the United States in all the cutting-edge technologies with the exception of armaments, aviation, and space. For Japan, the Western great powers were both the model and target it studied, imitated, and worked hard to catch up with and then overtake. The century of 'into-the-West' that began when Fukuzawa Yukichi first raised the slogan has ended.

This means that the framework of the Japanese world view will have to change. Ever since Japan's ports were opened by the West in the 1850s, the Japanese have always been implicitly and explicitly aware of a dichotomy between the 'advanced' West versus 'less developed' Japan. This dichotomy in various guises has been a theme that has threaded its way through every period since then: 'opening the country' versus 'expelling the barbarians' in the late Tokugawa period; 'the people's rights' versus 'the nation's rights' in the Meiji period; 'democracy' versus 'fascism' in the years between the two world wars; 'reform' versus 'conservatism' in the postwar period. These are just variations on the theme of whether it is better for Japanese to align themselves with 'the advanced West' or to cherish the values of 'backward Japan'. Does an inferiority complex toward the West lie at the root of this dichotomy? What is true, however, is that the values of the modern West have become part of the Japanese outlook on life.

Nowadays, this framework is losing its strength. After the war, books on history and political science by Ōtsuka Hisao and Maruyama Masao were full of misgivings about the dangers if Japanese modernisation continue unchanged and longed for the idea of the 'modern West', a longing backed up by a sense of mission to bring Japan closer to it. With the decline of Britain, its erstwhile champion, however, the modern West cannot be seen as Utopia or as *sollen*—an ideal or a moral imperative—and is a castle built upon sand.

As Japan has caught up materially, the pattern of being content simply to introduce the findings of Western research has lost any real meaning in academia. To overstate the case, what we are seeing in Japan is the decline of the modern West. When a historical event reaches its culmination, a sense of recognition is said to occur that allows us to see it in its entirety. What did the 'modern West' mean to Japan? Now that the West is approaching its twilight and Minerva's owl is about to take wing, it is time to explore the total significance of that question. Where is the intellectual horizon that will allow us to see the modern West's role in Japan in its entirety?

To oversimplify, the relationship between Japanese civilisation and the dominant civilisation, the modern West, is one of aspiration and confrontation. The aspiration stage has been a hundred-year cycle that is now drawing to a close. Henceforth, the focus will be on the elements of confrontation. Ever since the hundredth anniversary of the Meiji Restoration, a single world view has illuminated the whole picture in its entirety. This world view is the work of the group around Japanese ecologist and anthropologist Imanishi Kinji (1902–92). It is popularly called an ecological view of history to contrast it with the materialist view. The relationship between the materialist view and the ecological view in modern Japan might perhaps be compared to the relationship between Neo-Confucianism and the Kokugaku (National revival) School in Tokugawa Japan. Just as the world view of the Tokugawa period can be understood in its entirety only by tracing the process that began with the acceptance of Neo-Confucianism and culminated in the establishment of Kokugaku in opposition to it, so too the dynamism of the world view of modern Japan can only be grasped in its entirety by a coherent discussion of the materialist view of history and the ecological view of history that opposes it. For the present, we will fix our horizon here.

Appendices

Appendix 1. British Exports of Cotton Goods to India, China, and Japan

(i) Exports of Cotton Yarn from Britain to India, China, and Japan
—In Value (£'ooo) —

Year	Total Exports	China Hong Kong	China Treaty Ports	Japan	British India
1871	15,061	462	—	550	1,525
1872	16,697	424	170	738	1,738
1873	15,895	545	61	429	1,911
1874	14,517	749	52	351	2,501
1875	13,173	681	54	684	2,147
1876	12,782	531	—	703	2,062
1877	12,193	740	46	616	2,256
1878	13,017	403	48	985	2,107
1879	12,107	492	94	944	1,846
1880	11,902	743	121	1,130	2,833
1881	13,165	665	121	1,112	2,518
1882	12,865	558	59	766	2,625
1883	13,510	391	151	753	2,555
1884	13,813	492	124	836	2,796
1885	11,865	551	232	456	2,278
1886	11,487	216	151	534	2,471
1887	11,379	263	143	830	2,517
1888	11,657	375	258	1,007	2,712
1889	11,712	222	97	1,042	2,250
1890	12,341	269	289	983	2,564
1891	11,177	287	173	644	2,399
1892	9,693	179	82	836	1,755
1893	9,056	171	107	811	1,773
1894	9,286	192	97	663	1,643
1895	9,291	202	100	859	1,627
1896	10,045	143	140	1,109	2,061
1897	9,930	232	101	1,041	1,958
1898	8,923	209	156	699	1,595
1899	8,059	192	114	580	1,444
1900	7,741	56	29	699	1,485
——— Annual average per decade ———					
1871 /80	13,734 (100%)	577 (4.2%)	81 (0.6%)	713 (5.2%)	2,093 (15.2%)
1881 /90	12,379 (100%)	400 (3.2%)	163 (1.3%)	832 (6.7%)	2,529 (20.4%)
1891 /1900	9,320 (100%)	186 (2.0%)	110 (1.2%)	794 (8.5%)	1,774 (19.0%)

Source: Annual Statement of the Trade of the United Kingdom with Foreign Countries and British
Possessions for each year.

(ii) Exports of Cotton Cloth—Plain—from Britain to India, China, and Japan —In Value (£'ooo)—

Year	Total Exports	China Hong Kong	China Treaty Ports	Japan	British India
1871	33,303	1,306	4,779	453	9,825
1872	34,843	1,224	4,477	349	9,413
1873	34,273	1,414	2,919	262	11,187
1874	34,741	1,552	3,026	218	11,613
1875	33,255	1,802	3,026	361	10,920
1876	31,454	1,560	3,105	388	10,371
1877	31,810	1,463	2,429	183	11,962
1878	29,169	1,387	2,039	206	10,374
1879	29,254	1,571	2,700	446	10,029
1880	34,755	1,777	2,802	396	13,786
1881	37,170	1,818	3,464	397	14,298
1882	33,470	1,475	2,618	417	12,955
1883	34,151	1,343	2,239	311	13,689
1884	31,850	1,412	2,154	302	12,342
1885	30,565	1,597	2,785	275	11,736
1886	32,238	1,005	2,912	215	14,177
1887	32,814	1,162	3,511	391	12,983
1888	34,198	1,235	3,594	596	14,769
1889	32,348	973	3,128	540	13,589
1890	34,327	1,125	4,003	433	14,727
1891	33,014	1,065	3,664	441	13,473
1892	29,597	718	3,267	456	12,277
1893	26,979	601	2,286	371	12,243
1894	30,614	581	2,490	425	14,267
1895	27,341	802	3,000	614	10,121
1896	29,301	657	3,137	579	12,635
1897	27,408	737	2,395	548	11,190
1898	28,576	786	2,703	623	12,252
1899	28,830	922	2,994	498	12,364
1900	29,421	740	2,402	693	12,261
————— Annual average per decade —————					
1871 /80	32,686 (100%)	1,506 (4.6%)	3,130 (9.6%)	326 (1.0%)	10,948 (33.5%)
1881 /90	33,313 (100%)	1,315 (3.9%)	3,041 (9.1%)	388 (1.2%)	13,527 (40.6%)
1891 /1900	29,108 (100%)	761 (2.6%)	2,834 (9.7%)	525 (1.8%)	12,308 (42.3%)

Source: Annual Statement of the Trade of the United Kingdom with Foreign Countries and British Possessions for each year.

(iii) Exports of Cotton Cloth—Printed—from Britain to India, China, and Japan
—In Value (£'ooo)—

Year	Total	China		Japan	British India
	Exports	Hong Kong	Treaty Ports		
1871	19,564	196	221	—	1,642
1872	23,361	305	339	82	1,808
1873	21,581	476	449	97	1,812
1874	19,603	404	318	57	1,956
1875	19,901	143	332	243	2,459
1876	18,494	131	227	237	2,371
1877	20,219	175	340	240	2,288
1878	18,578	190	373	442	2,430
1879	17,253	176	360	311	2,375
1880	22,377	204	480	469	4,236
1881	21,235	194	489	384	3,159
1882	21,006	136	384	194	3,721
1883	20,831	97	424	218	3,771
1884	19,806	137	483	196	3,777
1885	17,706	261	648	220	3,741
1886	17,922	129	524	168	4,311
1887	18,924	141	812	308	3,473
1888	18,381	182	879	192	3,463
1889	19,036	105	424	304	3,811
1890	19,830	148	753	275	3,555
1891	19,417	149	869	236	3,266
1892	19,166	132	844	322	3,025
1893	20,302	113	659	341	3,537
1894	19,602	120	604	328	3,727
1895	19,417	134	684	296	2,486
1896	21,879	176	1,431	688	3,427
1897	18,395	135	944	448	2,283
1898	19,332	187	644	414	2,463
1899	22,029	309	1,043	462	4,148
1900	22,961	492	1,396	903	3,372
	———	Annual average per decade		———	
1871 /80	20,093 (100%)	240 (1.2%)	344 (1.7%)	218 (1.1%)	2,338 (11.6%)
1881 /90	19,468 (100%)	153 (0.8%)	582 (3.0%)	246 (1.3%)	3,678 (18.9%)
1891 /1900	20,250 (100%)	195 (1.0%)	912 (4.5%)	444 (2.2%)	3,173 (15.7%)

Source: Anuual Statement of the Trade of the United Kingdom with Foreign Countries and British Possessions for each year.

(iv) Exports of Cotton Yarn from Britain to India, China, and Japan
— In Volume ('ooo *lbs.*) —

Year	Total Exports	China Hong Kong	China Treaty Ports	Japan	British India
1871	193,695	8,262	—	10,217	21,892
1872	212,328	7,034	2,732	11,909	22,620
1873	214,779	9,410	1,081	7,663	25,971
1874	220,683	14,148	1,040	7,160	35,340
1875	215,610	13,504	1,055	14,810	30,352
1876	232,555	11,665	—	17,363	31,663
1877	227,651	16,970	992	15,125	36,030
1878	250,632	9,906	1,152	25,410	33,392
1879	235,626	11,913	2,431	24,608	29,363
1880	215,545	16,783	2,731	26,912	44,098
1881	254,940	16,232	2,917	28,330	40,183
1882	238,255	13,784	1,443	19,144	42,082
1883	264,772	9,489	3,882	20,129	42,172
1884	270,905	12,559	3,163	23,135	45,585
1885	245,810	14,230	6,144	12,687	41,521
1886	254,331	6,183	4,416	16,325	46,606
1887	251,026	7,778	4,104	23,473	48,852
1888	255,846	10,363	7,111	27,169	54,069
1889	252,436	6,180	2,649	26,891	45,354
1890	258,291	7,179	7,590	23,101	49,734
1891	245,259	8,316	4,829	14,804	49,991
1892	233,224	5,923	2,458	23,328	39,505
1893	206,546	5,544	3,225	18,963	38,538
1894	236,121	6,696	3,074	14,639	39,994
1895	251,989	7,667	3,558	21,266	41,071
1896	246,433	4,839	4,237	22,737	49,166
1897	252,547	8,081	3,165	23,143	47,693
1898	246,663	7,775	5,335	17,192	42,673
1899	213,125	7,419	3,925	12,524	39,015
1900	158,273	1,467	803	11,279	32,155
		— Annual average per decade —			
1871 /80	221,910 (100%)	11,960 (5.4%)	1,652 (0.7%)	16,118 (7.3%)	31,072 (14.0%)
1881 /90	254,661 (100%)	10,398 (4.1%)	4,342 (1.7%)	22,038 (8.7%)	45,616 (17.9%)
1891 /1900	229,018 (100%)	6,373 (2.8%)	3,461 (1.5%)	17,988 (7.9%)	41,980 (18.3%)

Source: Annual Statement of the Trade of the United Kingdom with Foreign Countries and British Possessions for each year.

(v) Exports of Cotton Cloth — Plain — from Britain to India, China, and Japan
— In Volume ('ooo yds.) —

Year	Total	China		Japan	British India
	Exports	Hong Kong	Treaty Ports		
1871	2,399,227	92,053	354,930	34,972	818,857
1872	2,379,968	76,241	295,878	24,413	749,687
1873	2,384,174	97,294	213,731	19,895	881,132
1874	2,586,710	117,198	242,085	17,983	998,427
1875	2,549,146	133,814	240,495	29,271	970,156
1876	2,667,423	133,692	296,293	35,368	1,017,594
1877	2,699,282	120,092	219,247	15,829	1,155,340
1878	2,539,166	117,213	193,869	18,697	1,028,660
1879	2,652,441	144,635	287,586	43,360	1,032,092
1880	3,057,966	152,411	258,834	35,501	1,361,256
1881	3,361,299	153,625	330,892	40,042	1,407,540
1882	2,959,883	127,458	242,977	40,808	1,245,171
1883	3,136,180	118,996	216,997	31,461	1,360,593
1884	3,095,354	137,341	215,281	31,533	1,335,083
1885	3,149,906	165,130	296,175	30,125	1,339,371
1886	3,497,866	98,767	309,588	22,866	1,712,058
1887	3,473,308	114,666	366,650	42,620	1,494,521
1888	3,607,991	127,595	369,110	62,669	1,694,319
1889	3,465,464	99,767	334,824	56,606	1,607,673
1890	3,581,715	108,107	395,774	43,707	1,675,333
1891	3,433,424	101,095	361,734	44,945	1,527,587
1892	3,329,037	76,484	349,652	52,315	1,527,993
1893	3,038,206	60,127	249,036	43,257	1,524,181
1894	3,668,386	74,205	295,505	50,293	1,863,128
1895	3,386,769	91,021	367,129	77,770	1,439,628
1896	3,403,843	70,018	345,095	63,465	1,665,390
1897	3,284,150	82,940	282,681	64,904	1,514,103
1898	3,547,874	90,736	331,309	76,710	1,720,670
1899	3,519,332	100,051	352,598	60,934	1,718,507
1900	3,233,126	74,480	258,181	70,973	1,548,664
	———	Annual average per decade	———		
1871 /80	2,591,550 (100%)	118,464 (4.6%)	260,295 (10.0%)	27,529 (1.1%)	1,001,320 (38.0%)
1881 /90	3,332,897 (100%)	125,145 (3.8%)	307,827 (9.2%)	40,244 (1.2%)	1,487,166 (44.6%)
1891 /1900	3,384,415 (100%)	82,116 (2.4%)	319,292 (9.4%)	60,557 (1.8%)	1,604,985 (47.4%)

Source: Annual Statement of the Trade of the United Kingdom with Foreign Countries and British Possessions for each year.

(vi) Exports of Cotton Cloth—Printed—from Britain to India, China, and Japan
—In Volume ('ooo yds.)—

Year	Total	China		Japan	British India
	Exports	Hong Kong	Treaty Ports		
1871	995,947	9,278	12,478	—	101,108
1872	1,137,626	12,416	16,813	3,335	111,376
1873	1,083,306	17,862	19,902	3,473	108,658
1874	1,003,101	17,579	16,341	2,347	120,571
1875	1,001,036	5,364	16,645	10,351	144,087
1876	990,147	6,009	11,804	10,308	148,098
1877	1,125,255	9,178	18,809	11,287	149,229
1878	1,067,298	9,300	19,702	23,533	159,552
1879	1,057,727	9,351	20,712	18,101	172,915
1880	1,416,348	10,894	25,501	25,539	308,406
1881	1,386,338	10,527	28,323	22,867	231,391
1882	1,349,875	7,885	25,517	12,112	276,306
1883	1,379,932	6,239	28,312	13,842	291,923
1884	1,321,646	10,147	31,815	13,822	307,639
1885	1,224,424	18,485	44,134	15,287	325,253
1886	1,351,977	9,355	38,113	11,763	406,758
1887	1,430,610	10,508	60,918	22,784	317,435
1888	1,430,249	12,999	64,844	15,188	340,820
1889	1,535,687	7,799	32,036	25,972	393,481
1890	1,543,206	11,013	55,404	20,372	345,696
1891	1,479,009	10,131	61,177	16,175	308,805
1892	1,543,965	9,004	62,261	22,866	322,879
1893	1,613,991	8,759	47,477	25,051	364,103
1894	1,553,843	8,513	47,216	21,218	413,096
1895	1,645,698	11,411	58,584	21,263	278,480
1896	1,813,748	13,915	113,787	41,819	372,357
1897	1,507,776	10,501	69,051	29,143	244,924
1898	1,668,060	15,707	48,312	28,241	363,022
1899	1,919,505	24,823	76,808	32,917	462,367
1900	1,798,518	31,416	90,214	48,483	329,142
	———	Annual average per decade	———		
1871	1,087,779	10,723	17,871	12,030	152,400
/80	(100%)	(1.0%)	(1.6%)	(1.1%)	(14.0%)
1881	1,395,394	10,496	40,942	17,401	323,670
/90	(100%)	(0.8%)	(2.9%)	(1.2%)	(23.2%)
1891	1,654,411	14,418	67,489	28,718	345,918
/1900	(100%)	(0.9%)	(4.1%)	(1.7%)	(21.0%)

Source: Annual Statement of the Trade of the United Kingdom with Foreign Countries and British
Possessions for each year.

Appendix 2. Imports of Cotton Yarn into British India, 1871–1910

Year	Quantity (*lbs*)	Year	Quantity (*lbs*)
1871	39,993,582	1891	50,970,950
1872	28,379,619	1892	50,404,318
1873	31,689,441	1893	38,276,545
1874	30,578,815	1894	42,806,991
1875	37,097,260	1895	41,482,747
1876	31,972,340	1896	46,354,766
1877	33,270,208	1897	50,173,890
1878	36,194,125	1898	58,290,717
1879	33,145,651	1899	45,545,668
1880	33,212,952	1900	42,621,854
1871–80 average	33,548,899	1891–1900 average	46,692,845
1881	45,876,575	1901	34,803,334
1882	40,761,751	1902	38,299,409
1883	44,859,175	1903	33,681,300
1884	45,378,956	1904	28,016,565
1885	44,799,637	1905	30,575,855
1886	45,915,123	1906	45,776,742
1887	49,013,979	1907	37,673,288
1888	51,542,549	1908	37,315,737
1889	52,587,181	1909	29,782,373
1890	46,382,525	1910	30,032,457
1881–90 average	46,711,745	1901–10 average	34,595,706

Source: *Parliamentary* (hereafter *Parl.*) *Papers 1881*, XCIII(c. 2976), *Parl. Papers 1890–91*, LXXXIX (c. 6502), *Parl. Papers 1902*, CXII (cd. 802): Statistical Abstract relating to British India from 1870/– to 1879/80, pp. 62–3 for 1871 to 1880; Statistical Abstract relating to British India from 1880/1 to 1889/90, pp. 214–5 for 1881 to 1890; Statistical Abstract relating to British India from 1890/91 to 1899/1900, pp. 210–1 for 1891 to 1900; *Parl. Papers 1904*, LXVII (cd. 1915): Tables relating to the Trade of British India with British Possessions and Foreign Countries, 1898/9 to 1902/3, p.16 for 1901 to 1903; *Parl. Papers 1909*, LXIV (cd. 4595): Tables relating to the Trade of British India with British Possessions and Foreign Countries 1903/4 to 1907/8, p. 13 for 1904 to 1908; *Parl. Papers 1914*, LXIII (cd. 7550): Tables relating to the Trade of British India with British Possessions and Foreign Countries 1908/9 to 1912/13, p. 7 for 1909 to 1910.

Appendix 3. The Revision of the Japanese Commercial Tariff on Cotton Manufactures in 1866

Shirtings, grey, white, and twilled, white spotted or figured; drills and jeans; white brocades; T-cloth; cambrics, muslins, lawns; dimities; quiltings, cottonets. All the above goods dyed, printed cottons, chintzes, and furnitures:

		(cents)	(£oos)
A. Not exceeding 34 inches wide	10 yards	$7^1/_2$	0
B. Not exceeding 40 inches wide	"	8 3/4	0
C. Not exceeding 46 inches wide	"	10	0
D. Exceeding 46 inches wide	"	$11^1/_4$	0
Taffachelas, not exceeding 31 inches	"	$17\ ^1/_2$	0
Ditto, exceeding 31 inches, and not exceeding 43 inches	"	25	0
Fustians, as cotton velvets, velveteens, satins, sattinets, and cotton damasks, not exceeding 40 inches	"	20	0
Ginghams, not exceeding 31 inches	"	6	0
Ditto, not exceeding 43 inches	"	9	0
Handkerchiefs	Dozen	5	0
Singlets and drawers	"	30	0
Table cloths	Each	6	0
Cotton thread, plain or dyed, in reel or ball	100 catties	50	7
Cotton yarn, plain or dyed	"	0	5

Note: This tariff remained unaltered until 1911, when Japan recovered tariff autonomy.

Source: *Parl. Papers 1867*, LXXIV (3758): Correspondence respecting the Revision of the Japanese Commercial Tariff, p. 5.

Appendix 4 (i). Distribution of English Shirtings to Japanese Localities (July 1878–June 1879)

Locality	Grey Shirting			
	Distribution from Yokohama		Distribution from Tokyo	
	Quantity	Value	Quantity	Value
	tan	*yen*	'000 *tan*	'000 *yen*
Tokyo	501,622	1,112,046	470	1,235
Kyoto	53,460	112,564	150	394
Osaka	145,812	340,664	50	131
Ise	950	3,046	3	8
Owari	12,401	26,135	32	84
Mikawa	–	–	2	5
Tōmi	–	–	6	16
Suruga	–	–	6	16
Kai	–	–	10	26
Izu	–	–	1	3
Sagami	–	–	6	16
Musashi	–	–	10	26
Kazusa	–	–	7	18
Shimousa	–	–	5	13
Hitachi	–	–	15	39
Kouzuke	–	–	7	18
Shimotsuke	–	–	20	53
Shinano	–	–	22	58
Iwaki	–	–	2	5
Iwashiro	–	–	9	24
Rikuzen	–	–	9	24
Rikuchū	–	–	2	5
Mutsu	200	565	–	–
Uzen	2,300	5,686	23	60
Ugo	–	–	5	13
Echigo	13,450	31,564	48	126
Total	730,195	1,642,270	920	2,417

Appendix 4 (ii). Distribution of English Shirtings to Japanese Localities (July 1878–June 1879)

Coloured Shirting			
Distribution from Osaka			
Locality	Quantity	Locality	Quantity
Saikyō	12,955 *tan*	Sanshū	4,011 *tan*
Kashū	17,058	Matsuyama	5,893
Okayama	14,976	Bungo	3,993
Etchū-Takaoka	6,018	Boushū	5,072
Kagoshima	9,987	Chikuzen	13,948
Geishū	9,978	Shimonoseki	4,927
Kumamoto	5,988	Nagoya	11,969
Kouchi	4,991	Saga	4,003
Tokushima	7,037	Sakushū	1,982
Nagasaki	6,975	Unshū	2,996
Himeji	7,897	Inhaku	3,985
Onomichi	5,024	Osaka	29,937
Total		198,640	

Source: *Shibusawa Eiichi Denki shiryō*, 17: 241–84; *Meiji-Taishō Ōsakashi-shi*, 7: 482–553.

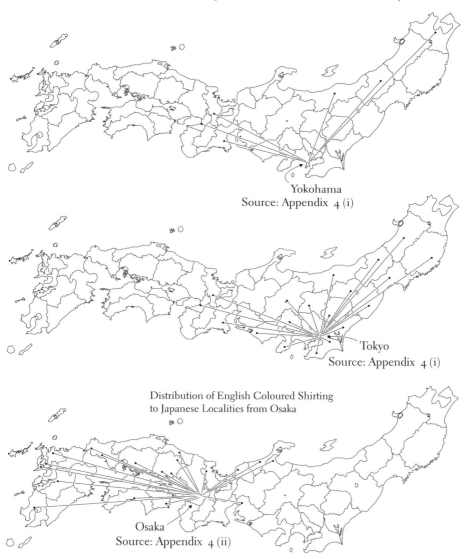

Distribution of English Grey Shirting
to Japanese Localities from Yokohama and Tokyo

Yokohama
Source: Appendix 4 (i)

Tokyo
Source: Appendix 4 (i)

Distribution of English Coloured Shirting
to Japanese Localities from Osaka

Osaka
Source: Appendix 4 (ii)

Appendix 4 (iii). Distribution of English Yarns to Japanese Localities
(July 1878–June 1879)

Locality	Distribution from Yokohama		Distribution from Tokyo	
	Quantity	Value	Quantity	Value
	kin	*yen*	*kin*	*yen*
Tokyo	11,205,600	3,340,771	5,000	575,000
Osaka	8,532,000	2,464,876	–	–
Saikyō	325,800	99,517	–	–
Nagoya	1,761,800	518,323	–	–
Ise	233,850	70,457	–	–
Mino	1,800	30,207	–	–
Mikawa	300	120	–	–
Tōmi	–	–	100	11,500
Suruga	600	186	200	23,000
Kai	128,965	36,997	–	–
Izu	–	–	1,000	25,000
Kouzuke	2,100	642	8,000	920,000
Shimotsuke	–	–	7,000	805,000
Shinano	900	223	2,000	23,000
Koube	2,400	642	–	–
Nagasaki	19,800	5,444	–	–
Rikuzen	21,900	6,819	600	69,000
Mutsu	51,300	14,230	–	–
Echigo	413,050	112,540	–	–
Uzen	8,700	5,454	400	46,000
Sagami	–	–	200	23,000
Musashi	–	–	10,000	250,000
Kazusa	–	–	300	34,500
Shimousa	–	–	200	23,000
Izumi	18,300	12,523	–	–
Hokkaido	–	–	5,000	575,000
Total	22,698,165	6,719,984	40,000	4,600,000

Appendix 4 (iv). Distribution of English Yarns to Japanese Localities
(July 1878–June 1879)

Distribution from Osaka			
Locality	Quantity	Locality	Quantity
	kin		*kin*
Yamato	12,887	Bichū	398
Izumi	5,242	Izumo	256
Iyo	3,624	Kawachi	189
Bizen	2,362	Buzen	270
Saikyō	1,876	Nagato	166
Osaka-City	1,552	Awaji	271
Awa	1,582	Echizen	143
Kii	1,389	Oumi	121
Harima	7	Hyūga	86
Chikuzen	927	Iga	122
Tosa	845	Bungo	155
Suou	885	Hizen	226
Ryūkyū	648	Mimasaka	87
Bigo	689	Tsushima	60
Aki	459	Tango	40
Chikugo	313	Hakushi	54
Etchū	307	Echigo	20
Sanuki	369	Wakasa	9
Higo	556	Inaba	37
Kaga	229	Tanba	33
	Total	40,400	

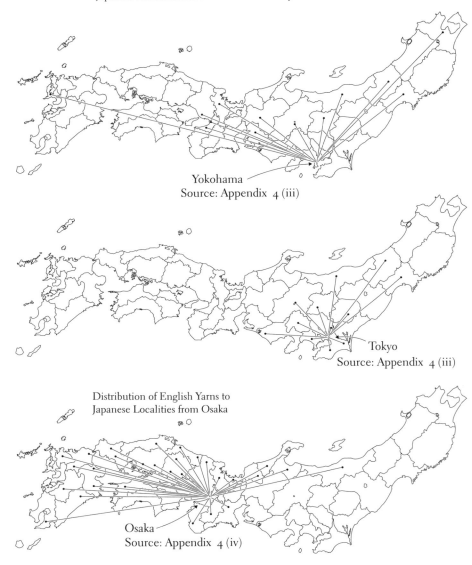

Distribution of English Yarns to
Japanese Localities from Yokohama and Tokyo

Yokohama
Source: Appendix 4 (iii)

Tokyo
Source: Appendix 4 (iii)

Distribution of English Yarns to
Japanese Localities from Osaka

Osaka
Source: Appendix 4 (iv)

Appendix 5. Dimensions of Samples of Japanese Cotton Piece Goods Forwarded in the Commercial Report on the Cotton Trade and Manufactures of Japan

(A) Various cotton cloths				(B) Various fancy cotton cloths			
	Length feet inches		Width inches		Length feet inches		Width inches
1. Mikawa momen	31	11/12	13 $^{1/2}$	1. Memmai Sen	34	9 $^{8/12}$	14 $^{1/4}$
2. Sarashi	31	11/12	12	2. Men Nambu	34	9 $^{8/12}$	14 $^{1/4}$
3. Hanzarashi	33	6 $^{1/12}$	13 $^{1/2}$	3. Futako momen	33	6 $^{9/12}$	14 $^{1/4}$
4. Mizufuri Mōka	34	9 $^{8/12}$	14 $^{1/4}$	4. Tamaire Futako	33	6 $^{9/12}$	14 $^{1/4}$
5. Akane	31	11/12	14 $^{1/4}$	5. Kinufuteko	33	6 $^{8/12}$	14 $^{1/4}$
6. Kon	31	11/12	13 $^{1/4}$	6. Riukiu	32	6 $^{8/12}$	14 $^{1/4}$
7. Moyogi	31	11/12	13 $^{1/2}$	7. Shin Riukiu	36	6 $^{9/12}$	13 $^{1/2}$
8. Cha	32	3 $^{10/12}$	13 $^{1/2}$	8. Hakata Yūki	36	6 $^{9/12}$	14 $^{1/4}$
9. Mimijiro	33	6 $^{9/12}$	14 $^{1/4}$	9. Hachijo	32	3 $^{10/12}$	13 $^{1/2}$
10. Tetsuiro	34	9 $^{8/12}$	14 $^{1/4}$	10. Asa no ha	33	6 $^{9/12}$	13 $^{1/2}$
11. Asagi	33	6 $^{8/12}$	13 $^{1/2}$	11. Nezumi	34	6 $^{8/12}$	14 $^{1/4}$
12. Kikiyo hanairo	33	6 $^{9/12}$	14 $^{1/4}$	12. Yuki	33	6 $^{9/12}$	14 $^{1/4}$
13. Ukon	31	11/12	12 $^{3/4}$	13. Hantenji	33	6 $^{9/12}$	14 $^{1/4}$
14. Momoiro	33	11/12	12	14. Mōka chingata	33	6 $^{9/12}$	14 $^{1/8}$
15. Kuro	33	6 $^{9/12}$	14 $^{1/4}$	15. Boseki tsumugi	34	9 $^{8/12}$	14 $^{1/4}$
16. Hanairo Mōka	33	6 $^{9/12}$	14 $^{1/4}$	16. Kokura ori	29	10	14 $^{1/4}$
17. Mekurajima	36	7/12	14 $^{1/4}$				
18. Unsai (white)	31	11/12	14 $^{1/4}$				
19. Unsai (dark blue)	29	10	14 $^{1/4}$				

(C) Samples of various fancy cotton cloths principally used for summer clothing

	Length feet inches		Width inches
1. Asagi ji chijimi Kōmon	33	6 $^{9/12}$	14 $^{1/4}$
2. Chōshi chijimi	34	9 $^{8/12}$	13 $^{1/2}$
3. Murayama kasuri	33	6 $^{9/12}$	13 $^{1/2}$
4. Yamato kasuri	32	3 $^{10/12}$	13 $^{1/2}$
5. Chijimi chingata	33	6 $^{9/12}$	14 $^{1/4}$
6. Chingata	33	6 $^{9/12}$	13 $^{1/2}$

Source: Parl. Papers 1887, LXXXII (c. 4924): Foreign Office Miscellaneous Series No. 49: Native Manufactures of Cotton Goods in Japan, pp. 17–22.

Appendix 6. Competition in the Far Eastern Yarn Markets between Lancashire and Bombay Cotton Spinning Industries

(i) Exports of Cotton Yarns from Britain and India to China (including Hong Kong) and Japan

(bales of 400 lbs.)

Year	Exports from England	Exports from India	Total	Percentage of English to Total Export (%)
1876	74,600	16,500	91,100	82
1877	82,670	34,460	117,130	71
1878	91,170	48,370	139,540	65
1879	97,560	60,950	158,510	63
1880	116,060	62,760	178,820	65
1881	118,700	71,600	190,300	62
1882	86,000	107,480	193,480	44
1883	83,750	118,220	201,970	41
1884	97,140	158,530	255,670	38
1885	82,650	189,090	271,740	34
1886	67,326	221,600	288,926	23
1887	88,387	274,900	363,287	24
1888	111,600	286,770	398,370	28
1889	89,300	316,910	406,210	22
1890	95,140	362,800	457,940	21
1891	70,000	413,350	483,350	15
1892	79,700	445,620	525,320	15
1893	69,350	332,000	401,350	17
1894	61,000	356,000	421,000	$14\frac{1}{2}$

Source: R. S. Gundry, *English Industries and Eastern Competition* (London, 1895), p. 17.

(ii) Exports of Cotton Yarns from Britain and India to China

('ooo lbs.)

From India		From the United Kingdom	
Year	Yarn	Year	Yarn
1876–77	6,334,719	1876	12,475,335
77–78	13,762,133	77	17,961,820
78–79	18,154,601	78	11,058,200
79–80	23,567,297	79	14,343,400
80–81	22,960,600	80	19,514,100
81–82	26,717,540	81	19,149,400
82–83	37,372,185	82	15,226,700
83–84	41,040,629	83	13,370,700
84–85	56,469,387	84	15,721,300
85–86	68,498,720	85	20,373,900
Percent increase in 1885-86 compared with 1876–77. (981.3%)		Percent increase in 1885 compared with 1876. (63.3%)	

Source: Parl. Papers 1887, LXII (c. 4932): Statement of the Trade of British India with British Possessions and Foreign Countries, for the five years 1881–82 to 1885–86, p. 500.

(iii) Exports of Cotton Yarns from Britain and India to Japan

('000 *piculs*)

Year	From Britain	From India	Total
1873	73		95
1874	99		105
1875	131		135
1876	131		147
1877	233	16	250
1878	177	31	209
1879	244	44	288
1880	253	33	286
1881	221	54	277
1882	185	65	253
1883	167	79	246
1884	146	65	212
1885	121	93	214
1886	136	111	246
1887	162	171	333
1888	233	242	474
1889	187	241	428
1890	179	140	319
1891	128	45	173
1892	160	83	243

Source: Yokohamashi-shi shiryōhen (History of Yokohama City, Documents), vol. 2.

(iv) Exports of Indian Yarns from Bombay

('000 *lbs.*)

Year	A	B	B/A
	Total Exports from India	From Bombay	(%)
1872/73–1874/75	2,368	2,220	94
1877/78–1879/80	20,928	20,749	93
1883–1885	61,754	65,307*	–
1888–1890	140,835	132,193	94
1893–1895	157,758	146,949	93
1898–1900	193,837	177,263	91

Note: Annual average of three years. (*Annual average of two years 1884-5)

Source: Parl. Papers 1876, LVII(c. 1616): Statement of the Trade of British India with British Possessions and Foreign Countries for the five years 1871–75, p. 96; *Parl. Papers 1881*, LXXXVIII(c. 2895): Statement of the Trade of British India with British Possessions and Foreign Countries for the five years 1875/76–1879/80, p. 165; Bombay Chamber of Commerce, *Report of the Bombay Chamber of Commerce for the year 1884–85* (Bombay, 1886), pp. 560, 564; Idem, *for the year 1890* (Bombay, 1891), pp. 772, 776; Idem, *for the year* 1895 (Bombay, 1896), pp. 854, 858; Idem, *for the year 1900* (Bombay, 1901), pp. 444, 448.

(v) Exports of Indian Yarns from Bombay to China and Japan

(bales)

Year	A	B	C	D	D
	Total Exports by Sea	To China	To Japan	Total to China & Japan	A (%)
1877	63,170	28,516	142	28,658	45
1878	82,791	45,933	1,745	47,678	58
1879	82,083	45,530	4,842	50,372	61
1880	106,546	63,194	4,527	67,721	64
1881	110,253	61,783	7,378	69,161	63
1882	132,790	81,434	9,854	91,288	69
1883	154,533	94,982	17,421	112,403	73
1884	189,390	127,318	13,846	141,164	75
1885	216,734	154,517	19,020	173,537	80
1886	265,053	199,407	20,543	219,950	83
1887	292,687	205,158	39,730	244,888	84
1888	336,557	234,071	52,697	286,768	85
1889	376,243	254,697	62,220	316,917	84
1890	429,983	325,060	37,722	362,782	84
1891	454,113	365,038	10,939	375,977	83
1892	476,763	385,771	21,445	407,216	85
1893	399,900	297,572	14,198	311,770	78
1894	455,309	338,703	10,743	349,446	77
1895	481,505	374,119	2,515	376,634	78
1896	573,367	471,023	2,467	473,490	83
1897	452,961	361,221	645	361,866	80
1898	546,811	437,645	475	438,120	80
1899	673,898	579,619	250	579,869	86
1900	341,429	253,331	100	253,431	74

Source: Bombay Chamber of Commerce, *Report of the Bombay Chamber of Commerce for the year 1900* (Bombay, 1901), p. 457; *Report of Bombay Chamber of Commerce for the year 1895* (Bombay, 1896), p. 867.

(vi) Bombay's Advantages over Lancashire

The following is the Report of the Board of the Manchester Chamber of Commerce, as the result of the inquiry undertaken by the Directors, in compliance with the resolution of the Quarterly General Meeting, held October 31st last (1887), the terms of which resolution were:

> "That, in view of the recent very rapid increase of cotton spinning in India, and the exports of yarn therefrom, more especially to China and Japan, while at the same time there has been a very serious check to the growth of Lancashire yarn exports to those countries, the Directors be requested to examine and report to a Special Meeting of the Chamber as to the causes and circumstances which have thus enabled Bombay spinners to supersede those of Lancashire."

The Committee, having held twenty-three meetings, and examined numerous well-informed witnesses; report as follows:

I. The principal circumstance that has favoured the rapid increase of mills in India, and enabled them to a great extant to supply China and Japan with yarns, which formerly were shipped from Lancashire, is their geographical position, which today gives them an advantage of at least $3/4$ d. per pound on the portion of their output that is shipped to China and Japan, and $13/16$ d. to $7/8$ d. per pound on what is consumed in India itself. This is an estimate of the nett advantage to the Indian spinner over his rival in England, arising from his proximity to the cotton-fields on the one hand, and to the consuming markets on the other; after allowing for his extra outlay for machinery, and consequently enhanced interest and depreciation, as well as greater expenditure in such items as imported coals, stores, etc.

II. Superadded to the geographical advantage which it enjoys, the Indian spinning industry, it will be remembered, was for a long time fostered by the import duty of $3^1/_2$ per cent levied on English yarn, which equalled about 7 per cent per annum on the capital invested in the mills.

This so assisted in stimulating the trade, that more mills were built than could profitably be employed, as shown by a fall of nearly 40 per cent, — on the average, — in the shares of 19 principal mills in Bombay during the six months ending March, 1885, and at the end of that year 35 out of 52 mills paid no dividend. It cannot be doubted that Indian-spun yarns, being thus thrown on the Eastern markets below cost price, had a further powerful influence in the direction of displacing English coarse yarns, and the former having practically gained a monopoly, the newest and best-appointed mills in Bombay are now earning very large profits, and, as might be expected, many new mills are in course of erection there.

III. The Committee have further had under consideration whether amongst the "cause and circumstances" that, as expressed in the resolution, have "enabled Bombay spinners to supersede those of Lancashire", the fall in the value of silver has had any important part. The advantage derived from this cause cannot extend to the main items of the cost of erecting and working mills, namely, machinery, cotton, coals, and imported stores, as the outlay on these in rupees increases in precise ratio to the fall in the gold value of silver; but wages, local taxation, and perhaps other small items, are not immediately affected by that fall, and whilst the process of adjustment is incomplete, the Bombay spinner is advantaged.

The advantage thus accruing to him has been represented by one witness as 30d. per lb., and by another as 51d., that is, on the assumption that no adjustment has taken place as between wages, etc., paid in silver in Bombay, and in gold in Lancashire, since exchange was at 24d., viz., in 1872. But, then, it is also in evidence before the Committee that at the earlier period just referred to, freight, and all other charges incidental to the transport of cotton and of yarns, were much higher, viz. 2.175d., then as against 1.060d. now, or, to put the case precisely, the Bombay spinner, after paying the then higher rates of freight and other transport charges on his machinery, coals, etc., had a greater nett advantage in such charges on cotton and yarn, in competing with Lancashire, than he possesses today by .99d., which it will be seen is more than double the benefit set down above as having accrued to him on the items of wages, etc., during the fall in exchange.

Accordingly, as might be expected, it has been shown in evidence that the most important and sudden expansion of the new industry took place in Bombay, when these high transport charges were current, and whilst exchange still remained at about the par of 24d.; whereas, during many subsequent years, almost no further extension took place, although exchange,—the while,—fell rapidly. It may even be added that so great were the advantages enjoyed by the Bombay spinner over his rival in Lancashire at the time referred to, that he was able to initiate, viz., in 1871–5, the competition with him which has since proved so formidable in the neutral markets of China and Japan, although he had then to pay the Indian Government an export duty of 3 per cent, from which the Lancashire spinner was, of course, exempt.

The Committee do not overlook the fact that the Indian spinner escapes the embarrassment to which his English competitor is subject, consequent on sudden fluctuations in the gold value of silver; but they are of opinion that apart from any benefit he has in this respect, or may derive from a low value of the rupee, the natural advantages that he has all along enjoyed, as set forth above, are sufficient to account for his having been able to obtain a virtual monopoly of the Eastern markets, as far as coarse yarns produced from Indian-grown cotton are concerned.

Source: Manchester Chamber of Commerce, *Bombay and Lancashire Cotton Spinning Inquiry*, (Manchester, 1888), pp. 356–9.

Appendix 7. Raw Cotton Imported into and Exported from India

(i) Quantity of Total Exports of Raw Cotton from India ('ooo cwt.)
— Official Years ended 31 March—

Year	Quantity	Year	Quantity	Year	Quantity
1871	5,157	1881	4,542	1891	5,925
1872	7,225	1882	5,630	1892	4,430
1873	4,413	1883	6,170	1893	4,789
1874	4,500	1884	5,987	1894	4,794
1875	5,600	1885	5,070	1895	3,387
1876	5,011	1886	4,192	1896	5,249
1877	4,558	1887	5,436	1897	5,217
1878	3,461	1888	5,375	1898	3,723
1879	2,967	1889	5,332	1899	5,412
1880	3,948	1890	6,323	1900	4,373
1871–80 average	4,684	1881–90 average	5,405	1891–1900 average	4,729

Source: *Parl. Papers 1881*, XCIII(c. 2976): Statistical Abstract relating to British India (hereafter contracted to *STBI*), 1870/1–1879/80, pp. 62-3; *Parl. Papers 1880–91*, LXXXIX(c. 6502): *STBI*, 1880/1–1889/90, pp. 222–3; *Parl. Papers 1902*, CXII(cd. 802): *STBI*, 1890/91–1899/1900, pp. 216–7.

(ii) Exports of Raw Cotton from India, distinguishing Presidencies from which exported.

	1887–88	1888–89	1889–90	1890–91	1891—92	1892–93
Bombay	73.1%	78.8%	76.3%	77.2%	80.1%	80.6%
Madras	12.2	11.2	13.6	14.3	13.4	10.6
Bengal	11.5	7.0	7.2	6.0	2.9	5.1
Sindh	2.4	2.4	2.3	2.0	3.4	3.3
Burma	0.7	0.6	0.7	0.5	0.2	0.4
Total (cwt. '000)	5,373	5,330	6,319	5,913	4,425	4,789

Source: *Parl. Papers 1893–94*, LXVI (c. 6886): *STBI*, p. 25; *Parl. Papers. 1893–94*, LXVI (c. 7280): *STBI*, p. 26.

(iii)-a. Exports of Raw Cotton from India, distinguishing Countries to which exported.
—In Volume—

To:	1880 /81 (%)	1882 /83 (%)	1883 /84 (%)	1884 /85 (%)	1887 /88 (%)	1888 /89 (%)	1889 /90 (%)	1890 /91 (%)	1891 /92 (%)	1892 /93 (%)
United Kingdom	44.5	46.4	45.0	42.1	40.0	33.3	34.3	25.7	16.0	11.0
Italy	14.0	15.2	14.7	14.6	14.4	14.6	15.1	13.9	13.3	14.8
Austria	12.3	12.4	10.1	11.4	12.8	14.2	11.7	12.1	12.4	12.4
Belgium		5.4	7.6	10.5	12.6	16.4	14.9	15.3	15.1	14.3
France	13.3	9.5	11.2	11.4	9.1	10.3	10.0	11.6	11.5	11.2
Germany		1.8	2.2	1.7	2.6	3.6	7.7	13.7	16.8	19.1
Russia					2.5	2.8	1.5	1.4	1.2	4.3
Spain					0.8	1.4	1.1	1.9	1.4	1.9
Other European Countries		2.5	2.6	2.0	0.7	0.2	0.1	0.2	0.3	1.3
China	8.2	6.0	5.2	4.7	3.8	2.3	3.0	2.0	2.5	1.0
Japan								1.0	1.3	9.1	9.3
Other Asia		0.6	1.1	1.6						
Total (cwt. '000)	4,542	6,170	5,987	5,070	5,375	5,332	6,323	5,925	4,430	4,789

Source: Parl. Papers 1882, LXVIII (c. 3139): STBI, p. xliv for 1880–81; Parl. Papers 1886, XLIX (c. 4729): STBI, p. xlvii for 1882–83 to 1884–85; Parl. Papers 1893–94, LXVI (c. 6886): STBI, p. 25 for 1887–88 to 1891–92; Parl. Papers 1893–94, LXVI (c. 7280): STBI, p. 26 for 1892–93; Parl. Papers 1890–91, LXXXIX (c. 6502): STBI, pp. 222-3, Parl. Papers 1902, CXII (cd. 802): STBI, pp. 216–7 for total.

(iii)-b. Exports of Raw Cotton from India, distinguishing Countries to which exported.
—In Value—

To:	1891 /92 (%)	1892 /93 (%)	1893 /94 (%)	1894 /95 (%)	1985 /96 (%)	1896 /97 (%)	1897 /98 (%)	1898 /99 (%)	1899 /1900 (%)
United Kingdom	15.1	10.2	9.8	8.8	11.1	6.8	4.8	3.7	2.1
Germany	16.8	19.0	21.6	20.6	19.1	16.8	16.1	15.6	11.5
Italy	13.2	14.8	13.7	15.9	12.2	12.5	12.8	11.0	8.2
Belgium	15.1	14.3	17.1	13.9	14.2	12.2	10.3	11.1	6.1
Austria-Hungary	12.8	12.7	13.1	12.1	13.9	10.6	8.9	8.1	4.3
France China	12.0	11.5	10.1	8.1	9.2	7.5	4.9	6.8	3.7
Hong Kong	2.5	1.0	0.1	0.8	1.1	1.9	3.0	2.8	3.0
Treaty Ports	–	0.0	0.0	–	0.0	1.2	1.0	2.6	3.6
Japan	9.3	9.9	8.2	14.7	17.3	29.0	36.7	36.8	56.4
Other Countries	3.3	6.6	6.3	5.1	1.9	1.5	1.5	1.5	1.1
Total	10,754	12,744	13,297	8,703	14,090	12,970	8,871	11,189	6,617
	(Tens of Rupees)								(£'000)

Source: Parl. Papers 1902, CXII (cd. 802): STBI from 1890/91 to 1899/1900, p. 243.

(iv) Imports of Raw Cotton into India—Official Years ended 31 March

Year	Total Imports	Imports into Bombay	Imports from Persia
	('000 *lbs*)		
1871	3,560 (100%)	3,521 (99%)	3,537 (99%)
1872	2,233 (100%)	2,215 (99%)	2,193 (98%)
1873	3,423 (100%)	3,294 (96%)	3,296 (96%)
1874	1,644 (100%)	1,487 (90%)	1,419 (86%)
1875	1,759 (100%)	1,723 (98%)	1,686 (96%)
1876	2,831 (100%)	2,565 (91%)	2,117 (75%)
1877	4,482 (100%)	4,354 (97%)	3,257 (73%)
1878	6,074 (100%)	5,946 (98%)	5,032 (83%)
1879	7,337 (100%)	7,222 (98%)	6,749 (92%)
1880	8,652 (100%)	8,608 (99%)	8,060 (93%)
1881	6,364 (100%)		6,040 (95%)
1882	4,656 (100%)		3,792 (81%)
1883	4,533 (100%)		4,414 (97%)
1884	5,384 (100%)		4,812 (89%)
1885	7,623 (100%)		7,106 (93%)
1886	8,487		
1887	6,395		
1888	6,123		
1889	7,238		
1890	12,992		

Year	(cwt)	Imports into Bombay	Asiatic	Other than Asiatic
1891	84,236		80,165	4,071
1892	81,258		64,123	17,135
1893	107,472 (100%)	106,982 (99.5%)	58,920	48,552
1894	94,492 (100%)	93,835 (99.3%)	57,624	36,868
1895	77,977 (100%)	77,836 (99.8%)	19,747	58,230
1896	117,394		51,474	65,920
1897	57,017		20,778	36,239
1898	46,213		16,376	29,837
1899	37,468		1,635	35,833
1900	188,795		27,644	161,151
1891–1900 average	89,232 (100%)		39,849 (45%)	49,384 (55%)

Source: Parl. Papers 1876, LVII (c. 1616): *STBI*, pp. 6, 37, 70 for 1871–75;
Parl. Papers 1881, LXXXVIII (c. 2895): *STBI*, pp. 58, 96 for 1876–80;
Parl. Papers 1886, XLIX (c. 4729): *STBI*, pp. 10, 111 for 1881–85;
Parl. Papers 1890–1, LXXIX (c. 6502): *STBI*, p. 215 for 1886–90;
Parl. Papers 1896, LXII (c. 7997): *STBI*, p. 90 for 1891–95;
Parl. Papers 1901, L (cd. 485): *STBI*, p. 14 for 1896–1900;
Bombay Chamber of Commerce, *The Report of Bombay Chamber of Commerce for the year 1895*, p. 848 for imports into Bombay for the years 1893 to 1895.

NOTES

In citing works in the notes, short titles have generally been used. Works frequently cited have been identified by the following abbreviations:

ASTUK   Annual Statement of the Trade of the United Kingdom with Foreign Countries and British Possessions

STBI   Statement of the Trade of British India with British Possessions and Foreign Countries

Introduction

1. See N. D. Kondratieff, 'The Long Waves in Economic Life', *Review of Economic Statistics*, 17,6 (1935); H. L. Beales, 'The "Great Depression" in Industry and Trade', *Economic History Review*, 5,1 (1934); see also S. B. Saul, *The Myth of the Great Depression, 1873–1896* (London, 1969) as a review on this subject.
2. *Bombay and Lancashire Cotton Spinning Inquiry* ([Manchester], 1888), p. 356. See Appendix 6 (vi).
3. T. Ellison, 'Lancashire and her Competitors', *Cotton Movement and Fluctuation 1889–1894*, 21st edn. (New York, 1894), p. 35.
4. R. S. Gundry, *English Industries and Eastern Competition* (London, 1895), p. 18.
5. & 6. These figures are taken from M. Kajinishi, ed., *Gendai Nihon sangyō hattatsushi: Sen'i* [History of the development of modern industry in Japan: Textiles] (Tokyo, 1964), Appendix p. 50. (Hereafter contracted to *Sen'i*).
7. L. G. Sandberg, *Lancashire in Decline* (Columbus, 1974), p. 170.

8. S. B. Saul, *Studies in British Overseas Trade, 1870–1914* (Liverpool, 1960), pp. 43–64; A. J. H. Latham, *The International Economy and the Undeveloped World 1865–1914* (London, 1978), pp. 65–101.

9. E. Lipson, *The Economic History of England*, 6th edn., vol. 2 (London, 1956), p. 93.

10. Quoted from P. J. Thomas, *Mercantilism and the East India Trade* (London, 1926), p. 165.

11. For a critical survey on Asian economic history, see Y. Komatsu, 'The Study of Economic History in Japan', *Economic History Review*, new series, 14,1 (1961) for Japan; C. M. Hou, 'Some Reflections on the Economic History of Modern China (1840–1949)', *Journal of Economic History*, 23,4 (1963) for China; M. D. Morris, 'The Economic History of India: A Bibliographic Essay', *Journal of Economic History*, 21,2 (1961) for India.

12. Quoted from the English translation of the Preface to the first German edition of *Das Kapital*.

13. *Capital*, Everyman edn., vol. 1 (London, 1930), p. 3.

14. Ibid.

15. Ibid., p. 4.

16. Ibid., p. 6.

17. Ibid., pp. 484–5.

18. *Parliamentary Papers 1859*, XXXIII (c. 2571): Correspondence Relative to the Earl of Elgin's Special Missions to China and Japan, 1857–1859, p. 244.

19. Apart from classic works by T. Ellison, G. von Schulze-Gaevernitz, and S. Chapman, representative works on this subject, among others, are Sandberg, *Lancashire in Decline*; D. A. Farnie, *The English Cotton Industry and the World Market, 1815–1896* (Oxford, 1979).

20. The result of this price comparison was published in 1976: H. Kawakatsu, 'Price of Domestic and Imported Cotton Cloth in the Early Meiji Era, 1873–1893' (in Japanese), *Waseda Seiji Keizaigaku Zasshi* [*The Waseda Journal of Political Science and Economics: Essays in Honour of Retiring Professor Yoshitaka Komatsu*], 244–5 (1976).

21. K. Marx & F. Engels, *Manifesto of the Communist Party*, Progress Publishers edn. (Moscow, 1971), p. 40.

22. H. Kawakatsu, 'Qualities of Domestic and Imported Cotton Products in the Early Meiji Era' (in Japanese), *Waseda Seiji Keizaigaku Zasshi* [*The Waseda Journal of Political Science and Economics*], 250–1 (1977).

23. A paper on this subject was read at the annual conference of Japanese Social and Economic History Society, Tokyo, 5 October 1980, and was published in its journal: 'The English Cotton Industry and its Market in East Asia in the Late Nineteenth Century' (in Japanese), *Shakai Keizai Shigaku* [Socio-Economic History Review], 47,2 (1981).

Chapter One

The Eastward and Westward Spread of Cotton Cultivation

1. *Encyclopaedia Britannica*, 9th edn., vol. 6 (1877), p. 482; 11th edn., vol. 7 (1910), p. 257.
2. C. P. Brooks, *Cotton Manufacturing* (London, 1888), p. 17.
3. *Encyclopaedia Britannica*, 11th edn., 7: 256.
4. G. Watt, *The Wild and Cultivated Cotton Plants of the World* (London, 1907).
5. Watt wrote supplementary articles to the work in 1926 and 1927, both entitled 'Gossypium', which appeared in *Kew Bulletin*.
6. G. S. Zaitzev, 'A Contribution to the Classification of the Genus Gossypium L.', *Bulletin of Applied Botany of Genetics and Plant Breeding*, 18,1 (1927–8), 37–65 (translated from *Trudy Po Prikladnoi Botanike, Genetike I Selektsii*, 1928).
7. Ibid., pp. 45–6.
8. In fact, as early as 1905, Professor Gammie found, through his field observations of Indian cottons, that 'All Indian cottons can be hybridized freely by artificial means, and the progeny, exhibiting an equal blending of the qualities and characters of their parents, do not fall off in fertility. Out of the numerous crosses made by me none between an American and Indian variety has survived with the solitary exception of one between G. *hirsutum* [and] G. *herbaceum*. Even in this instance doubts are now entertained whether the plant may not be of the nature of a sport.' G. A. Gammie, *The Indian Cottons* (Calcutta, 1905), p. 22.
9. Zaitev, 'Contribution to the Classification', pp. 46–7.
10. Ibid., pp. 55–64.
11. S. C. Harland, 'The Genetical Conception of the Species', *Biological Reviews*, 11,1 (1936), 91–6.
12. R. A. Silow, 'The Genetics of Species Development in the Old World Cottons', *Journal of Genetics*, 46 (1944), 62–73; G. *herbaceum* was confined almost entirely to the drier and cooler season, while races of G. *arboreum* were more generally grown in the wetter, warmer *kharif* (monsoon) season. *The Evolution of Gossypium and the Differentiation of the Cultivated Cottons*, ed. J. B. Hutchinson et al. (London, 1947), p. 95.
13. J. B. Hutchinson, *The Application of Genetics to Cotton Improvement* (Cambridge, 1959), p. 17; for example, forms of G. *herbaceum* race *wightianum* were found growing mixed with G. *arboreum* race *bengalense* in western India, and with G. *arboreum* race *indicum* in Madras. Similar mixtures of G. *herbaceum* race *kuljianum* and G. *arboreum* race *sinense* were reported from western China. In these mixed crops the two species maintain their integrity in spite of some crossing. Silow, 'Genetics of Species Development', p. 71.

14. Hutchinson, *Application of Genetics*, p. 17.
15. J. B. Hutchinson, 'New Evidence on the Origin of the Old World Cottons', *Heredity*, 8, 2 (1954), 238. For example, genetic breakdown in F2 and later generations was demonstrated in crosses between G. *herbaceum* race *persicum* and G. *arboreum* race *bengalense*. Moreover, attempts to produce agriculturally acceptable cottons from G. *herbaceum* race *wightianum* x G. *arboreum* race *indicum* crosses failed repeatedly.
16. Watt, *Wild and Cultivated Cotton Plants*, p. 322.
17. Hutchinson et al., *The Evolution of Gossypium*, p. 82.
18. According to Zaitzev, 'with a few exceptions, all these places lie within the limits of the northern and southern isotherm of the coldest month showing 18°C (64½ degrees Fahrenheit), i.e., within the region that is considered to be the region of the tropical countries.' 'Contribution to the Classification', p. 40.
19. Hutchinson et al., *The Evolution of Gossypium*, p. 81.
20. Ibid., p. 88.
21. The development of annual types brought about a fundamental change in the whole physiology of the plant. They could be grown as an annual in areas where there was a long dry season or which were subject to frost. Even in the tropics where perennials could make satisfactory growth, a demand arose for annual forms in order to ensure the production of cotton of the best quality, to facilitate the way in which the plants were managed, and to keep insects and pests in check. Hutchinson et al., *The Evolution of Gossypium*, p. 82; *Encyclopaedia Britannica*, 11th edn., 7: 256. There can be little doubt that commercial pressures led to the establishment of annual cropping. J. B. Hutchinson, *Evolutionary Studies in World Crops* (Cambridge, 1974), p. 154.
22. Hutchinson et al., *The Evolution of Gossypium*, p. 84.
23. Hutchinson, 'New Evidence', p. 235.
24. Hutchinson, *Application of Genetics*, p. 17.
25. Hutchinson, 'New Evidence', pp. 232–3.
26. Hutchinson, *Application of Genetics*, p. 12.
27. Hutchinson, *Evolutionary Studies in World Crops*, p. 90; it is also accepted that a form of one of the Old World cottons, the South African G. *herbaceum* race *africanum*, alone is an ancient, truly wild plant, and is the modern representative of the wild ancestor of all diploid cottons. Hutchinson, 'New Evidence', p. 229.
28. J. B. Hutchison, 'Changing Concepts in Crop Plant Evolution', *Experimental Agriculture*, 7,4 (1971), 274.
29. Hutchinson, 'New Evidence', p. 235.
30. J. B. Hutchinson, 'A Note on Some Geographical Races of Asiatic Cottons', *Empire Cotton Growing Review*, 27,2 (1950), 125.
31. Ibid.

32. J. B. Hutchinson and R. L. M. Ghose, 'The Composition of the Cotton Crops of Central India and Rajputana', *The Indian Journal of Agricultural Science*, 7 (1937), 24.

33. Marco Polo, *The Travels*, trans. Ronald Latham (Harmondsworth, 1958), p. 291.

34. J. B. Hutchinson, 'The Distribution of Gossypium and the Evolution of the Commercial Cottons', Papers Read and Summary of Proceedings, Indian Central Cotton Committee, *First Conference of Scientific Research Workers on Cotton in India* (Bombay, 1938), p. 359.

35. *Parliamentary Papers 1847*, XLII (c. 439): A Return 'of Papers in the Possession of the East India Company, showing what Measures have been taken since 1836 to promote the Cultivation of Cotton in India, with the Particulars and Result of any Experiments which have been made by the said Company, with a view to introduce the Growth of American Cotton, or to encourage the Production of Native Cotton in India', with Plans, & c., No. 199 (Mr. Price to Mr. Secretary Halliday), p. 269.

36. Nazir Ahmad, 'Discussion', Indian Central Cotton Committee, *First Conference of Scientific Research Workers on Cotton in India*, p. 36.

37. Hutchinson, *Evolutionary Studies in World Crops*, p. 91. The development of the annual variety can be fairly well dated. Dr. Hove collected the annual *G. herbaceum* race *wightianum* in Gujarat in 1787. Watt noted, 'Dr. Hove's specimens are in the British Museum, and it has to be admitted that they could not be separated botanically from any corresponding set of more recent data'. Watt, *Wild and Cultivated Cotton Plants*, p. 137. With the knowledge now available about the origin of the annual habit it may be postulated with some confidence that *G. herbaceum* race *wightianum* was developed in western India following the introduction of annual, open-bolled forms of the species from Persia in the early eighteenth century. See Hutchinson, *Application of Genetics*, p. 16.

38. Hutchinson and Govande calculated that the mean hair length in inches of northern *arboreum* was 0.77, while that of southern *arboreum* was 0.85, and that the highest standard warp count of the former was 15.5s, while the latter was 28s. J. B. Hutchinson and G. K. Govande, 'Cotton Botany and the Spinning Value and Hair Properties of Cotton Lint', *The Indian Journal of Agricultural Science*, 8 (1938), 35.

39. Ginning percentages higher than 28 were very rare in India in 1840, but the range of ginning percentage of the northern annual type was from 28 to 40. Hutchinson, 'Distribution of *Gossypium*', p. 35; Hutchinson et al., *The Evolution of Gossypium*, p. 94.

40. Hutchinson and Ghose, 'The Composition of the Cotton Crops', p. 32.

41. The first shipment to China was made in 1704 by the East India Company. The amount exported rose continuously until it reached a peak level, about a half-million *piculs* in the 1830s (1 *picul* is approximately equal to 60.48

kg.). See K. Chao, *The Development of Cotton Textile Production in China* (Cambridge, MA, 1977), pp. 102–4.

42. *Parliamentary Papers 1847*, XLII (c. 439): no. 205 (Mr. Price to Mr. Secretary Halliday), p. 275.

43. Hutchinson, *Evolutionary Studies in World Crops*, p. 92.

44. Hutchinson et al., *The Evolution of Gossypium*, p. 95.

45. J. B. Hutchinson, 'The History and Relationships of the World's Cottons', *Endeavour* 21 (1962), 7–8.

46. Hutchinson, 'Distribution of Gossypium', p. 35.

47. Hutchinson, *Evolutionary Studies in World Crops*, p. 92.

48. Hutchinson, 'History and Relationships of the World's Cottons', p. 8.

49. Silow, 'Genetics of Species Development', pp. 68–9.

50. Hutchinson et al., *The Evolution of Gossypium*, p. 94.

51. Hutchinson, *Application of Genetics*, p. 19.

52. Hutchinson, 'History and Relationships of the World's Cottons', p. 7.

53. Hutchinson, 'Note on Some Geographical Races of Asiatic Cottons', p. 125.

54. Chao, *Development of Cotton Textile Production in China*, pp. 4–10.

55. Marco Polo, *The Travels*, p. 232.

56. Paul Pelliot, *Notes on Marco Polo*, vol. 1 (Paris, 1959), pp. 499–507.

57. See Hutchinson, 'Distribution of Gossypium', p. 354.

58. Chao, *Development of Cotton Textile Production in China*, p. 11.

59. Pelliot, *Notes on Marco Polo*, 1: 506.

60. S. Nishijima, *Chūgoku keizaishi kenkyū* [Studies in Chinese economic history] (Tokyo, 1966), p. 760.

61. S. Katō, *Shina keizaishi kōshō*, vol. 2 [Studies in Chinese economic history] (Tokyo, 1952), pp. 711–12.

62. Nishijima, *Chūgoku keizaishi kenkyū*, pp. 732–50.

63. M. Elvin, *The Pattern of the Chinese Past* (Stanford, 1973), pp. 214–15.

64. K. Sudō, 'Kōrai makki yori Chōsen shoki ni itaru orimonogyō no hatten' [Development of the textile industry from the late Kōryū dynasty to the early Yi dynasty], *Shakai Keizai-Shigaku* [Socio-economic History], 12 (1942), 5–8.

65. Ibid., pp. 8–10.

66. T. Sawamura, 'Li-chō kōki momen no chōshū chiiki to seisan ritchi' (Cotton growing conditions in localities where tax on cottons was imposed in the Yi dynasty), *Keizaishi Kenkyū* (Study of Economic History), 28 (1942), 50–1.

67. Sudō, 'Kōrai makki yori Chōsen shoki ni itaru orimonogyō no hatten', pp. 24, 28.

68. S. J. Koh, *Stages of Industrial Development in Asia: A Comparative History of the Cotton Industry in Japan, India, China, and Korea* (Philadelphia, ca. 1966), p. 289.

69. Ibid., pp. 290–1.

70. As the government had prohibited commerce with Japan in 1523, trade in cotton cloth was carried out by Chinese smugglers from Fujian. Cotton cloth from China flooded into Japan in the 1570s, and exceeded that from Korea. Koh, *Stages of Industrial Development in Asia*, p. 293; K. Ōno, *Nihon sangyō hattatsu-shi no kenkyū* [Studies in Japanese industrial development] (Tokyo, 1941), pp. 326–8.

71. The Sō of Tsushima was the only daimyō family allowed to trade with Korea by both the Japanese and Korean governments.

72. T. Sawamura, 'Li-chō jidai momen yushutsu no shūmatsu' (The end of cotton textile exports in the Yi dynasty), *Keizaishi Kenkyū*, 31 (1944), 1–20.

73. Koh, *Stages of Industrial Development in Asia*, pp. 312–13.

74. K. Shiba, 'Momen no seisan-bunpai ni kansuru kyokutō-kōtsū-bunkashiteki kōsatsu (1)' [A note on production and distribution of cottons in the commercial and cultural history of the Far East 1], *Kōtsu Bunka* (Transportation Culture), 2 (1938), 138–9.

75. Ōno, *Nihon sangyō hattatsu-shi no kenkyū*, pp. 345–9.

76. T. Furushima, *Nihon hōken nōgyōshi* [Agricultural history of feudal Japan] (Tokyo, 1941), pp. 197–215; *Kinsei Nihon nōgyō no kōzō* [The structure of pre-modern Japanese agriculture] (Tokyo, 1943), pp. 273–9; *Kinsei nōgyō gijutsushi* [History of agricultural technology in pre-modern Japan] (Tokyo, 1953), pp. 357–9, 538.

77. Ōno, *Nihon sangyō hattatsu-shi no kenkyū*, pp. 356, 367.

78. See, for example, the discussion by W. B. Hauser, *Economic Institutional Change in Tokugawa Japan* ([London, New York, 1974]).

79. A. M. Watson, 'The Arab Agricultural Revolution and its Diffusion, 700–1100', *Journal of Economic History*, 34 (1974).

80. T. H. Kearney, 'Cotton Plants, Tame and Wild', *Journal of Heredity*, 21, 5 (1930), 196–7; Hutchinson notes the 'great wealth of cotton fabrics of outstanding design and technical competence' found in Peru; 'History and Relationships of the World's Cottons', p. 8.

81. Kearney, 'Cotton Plants, Tame and Wild', p. 196.

82. Ibid., p. 197.

83. Hutchinson, 'Changing Concepts in Crop Plant Evolution', p. 24.

84. Hutchinson, 'History and Relationships of the World's Cottons', p. 8; Kearney, 'Cotton Plants, Tame and Wild', p. 197.

85. Hutchinson, *Evolutionary Studies in World Crops*, p. 91.

86. Hutchinson, 'History and Relationships of the World's Cottons', pp. 8–9.

87. Ibid.

88. Kearney, 'Cotton Plants, Tame and Wild', pp. 197–9.

89. Hutchinson, 'History and Relationships of the World's Cottons', p. 10.

90. Hutchinson et al., *The Evolution of Gossypium*, p. 106.

91. Hutchinson, 'History and Relationships of the World's Cottons', p. 10.

92. Hutchinson et al., *The Evolution of Gossypium*, p. 108.
93. J. B. Hutchinson and H. L. Manning, 'The Sea Island Cottons', *The Empire Journal of Experimental Agriculture*, 13 (1945), 80.
94. Hutchinson, 'History and Relationships of the World's Cottons', p. 11.
95. Hutchinson and Manning, 'The Sea Island Cottons', p. 80.
96. Ibid.
97. Ibid., p. 81.
98. Hutchinson et al., *The Evolution of Gossypium*, p. 106.
99. Mohammad Afzal, 'Cotton Growing in Egypt', *The Indian Cotton Growing Review*, 1 (1947), 169; V. G. von Panse, 'Cotton in Egypt', *The Indian Cotton Growing Review*, 3 (1949), 2.
100. Hutchinson, *Evolutionary Studies in World Crops*, pp. 89–90.
101. Hutchinson, 'Note on Some Geographical Races of Asiatic Cottons', pp. 123–4; Hutchinson and Ghose, 'Composition of the Cotton Crops', p. 354.
102. von Panse, 'Cotton in Egypt', p. 2.
103. E. R. J. Owen, *Cotton and the Egyptian Economy, 1820–1914* (Oxford, 1969), p. 352.
104. Afzal, 'Cotton Growing in Egypt', p. 169.
105. Hutchinson, 'History and Relationships of the World's Cottons', p. 11.
106. The importance of cotton to the Egyptian economy was negligible before 1820, as indicated in the following table.

Total Crop in *Kantars*.
(one kantar = 100 lbs lint.)

1820	944
1830	186,675
1840	193,507
1850	384,493
1860	596,200
1870	196,215
1880	2,792,184
1890	4,159,405
1900	5,435,480

Source: M. Afzal, 'Cotton Growing in Egypt', p. 170.

107. Production rose to 88,000 tons in 1864, and exports in 1865 were over four times the total for 1861, von Panse, 'Cotton in Egypt', pp. 2–3; Owen, *Cotton and the Egyptian Economy*, pp. 89–121.
108. Ashmouni was a new variety derived from a natural cross between Sea Island and Jumel and introduced into commercial cultivation in 1868, holding the

field as the most extensively grown variety in Egypt as late as 1949, von Panse, 'Cotton in Egypt', p. 3.

109. Hutchinson, 'History and Relationships of the World's Cottons', p. 11.

110. Hutchinson et al., *The Evolution of Gossypium*, pp. 1–3.

111. For a discussion of the test, see 'Spinning Tests': Editorial, *The Empire Cotton Growing Review*, 9,4 (1932), 261–8; A. J. Turner and C. Underwood conducted fibre tests, including measurements of length, variability of length, fibre weight per centimeter, and immaturity, on three cottons: Indian, Empire, and Egyptian. The results of the test show very close correlation between fibre length and counts. See, for example, the following table:

Highest standard	Effective length* counts (1/32 inch)
10 – 29	28 – 33
30 – 49	34 – 37
50 – 69	38 – 41
70 – 89	42 – 45
90 – 109	46 – 49
110 – 129	50 – 53
130 – 159	54 – 61

Note: * Effective length is obtained by a simple geometrical construction from the Baer Sorter. Its value is approximately the same as the grader's 'staple'. The figures are accurate to about 3 per cent—i.e., in cottons of about 1-inch staple, differences of more than 1/32 inch can be considered real. (p. 265)

Source: Turner and Underwood, 'The Relation between Fibre Properties and Spinning Value', *Report and Summary of Proceedings, Empire Cotton Growing Corporation, Second Conference of Workers on Cotton-Growing Problems* (1934), p. 283.

112. Hutchinson and Govande, 'Cotton Botany and the Spinning Value and Hair Properties of Cotton Lint', p. 42.

113. Ibid., p. 35.

114. Ibid., p. 42.

Chapter Two

The Spread of Cotton Textiles to the West

1. P. J. Thomas, *Mercantilism and the East India Trade* (London, 1926), p. 31.

2. J. H. Parry, *The Age of Reconnaissance*, 2nd edn. (London, 1966), p. 19.

3. These tropical 'drugs' seem to have been believed by medieval Europeans to be efficacious against diseases. Although this is not the place to enter into detail on this subject, if that were the case, the spice trade would be connected to the plague which frequently struck Europe in the late Middle Ages. At the moment, this is mere speculation, but I. Origo, *The Merchant of Prato*, rev. edn. (London, 1963), pp. 293–5, mentions that various kinds of spices such as saffron, pepper, ginger, cinnamon, cloves, nutmeg, cassia, and even sugar were used more for medicinal purposes than to disguise the taste of imperfectly cured fish and meat. R. T. Gunter, *Early Science in Oxford*, vol. 1 (Oxford, 1923), pp. 3–5, shows that in the early fourteenth century, the first apothecary shop in England (then called the '*apothecaria et spiceria*') sold spices, that the *spiceria* was situated in the High Street between All Saints and St. Mary's churches, and 'belonged to St. John's Hospital', and also that similar sorts of apothecary shops stocked with remedies prepared from plants had already sprung up in Spain and southern Italy in the eleventh century and a little later in Germany. H. Saye, 'Translation of a Fourteenth Century French Manuscript dealing with Treatment of Gout', *Bulletin of the Institute of the History of Medicine*, 2 (1934), mentions cloves, saffron, and cinnamon as cures for gout. D. V. S. Reddy, 'Medicine in India in the Middle of the XVI Century', *Bulletin of the History of Medicine*, 8 (1940), 53, draws up a list of 'the most important herbs and drugs' in sixteenth-century India, which includes cloves, ginger, nutmeg, pepper, and other spices, and suggests that these 'drugs' were used in Europe, too; see also Walter Bailey, *A Short Discourse of the Three Kindes of Peppers in Common Use, and Certaine Special Medicines Made of the Same, Tending to the Preservation of Health* (London, 1588; facs. Amsterdam, 1972).

4. The fact that the triangular structure of the intra-Asiatic trade remained the same until the end of the seventeenth century is a well-accepted fact. See W. H. Moreland, 'Indian Exports of Cotton Goods in the Seventeenth Century', *Indian Journal of Economics*, 5,3 (1925), 225; J. Irwin, 'Indian Textile Trade in the Seventeenth Century: (2) Coromandel Coast', *Journal of Indian Textile History*, 2 (1956), 24; idem, 'Indian Textile Trade in the Seventeenth Century: (3) Bengal', *Journal of Indian Textile History*, 3 (1957), 59–60; J. Irwin & M. Hall, *Indian Painted and Printed Fabrics* (Ahmedabad, 1971), Chapter 4: 'Export Fabrics', p. 36. The main islands of the Malay Archipelago were the Moluccas, Java, Sumatra, and Borneo. Cloves were grown in the islands of the Moluccas. The independent kingdom of Banda yielded nutmeg and mace. Java yielded all sorts of spices such as nutmeg, cloves, mace, pepper, but in small quantity. The principal product in Sumatra was pepper. The realm of Succadana in Borneo yielded pepper in great quantity, cloves, and nutmegs as well. These spices and pepper of

the Archipelago had the highest reputation. The pepper of Sumatra, for instance, was bigger and heavier than that from Malabar in India according to B. Krishna, *Commercial Relations between India and England, 1601–1757* (London, 1924), pp. 29–33, while the Indian Coromandel pepper was poor in quality but dear in price. Indian spices were also inferior to those of the Archipelago, so that it is not surprising that the English East India Company found no considerable trade possible for them. Nor was India suitable for the cultivation of spices. In other words, merchants who wanted to acquire spices and pepper of good quality and low price had to sail to the Malay Archipelago, popularly known at that time as the Spice Islands, S. A. Khan, *The East India Trade in the XVIIth Century* (Oxford, 1923), p. 264. The Spice Islands of the Archipelago in turn required Indian fabrics in abundance. All these regions used cotton cloth. Ralph Fitch, an English traveller, observed in 1585 that famous Dacca muslin was sent to 'all India, Ceilon, Pegu [Burma], Malacca, Sumatra', in W. Foster, ed., *Early Travels in India, 1583–1619* (London, 1921), p. 28. Cambay, Bengal, and Coromandel sent their textiles to these islands 'to exchange them for cloves, mace, and nutmegs', J. N. Varma, 'History of the Cotton Industry from the Earliest Times to the Battle of Plassey', University of London, M.Sc. thesis (1921), p. 218. Indian cloth was practically the only commodity which was readily acceptable to the producers of spices. S. Chaudhuri, 'The Financing of Investments in Bengal: 1650–1720', *The Indian Economic and Social History Review*, 8 (1971), 110.

5. K. Glamann, *Dutch-Asiatic Trade 1620–1740* (Copenhagen, 1958), p. 132.
6. J. Irwin, 'Indian Textile Trade in the Seventeenth Century: (1) Western India', *Journal of Indian Textile History*, 1 (1955), 6–8; F. J. Fisher, 'London's Export Trade in the Early Seventeenth Century', in W. E. Minchinton, ed., *The Growth of English Overseas Trade in the 17th and 18th Centuries* (London, 1969), p. 72.
7. The Dutch East India Company also regularly paid for 80 to 90 per cent of their purchases with gold and silver coins. J de Vries, *The Economy of Europe in an Age of Crisis, 1600–1750* (Cambridge, 1976), p. 135.
8. Moreland, 'Indian Exports of Cotton Goods in the Seventeenth Century', p. 225.
9. Quoted in Khan, *The East India Trade in the XVIIth Century*, p. 153.
10. Ibid., pp. 7 & 154.
11. J. Irwin, 'Indian Textile Trade in the Seventeenth Century: (4) Foreign Influences', *Journal of Indian Textile History*, 4 (1959), 57–8. These methods, however, did not work well; Thomas, *Mercantilism and the East India Trade*, pp. 40–1.
12. A. W. Douglas, 'Cotton Textiles in England: The East India Company's Attempt to Exploit Developments in Fashion 1660–1721', *Journal of British Studies*, 8 (1969), 29–30.

13. Ibid., p. 33.

14. Fisher, 'London's Export Trade in the Early Seventeenth Century', p. 68.

15. Quoted in Thomas, *Mercantilism and the East India Trade*, p. 28.

16. Irwin & Hall, *Indian Painted and Printed Fabrics*, p. 36.

17. R. Davis, 'English Foreign Trade, 1660-1700', *Economic History Review*, new series, 7,2 (1954), 153.

18. Khan, *The East India Trade in the XVIIth Century*, p. 157.

19. V. Slomann, *Bizarre Designs in Silks, Trade and Traditions*, trans. by E. M. Wendt (Copenhagen, 1953), p. 116.

20. J. Cary, *A Discourse Concerning the East India Trade* (1699), p. 4, quoted in Slomann, *Bizarre Designs in Silks*, p. 104.

21. Defoe's *Review*, 3 January 1713, quoted in R. Davis, 'English Foreign Trade, 1700–1774', *Economic History Review*, new series, 15 (1962), 294.

22. S. D. Chapman & S. Chassagne, *European Textile Printers in the Eighteenth Century* (London, 1981), pp. 5–6.

23. Thomas, *Mercantilism and the East India Trade*, p. 30.

24. A. P. Wadsworth & J. de L. Mann, *The Cotton Trade and Industrial Lancashire, 1600–1780* (Manchester, 1931), p. 117.

25. Quoted in H. Heaton, *Economic History of Europe*, rev. edn. (New York, 1948), p. 316.

26. This imitation by printing began almost simultaneously in France, Holland, and England. Switzerland and Germany also became the leading printing countries. Wadsworth & Mann, *The Cotton Trade and Industrial Lancashire*, pp. 131 & 151. See also Chapman & Chassagne, *European Textile Printers in the Eighteenth Century*.

27. Wadsworth & Mann, *The Cotton Trade and Industrial Lancashire*, p. 143.

28. Slomann, *Bizarre Designs in Silks*, p. 102.

29. Khan, *The East India Trade in the XVIIth Century*, p. 277.

30. Ibid., pp. 227–8.

31. See, for example, D. A. Farnie, 'The Commercial Empire of the Atlantic, 1607–1783', *Economic History Review*, new series, 15,2 (1962), 205–18.

32. Quoted in Wadsworth & Mann, *The Cotton Trade and Industrial Lancashire*, pp. 151–2.

33. Ibid., p.160.

34. Thomas, *Mercantilism and the East India Trade*, pp. 44–5.

35. Calicoes include all cottons without silk admixture.

36. Davis, 'English Foreign Trade, 1700–1774', pp. 302–3.

37. Three to five spinners were required to keep one weaver supplied with yarn before the invention of Kay's flying shuttle (1733), and the latter increased the disparity. R. Patterson, 'Spinning and Weaving', in C. Singer et al., eds., *A History of Technology*, vol. 3 (Oxford, 1957), p. 161.

38. Wadsworth & Mann, *The Cotton Trade and Industrial Lancashire*, p. 185.

39. Colquhoun, 'An Important Crisis, in the Callico and Muslin Manufactory in Great Britain, Explained' ([London?], 1788), pp. 8–9.

40. E. Baines, *History of the Cotton Manufacture in Great Britain*, 2nd edn. (London, 1966), p. 301.

41. Ibid., p. 302.

42. M. M. Edwards, *The Growth of the British Cotton Trade, 1780–1815* (Manchester, 1967), p. 89.

43. Ibid., p. 252.

44. Ibid., p. 89.

45. H. Catling, *The Spinning Mule* (Newton Abbot, 1970), p. 21.

46. S. D. Chapman, *The Cotton Industry in the Industrial Revolution* (London, 1972), p. 21.

47. Ibid.

48. Catling, *The Spinning Mule*, p. 37.

49. *Cyclopaedia*, vol. 10 (1819), s.v. 'Cotton'.

50. Catling, *The Spinning Mule*, p. 115.

51. J. W. McConnel, *A Century of Fine Cotton Spinning 1790–1906* (Manchester, 1906), pp. 11 & 35.

52. Baines, *History of the Cotton Manufacture in Great Britain*, p. 376.

53. Catling, *The Spinning Mule*, p. 115.

54. Chapman, *The Cotton Industry in the Industrial Revolution*, p. 22.

55. Catling, *The Spinning Mule*, p. 40.

56. Ibid., p. 39.

57. G. Unwin, *Samuel Oldknow and the Arkwrights*, 2nd edn. (Manchester, 1968), p. 4.

58. Ibid., p. 6. At this time muslins were made from yarns of counts between 50s and 70s, but in the early 1790s the general level of the counts rose to between 90s and 120s. Ibid., pp. 43 & 134.

59. Chapman, *The Cotton Industry in the Industrial Revolution*, p. 21.

Chapter Three

British Expansion into Asian Markets

1. Marx, *Capital*, 1: 4.

2. Ibid., p. 333.

3. Ibid., p. 462.

4. M. D. Morris, 'Trends and Tendencies in Indian Economic History', *The Indian Economic and Social History Review*, 5,4 (1968), 383; Sandberg, *Lancashire in Decline*, p. 166.

5. For a discussion of this classical view see M. D. Morris, 'Economic Change and Agriculture in Nineteenth Century India', *The Indian Economic and Social History Review*, 3,2 (1966), 187–92.

6. Marx & Engels, *Manifesto of the Communist Party*, p. 40.

7. Saul, *Studies in British Overseas Trade*, Chapter 3; Latham, *The International Economy and the Undeveloped World*, Chapter 3.

8. Saul, *Studies in British Overseas Trade*, p. 58.

9. Farnie, *The English Cotton Industry and the World Market*, p. 91.

10. Calculated from Annual Statement of the Trade of the United Kingdom with Foreign Countries and British Possessions (hereafter contracted to ASTUK).

11. R. E. Tyson, 'The Cotton Industry', in D. H. Aldcroft, ed., *The Development of British Industry and Foreign Competition, 1875–1914* (London, 1968), p. 110.

12. Calculated from ASTUK.

13. *Parliamentary Papers 1909*, CII (c. 4896): Census of Production (1907), p. 22.

14. Calculated from ASTUK.

15. Kajinishi, ed., *Sen'i*, Appendix III-6.

16. S. D. Mehta, *The Cotton Mills of India, 1854 to 1954* (Bombay, 1954), p. 47.

17. *Parliamentary Papers 1876*, LVII (c. 1616): Statement of the Trade of British India with British Possessions and Foreign Countries, for the Five Years 1870–71 to 1874–75, p. 96.

18. Metha, *The Cotton Mills of India*, p. 47.

19. T. Ellison, *The Cotton Trade of Great Britain* (London, 1886), p. 317.

20. *Parliamentary Papers 1887*, LXII (c. 4932): Statement of the Trade of British India with British Possessions and Foreign Countries for the Five Years 1881–82 to 1885–86, p. xlii.

21. Ibid.

22. *Parliamentary Papers 1895*, LXXII (c. 7602): Papers relating to the Indian Tariff Act and the Cotton Duties, 1894, p. 7.

23. S. D. Mehta, *The Indian Cotton Textile Industry* (Bombay, 1953), pp. 86–120.

24. *Parliamentary Papers 1895*, LXIII (c. 7602): p. 8.

25. *Report of the Bombay Chamber of Commerce for the Year 1873–74* (Bombay, 1875), p. 45.

26. *Parliamentary Papers 1895*, LXIII (c. 7602): pp. 9–10.

27. See Appendix 2.

28. *The Indian Economic and Social History Review*, 5,1 (1968), 1–100.

29. M. D. Morris, 'Towards a Reinterpretation of Nineteenth-Century Indian Economic History', *Journal of Economic History*, 23 (1963), 613.

30. T. Raychaudhuri, 'A Re-interpretation of Nineteenth Century Indian Economic History?', *The Indian Economic and Social History Review*, 5,1 (1968), 93.

31. D. R. Gadgli, *The Industrial Evolution of India in Recent Times, 1860–1939*, 5th edn. (Delhi, 1971), pp. 33, 43.

32. G. Watt, ed., *A Dictionary of the Economic Products of India*, vol. 4 (London, 1890), p. 158.

33. G. Watt, *The Commercial Products of India* (London, 1908), p. 616.

34. Ibid., p. 79; M. D. Morris and B. Stein, 'The Economic History of India: A Bibliographic Essay', *The Journal of Economic History*, 21,2 (1961), 195–6; Morris, 'Trends and Tendencies', pp. 384–5.

35. Trade figures for China are taken from L. L. Hsiao, *China's Foreign Trade Statistics, 1864–1949* (Cambridge, MA, 1974).

36. M. Koyama, 'Shinmatsu Chūgoku ni okeru gaikoku menseihin no ryūnyū' [The influx of foreign cotton goods in the late Qing period], *Kindai Chūgoku kenkyū* [Modern China studies], 4 (Tokyo, 1960).

37. *Report of the Mission to China of the Blackburn Chamber of Commerce, 1896–7* (Blackburn, 1898), p. 212.

38. R. H. Myers, 'Cotton Textile Handicraft and the Development of the Cotton Textile Industry in Modern China', *Economic History Review*, new series, 18,3 (1965), 620.

39. Ibid.

40. Ibid., p. 624.

41. Hou, 'Some Reflections on the Economic History of Modern China', p. 599.

42. A. Feuerwerker, 'Handicraft and Manufactured Cotton Textiles in China, 1871–1910', *The Journal of Economic History*, 30,2 (1970), 358–9.

43. A. Feuerwerker, 'Economic Trends in the Late Ch'ing Empire, 1870–1911', in D. Twitchett and J. K. Fairbank, eds., *The Cambridge History of China*, vol. 11 (Cambridge, 1980), p. 25.

44. *Dai Nihon menshi bōseki dōgyō rengōkai geppō* [Monthly report of the Japanese Millowners' Association], 190 (1908), quoted from E. Soejima, 'Nippon bōsekigyō to Chūgoku shijō' [The Japanese spinning industry and its Chinese markets], *Jinbun Gakuhō* (Journal of Humanistic Studies), 33 (1972), 107.

45. C. M. Hou, 'Economic Dualism: The Case of China 1840–1937', *The Journal of Economic History*, 23,3 (1963), 286–7.

46. A summary of these studies is found in K. Chao, 'The Growth of a Modern Cotton Textile Industry and the Competition with Handicrafts', in D. H. Perkins, ed., *China's Modern Economy in Historical Perspective* (Stanford, 1975), pp. 173–5.

47. For example, see M. Shinohara, *Chōki keizai tōkei* / 'Estimates of Long-term Economic Statistics of Japan since 1868', vol. 10 (Tokyo, 1872), p. 196. This book is written in English as well as in Japanese.

48. S. Nakamura, *Meiji Ishin no kiso kōzō* [The underpinnings of the Meiji Restoration] (Tokyo, 1968), Appendix 3.

49. T. Sawamura, 'Richō jidai momen yushutsu no shūmatsu' (The end of cotton textile exports in the Yi dynasty), *Keizaishi kenkyū* (Study of economic history), 31 (1944), 29–30.

50. T. Sawamura, 'Igirisu menseihin no Tōyō shinshutsu to Chōsen mengyō' [The effect on the Korean cotton industry of the acquisition of the Far Eastern markets by the British], *Shakai Keizai Shigaku* [Socio-economic History], 17, (1951), 72.

51. H. Kajimura, *Chōsen ni okeru shihonshugi no keisei to tenkai* [Formation and development of capitalism in Korea] (Tokyo, 1977), pp. 39–126.

52. M. Yoshino, 'Richō makki ni okeru menseihin yunyū no tenkai' [Development of imports of cotton manufactures in the late Yi dynasty], *Chōsen rekishi ronshū* [Journal of Korean history], 2 (Tokyo, 1979); H. Miyajima, 'Chōsen kōgo kaikaku igo no shōgyōteki nōgyō' [Commercialised agriculture after the Korean Gabo reform], *Shirin* [The Society of Historical Research] 57 (1974); K. Murakami, 'Nihon shihonshugi ni yoru Chōsen mengyō no saihensei' [Re-organisation of the Korean cotton industry under Japanese capitalism], in R. Kojima, ed., *Nihon teikokushugi to Higashi Ajia* [Japanese imperialism and East Asia] (Tokyo, 1979).

Chapter Four

Comparison of Prices between British and Japanese Cotton Cloths

1. L. J. Zimmerman, 'The Distribution of World Income 1860–1960', in E. de Vries, ed., *Essays on Unbalanced Growth* ('s-Gravenhage, 1962), pp. 48–9.

2. *Parliamentary Papers 1859*, XXXIII (c. 2571): Correspondence Relative to the Earl of Elgin's Special Missions to China and Japan, 1857–1859, p. 243.

3. Ibid., p. 244.

4. Ibid.

5. *Parliamentary Papers 1860*, LXIX (c. 2589): Treaty of Peace, Friendship, and Commerce between Her Majesty and the Tycoon of Japan, signed . . . at Yedo, August 26, 1858. Japan was forced to conclude similar treaties with the United States, Holland, Russia, and France in the same year. All of these included the 'most favoured nation' clause, and a clause of extraterritoriality to foreigners. These treaties also deprived Japan of tariff autonomy.

6. Ibid., p. 4.

7. Ibid., p. 8. This rate was revised in 1866 (see Appendix 3), so that it might become more favourable to Britain.

8. *Parliamentary Papers 1862*, LVIII (c. 3054): Despatch from Mr. Alcock, Her Majesty's Minister in Japan, April 26, 1860, p. 88.

9. *Parliamentary Papers 1862*, LVIII (c. 3054): Report by Captain Howard Vyse, *British Acting- Consul at Yokohama, on the Trade of that Port during the year 1860*, p. 283.

10. *Parliamentary Papers 1866*, LXXI (c. 3707): Sir H. Parkes to the Earl of Clarendon, Yokohama, May 16, 1866, p. 241.

11. In contrast to Japan, in India and China cotton cloth remained the principle item of import. See below.

Imports of Cotton Goods into India

1870–71–78/80: £ ('000)
1880/81–98/99: Tens of Rupees ('000)

	A Total Value of Imports	B Value of Imports of Cotton Goods	B/A (%)	C Composition of B (%)	
				cloth	yarn
On average					
1870/71–79/80	34,901	18,568	53	85	15
1880/81–89/90	55,915	26,742	48	87	13
1890/91–96/99	69,012	28,835	42	89	11

Source: Calculated from *Parliamentary* Papers 1881, XCIII: Statistical Abstract related to British India (hereafter contracted to SABI) from 1870/71 to 1879/80, pp. 60–61; *Parliamentary* Papers 1890–91, LXXXIX: SABI from 1880/81 to 1889/90, pp. 212–213; *Parliamentary* Papers 1902, CXII: SABI from 1890–91 to 1899/1900, pp. 208–209.

Imports of Cottons in China

Before 1874 in Taels ('000)
1874–1909 in Haikwan Taels ('000)

	A Total Value of Imports	B Value of Imports of Cottons	B/A (%)	C Composition of B (%)		
				cloth	yarn	raw cotton
On average						
1870–79	72,078	26,025	36	83	10	7
1880–89	92,762	38,717	41	73	20	4
1890–99	181,747	93,866	52	68	30	2
1900–09	367,728	183,039	50	69	30	1

Source: Calculated from L. L. Hsiao, *China's Foreign Trade Statistics, 1864–1949*, pp. 22–23, 38–39 (Cambridge, MA, 1974)

12. *Parliamentary Papers 1868–69*, LX (c. 4138): Commercial Report on Kanagawa, 1868, p. 3, stated, 'cotton yarn continued in much request throughout the year, it is woven with hand-spun thread'; *Parliamentary Papers 1873*, LXVI (c. 863): Commercial Report on Kanagawa, 1872, p. 34, noted, 'the consumers of [imported] yarn are for the most part amongst the farmers'; *Parliamentary Papers 1878–79*, LXXII (c. 2358): Commercial Report on Kanagawa, 1878, p. 35. See also T. Furushima, *Sangyō-shi* [History of industry], vol. 3 (Tokyo, 1966), pp. 64–6.

13. *Parliamentary Papers 1878–79*, LXXII (c. 2358): Commercial Report on Kanagawa, 1878.

14. The 'backward linkage effect' is defined as 'every non-primary economic activity [that] will induce attempts to supply through domestic production the

inputs needed in that activity.' A. O. Hirschman, *The Strategy of Economic Development* (New Haven, 1958), p. 100.

15. S. Nakayasu, '"Zairai-men" orimonogyō no tenkai to bōseki-shihon' [The development of the traditional weaving industry and the modern spinning industry], *Tochiseido-shigaku* (Journal of agrarian history), 14 (1962).

16. *Parliamentary Papers 1887*, LXXXII (c. 4924): On Native Manufactures of Cotton Goods in Japan, p. 10.

17. Kōmu-Kyoku [Dept. of Technology], *Daini-kangyōkai kōmubu nisshi* [Record of the second industrial exhibition] (1885), pp. 22–3; *Rengō bōseki geppō* [Monthly review of the Cotton Millowners' Association], 4 (1889), 11–12; 'Wakayama-ken kangyō chakushu gaikyō' [General report on industrial enterprise in Wakayama Prefecture], in T. Tsuchiya, ed., *Gendai Nihon kōgyōshi shiryō* [Documents on the history of modern Japanese industry], vol. 1 (Tokyo, 1949), p. 193.

18. This was in sharp contrast to China, where *likin* was imposed on foreign goods. Although Article XVI of the treaty signed between British and Japan in 1859 secured free transit, duty had, in fact, ceased to exist in Japan as early as the late sixteenth century. Feudal lords did not have the right to impose transit dues on any merchandise during the Edo period (1603–1868). This situation of free circulation of all merchandise did not change after the Meiji Restoration (1868).

19. K. Hattori, 'Yunyūhin no hanro' [Markets for imported goods], *Yokohamashi-shi shiryōhen* 4(2) [History of Yokohama City, documents] (Yokohama, 1963), pp. 267–79. See also Appendix 4.

20. As to the fact that Japanese cotton goods were distributed throughout the country, see 'Naikoku-bōeki no bunseki' [Analysis of internal trade], in K. Yamaguchi, *Meiji zenki keizai no bunseki* [Analysis of the early Meiji economy] (Tokyo, 1963).

21. K. Yamaguchi, *Bakumatsu bōekishi* [The history of late Tokugawa foreign trade] (Tokyo, 1943), pp. 155–7, 219–21; T. Ishii, *Bakumatsu bōekishi no ken-kyū* [A study of the history of late Tokugawa foreign trade] (Tokyo, 1944), pp. 1–30; *Yokohamashi-shi shiryōhen* 2 (Yokohama, 1962), p. 532; 4(2): 245.

22. Furushima, *Sangyōshi*, 3: 41.

23. N. Takamura, *Nihon bōsekigyōshi josetsu* [Introduction to the history of the Japanese cotton spinning industry] (Tokyo, 1971), p. 17.

24. Satoru Nakamura is most explicit about this point in his essay, 'Sekaishihonshugi to Nihonmengyō no henkaku' [The capitalist world economy and the transformation of the Japanese cotton industry], in his *Meiji Ishin no kiso kōzō*, p. 254.

25. *Yokohamashi-shi shiryōhen*, 2: 7–9.

26. Yamaguchi, *Meiji zenki keizai no bunseki*, p. 200.

27. Ibid.

28. Nagoya Revenue Office, *Kannai orimono kaisetsu* [Introduction to textiles in Aichi Prefecture] (Nagoya, 1914), p. 423.

29. Ibid., p. 67.
30. This, though incomplete, is the only available source of statistics concerning imports of local cotton cloths into Tokyo.
31. This amounts to one-tenth of the total output of cotton textiles throughout the country, 20 million *tan*, the figure given in *Meiji shichinen fuken bussan-hyō* [Prefectural production in 1874] (Tokyo, 1959). Thus Tokyo played a vital role in the imports of Japanese textiles as well as in the imports of foreign textiles.
32. Japan in 1874 contained 65 prefectures.
33. *Momen* means 'cotton cloth', and *kishiro* means 'unbleached white'.
34. *Parliamentary Papers 1887*, LXXXII (c. 4924): Foreign Office Miscellaneous Series No. 49: Report on the Native Manufactures of Cotton Goods in Japan, p. 17.
35. Nagoya Revenue Office, *Kannai orimono kaisetsu*, pp. 68–9; *Aichi-ken shi* [History of Aichi Prefecture] (Nagoya, 1980/1), p. 442; S. Hattori & S. Shinobu, *Meiji senshoku keizaishi* [Economic history of Meiji era textiles] (Tokyo, 1937), p. 405.
36. Ministry of Finance, *Gaikoku bōeki gairan* [Annual survey of foreign trade] (1892), p. 387; idem, (1896), p. 52.
37. T. Ichikawa & Y. Irimajiri, 'Orimono-gyō' [Textile industry], in *Nihon sangyō-shi taikei* [History of Japanese industries series], vol. 1 (Tokyo, 1961), p. 252.
38. See Appendix 5.
39. *Parliamentary Papers 1887*, LXXXII (c. 4924): p. 14.
40. *Parliamentary Papers 1887*, LXXXII (c. 4924): Foreign Office Miscellaneous Series No. 7: Report on the Import Trade of Great Britain with Japan, p. 7.
41. Tōyō Keizai Shinpō, ed., *Nihon bōeki seiran* [Foreign trade of Japan, a statistical survey] (Tokyo, 1975), p. 241.
42. M. Umemura et al., eds., *Chōki keizai tōkei* with the English subtitle 'Estimates of Long-Term Economic Statistics of Japan since 1868' (hereafter contracted to LTES), vol. 9 (Tokyo, 1966), p. 195.
43. K. Ōkawa et al., eds., LTES, vol. 6 (Tokyo, 1967), pp. 132–41.
44. *Parliamentary Papers 1859*, XXXIII (c. 2571): pp. 246–7.
45. Chao, 'The Growth of a Modern Cotton Textile Industry', pp. 179–80, 199–201; idem, *The Development of Cotton Textile Production in China*, pp. 174–6.
46. Chao, 'The Growth of a Modern Cotton Textile Industry', p. 179.
47. *Parliamentary Papers 1862*, LVIII (c. 2960): Report by Lieutenant-Colonel Neale, Peking, 1861, pp. 378–9.
48. Kang, *The Development of Cotton Textile Production in China*, p. 353.
49. Kajinishi, ed., *Sen'i*, pp. 43–4.

Chapter Five

Quality Differences between Cotton Goods

1. In 1860, English shirtings formed 54 per cent of Japanese imports of cotton textiles, and remained the principal choice among imported cloths in the following few decades. See *Yokohamashi-shi*, 2: 388, and Table N-5.
2. K. Yanagita, 'Meiji Taishō shi' [History of the Meiji and Taishō eras], *Teihon Yanagita Kunio shū* [Collected works of Yanagita Kunio], vol. 24 (Tokyo, 1963), p. 146.
3. *Parliamentary Papers 1887*, LXXXII (c. 4924): On Native Manufactures of Cotton Goods in Japan, p. 12.
4. *Meiji-Taishō Osakashi-shi* [History of Osaka City in the Meiji and Taishō eras], vol. 7 (Osaka, 1933), pp. 523–33.
5. Ministry of Finance, *Gaikoku bōeki gairan* [Annual survey of foreign trade] (Tokyo, 1890), pp. 186–9.
6. *Parliamentary Papers 1859*, XXXIII (c. 2571): Correspondence Relative to the Earl of Elgin's Special Missions to China and Japan, 1857–1859, p. 246.
7. *Parliamentary Papers 1862*, LVIII (c. 2960): Report by Lieutenant-Colonel Neale, Peking, 1861, p. 383.
8. *Parliamentary Papers l887*, LXXXII (c. 4924): Report on the Native Cloths in use in the Amoy consular district, p. 4.
9. Ibid., p. 17.
10. Kajimura, *Chōsen ni okeru shihonshugi no keisei to tenkai*, pp. 43–58.
11. Brooks, *Cotton Manufacturing*, p. 82.
12. Baines, *History of the Cotton Manufacture in Great Britain*, pp. 376–7.
13. J. R. McCulloch, *A Descriptive and Statistical Account of the British Empire*, 4th edn. (London, 1854), pp. 685–6.
14. McConnel, *A Century of Fine Cotton Spinning*, p. 12.
15. D. A. Farnie, 'The Textile Industry: Woven Fabrics', in C. Singer et al., eds., *A History of Technology*, vol. 5 (Oxford, 1958), p. 576.
16. J. de L. Mann, 'The Textile Industry: Machinery for Cotton, Flax, Wool, 1760–1850', in C. Singer et al., eds., *A History of Technology*, vol. 4 (Oxford, 1958), p. 298.
17. Tyson, 'The Cotton Industry', pp. 104–5.
18. D. A. Farnie, 'The English Cotton Industry 1850–1896', University of Manchester, MA thesis (1953), p. 196.
19. Brooks, *Cotton Manufacturing*, pp. 12–24.
20. *Indian Textile Journal*, 3 (1892/93), 243.
21. Farnie, 'The English Cotton Industry 1850–1896', p. 177.

22. 'Mr. T. Comber's Evidence before Royal Commission on Gold and Silver on Nov. 18, 1887', quoted by Manchester Chamber of Commerce, *Bombay and Lancashire Cotton Spinning Inquiry*, p. 109.
23. See Farnie, *The English Cotton Industry and the World Market*, pp. 334–5, for a general introduction to Worrall's Directories.
24. Ministry of Agriculture & Commerce, *Kōgyō iken* [Advice on the promotion of industry], vol. 1 (Tokyo, 1884), p. 488.
25. I. Ishikawa, *Jūyō shōhinshi* [Survey of important commodities] (Tokyo, 1897), p. 87.
26. McConnel, *A Century of Fine Cotton Spinning*, p. 11.
27. *Parliamentary Papers 1874*, LXVIII (c. 1081): Commercial Report (hereafter CR) on Hyogo and Osaka, 1873, p. 18.
28. Ibid.
29. *Parliamentary Papers 1875*, LXXVIII (c. 1362): CR on Hyogo and Osaka, 1874, p. 52.
30. *Parliamentary Papers 1876*, LXXVI (c. 1603): CR on Kanagawa, 1875, p. 40.
31. *Parliamentary Papers 1878–79*, LXXII (c. 2358): CR on Kanagawa, 1878, p. 35.
32. *Parliamentary Papers 1883*, LXXV (c. 3799): CR on Hyogo and Osaka, 1882, p. 11.
33. *Parliamentary Papers 1895*, LXXII (c. 7602): Papers relating to the Indian Tariff Act and the Cotton Duties, 1894, p. 7.
34. See Appendix 4.
35. See Appendix 4.
36. *Parliamentary Papers 1878–79*, LXXII (c. 2358): CR on Kanagawa, 1878, p. 35.
37. *Parliamentary Papers 1882*, LXXII (c. 3349): CR on Kanagawa, 1881, p. 32.
38. *Parliamentary Papers 1883*, LXXV (c. 3799): CR on Hyogo and Osaka, 1882, p. 11.
39. Kenshi Orimono Tōshikki Kyōshinkai, ed., *Menshi Shūdan-kai kiji* [Proceedings of the conference on cotton yarn] (Tokyo, 1885), p. 8.
40. *Parliamentary Papers 1884–5*, LXXXI (c. 4596): CR on Osaka, 1885, p. 19.
41. Kenshi Orimono Tōshikki Kyōshinkai, ed., *Kenshi Orimono Tōshikki Kyōshinkai shinsa hōkoku, Dainiku, Dainirui, Menshi* [Records of the conference on the promotion of raw-silk, textiles and pottery, part 2, section 2: cotton yarn] (Tokyo, 1885), p. 117.
42. *Parliamentary Papers 1887*, LXXXII (c. 4924): On Native Manufactures of Cotton Goods in Japan, p. 10.

43. Shares of Output of Japanese Cotton Yarn by Counts (%)

	1892	1894	1897	1903
10s and under	3.8	4.6	6.1	2.1
10–20s	93.8	87.3	88.3	86.1
20–40	3.3	7.0	4.0	5.1
40s and above	–	0.1	–	4.7

Source: K. Sanpei, Nihon mengyō hattatsu-shi (History of the development of the Japanese cotton industry) (Tokyo, 1941), p. 83.

44. Nakamura Tsutomu, Nihon gara-bōshiwa [Story of the history of the Japanese garabo] (Tokyo, 1942), p. 133.

45. He introduced the first English spinning machinery to Japan in 1867.

46. T. Kinugawa, Honpō menshi bōsekishi [History of the Japanese cotton spinning industry], vol. 1 (Tokyo, 1937), p. 79.

47. See Appendix 6.

48. The Textile Manufacturer (Manchester, 1877), 171.

49. Manchester Chamber of Commerce, Proceedings of the Manchester Chamber of Commerce 1885–1890 (Manchester), p. 418. Meetings were held frequently on this matter (November 1st, 4th, 11th, 15th, 24th, 25th, 28th, and 30th), and showed the members' serious concern with Bombay competition. See ibid., pp. 424–54.

50. Ibid., p. 418.

51. M. Yamada, Nihon shihonshugi bunseki [Analysis of Japanese capitalism] (Tokyo, 1934), pp. 24–5; S. Ōe, ed., Nihon no sangyō kakumei [Japan's industrial revolution] (Tokyo, 1968), pp. 225–6.

52. O. Kitagawa, 'Nisshin-sensō madeno Nissen-bōeki' (Japanese-Korean foreign trade up to the Sino-Japanese War), in Ōe, ed., Nihon no sangyō kakumei, pp. 197–208.

53. Parliamentary Papers 1883, LXXV (c.3459): Memorandum respecting the Trade between Japan and Corea, 1877–82, p. 5.

54. See Table 3.13 in Chapter Three.

55. The average unit-value of British yarn exported to India was similar to that exported to Southeast Asia (see Table 3.1 in Chapter Three). Therefore, the quality would also have been similar, though the quantity was only one-tenth of the yarn exported to British India.

56. Parliamentary Papers 1896, LXII (c. 7997): Review of the Trade, and Navigation of British India by J. E. O'Conor, pp. 18–19.

57. Bombay Chamber of Commerce, Report of the Bombay Chamber of Commerce for the Year 1875–76, Appendix O, pp. 186–9.

58. Parliamentary Papers 1878–79, LXVIII (c. 2400): Statement of the Trade of British India with British Possessions and Foreign Countries for the five years 1873–74 to 1877–78, p. xviii.

59. *Parliamentary Papers 1895*, LXXII (c. 7602): Papers relating to the Indian Tariff Act and the Cotton Duties, 1894, p. 9.
60. *Parliamentary Papers 1878–79*, LV (241): Further Papers relating to the Import Duties upon Cotton Goods, and to Other Articles in the Tariff of India, p. 18.
61. Tyson, 'The Cotton Industry', pp. 104–5.
62. L. G. Sandberg, 'American Rings and English Mules: The Role of Economic Rationality', *Quarterly Journal of Economics*, 83,1 (1969), 25–43.
63. M. T. Copeland, *The Cotton Manufacturing Industry of the United States* (Cambridge, MA, 1912), p. 301.
64. *The Textile Manufacturer* (15 October 1877), 315.
65. Copeland, *The Cotton Manufacturing Industry of the United States*, p. 21.
66. Ibid., p. 35.
67. Ibid., pp. 51, 221–4.
68. Ibid., p. 235.
69. Ibid., p. 283.
70. Tyson, 'The Cotton Industry', p. 106.
71. *The Textile Recorder*, 112 (15 August 1892), 78.
72. *The Northern Finance and Trade* (28 July 1877), 50; (4 August 1877), 76; (17 November 1877), 416.
73. Tariff Commission, *Report of the Tariff Commission*, vol. 2, Textile Trades, part 1, The Cotton Industry (1905), para. 14 to 28; S. J. Chapman, *A Reply to the Report of the Tariff Commission* (Manchester, 1905), pp. 5–6.
74. L. G. Sandberg, 'Movements in the Quality of British Cotton Textile Exports, 1815–1913', *Journal of Economic History*, 28,1 (1968), 13–15. Naturally there were variations. Italy, for example, produced rather low counts. 'The average counts in 1876 were 16's and in 1898 about 22's, though some mills indeed were turning out finer yarn up to 120's and even 160's.' S. J. Chapman, *Work and Wages*, Part 1, *Foreign Competition* (London, 1904), p. 147. But no Far Eastern country could spin as high a count as 120s.
75. 'The hand-loom weavers . . . now very extensively use the finer qualities of imported yarns for the weaving of the better and special qualities of cloth worn by the wealthier classes', *Parliamentary Papers 1878–79*, LXVIII (c. 2400): Review of the Trade of British India for the official year 1877–78, p. xix; 'At the time of Independence about 20% of handlooms were producing both high count and the more complicated fabrics.' Morris, 'Trends and Tendencies', p. 381.
76. Ellison, *The Cotton Trade of Great Britain*, p. 60.
77. Farnie, *The English Cotton Industry and the World Market*, p. 132.
78. Tyson, 'The Cotton Industry', p. 103.
79. Farnie, *The English Cotton Industry and the World Market*, p. 132.
80. The gross value of home consumption of cotton products was: £11.9 million in 1876/80, £13.7 million in 1881/85, £15.2 million in 1886/90, £15.1 million in

1891/95, and £17.5 million in 1896/1900 (the quinquennial averages). Tariff Commission, *Report of the Tariff Commission*, para. 40.

81. Farnie, *The English Cotton Industry and the World Market*, p. 134.

82. In 1840 in the United States, the best and the finest counts were Nos. 50–60, and 'the finest yarn spun in the United States, of which I [Montgomery] have been able to obtain any account, is only No. 60'. J. Montgomery, *A Practical Detail of the Cotton Manufacture of the United States of America . . . contrasted and compared with that of Great Britain . . .* (Glasgow, 1840), pp. 31, 67; but in the 1900s, 'several American mills are spinning 120's'. Copeland, *The Cotton Manufacturing Industry of the United States*, p. 69.

83. P. Mathias, *The First Industrial Nation* (London, 1988), p. 374.

Chapter Six

Quality Differences in Raw Cotton

1. Sandberg, *Lancashire in Decline*, p. 117 n65.

2. Marx, *Capital* 1: 177.

3. This is a general statement and, of course, is true of cotton manufacturing, too. H. Monie, Jr., *The Cotton Fibre—its Structure, Etc.* (Manchester, 1890), p. vii, states: 'it is obvious that our workpeople must obtain a more intimate knowledge of the material and the mechanical structure of the fibres, as in this way any part of the process which might be calculated to injure or reduce the natural qualities could be avoided'. Indeed, any change in the type of cotton used required particularly difficult adjustments to the machinery. 'According to a statement made in 1912 by W. Howarth, a leading cotton-spinner, when a mill was fitted up for spinning cotton of one staple length, "it [was] fixed definitely for at least twenty years"'; Owen, *Cotton and the Egyptian Economy*, p. 200.

4. *Cyclopaedia*, 'Cotton, in Commerce', vol. 10 (1819), paragraphs 7–9.

5. Baines, *History of the Cotton Manufacture in Great Britain*, pp. 310–11.

6. W. I. Hannan, *The Textile Fibres of Commerce* (London, 1902), p. 105.

7. The measure of staple length used in England was the effective length, which was neither the mean length nor the most frequent length but a measure closely approximating to the 'hand staple' length (or grader's length). The apparatus used for determining the effective length was the Baer Sorter. This estimation was based on fibre length distribution by number and not by weight; however, the difference between the average lengths obtained by the two methods rarely exceeded about three per cent for the same cotton. C. Nanjundayya, 'Staple Length of Cotton', *The Indian Cotton Growing Review*, 7,1 (1953), 19.

8. Ibid., pp. 12–15.

9. W. H. Evans, 'Botany of Cotton', in A. C. True, ed., *The Cotton Plant*, U.S. Department of Agriculture, Bulletin No. 33 (Washington, 1896), p. 77; K. M. Simlote, 'Effect of Rainfall on the Staple Length of Malvi 9', *The Indian Cotton Growing Review*, 4,3 (1950), 143, wrote: 'the value of cotton depends upon the length and grade of its staple, that is, its quality. Of these, the length of the lint is considered of greater importance'.

10. Similar tables were compiled by various specialists. See Hannan, *The Textile Fibres of Commerce*, pp. 94–6; J. A. Todd, *The World's Cotton Crops* (London, 1915), p. 17; Monie, *The Cotton Fibre*, pp. 96–8. We have reproduced Brooks' table because it is more comprehensive than the others.

11. W. H. Evans made a careful study on this point with the principal cotton fibres—Sea Island, New Orleans, Texas, Upland, Egyptian, Brazilian, and Indian varieties. He concludes that 'as a rule, the longer the fiber the less its diameter. The extreme variation in length of the above fibers . . . is from 0.25 to 0.30 inch. In proportion to their size the variation in diameter is much greater than that shown for the length'; see *The Cotton Plant*, p. 77. This means that a certain difference in the length of fibres indicates a greater difference in their fineness. See also Monie, *The Cotton Fibre*, pp. 39–92; he concludes his observation on different cottons as follows: 'as a general rule, the cottons which had the longest fibres were also the smallest in diameter, the silkiest in appearance' (p. 92).

12. For these relations, see also tables compiled by Hannan, *The Textile Fibres of Commerce*, pp. 94–6, and also by Todd, *The World's Cotton Crops*, p. 17.

13. Ibid.

14. Hannan, *The Textile Fibres of Commerce*, p. 88.

15. J. Winterbottom, *Cotton Spinning Calculations and Yarn Costs*, 2nd edn. (London, 1921), pp. 235–6. For a comparative analysis of factor costs between rings and mules using Winterbottom's figures, see Sandberg, *Lancashire in Decline*, pp. 35–43.

16. G. Ōsumi, *Bōshoku genryōgaku* [Study of the raw materials of textiles] (Tokyo, 1917), p. 25.

17. Winterbottom, *Cotton Spinning Calculations and Yarn Costs*, p. 232.

18. *Economist* (23 May 1857), 559ff, quoted in A. Silver, *Manchester Men and Indian Cotton, 1847–1872* (Manchester, 1966), Appendix A, pp. 292 & 294.

19. E. Leigh, *The Science of Modern Cotton Spinning*, vol. 1 (Manchester, 1871), pp. 2–3.

20. H. B. Heylin, *The Cotton Weaver's Handbook* (London, 1908), p. 168.

21. *Parliamentary Papers 1878–79*, LXVIII (c. 2400): Review of the Trade of British India for the official year 1877–78 by J. E. O'Conor, p. xvii.

22. *Parliamentary Papers 1895*, LXII (c. 7602): Papers relating to the Indian Tariff Act and the Cotton Duties, 1894, pp. 7–8.

23. *Kenshi Orimono Tōshikki Kyōshinkai shinsa hōkoku, Dainiku, Dainirui, Menshi* [Report of the of conference on promotion of raw-silk, textiles and pottery, part 2, section 2, cotton yarn] (Tokyo, 1885).

24. Japanese Millowners' Association, *Menka yunyū-kanzei kenmen seigan no yōshi* [Petition to the Government on lifting the import duty on raw cotton] (Tokyo, 1891), pp. 15–16.

25. Ministry of Finance, *Meiji 27-nen gaikoku bōeki gairan* [Annual survey of Japanese foreign trade for 1894] (Tokyo, 1894), p. 395.

26. K. Okumura, *Bōseki kaikyū-dan* (A talk about spinning in the old days] (Osaka, 1932), p. 44.

27. Farnie, 'The Textile Industry: Woven Fabrics', p. 574.

28. McConnel, *A Century of Fine Cotton Spinning*, p. 12.

29. Mann, 'The Textile Industry: Machinery for Cotton, Flax, Wool', p. 297.

30. E. Leigh, *The Science of Modern Cotton Spinning*, vol. 2 (Manchester, 1873), p. 162.

31. Quoted in S. Smiles, *Self-help* (London, 1866; rept. Rockville, MD, 2008), p. 51.

32. Farnie, *The English Cotton Industry and the World Market*, pp. 10–13.

33. The initial consequence was the revival of imports of long-stapled cottons. D. A. Farnie wrote in an unpublished article on Heilmann's combing machine, that 'Sea Island cotton doubled in price at Charleston between 1848 and 1853 and first surpassed in 1860 the quantity of its exports in 1827. Egypt increased its exports of cotton, and the volume imported into Britain rose by 43% between 1853 and 1856.'

34. J. A. Todd, 'The Market for Egyptian Cotton in 1909–1910', *L'Egypte Contemporaine*, 5 (1911), 11. From these 'lower grades', such high counts as 60s, 70s, or even 80s were spun (ibid., p. 2); Owen, *Cotton and the Egyptian Economy*, pp. 198–9.

35. J. A. Todd, 'The Demand for Egyptian Cotton', *L'Egypte Contemporaine*, 1 (1910), 278.

36. Owen, *Cotton and the Egyptian Economy*, pp. 199–200.

37. Quantities of raw cotton exported from India were 392 million lbs. in 1861/2, and rose to 893 million lbs. in 1865/6. P. Harnetty, 'Cotton Exports and Indian Agriculture, 1861–1870', *Economic History Review*, new series, 24 (1971), 414.

38. Ellison, *The Cotton Trade of Great Britain*, Table 1 in Appendix.

39. Ibid.

40. Farnie, *The English Cotton Industry and the World Market*, p. 149.

41. G. Watt, *A Dictionary of the Economic Products of India*, 4: 48.

42. The following table, summarised from the handbook to the Imperial Cotton Exhibition (1905), giving the length of staple and value on 16 January 1905, will serve to indicate the comparative values of some of

the principal commercial cottons. The actual value, of course, fluctuated greatly. The close relationship between the length of the staple and the market price will be at once apparent: Indian cottons were the cheapest in price and the shortest in length.

	Length of Staple (Inches) s. d.	Value (per lb.)
Sea Island Cotton	Carolina Sea Island 1.8 1 3	
	Florida 1.8 1 0	
	Georgia 1.7 11 1/4	
	Barbados 2.0 1 3	
Egyptian Cottons	Yannovitch 1.5 9 4/5	
	Abbassi 1.5 8 3/4	
	Good Brown Egyptian 1.2 7 1/2	
American Cotton	Good middling Memphis 1.3 4 2/5	
	Good middling Texas 1.0 4 1/5	
	Good middling Upland 1.0 4	
Indian Cottons	Fine Tinnevelly 0.8 4 1/4	
	Fine Bhaunagar 1.0 3 1/4	
	Fine Amaraoti 1.0 3 7/8	
	Fine Broach 0.9 3 15/16	
	Fine Bengal 0.9 3 11/16	
	Fine ginned Sind 0.8 3 11/16	
	Good ginned Kumta 1.0 3 1/2	

Source: *The Encyclopaedia Britannica*, 11th edn., vol. 7 (Cambridge, 1910), p. 258.

43. Silver, *Manchester Men and Indian Cotton*, p. 294.
44. Ibid., pp. 32–3. There was 20–25 per cent wastage with Indian cotton compared with up to 10 per cent for American prior to 1858 (ibid., p. 294).
45. A. M. Vicziany, 'The Cotton Trade and the Commercial Development of Bombay, 1855–1875', University of London, Ph.D. thesis (1975), pp. 42–52.
46. Baines, *History of the Cotton Manufacture in Great Britain*, p. 317.
47. Of the output of raw cotton, 7 to 25 per cent was exported from Japan to Britain between 1862 and 1864.
48. *Parliamentary Papers 1863*, LXX (c. 3929): Report by Mr. Consul Howard Vyse on the Trade for the year 1862.
49. *Parliamentary Papers 1865*, LIV (c. 3487): Commercial Report on Yokohama and Kanagawa, p. 13.
50. For a discussion of this point and others, see Vicziany, 'The Cotton Trade and the Commercial Development of Bombay', pp. 42–52.

51. Ellison, *The Cotton Trade of Great Britain*, Appendix; idem, *Ellison's Annual Review of Cotton Trade* (1904/5), 3.

52. E. J. Helm, 'The British Cotton Industry', in W. J. Ashley, ed., *British Industries* (London, 1903), p. 75.

53. Ellison, *The Cotton Trade of Great Britain*, Table nos. 4 and 5 in Appendix.

54. These percentages are calculated on the figures taken from ibid., and from *Ellison's Annual Review of the Cotton Trade* (1904/5), 3.

55. Ibid.

56. & 57. See Tables 6.3 and 6.4.

58. W. Woodruf, *Impact of Western Man* (London, 1966), Table VII/5 in Appendix.

59. Ibid., Table VII/7 in Appendix.

60. Bombay always played an extremely important role in this trade. See Vicziany, 'The Cotton Trade and the Commercial Development of Bombay', pp. 72–74; see also below Appendix 7.

61. D. A. Farnie, *East and West of Suez* (Oxford, 1969), pp. 97–101.

62. See Appendix 7 (iii).

63. 4.7 million cwts. in the 1870s, 5.4 million cwts. in the 1880s, and 4.7 million cwts. in the 1890s; see also Appendix 7 (i).

64. Vicziany, 'The Cotton Trade and the Commercial Development of Bombay', p. 79.

65. See Appendix 7 (iii).

66. *Parliamentary Papers 1886*, XLIX (c. 4729): STBI for the five years 1880–81 to 1884–5, p. xlviii; Parliamentary Papers 1889, LVII (c. 5680): STBI for the five years 1886–7 to 1890–1, p.10.

67. See Appendix 7 (iii).

68. *Parliamentary Papers 1889*, LVII (c. 5680): p. 12; Parliamentary Papers 1892, LVIII (c. 6646): p. 10.

69. See Appendix 7 (iii).

70. Exports of raw cotton from India:

(£ '000)

	1903/4	1912/13
Britain	1,373	717
Industrial Europe	10,028	9,665
Japan	3,156	9,665
Total	16,251	18,890

Source: S. B. Saul, *Studies in British Overseas Trade, 1870–1914*, p. 191.

71. Todd, *The World's Cotton Crops*, p. 53.

72. Ibid., p. 60.

73. *Parliamentary Papers 1863*, LXX (c. 3299): p. 212.

74. R. B. Handy, 'History and General Statistics of Cotton', *The Cotton Plant*, U.S. Department of Agriculture, Bulletin No. 33 (Washington, 1896), p. 60.

75. T. Furushima, *Shihonsei seisan no hatten to jinushisei* [The landlord system and the development of capitalist production] (Tokyo, 1963), p. 154.

76. See Table 3.11 in Chapter Three.

77. Kang, *The Development of Cotton Textile Production in China*, p. 102.

78. A. Feuerwerker, 'Handicraft and Manufactured Cotton Textiles in China, 1871–1910', p. 349. Five million *piculs* amount to 1.3 million bales (a *picul* = 133.33 lbs.). The figure is near to Todd's independent estimates, 1.2 million bales (see Table 4.8 in Chapter Four).

79. S. S. Chong, *The Foreign Trade of China* (New York, 1919; rept. 1970), p. 323. This pattern remained the same in the twentieth century. See Kang, *The Development of Cotton Textile Production in China*, p. 105.

80. Kang, *The Development of Cotton Textile Production in China*, pp. 24–7.

81. Vicziany, 'The Cotton Trade and the Commercial Development of Bombay', p. 41.

82. *Parliamentary Papers 1876*, LVI (c. 56): Copy of Correspondence relating to the Indian Tariff Act of 1875, p. 9.

83. See Appendix 5.

84. *Parliamentary Papers 1876*, LVII (c. 1616): STBI for the five years 1870–71 to 1875–76, p. xli.

85. Mehta, *The Cotton Mills of India*, p. 45.

86. *Parliamentary Papers 1895*, LXXII (c. 7602): Papers relating to the Indian Tariff Act and the Cotton Duties, 1894, p. 10.

88. Mehta, *The Cotton Mills of India*, p. 45.

89. See Appendix 7 (iv).

90. See Appendix 7 (i).

91. Handy argued that 'the increased exportation . . . was at the expense of home consumption' ('History and General Statistics of Cotton', p. 45), whereas Vicziany maintains that 'exports formed only a small part of total production' ('The Cotton Trade and the Commercial Development of Bombay', p. 41). The former represents the classical view; for a discussion thereof, see M. D. Morris, 'Economic Change and Agriculture in Nineteenth Century India', *The Indian Economic and Social History Review*, 3,2 (1966), 187–192.

92. Harnetty, 'Cotton Exports and Indian Agriculture', pp. 414–19.

93. Ellison, *The Cotton Trade of Great Britain*, p. 317.

94. *Parliamentary Papers 1889*, LVII (c. 5680): STBI for the 1883–84 to 1887–88, p. 12.

95. Gammie, *The Indian Cottons*, pp. 28–38, quotation on p. 1. Gammie was professor of botany at the Poona College of Science.

96. Ibid., pp. 29, 38.

97. S. M. Tracy, 'Cultivated Varieties of Cotton', *The Cotton Plant*, U.S. Department of Agriculture, Bulletin No. 33 (1896), 198–210. 'The word "variety" as used [here] refers exclusively to various forms and kinds which are called "varieties"

by cotton planters, and is not restricted to the more marked and permanent types which are recognized by the botanists' (ibid., p. 197).

98. S. Leacock & D. G. Mandelbaum, 'A Nineteenth Century Development Project in India: The Cotton Improvement Program', *Economic Development and Cultural Change*, 3,4 (1955), 338.

99. Ibid.

100. Ibid., pp. 338–9. The only successful attempt to introduce American cotton into India took place at Dharwar in the southern Bombay Presidency (ibid., p. 340.)

101. The Association was a forerunner of the British Cotton Growing Association and the Empire Cotton Growing Corporation. W. O. Henderson, 'The Cotton Supply Association, 1857–1872', *The Empire Cotton Growing Review*, 9,2 (1932), 133.

102. Quoted by Henderson, pp. 133–4.

103. Ibid., p. 134.

104. P. Harnetty, 'The Cotton Improvement Program in India, 1865–1875', *Agricultural History*, 44,4 (1970), 392.

105. Vicziany, 'The Cotton Trade and the Commercial Development of Bombay', p. 115.

106. For a discussion of these and other points, see Leacock & Mandelbaum, 'A Nineteenth Century Development Project in India', pp. 331–51, and see also Harnetty, 'The Cotton Improvement Program in India', pp. 379–92.

107. Hutchinson, *Evolutionary Studies in World Crops*, p. 97. The substitution of American varieties for the indigenous plants became successful after the War. In 1969/70, 50 per cent of Indian cotton acreage came under such varieties.

108. Winterbottom, *Cotton Spinning Calculations and Yarn Costs*, p. 235.

109. J. F. Royle, *Lectures on the Results of the Great Exhibition of 1851* (London, 1852), p. 492.

110. Quoted in Handy, 'History and General Statistics of Cotton', p. 20.

111. Quoted in Thomas, *Mercantilism and the East India Trade*, p. 33.

112. W. Ward, *View of the History, Literature, and Mythology of the Hindoos*, 3rd edn., vol. 3 (London, 1822), p. 127, quoted by Handy, 'History and General Statistics of Cotton', p. 20.

113. J. Blanch, *The Naked Truth in an Essay upon Trade* (London, 1696), p. 11, quoted in Handy, p. 20. An amusing story is told: 'The Emperor Aurangzeb [r. 1657–1707] was once angry with his daughter for showing her skin through her clothes; whereupon the young princess remonstrated in her justification that she had seven *jamahs* (suits) on'; Thomas, *Mercantilism and the East India Trade*, p. 33.

114. Baines, *History of the Cotton Manufacture in Great Britain*, p. 56.

115. Ellison, *The Cotton Trade of Great Britain*, p. 2.

116. Royle, *Lectures on the Results of the Great Exhibition of 1851*, pp. 488–9.

117. A. Ure, The Cotton Manufacture of Great Britain, vol. 1 (London, 1836), p. 83.

118. J. G. Borpujari, 'The British Impact on the Indian Cotton Textile Industry: 1757–1865', Cambridge University Ph.D. thesis (1969), p. 25.

119. Gadgli, *The Industrial Evolution of India in Recent Times*, pp. 36–46.

120. Ibid., p. 34; K. N. Chaudhuri, 'The Structure of Indian Textile Industry in the Seventeenth and Eighteenth Centuries', *Indian Economic and Social History Review*, 11 (1974), 171.

121. Royle, *Lectures on the Results of the Great Exhibition of 1851*, p. 487.

122. Chaudhuri, 'The Structure of Indian Textile Industry', p. 178.

123. Ellison, *The Cotton Trade of Great Britain*, p. 51.

124. J. Forbes Watson, *The Textile Manufactures and the Costumes of the People of India* (London, 1866), p. 26.

125. Varma, 'History of the Cotton Industry of India', p. 291.

Conclusion

1. K. N. Chaudhuri, *The Trading World of Asia* (Cambridge, 1978).

2. R. A. Silow, "The Genetics of Species Development in the Old World Cottons," *Journal of Genetics*, vol. 46 (1944), .pp. 68–69; *Evolution of Gossypium*, eds., J. B. Hutchinson, et al., (Oxford, 1947), p. 94; J.-B. Hutchinson, *The Application of Genetics to Cotton Improvement* (Cambridge, 1959), p. 19; idem, "The History and Relationships of the World's Cottons," Endeavour, vol. 21, (1962), p. 8.

3. Mark Elvin, *The Pattern of the Chinese Past* (Stanford, 1973), pp. 214–5. Other Social factors also tended to inhibit technological innovations (ibid ., pp. 276–284).

4. Sung Jae Koh, *Stages of Industrial Development in Asia* (Philadelphia, 1966), pp. 312–3.

5. William B. Hauser, *Economic Institutional Change in Tokugawa Japan* (Cambridge, 1974.)

6. T. Furushima, *Nihon Hoken Nōgyō-shi*, pp. 197–215; *Kinsei Nihon Nōgyō no Kōzō*," pp. 273–9, 378; idem., *Kinsei Nōgyō Gijutushi*, pp. 357–9, 538. (These pages are from his collected works.)

7. K. Sugihara, "Patterns of Intra-Asiatic Trade, 1898–1943," *Osaka City University Economic Review*, no. 16, 1980.

8. S. B. Saul, op. cit., p. 188.

9. For discussion that Asian experiences during the period between 1864 and 1914 do not fit Frank's thesis, see A. J. H. Latham, "Merchandise Trade Imbalances and Uneven Economic Development in India and China," *Journal of European Economic History*, vol. 7, no. l (1978).

Epilogue
Two Modes of 'Escape-from-Asia'

1. F. List, *The National System of Political Economy*, trans. S. S. Lloyd (London, 1909; rept. Fairfield, NJ, 1991), p. 103.
2. W. Rostow, *The Stages of Economic Growth* (Cambridge, 1960; rept. 1990), p. 4.
3. Morishima Michio, *Why Has Japan 'Succeeded'?: Western Technology and the Japanese Ethos* (Cambridge, 1989); *Satchō jidai no Igirisu: sono seiji keizai kyōiku* [Britain in the Thatcher era: its politics, economy, and educational system] (Tokyo, 1988); *Igirisu to Nihon: sono kyōiku to keizai* [Britain and Japan: their educational systems and economies] (Tokyo, 1978/9).
4. Immanuel Maurice Wallerstein, *Capitalist Agriculture and the Origins of the European World-Economy in the Sixteenth Century*, The Modern World-System 1 (New York, 1974; rept. Berkeley, 2011); *Mercantilism and the Consolidation of the European World-Economy, 1600–1750*, The Modern World-System 2 (New York, 1980; rept. Berkeley, 2011); *The Second Era of Great Expansion of the Capitalist World-Economy, 1730s–1840s*, The Modern World-System 3 (New York, 1985; rept. Berkeley, 2011); *Centrist Liberalism Triumphant, 1789–1914*, The Modern World-System 4 (Berkeley, 2011).
5. Morishima, *Why Has Japan 'Succeeded'?*, p. 19.
6. Max Weber, *The Protestant Ethic and the Spirit of Capitalism*, trans. Talcott Parsons (London, 1930).
7. Weber, *The Religion of China: Confucianism and Taoism*, trans. Hans Heinrich Gerth (New York, 1951).
8. Reg Little & Warren Reed, *The Confucian Renaissance* (Annandale, NSW, 1989); Dai Hongchao, *Confucianism and Economic Development: An Oriental Alternative?* (Washington, DC, 1989). In 1989, the Academia Sinica's Institute of Economic Studies held an international symposium in Taipei on the theme of Confucianism and East Asian economic growth.
9. Werner Sombart, *Luxury and Capitalism*, trans. Philip Siegelman (Ann Arbor, 1967).
10. Robert N. Bellah, *Tokugawa Religion: The Values of Pre-Industrial Japan* (Glencoe, 1957; rept. 2014).
11. Maruyama Masao's review in *Kokka Gakkai Zasshi* [Journal of the Association of Political and Social Sciences] 72,4 (1958), and see Bellah's comments in the Introduction to the paperback edition of *Tokugawa Religion* (1985).
12. Morishima, *Why Has Japan 'Succeeded'?*, pp. 3–9.
13. George Sansom, *Japan in World History* (New York, 1951), p. 33.
14. Morishima, *Why Has Japan 'Succeeded'?*, pp. 6, 48, 105.
15. Ibid., pp. 60, 64.

16. Ibid., pp. 59–60.

17. Ibid., p. 64.

18. Watsuji Tetsurō, *Sakoku: Nihon no higeki* [National isolation: Japan's trag-edy] (Tokyo, 1950; rept. 1964), p. 1.

19. Ibid., p. 401.

20. Engelbert Kaempfer, *The History of Japan*, trans. John Gaspar Scheuchzer, vol. 3 (London, 1727; rept. 1993), p. 336.

21. This theory was proposed by David Ricardo (1771–1823) to explain the principles of international trade and the origins of an international division of labour. Suppose, for example, it is cheaper to produce rice but more expensive to make cars in the United States than it is in Japan. Conversely, production costs in Japan are higher for rice but lower for automobiles than in the United States. In this case it would be more advantageous for both sides if the United States produced rice and Japan produced cars and the two countries traded with each other. Even when the cost of production is advantageous in absolute terms but disadvantageous in relative terms, it is more advantageous to import a product rather than produce it. This theory attempts to explain the conduct of interna-tional trade based on comparative advantage in the cost of production.

22. See Tsunoyama Sakae, *Tokei no shakaishi* [A social history of clocks] (Tokyo, 1984).

23. Okumura Shōji, *Hinawajū kara Kurofune made: Edo jidai gijutsushi* [From matchlocks to the Black Ships: a history of Edo period technology] (Tokyo, 1970), p. 10.

24. Morishima, *Why Has Japan 'Succeeded'?*, p. 60.

25. Vasilii Golovnin, *Memoirs of a Captivity in Japan*, vol. 3 (London, 1824; rept. London, 1984), 150–53.

26. See, for example, Tanaka Masatoshi, *Chūgoku kindai keizaishi kenkyū josetsu* [An introduction to research on modern Chinese economic history] (Tokyo, 1973).

27. K. Marx & F. Engels, 'Manifesto of the Communist Party', in Marx & Engels, *Selected Works in Two Volumes* (Moscow, 1958), p. 38.

28. K. Marx, 'Revolution in China and Europe', *New York Daily Tribune* (June 14, 1853), online at https://www.marxists.org/archive/marx/works/1853/06/14.htm.

29. K. Marx, 'Trade and the Treaty', *New York Daily Tribune* (October 5, 1858), online at https://www.marxists.org/archive/marx/works/1858/10/05.htm.

30. K. Marx, 'Letter to Engels', 8 October 1858, in McLellan, ed., *Selected Writings*, p. 371.

31. Shōda Ken'ichirō & Sakudō Yōtarō, *Gaisetsu Nihon keizaishi* [Overview of Japanese economic history] (Tokyo, 1978).

32. See Tsunoyama Sakae, *Cha no sekaishi* [World history of tea] (Tokyo, 1960) and *Karasa no bunka, amasa no bunka* [Cultures of piquancy, cultures of sweetness] (Tokyo, 1987).

33. *The Suma Oriental of Tomé Pires*, trans. Arnoldo Cortesão, vol. 2 (London, 1944), p. 268.

34. K. N. Chaudhuri, *Trade and Civilisation in the Indian Ocean* (Cambridge, 1985).

35. Celso Furtado, quoted in Wallerstein, *The Modern World-System*, 1: 301.

36. Kobata Atsushi, *Kingin bōekishi no kenkyū* (A study of the history of the trade in gold and silver] (Tokyo, 1976), p. 5.

37. Iwao Seiichi, *Sakoku* [National seclusion] (Tokyo, 1966; rept. 1981), p. 223.

38. Hoshikawa Kiyochika, *Saibai shokubutsu no kigen to denpa* [The origins and diffusion of cultivated plants] (Tokyo, 1978); N. W. Simmonds, ed., *Evolution of Crop Plants* (London, 1976).

39. Tsunoyama, *Karasa no bunka, amasa no bunka*, p. 201.

40. *Kindai Nihon tōgyōshi* 1 [The history of the sugar industry in modern Japan 1] (Tokyo, 1962).

41. Yanaihara Tadao, *Teikokushugika no Taiwan* [Taiwan under imperialism] (Tokyo, 1934).

42. L. H. Brockway, *Science and Colonial Expansion: The Role of the British Royal Botanic Gardens* (New York, 1979), p. 48.

43. W. Sombart, *Luxury and Capitalism* (Ann Arbor, 1967), p. 99.

44. Tsunoyama, *Cha no sekaishi.*

45. Ueyama Shunpei, et al., eds., *Zoku shōyō jurin bunka* [Sequel to the culture of glossy-leaf forests] (Tokyo, 1976), p. 8.

46. Matsushita Satoru, *Nihoncha no denrai* [The introduction of Japanese tea] (Kyoto, 1978).

47. Itō Hiroshi, *Kōhī tansaku* [The quest for coffee] (Tokyo, 1974).

48. M. Medley, *The Chinese Potter*, 2nd edn. (Oxford, 1980).

49. T. Volker, *Porcelain and the Dutch India Company* (Leiden, 1971).

50. *Zuroku Nihon no kahei* 1: *genshi, kodai, chūsei* [Japanese currency illustrated 1: prehistoric, ancient and medieval] (Tokyo, 1972).

51. Mori Katsumi & Tanaka Takeo, *Kaigai kōshō no shiten* 1 [Perspectives on international negotiations] (Tokyo, 1975).

52. Arai Hakuseki, *Told Round a Brushwood Fire*, trans. J. I. Ackroyd (Princeton, 1979), p. 241.

53. *Zuroku Nihon no kahei* 2: *Kinsei heisei no seiritsu* [Japanese currency illustrated 2: The establishment of the early modern coinage system] (Tokyo, 1973); Yamaguchi Kazuo, *Kahei no kataru Nihon no rekishi* [Japanese history as told through its currency] (Tokyo, 1979).

54. K. Glamann, *Dutch-Asiatic Trade, 1620–1740* (Copenhagen, 1958).

55. See Tsunoyama Sakae, ed., *Nihon ryōji hokoku no kenkyū* [Studies of Japanese consular reports] (Kyoto, 1986) and especially the essay by Yamamoto Yūzō, 'Eiryō kaikyō shokuminchi ni okeru engin ryūtsū to sono shūen' [The circulation of yen in British colonies along the straits and its demise].

56. Marx, *Capital*, 1: 88.

57. Kitō Hiroshi, *Nihon nisennen no jinkōshi* [2000 years of the history of population in Japan] (Kyoto, 1983).

58. Saitō Osamu, *Puroto kōgyōka no jidai* [The age of proto-industrialisation] (Tokyo, 1985).

59. Hayami Akira, 'Keizai shakai no seiritsu to sono tokushitsu' [The formation of an economic society and its distinctive features], in Shakai Keizai Shigakkai, ed., *Atarashii Edo jidaishi zō o motomete* [In search of a new image of the history of the Edo period] (Tokyo, 1977), pp. 12–13.

60. Furushima Toshio, *Nihon nōgakushi* [History of Japanese agriculture], in *Furushima Toshio Chosakushū* 5 [The collected works of Furushima Toshio 5] (Tokyo, 1974), pp. 425–6.

61. Ibid., p. 454.

62. Saitō Osamu, 'Daikaikon, jinkō, shōnō keizai' [Major land clearing, population, and the economics of peasant farming], in Hayami Akira & Miyamoto Matao, eds., *Nihon keizaishi* 1 [Japanese economic history 1] (Tokyo, 1988).

63. R. Davis, *The Industrial Revolution and British Overseas Trade* ([Leicester], 1979).

64. J. Schumpeter, *Business Cycles*, vol. 1 (New York, 1939), p. 134.

65. Giovanni Boccaccio, *The Decameron*, trans. F. Winwar (New York, 1955), pp. xxiii–xxix.

66. M. W. Dols, *The Black Death in the Middle East* (Princeton, 1977).

67. W. H. McNeill, *Plagues and Peoples* (New York, 1998), pp. 173–4.

68. Amino, *Nihon chūsei no minshuzō*, p. 171.

69 W. Woodruff, *A Concise History of the Modern World* (London, 1991), p. 7.

70. F. Braudel, *Civilization and Capitalism in the 15th–18th Century: The Structure of Everyday Life* (Berkeley, 1981), p. 187.

71. P. Bairoch, 'Historical Roots of Economic Underdevelopment', in W. J. Mommsen & J. Osterhammel, eds., *Imperialism and After* (London, 1986), p. 194.

72. G. Parker, *The World: An Illustrated History* (London, 1986), p. 5.

73. See, for example, Murakami Yōichirō, *Pesuto dairyūkō* [Plague pandemic] (Tokyo, 1983).

74. Amino, *Nihon chūsei no minshuzō*, pp. 171, 178.

75. Thomas Mun, 'A Discourse of Trade from England unto the East-Indies', in J. R. McCulloch, ed., *A Select Collection of Early English Tracts on Commerce from the Originals* . . . (London, 1856; rept. 1995), p. 8.

76. See, for example, W. Woodruff, *Impact of Western Man* (London, 1966).

77. Tsunoyama Sakae, 'Cha to Yoroppa shokuji bunkashi' [Tea and the history of European food culture], in Morita Takeshi, ed., *Cha no bunka: sono sōgōteki kenkyū* 1 [The culture of tea: a comprehensive study] (Kyoto, 1981), pp. 169–70.

78. Watanabe Minoru, *Nihon shokuseikatsushi* [History of the Japanese diet] (Tokyo, 1964), p. 39.

BIBLIOGRAPHY

(A) PRIMARY SOURCES

1. Manuscript Sources

Jardine, Matheson Archives, deposited in the Cambridge University Library. Prices Current and Market Reports 1821–1899 are used most.

Proceedings of the Manchester Chamber of Commerce deposited in the Manchester Central Library. Four volumes for 1858–67, 1867–72, 1885–90, and 1894–1902 are used, together with Minute Book: China and Far East section.

2. Theses

Borpujari, Jitendra Gopal, 'The British Impact on the Indian Cotton Textile Industry: 1757–1865' (Cambridge Univ. Ph.D. thesis 1969).

Farnie, D. A., 'The English Cotton Industry 1850–1896' (Manchester Univ. M.A. thesis 1953).

Kraus, Richard A., 'Cotton and Cotton Goods in China, 1918–36' (Harvard Univ. Ph.D. thesis 1968).

Smith, Roland, 'A History of the Lancashire Cotton Industry between the Years 1873 and 1896' (Birmingham Univ. Ph.D. thesis 1954) .

Varma, J. N., 'History of the Cotton Industry from the Earliest Times (1800 B.C.) to the Battle of Plassey (1757 A.D.)' (London Univ. M.Sc. thesis 1921).

3. Parliamentary Papers and Official Contemporary Printed Sources

Annual Statement of the Trade of the United Kingdom with Foreign Countries and British Possessions for relevant years.

Parl. Papers 1847, XLII (439): Return of the Papers in the Possession of the East India Company, showing what measures have been taken since 1836 to promote the cultivation of cotton in India, with the particulars and result of any experiments which have been made by the said Company, with a view to introduce the growth of American cotton, or to encourage the production of native cotton in India, Nos. 199 & 205.

Parl. Papers 1859, XXXIII (2571): Correspondence relative to the Earl of Elgin's Special Missions to China and Japan, 1857–1859.

Parl. Papers 1869, LXIX (2589): Treaty of Peace, Friendship, and Commerce between Her Majesty and the Tycoon of Japan, signed at Yedo, August 26, 1858.

Parl. Papers 1862, LVIII (2960): Report by Lieutenant-Colonel Neale, Peking, 1861.

Parl. Papers 1862, LVIII (3054): Despatch from Mr. Alcock, Her Majesty's Minister in Japan, April 26, 1860.

Parl. Papers 1862, LVIII (3054): Report by Captain Howard Vyse, British Acting Consul at Yokohama, on the trade of that port during the year 1860.

Parl. Papers 1863, LXX (3929): Report by Mr. Consul Howard Vyse on the trade for the year 1862.

Parl. Papers 1864, XXII (8430): Reports of the Inspectors of Factories, October 31, 1863.

Parl. Papers 1865, LIV (3487): Commercial Report on Yokohama and Kanagawa.

Parl. Papers 1866, LXXI (3703): Sir H. Parkes to the Earl of Clarendon, Yokohama, May 16, 1866.

Parl. Papers 1867, LXXIV (3758): Correspondence respecting the Revision of the Japanese Commercial Treaty.

Parl. Papers 1868–69, LX (4138): Commercial Report on Kanagawa, 1868.

Parl. Papers 1873, LXVI (c.863): Commercial Report on Kanagawa, 1872.

Parl. Papers 1874, LXVIII (c.1081): Commercial Report on Hyogo and Osaka, 1873.

Parl. Papers 1875, LXXVIII (c.1362): Commercial Report on Hyogo and Osaka, 1874.

Parl. Papers 1876, LVI (56): Copy of correspondence relating to the Indian Tariff Act of 1875.

Parl. Papers 1876, LVII (c.1616): Statement of the Trade of British India with British Possessions and Foreign Countries for the five years 1870–71 to 1874–75.

Parl. Papers 1876, LXXVI (c.1603): Commercial Report on Kanagawa, 1875.

Parl. Papers 1878–79, LV (241): Further papers relating to the import duties upon cotton goods and to other Articles in the Tariff of India.

Parl. Papers 1878–79, LXXII (c.2358): Commercial Report on Kanagawa, 1878.

Parl. Papers 1878–79, LXVIII (c.2400): Review of the Trade of British India for the official year 1877–78.

Parl. Papers 1878–79, LXVIII (c.2400): Statement of the Trade of British India with British Possessions and Foreign Countries for the years 1873–74 to 1877–78.

Parl. Papers 1881, LXXXVIII (c.2895): Statement of the Trade of British India with British Possessions and Foreign Countries for the five years 1875–76 to 1879–80.

Parl. Papers 1881, XCIII (c.2976): Statistical Abstract relating to British India from 1870–71 to 1879–80.

Parl. Papers 1882, LXVIII (c.3139): Statement of the Trade of British India with British possessions and Foreign Countries for the years 1876–77 to 1879–80.

Parl. Papers 1882, LXXII (c.3349): Commercial Report on Kanagawa, 1881.

Parl. Papers 1883, LXXV (3459): Memorandum respecting the trade between Japan and Corea.

Parl. Papers 1883, LXXV (3799): Commercial Report on Hyogo and Osaka, 1882.

Parl. Papers 1884–85, LXXXI (c.4596): Commercial Report on Osaka, 1885.

Parl. Papers 1886, XLIX (c.4729): Statement of the Trade of British India with British Possessions and Foreign Countries for the years 1880–81 to 1884–85.

Parl. Papers 1887, LXII (c.4932): Statement of the Trade of British India with British Possessions and Foreign Countries for the years 1881–82 to 1885–86.

Parl. Papers 1887, LXXXII (c.4924): On Native Manufactures of Cotton Goods in Japan.

Parl. Papers 1889, LVII (c.5680): Statement of the Trade of British India with British Possessions and Foreign Countries for the years 1883–84 to 1887–88.

Parl. Papers 1890–91, LXXXIX (c.6502): Statistical Abstract relating to British India from 1880–81 to 1889–90.

Parl. Papers 1892, LVIII (c.6646): Statement of the Trade of British India with British Possessions and Foreign Countries for the years 1886–87 to 1890–91.

Parl. Papers 1893–94, LXVI (C.6886): Statement of the Trade of British India with British Possessions and Foreign Countries for the years 1887–88 to 1891–92.

Parl. Papers 1895, LXXII (c.7602): Papers relating to Indian Tariff Act and the Cotton Duties, 1894.

Parl. Papers 1896, LXII (c.7997): Review of the Trade, and Navigation of British India by J. E. O'Conor.

Parl. Papers 1901, L (cd.485): Tables relating to the Trade of British India with British Possessions and Foreign Countries for the years 1895–96 to 1899–1900.

Parl. Papers 1902, CXII (cd. 802): Statistical Abstract relating to British India from 1890–91 to 1899–1900.

Parl. Papers 1904, LXVII (cd.1915): Tables relating to the Trade of British India with British Possessions and Foreign Countries for the years 1898–99 to 1902–03.

Parl. Papers 1909, LXIV (cd.4595): Tables relating to the Trade of British India with British Possessions and Foreign Countries for the years 1903–04 to 1907–08.

Parl. Papers 1909, CII (cd. 4896): Census of Production.

Parl. Papers 1914, LXIII (cd. 7550): Tables relating to the Trade of British India with British Possessions and Foreign Countries for the years 1908–09 to 1912–13.

Tariff Commission, *Report of the Tariff Commission, II, The Textile Trade Part 1, The Cotton Industry* (London, 1905)
The United States Department of Agriculture, Office of Experiment Stations, Bulletin No. 33, *The Cotton Plant: Its History, Botany, Chemistry, Culture, Enemies, and Uses,* (Washington, 1896); the following three reports in it are cited:
    R. B. Handy, 'History and General Statistics of Cotton,'
    Walter H. Evans, 'Botany of Cotton,'
    S. M. Tracy, 'Cultivated Varieties of Cotton.'

4. Non-Official Contemporary Printed Sources
Blackburn Chamber of Commerce, *Report of the Mission to China of the Blackburn Chamber of Commerce, 1896–97* (Blackburn, 1898).
Bombay Chamber of Commerce, *Report of the Bombay Chamber of Commerce,* for relevant years, (Bombay).
Economist, May 23, 1859.
Ellison's Annual Review of the Cotton Trade for the Season 1904–5 (Liverpool, 1905).
Manchester Chamber of Commerce, *Bombay and Lancashire Cotton Spinning Inquiry* (Manchester, 1888).
Northern Finance and Trade, July 7, 14, 28, Aug. 4, 11, 18, Sep. 9, 22, 29, Oct. 6, 13, 27, Nov. 3, 10, 17 for 1897, and Jan. 5 for 1898.
Oldham Incorporated Chamber of Commerce, *Annual Report of the Council and Statement of Accounts,* for relevant years.
Textile Investigation Chamber, *Textile Investigations* (Manchester, 1911)
Textile Manufacturer, Mar., May, Sep., Oct. for 1875, Feb., Mar., Apr., May., Jun., July, Aug., Sep., and Oct. for 1876, Jan., Mar., May., Jun., July, Oct., and Dec. for 1877, and Jan. for 1878 (Manchester).
Textile Recorder (August 15, 1892).
Worrall, John, *The Cotton Spinners' and Manufacturers' Directory* for the years 1887 and 1908 (Oldham).

(B) SECONDARY SOURCES

1. Books and Articles published up to 1918
Baines, E., *History of the Cotton Manufacture in Great Britain* (2nd. edn., London, 1966)
British Industries, ed. W. J. Ashley (London, 1903).
Brooks, C. P., *Cotton Manufacturing* (London, 1888).
———. *Cotton* (London, 1898).
Chapman, S. J., *The Lancashire Cotton Industry* (Manchester, 1904).
———. *Work and Wages, Part I: Foreign Competition* (London, 1904).

——. *A Reply to the Report of the Tariff Commission* (Manchester, 1905).

——. *The Cotton Industry and Trade* (London, 1905).

Copeland, M. T., *The Cotton Manufacturing Industry of the United States* (Cambridge, 1912).

Cyclopaedia, Vol. X (London, 1819).

Ellison, Thomas, *The Cotton Trade of Great Britain* (London, 1968, lst edn 1886).

——. 'Lancashire and Her Competitors,' *Cotton Movement and Fluctuation 1889–1894* (New York, 1894).

Encyclopaedia Britanica Vol. 7 (11th edn., Cambridge, 1910).

Gammie, G. A., *The Indian Cottons* (Calcutta, 1905).

Gundry, R. S., *English Industries and Eastern Competition* (London, 1895).

Handbook to the Imperial Cotton Exhibition (1905).

Hannan, William, *The Textile Fibres of Commerce* (London, 1902).

Helm, Elijah, 'The British Cotton Industry,' *British Industries*, ed. E. J. Ashley (London, 1903).

Heylin, Henry Brougham, *Buyers and Sellers in the Cotton Trade* (London, 1913).

Leigh, Evan, *Science of Modern Cotton Spinning*, Vol. 1 (Manchester, 1871).

Marx, Karl, and Engels, F., *Manifesto of the Communist Party* (Progress Publishers edn., Moscow, 1971).

Marx, Karl, *Capital*, Vol. 1 (Everyman edn., London, 1930).

McConnel & Co., *A Century of Fine Cotton Spinning 1790–1906* (Manchester, 1906).

McCulloch, J. R., *A Description and Statistical Account of the British Empire* (3rd edn., London, 1847).

Monie, Hugh, Jr., *The Cotton Fibre* (Manchester, 1890).

Montgomery, James, *A Practical Detail of the Cotton Manufacture of the United States of America Contrasted and Compared with that of Great Britain* (Glasgow, l840).

Mortimer, John, *Cotton Spinning* (Manchester, 1895).

——. *Mercantile Manchester* (Manchester, 1896).

Royle, J. F., *The Culture and Commerce of Cotton in India* (London, 1851).

——. 'The Arts and Manufactures of India,' *Lectures on the Results of the Great Exhibition of 1851* (London, 1852).

Todd, J. A., 'The Demand for Egyptian Cotton,' *L'Egypte Contemporaine*, Vol. 1 (1910).

——. 'The Market for Egyptian Cotton in 1909–1910,' *L'Egypte Contemporaine*, Vol. 2, (1911).

——. *The World's Cotton Crop* (London, 1915).

Ure, Andrew, *The Cotton Manufacture of Great Britain*, Vol. 1 (London, 1839).

Watkins, J. L., *King Cotton, A Historical and Statistical Review, 1790–1908* (London, 1908).

Watson, J. Forbes, *The Textile Manufactures and the Costumes of the People of India* (London, 1866).

Watt, George, *A Dictionary of the Economic Products of India*, Vol. 4 (London & Calcutta, 1890).

———. *The Wild and Cultivated Cotton Plants of the World* (London, 1907).

———. *The Commercial Products of India* (London, 1908).

Watts, I., 'Cotton,' *The Encyclopaedia Britanica*,Vol. 6 (9th edn., Edinburgh, 1877).

2. Books and Articles published after 1918

Afzal, Mohammad, 'Cotton Growing in Egypt,' *Indian Cotton Growing Review*, Vol. 1, (1947).

Ahmad, Nazir, 'Discussion,' Indian Central Cotton Committee, *First Conference of Scientific Research Workers on Cotton in India* (Bombay, 1938).

Ashtor, E., 'The Venetian Cotton Trade in Syria in the Later Middle Ages,' *Studi Medievali* (1974).

Bagchi, A. K., *Private Investment in India 1900–1939* (Cambridge, 1972).

Catling, H., *The Spinning Mule* (Newton Abbot, 1970).

Chapman, S. D., *The Cotton Industry in the Industrial Revolution* (London, 1972).

Chaudhuri, K. N., "The Structure of Indian Textile Industry in the Seventeenth and Eighteenth Centuries,' *Indian Economic and Social History Review*, Vol. XI (1974).

———. *The Trading World of Asia and the English East India Company 1660–1760* (Cambridge, 1978).

Chaudhuri, Susil, 'The Financing of Investment in Bengal: 1650–1720,' *The Indian Economic and Social History Review*, Vol. VIII (1971).

Davis, Ralph, 'English Foreign Trade, 1660–1700,' *Economic History Review*, 2nd series, Vol. VII, No. 2 (1954).

———. 'English Foreign Trade, 1700–1774,' *Economic History Review*, 2nd series, Vol. XV (1962).

———. 'English Imports from the Middle East 1580–1780,' *Studies in the Economic History of the Middle East*, ed. M. A. Cook (Oxford, 1970).

———. *The Industrial Revolution and British Overseas Trade* (Leicester, 1979).

Deane, P., and W. A. Cole, *British Economic Growth 1688–1959* (2nd edn., Cambridge, 1969).

Douglas, A. W., 'Cotton Textiles in England: the East India Company's Attempt to Exploit Developments in Fashion 1660–1721,' *Journal of British Studies*, Vol. VIII (1969).

Edwards, M. M., *The Growth of the British Cotton Trade 1780–1815* (Manchester, 1967).

Elvin, Mark, *The Pattern of the Chinese Past* (Stanford, 1973).

Farnie, D. A., 'The Textile Industty: woven fabrics,' *A History of Technoloov*, eds. E. J. Holmyard, et al. (Oxford, 1958).

——. 'The Commercial Empire of the Atlantic, 1607–1783,' *Economic History Review*, 2nd series , Vol. XV (1962).

——. *East and West of Suez* (Oxford, 1969).

——. *The English Cotton Industry and the World Market 1815–1896* (Oxford, 1979).

Feuerwerker, A., 'Handicraft and Manufactured Cotton Textiles in China 1871–1910,' *Journal of Economic History*, Vol. 30 (1970).

——. '"Economic Trade in the Late Ch'ing Empire, 1870–1911,' *The Cambridge History of China*, Vol. 11, eds., Denis Twitchett, et al.

Fisher, F. J., 'London's Export Trade in the Early Seventeenth Century,' *The Growth of English Overseas Trade in the 17th and 18th Centuries*, ed. W. E. Minchinton (London, 1969).

Gadgil, D. R., *The Industrial Evolution of India in Recent Times 1860–1939* (5th edn., Oxford, 1971).

Geijer, Agnes, 'Some Evidence of Indo-European Cotton Trade in Pre-Mughal Times,' *Journal of Indian Textile History*, No. 1 (1955).

Glamann, K., *Dutch-Asiatic Trade 1620–1740* (Copenhagen, 1958).

Harland, S. C., 'The General Conception of the Species,' *Biological Reviews of the Cambridge Philosophical Society*, Vol. 11, No. 1 (1936).

Harnetty, Peter, 'The Cotton Improvement Program in India 1865–1875,' *Agricultural History*, Vol. XLIV (1970).

——. 'Cotton Exports and Indian Agriculture, 1861–1870,' *Economic History Review*, 2nd series, Vol. 24 (1971).

——. *Imperialism and Free Trade* (Manchester, 1972).

Heaton, H., *Economic History of Europe* (revised edn., New York, 1948).

Henderson, W. O., 'The Cotton Supply Association, 1857–1872,' *The Empire Cotton Growing Review*, Vol. IX (1932).

Heylin, Henry Brougham, *Buyers and Sellers in the Cotton Trade* (London, 1913).

Hirschman, Albert O., *The Strategy of Economic Development* (New Haven, 1958).

Hou, Chi-ming, 'Some Reflections on the Economic History of Modern China,' *Journal of Economic History*, Vol. XXIII (1963).

——. 'Economic Dualism: The Case of China 1840–1947,' *Journal of Economic History*, Vol. XXIII (1963).

Hsiao, Liang-lin, *China's Foreign Trade Statistics 1864–1949* (Cambridge, Mass, 1974).

Hutchinson, J. B., 'Changing Concepts in Crop Plant Evolution,' *Experimental Agriculture Review*, Vol.13 (1971).

——. 'The Distribution of Gossypium and the Evolution of the Commercial Cottons,' Papers Read and Summary of Proceedings, Indian Central Cotton

Committee, *First Conference of Scientific Research Workers on Cotton in India* (Bombay, 1938).

——. 'New Evidence on the Origin of the Old World Cottons,' *Heredity*, Vol. 8 (1954).

——. 'The History and Relationships of the World's Cottons,' *Endeavour*, Vol. XXI (1962).

——. 'A Note on Some Geographical Races of Atlantic Cottons,' *Empire Cotton Growing Review*, Vol. XXVII (1950).

——. 'The Sea Island Cottons,' *Empire Journal of Experimental Agriculture*, Vol. VIII (1945).

——, and R. L. M. Ghose, 'The Composition of the Cotton Crops of Central India and Rajputana,' *Indian Journal of Agricultural Science*, Vol. VII (1937).

——, and Govande, G. K., 'Cotton Botany and the Spinning Value and Hair Properties of Cotton Lint,' *Indian Journal of Agricultural Science*, Vol. VIII (1938).

—— et al., *The Application of Genetics to Cotton Improvement* (Cambridge, 1959).

—— et al., *The Evolution of Gossypium* (Oxford, 1947).

—— et al., *Evolutionary Studies in World Crops* (Cambridge, 1974).

Irwin, J., 'Indian Textile Trade in the Seventeenth Century I Western India.' *Journal of Indian Textile History*, No. 1 (1955).

——. 'Indian Textile Trade in the Seventeenth Century, II Coromandel Coast,' *Journal of Indian Textile History*, No. 2 (1956).

——. 'Indian Textile Trade in the Seventeenth Century, III Bengal,' *Journal of Indian Textile History*, No.3 (1957).

——. 'Indian Textile Trade in the Seventeenth Century, IV Foreign Influence,' *Journal of Indian Textile History*, No. 4 (1959).

—— and M. Hall, *Indian Painted and Printed Fabrics*, Chapter IV, 'Export Fabrics' (Ahmedabad, 1971).

Jewkes, J., and Gray, E. M., *Wages and Labour in the Lancashire Cotton Spinning Industry* (Manchester, 1935).

Jones, G. J., *Increasing Return* (Cambridge, 1933).

Kang, Chao, 'The Growth of a Modern Cotton Textile Industry and the Competition with Handicrafts,' *China's Modern Economy in Historical Perspective*, ed. Dwight H. Perkins (Stanford, 1975).

——. *The Development of Cotton Textile Production in China* (Cambridge, Mass., 1977).

Kearney, Thomas, H., 'Cotton Plants, Tame and Wild,' *Journal of Heredity*, Vol. XXI (1930).

Khan, S. A., *The East India Trade in the Seventeenth Century* (Oxford, 1923).

Krishna, Bal., *Commercial Relations between India and England* (London, 1924).

Latham, A. J. H., *The International Economy and the Underdeveloped World 1865–1914* (London, 1978).

———. 'Merchandise Trade Imbalances and Uneven Economic Development in India and China,' *Journal of European Economic History*, Vol. 7, No. 1 (1978).

Leacock, Seth, and Mandelbaum David G., 'A Nineteenth Century Development Project in India: The Cotton Improvement Project,' *Economic Development and Cultural Change*, Vol. III (1955).

Le Fevour, Edward, *Western Enterprise in Late Ch'ing China: a selective survey of Jardine, Matheson and Company's operations, 1842–1895* (Cambridge, Mass., 1970).

Lipson, E., *An Introduction to the Economic History of England* (London, 1920).

Lopez, R. et al,, 'England to Egypt, 1350–1500: Long-term Trends and Long-distance Trade,' *Studies in the Economic History of the Middle East*, ed. M. A. Cook (Oxford, 1970).

Mann, Julia de Lacy, 'The Textile Industry: Machinery for Cotton Flax, Wool, 1760–1850,' *A History of Technology*, Vol. 4, ed. C. Singer (Oxford, 1958).

Mathias, Peter, *The First Industrial Nation* (London, 1969, 2nd edn. 1983) .

Mazzaoui, M. F., 'The Cotton Industry of Northern Italy in the late Middle Ages: 1150–1450,' *Journal of Economic History*, Vol. XXXII (1972).

———. *The Italian Cotton Industry in the Later Middle Ages 1100–1600* (Cambridge, 1981).

Mehta, S. D., *The Indian Cotton Textile Industry* (Bombay, 1953).

———. *The Cotton Mills of India 1854–1954* (Bombay, 1954).

Mitchell, B. R., and P. Deane, *Abstract of British Historical Statistics* (Cambridge, 1962).

Moreland, W. H., 'Indian Exports of Cotton Goods in the Seventeenth Century,' *Indian Journal of Economics*, Vol. V, Part 3 (1925).

Morris, Morris D., 'The Economic History of India: A Bibliographic Essay,' *Journal of Economic History*, Vol. 21 (1961).

———. 'Towards a Reinterpretation of Nineteenth-Century Indian Economic History,' *Journal of Economic History*, Vol. 23 (1963).

———. 'Economic Change and Agriculture in Nineteenth Century India,' *Indian Economic and Social History Review*, Vol. 3 (1966).

———. 'Trends and Tendencies in Indian Economic History,' *Indian Economic and Social History Review*, Vol. 5 (1968).

Myers, Ramon H., 'Cotton Textile Handicraft and the Development of the Cotton Textile Industry in Modern China,' *Economic History Review*, 2nd series, Vol. 18 (1965).

Nanjundayya, C., 'Staple Length of Cotton,' *Indian Cotton Growing Review*, Vol. 7 (1953).

Owen, Roger, *Cotton and the Egyptian Cotton Economy 1820–1914* (Oxford, 1969).

Panse, V. G., 'Cotton Growing Review,' *Indian Cotton Growing Review*, Vol. III (1949).

Parry, J. H., *The Age of Reconnaissance* (2nd edn., London, 1966).

Patterson, R., 'Spinning and Weaving,' *History of Technology*, Vol. II, ed. C. Singer (Oxford, 1956); Vol. III (1957).

Pelliot, Paul, *Notes on Marco Polo*, I (Paris, 1959).

Polo, Marco, *The Travels* (Harmondsworth, 1958).

Raychaudhuri, T., 'A Re-interpretation of Nineteenth Century Indian Economic History?' *Indian Economic and Social History Review*, Vol. 5 (1968).

Redford, Arthur, *Manchester Merchants and Foreign Trade*, Vol. II (Manchester, 1956).

Ryan, John, 'Machinery Replacement in the Cotton Trade,' *Economic Journal*, Vol. XL (1930).

Sandberg, L. G., 'Movements in the Quality of British Cotton Textile Exports, 1815–1913,' *Journal of Economic History*, Vol. 28, No. 1 (1968).

——. 'American Rings and English Mules,' *Quarterly Journal of Economics* (Feb., 1969).

——. *Lancashire in Decline* (Ohio, 1974).

Saunders, J. H., *The Wild Species of Gossypium and Their Evolutionary History* (Oxford, 1961).

Saul, S. B., *Studies in British Overseas Trade 1870–1914* (Liverpool, 1960).

Saxelby, C. H., *Bolton Survey* (Bolton, 1953).

Saxonhouse, Cary, 'A Tale of Japanese Technological Diffusion in the Meiji Period,' *Journal of Economic History*, Vol.34, No. 1 (1974).

See, Chong Su, *The Foreign Trade of China* (New York, 1970).

Silow, R. A., 'The Genetics of Species Development in the Old World Cottons,' *Journal of Genetics*, Vol. 46 (1944).

Silver, Arthur, *Manchester Men and Indian Cotton 1847–72* (Manchester, 1966).

Slater, W. H., 'World Cotton Spinning Capacity,' *Textile Recorder* (15 Jan., 1930).

Slomann, V., translated by Eve M. Wendt, *Bizarre Designs in Silk: Trade and Tradition* (Copenhagen, 1953).

'Spinning Test,' editorial, *The Empire Cotton Growing Review*, Vol. IX (1932).

Smith, Roland, 'An Oldham Limited Liability Company 1875–1896,' *Business History*, Vol. IV, No. 1 (1961).

Thomes, P. J., *Mercantilism and the East India Trade* (London, 1926).

Tyson, R. E., 'The Cotton Industry,' *The Development of British Industry and Foreign Competition 1875–1914*, ed. Derek H. Aldcroft (London, 1968).

Unwin, G., *Samuel Oldknow and the Arkwrights* (2nd edn., Manchester, 1968).

Utley, Freda, *Lancashire and the Far East* (London, 1931).

Vicziany, A. M., 'The Cotton Trade and the Commercial Development of Bombay, 1855–1875' (London Univ. Ph.D. thesis 1875).

Vries, Jan de, *Economy of Europe in an Age of Crisis* (Cambridge, 1976).

Wadsworth, A. P., and Mann, Julia de L., *The Cotton Trade and Industrial Lancashire 1600–1780* (Manchester, 1931).

Wallerstein, I., *The Modern World-System I* (New York, 1974).

Watson, A. M., 'The Arab Agricultural Revolution and Its Diffusion, 700–1100,' *Journal of Economic History*, Vol. XX–IV (1974).

Wescher, H., 'Fustian Weaving in South Germany from the Fourteenth to the Sixteenth Century,' *Ciba Review*, 64 (1948).

——. 'Schürlitz Weaving in Switzerland,' *Ciba Review*, 64 (1948).

——. 'Cotton Growing and Cotton Trade in the Orient during the Middle Ages,' *Ciba Review*, 64 (1948).

Winterbottom, James, *Cotton Spinning Calculations and Yarn Costs* (2nd edn., London, 1921).

Woodman, Harold, *King Cotton and His Retainers* (Lexington, 1968).

Woodruff, William, *Impact of Western Man* (London, 1966).

Zaitzev, G. S., 'A Contribution of the Classification of the Genus Gossypium,' *Bulletin of Applied Botany and Plant Breeding*, Vol. 18 (1928).

(C) JAPANESE SOURCES (WHICH ARE CITED.)

1. Primary Sources
i) Official Sources

Dai ni-ji Kangyōkai Kōmubu Nisshi (records of the second industrial exhibition), (1885).

Dai jūichi-ji Nōshōmu Tōkeihyō (the 11th statistical survey on agriculture and commerce) (Tokyo, 1896).

Gaikoku Bōeki Gairan (annual survey of foreign trade) (Tokyo, 1890, 1892).

Kannai Orimono Kaisetsu (introduction to textiles in Aichi Prefecture) (Nagoya, 1914).

Kenshi Orimono Tōshikki Kyōshinkai Hōkoku: Menshi (records of conference on promotion of raw-silk textiles and pottery: cotton yarn) (Tokyo, 1885).

Meiji shichi-nen Fuken Bussanhyō (prefectural production in 1874) (Tokyo, 1874).

Meiji-Taishō Ōsakashi-shi (history of Osaka city), Vol. 7 (Osaka, 1933).

Menshi Shūdan-kai kiji (proceedings of conference on cotton yarn) (Tokyo, 1885).

Mentō Kyōshinkai Hōkoku (report on cotton goods and sugar), No. 2 (Tokyo, 1880).

Nōshōmu Tōkeihyō (statistics relating to agriculture and commerce), No. 2 & 3 (Tokyo, 1888, 1889).

Tokyo 100-nen-shi (history of a century of Tokyo), Vol. 2 (Tokyo, 1972).
Wakayama-ken Kangyō Chakushu Gaikyō (general report of industrial enterprise in Wakayama Prefecture) (Wakayama, 1877).
Yokohamashi-shi: Shiryōhen (history of Yokohama city: documents), Vol. 2 (Yokohama, 1962).

ii) Non-Official Sources
Chōki Keizai Tōkei with English subtitle of *Estimates of Long-Term Economic Statistics of Japan since 1868*, eds. M. Umemura, et al. (Tokyo, 1966).
Chūgai Bukka Shinpō (domestic and foreign prices current) (Tokyo, 1878–1882).
Dainihon Menshi Bōeki Dōgyō Rengōkai Geppō (monthly report on the Japanese mill owners' association), No. 190 (Osaka, 1980).
Tokyo Keizai Zasshi (Tokyo Economic Journal) (1883–1890).
Nihon Bōeki Seiran (foreign trade of Japan), ed. Tōyōkeizai Shinpō (Tokyo, 1975).
Rengō Bōseki Geppō (monthly review of cotton mill owners' association), No. 4 (Osaka, 1889).
Shibusawa Eiichi Denki Shiryō (documents relating to Shibusawa Eiichi), Vol. 17 (Tokyo, 1957).
Tōkei Hōkoku (statistical reports), Nos. 1–5 (Tokyo, 1885–1889).

2. Secondary Sources
Furushima, T., *Nihon Hōken Nōgyō-shi* (agricultural history of feudal Japan) (Tokyo, 1941).
———. *Kinsei Nihon Nōgyō no Kōzō* (structure of pre-modern Japanese agriculture) (2nd. edn., Tokyo, 1974; 1st edn. 1943).
———. *Shihonsei Seisan no Hattatsu to Jinushisei* (development of capitalistic production and landlordism) (Tokyo, 1962).
———. *Sangyōshi* (history of industry), Vol. 3 (Tokyo, 1966).
———. *Kinsei Nōgyō Gijyutsu-shi* (history of agricultural technology of pre-modern Japan) (2nd edn., Tokyo, 1975).
Gendai Nihon Sangyō Hattatsu-shi: Sen'i (history of Japanese modern industry: textiles) ed. M. Kajinishi (Tokyo, 1964).
Hattori, K., 'Yunyūhin no Hanro' (markets for imported goods), *Yokohamashi-shi* (history of Yokohama city), Vol. 4 (Yokohama, 1965).
Hattori, Shisō and Shinobu Seizaburō, *Meiji Senshoku Keizaishi* (textile history of the Meiji Era) (Tokyo, 1937).
Ichikawa, K. and Irimajiri K., 'Orimono-gyō' (textile industry), *Nihon Sangyō-shi Taikei* (series of history of Japanese industry), Vol. 1 (Tokyo, 1961).
Ishii, T., *Bakumatsu Bōeki no Bunseki* (a study of late Tokugawa foreign trade) (Tokyo, 1944).
Ishikawa, G., *Jūyō Shōhin-shi* (survey of important commodity) (Tokyo, 1897).

Kajimura, H., *Chōsen niokeru Shihonshugi no Keisei to Tenkai* (formation and development of capitalism in Korea) (Tokyo, 1977).

Katō, Shigeru, *Shina Keizaishi Kōshō* (studies in Chinese economic history), Vol. II (Tokyo, 1953).

Kinugawa, T., *Honpō Menshi Bōsekishi* (history of the Japanese cotton spinning industry), Vol. 1 (Tokyo, 1937).

Kitagawa, O., 'Nisshin-sensō madeno Nissen-bōeki' (Japanese-Korean foreign trade up to the Sino-Japanese War), *Nihon no Sangyō Kakumei* (Japanese industrial revolution), ed. S. Ōe (Tokyo, 1977).

Koike, Kenji., 'Indo Mengyō to Shijōmondai' (the structure of Bombay cotton mills' markets), *Ajia Keizai*, Vol. XVI; No. 9 (Tokyo, 1975).

——. *Keiei Dairi Seido* (managing agency system) (Tokyo, 1979).

Koyama, M., *Shinmatsu Chūgoku niokeru Gaikoku Menseihin no Ryūnyū* (the influx of foreign cotton goods in the late Ch'ing period), *Kindai Chūgoku Kenkyū*, Vol. IV (Tokyo, 1960).

Minabe, S., 'Meiji Shoki niokeru Wagakuni Menkaseisan no Chōraku' (decline in cotton growing in the Meiji period), *Keio Keizai Shigaku Kiyō*, Vol. 1 (Tokyo, 1937).

Miyajima, H., 'Chōsen Kōgyō Kaikakuigo no Shōgyōteki Nōgyō' (commercialized agriculture after the reform in Korea in 1894), *Shirin*, Vol. 57 (Tokyo, 1974).

Murakami, K., 'Nippon Mengyō niyoru Chōsen Mengyō no Saihensei' (re-organization of the Korean cotton industry by Japanese cotton manufacturing interests), *Nippon Teikokushugi to Asia*, ed. R. Kojima (Tokyo, 1979).

Nakamura, Satoru, 'Sekai Shihonshugi to Nihon Mengyō no Henkaku' (the capitalist world economy and the transformation of the Japanese cotton industry), *Meiji Ishin no Kiso Kōzō* (infrastructure of the Meiji Restoration) (Tokyo, 1968).

Nakamura, Sei, *Nihon Garabo-shi-wa* (story of Japanese *gara-bo*) (Tokyo, 1942).

Nakayasu, Sadako, 'Zairai Men'orimonogyō no Tenkai to Bōsekishihon' (the development of the traditional weaving industry and the modern spinning industry), *Tochi Seido Shigaku*, Vol. 14 (Tokyo, 1962).

Nihon no Sangyō to Bōeki no Hatten (development of Japanese industry and trade), ed. Mitsubishi Institute of Economic Research (Tokyo, 1935).

Nishijima, S., *Chūgoku Keizaishi Kenkyū* (studies in Chinese economic history) (Tokyo, 1966).

Nishimura, Hatsu, 'Mengyō' (cotton industry), *Nihon Sangyō Kakumei no Kenkyū* (studies of the Japanese industrial revolution) ed. K. Ōishi, Vol. 1 (Tokyo, 1975).

Ōno, Kazuichirō, 'Dai ichi-ji Taisenzengo no Gaikokubōeki' (foreign trade around World War I), *Kōza Nihon Shihonshugi Hattatsushi-ron* (studies of the development of Japanese capitalism), Vol. II (Tokyo, 1968).

Ōe, Shinobu, *Nihon no Sangyō Kakumei* (Japanese industrial revolution) (Tokyo, 1968).

Okamura, Katsumasa, *Bōseki Kaikyūdan* (a talk about old days of spinning) (Tokyo, 1932).

Ono, Kōji, 'Honpō Momenkigyō Seiritsu no Katei' (how the Japanese cotton textile industry emerged), *Nihon Sangyō Hattatsushi no Kenkyū* (studies in Japanese industrial development) (Tokyo, 1941).

Ōsumi, Gohachi, *Bōshoku Genryōgaku* (raw materials of textiles) (Tokyo, 1936).

Sanpei, Takako, *Nihon Mengyō Hattatsushi* (development of the Japanese cotton industry) (Tokyo, 1941).

Sawamura, Tōhei, 'Li-chō Kōki Momen no Chōshū Chiiki to Seisan Ritchi' (cotton growing conditions of localities where tax on cottons was imposed in the late Yi dynasty), *Keizaishi Kenkyū*, No. 28 (Tokyo, 1942).

———. 'Richōjidai Momen Yushutsu no Shūmatsu' (the end of the exports of cotton textiles in the era of Yi dynasty), *Keizaishi Kenkyū*, No. 31 (Tokyo, 1944).

———. 'Igirisu Menseihin no Tōyō Shinshutsu to Chōsen Mengyō' (exports of British cotton manufactures to Asia and the Korean cotton industry), *Shakai Keizai Shigaku*, Vol. 17 (Tokyo, 1951).

Shiba, Kentarō, 'Momen no Seisan Bunpai nikansuru Kyokutō Kōtsu Bunkashi-teki Kōsatsu (1)' (a note on production and distribution of cottons in the commercial and cultural history of the Far East), *Kōtsūbunka*, No. 2 (Tokyo, 1938).

Shinohara, Miyohei, *Chūki Keizai Taikei (6): Kojin Shōhi Shishutsu* (estimates of long-term economic statistics of Japan (6): consumption expenditure) (Tokyo, 1972).

Shōda, Ken'ichirō, *Nihon Shihonshugi to Kindaika* (Japan's capitalism and modernization) (Tokyo, 1971).

Soejima, Enshō, 'Nippon Bōsekigyō to Chūgoku Shijō' (Japanese spinning industry and Chinese market), *Jinbun Gakuhō*, No.33 (Tokyo, 1972).

Sudō, Kichiyuki, 'Kōrai Makki yori Chōsen Shoki ni itaru Orimonogyō no Hattatsu' (development of the textile industry from the late Koryo dynasty to the early Yi dynasty), *Shakai Keizai Shigaku*, Vol. 12 (Tokyo, 1942).

Takamura, Naosuke, *Nihon Bōsekigyō-shi Josetsu* (history of Japanese cotton spinning industry), Vol. 1 (Tokyo, 1971).

Yamada, Moritarō, *Nihon Shihonshugi Bunseki* (analysis of Japanese capitalism) (Tokyo, 1934).

Yamaguchi, Kazuo, *Meijizenki Keizai no Bunseki* (analysis of early Meiji economy) (Tokyo, 1963).

Yanagita, Kunio, *Meiji Taishō-shi* (history of the Meiji and Taishō eras) in his
   collected works, Vol. 24 (Tokyo, 1963).
Yoshino, M., 'Richō Makki ni okeru Menseihin Yunyū no Tenkai (development
   of imports of cotton manufactures in the late Yi dynasty); *Chōsen Rekishi
   Ronshū*, Vol. II (Tokyo, 1979).

INDEX